GOLD IN THE FURNAC
life in occupied Germany i
travels and interviews conc

Savitri Devi is scath
hypocrisy: countless Germ ... millions
perished after the war, driven from their homes by Russians, Czechs, Poles, and others; more than a million prisoners of war perished from planned starvation or outright murder in Allied concentration camps; untold thousands more disappeared into slave labour camps from the Congo to Siberia.

Savitri Devi describes in vivid detail how individual National Socialists were subjected to "de-Nazification" by Germany's democratic liberators. Party and military leaders were subjected to summary execution, torture, starvation, show-trials, imprisonment, and execution. Ordinary party members were subjected to petty indignities and recantations extorted under the threat of imprisonment, hunger, and the denial of livelihood. She also chronicles the systematic plunder of Germany by the Allies: the clear-cutting of ancient forests, the dismantling of factories, and the theft of natural resources.

In spite of the disaster, Savitri Devi did not view it as the end of National Socialism, but as a purification—a trial by fire separating the base metal from the gold—and a prelude to a new beginning. Thus she also devotes chapters to presenting the basic philosophy and constructive political programme of National Socialism.

Gold in the Furnace is a valuable historical document of the National Socialists who never lost faith, despite suffering, persecution, and martyrdom; of the ordinary Germans who revered Hitler even after the war; of the widespread rumours of Hitler's survival; of the hopes of imminent National Socialist revival, perhaps in the aftermath of a Third World War; of the expectations of Soviet victory in such a war; and of the philosophy, experiences, and unique personality of a remarkable woman.

Gold in the Furnace is one of the first "revisionist" books on World War II and its aftermath. But although Savitri Devi challenged many claims about the concentration camps, she believed that there had been a programme of mass-extermination of Jews and that the methods of extermination included homicidal gas chambers. (She later rejected these claims.)

For many years, *Gold in the Furnace* was almost impossible to find. Published in a tiny edition by Savitri Devi's husband A.K. Mukherji in Calcutta in 1952, it was distributed privately by the authoress to her friends and comrades. A German translation appeared in 1982, a Spanish translation in 1995, and an Italian translation in 2015. In 2005, a second English edition was published in England, in commemoration of the 100th anniversary of Savitri Devi's birth, on 30 September 1905. In 2006, the Savitri Devi Archive published a definitive third edition correcting a number of errors in the second edition (including the omission of the frontispiece and two entire pages of text), and including several new photographs. This fourth edition from Counter-Currents reprints the third edition with a few corrections.

The Savitri Devi Archive

The Centennial Edition of Savitri Devi's Works
R.G. Fowler, General Editor

Each volume will be released in a limited cloth edition of 200 numbered copies.

Volume One:
AND TIME ROLLS ON
The Savitri Devi Interviews

Volume Two:
GOLD IN THE FURNACE
Experiences in Post-War Germany

Volume Three:
FOREVER AND EVER
Devotional Poems

Volume Four:
DEFIANCE
The Prison Memoirs of Savitri Devi

Volume Five:
THE LIGHTNING AND THE SUN
(complete and unabridged)

Volume Six:
PILGRIMAGE

Future Volumes:

MEMORIES AND REFLECTIONS OF AN ARYAN WOMAN

THE LOTUS POND
Impressions of India

HARD AS STEEL

LONG-WHISKERS AND THE TWO-LEGGED GODDESS
or, the True Story of a "Most Objectionable Nazi" and...
Half-a-Dozen Cats

IMPEACHMENT OF MAN

A SON OF GOD
The Life and Philosophy of Akhnaton, King of Egypt
(complete and unabridged)

AKHNATON'S ETERNAL MESSAGE
(and other writings on Akhnaton)

A WARNING TO THE HINDUS
(and The Non-Hindu Indians and Indian Unity)

NOT "FOR NOTHING": LETTERS OF SAVITRI DEVI, VOLUME 1

SAINT SAVITRI: LETTERS OF SAVITRI DEVI, VOLUME 2

SAVITRI DEVI

GOLD IN THE FURNACE
EXPERIENCES IN POST-WAR GERMANY

EDITED BY R.G. FOWLER

A Savitri Devi Archive Book
Counter-Currents Publishing, Ltd.
San Francisco

Savitri Devi
(*née* Maximine Portaz, a.k.a. Maximiani Portas)
1905-1982
Gold in the Furnace: Experiences in Post-War Germany
Edited with Preface by R.G. Fowler
Includes index

Copyright © 2021
Counter-Currents Publishing

Cover by Kevin I. Slaughter

ISBNs:
Non-Limited Hardcover Edition: 978-1-64264-112-7
Paperback Edition: 978-1-64264-113-4

Fourth Edition

First Edition: *Gold in the Furnace*. Calcutta: A.K. Mukherji, 1952.
German Translation: *Gold im Schmelztiegel: Erlebnisse im Nachkriegsdeutschland. Eine Huldigung an Deutschland.* Trans. Lotte Asmus. Padua: Edizioni di Ar/Mohrkirch: Nordwind Verlag, 1982.
Spanish Translation: *Oro en el Crisol: Vivencia en la postguerra Alemania. Un homenage de Alemania.* Trans. Ramiro R.B. (from the German translation by Lotte Asmus). Spain: Diffussion Eneese, 1995, rev. ed. 2001.
Second Edition: *Gold in the Furnace: Experiences in Post-War Germany.* Ed. R.G. Fowler. Uckfield, Sussex, England: Historical Review Press, 2005.
Third Edition: *Gold in the Furnace: Experiences in Post-War Germany.* Ed. R.G. Fowler. Atlanta, Georgia: The Savitri Devi Archive, 2006.
Italian Translation: *Oro nel crogiolo.* Ed. Marco Linguardo. Trans. Stefania Labruzzo. Rome: Thule Italia, 2015.
French Translation: *L'or dans le fourneau.* Ed. R. G. Fowler. Trans. Pierre Bergeron. Contre le temps, 2020.

Dedicated
to the Martyrs of Nuremberg.

The Werl prison,

in which so many Germans were—and still are, to this day—detained for having done their duty faithfully and thoroughly, as one should.

"Muß eine militärische Niederlage zu einem so restlosen Niederbruch einer Nation und eines Staates führen? Seit wann ist dies das Ergebnis eines unglücklichen Krieges? Gehen denn überhaupt Völker an verlorenen Kriegen an und für sich zugrunde?

"Die Antwort darauf kann sehr kurz sein: Immer dann, wenn Völker in ihrer militärischen Niederlage die Quittung für ihre innere Fäulnis, Feigheit, Charakterlosigkeit, kurz Unwürdigkeit erhalten. *Ist es nicht so, dann wird die militärische Niederlage eher zum Antrieb eines kommenden größeren Aufstiegs als zum Leichenstein eines Völkerdaseins.*

"Die Geschichte bietet unendlich viele Beispiele für die Richtigkeit dieser Behauptung."

—Adolf Hitler, *Mein Kampf* [1]

---

[1] "Must a military defeat lead to a complete collapse of a nation and a state? Since when is this the result of an unfortunate war? Do peoples perish in consequence of lost wars as such?

"The answer to this can be very brief: always, when military defeat is the payment meted out to peoples for their inner rottenness, cowardice, lack of character, in short, unworthiness. *If this is not the case, the military defeat will rather be the inspiration of a great future resurrection than the tombstone of a national existence.*

"History offers innumerable examples for the truth of this assertion" (Adolf Hitler, *Mein Kampf* [Munich: Zentralverlag der NSDAP, Franz Eher Nachf., 1939], vol. I, ch. x, p. 250; English trans. by Ralph Mannheim [Boston: Houghton Mifflin, 1943], p. 229). Emphasis added by Savitri—Ed.

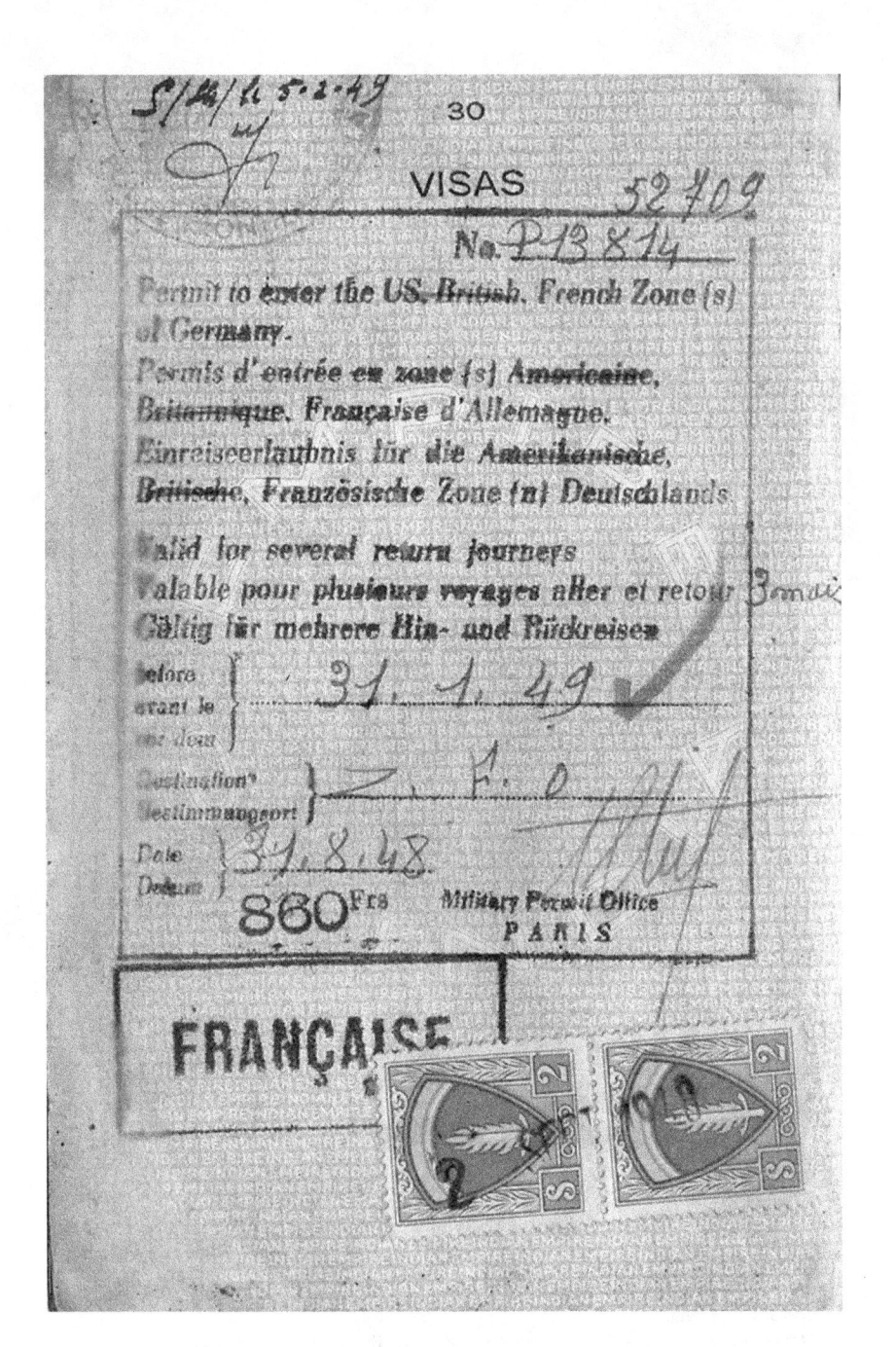

Savitri's military permit to enter French-occupied Germany, issued 31 August 1948.

Contents

Editor's Preface	iii
Foreword	xiii
Introduction	xv
1. The Philosophy of the Swastika	1
2. Brief Days of Glory	13
3. Now, the Trial	18
4. The Unforgettable Night	33
5. De-Nazification	51
6. Chambers of Hell	68
7. Plunder, Lies, and Shallowness	89
8. A Peep into the Enemy's Camp	123
9. The Élite of the World	142
10. Divine Vengeance	170
11. The Constructive Side	182
12. The Holy Forest	223
13. Echoes from the Russian Zone	243
14. Against Time	265
Index	289
About the Authoress	294

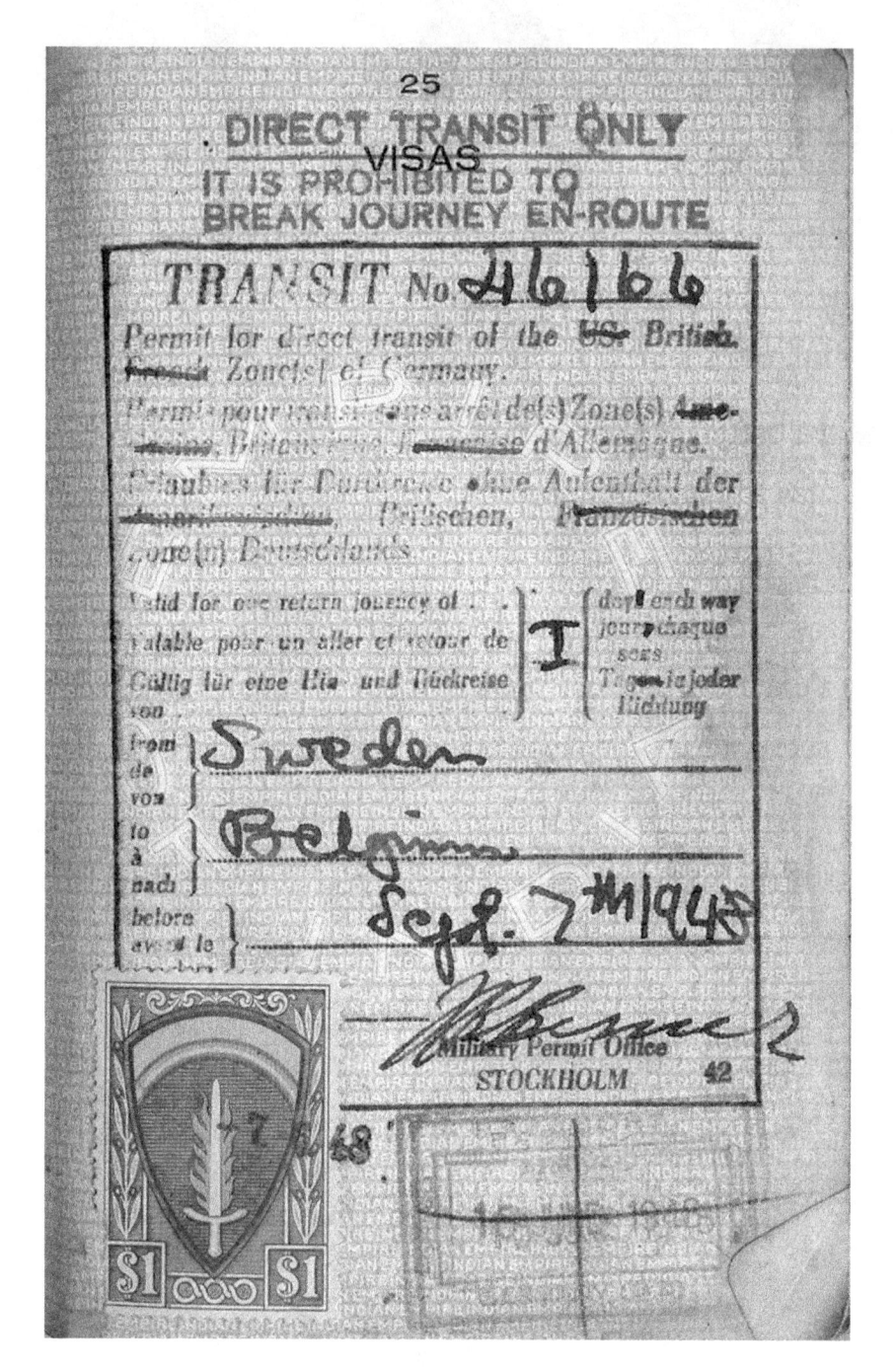

Savitri's permit to pass through British-occupied Germany, on 15 June 1948. (See Chapter 4.)

Editor's Preface

Savitri Devi (1905-1982) was an ardent National Socialist. She regarded Hitler's Germany as a Holy Land for all Aryans. But Savitri never saw National Socialist Germany in its days of glory.[1] She saw it only in ruins. *Gold in the Furnace* is the record of her experiences.

My purpose in this Preface is not to provide a summary, analysis, or critique of *Gold*, but to tell the story of its creation based primarily on *Defiance*, Savitri's gripping and powerful account of her arrest, trial, and imprisonment in 1949 for distributing National Socialist propaganda in occupied Germany. *Defiance* is something of a companion volume to *Gold* since it tells the story of its creation.[2]

Savitri first entered Germany on the night of 15-16 June 1948. She was working as a dresser in the dance company of Ram Gopal.[3] The company was returning to London after a Scandinavian tour on the Nord Express, which entered Germany from Denmark at Flensburg, passed through Hamburg, Düsseldorf, and Cologne, and crossed the Belgian frontier near Aachen (Aix-la-Chapelle). In solidarity with the German people, many of whom were starving, Savitri neither ate nor drank. Nor did she sleep. She spent the night throwing packets of food and cigarettes and hand-lettered National Socialist leaflets from the windows of the train. She describes her experiences in Chapter 4 of *Gold*, "The Unforgettable Night."

Savitri returned to Germany on 7 or 11 September 1948[4] with eleven thousand posters and leaflets printed for her in London by Count Geoffrey Potocki de Montalk, a pro-German poet, printer, and pretender to the throne of Poland whom Savitri had met in London in 1945 or 1946.[5] In addition to stealthily distributing National Socialist

---

[1] "Savitri Devi" is a *nom de plume* meaning "Sun Goddess." ("Savitri" = sun; "Devi" = goddess.) It may seem like undue familiarity to refer to her, for the sake of verbal economy, as "Savitri" rather than as "Devi," but "Devi" is not a surname, but a title analogous to "Saint," and just as one refers to Saint Paul as Paul for short, rather than as Saint, one refers to Savitri Devi as Savitri, not Devi. Savitri's surname, after her marriage, was Mukherji, Mukherji being a contraction of Mukhopadhyaya.

[2] Savitri Devi, *Defiance* (Calcutta: A.K. Mukherji, 1951).

[3] Ram Gopal (1912-2003) was one of the leaders of the revival of classical Indian dance and one of the most celebrated and widely travelled dancers of the twentieth century.

[4] In *Defiance* (51), Savitri gives her date of return as 7 September 1948; in *Gold* (123) she gives the date as 11 September.

[5] Count Geoffrey Wladyslaw Vaile Potocki de Montalk (1903-1997).

propaganda, Savitri had three other goals: to contact die-hard National Socialists, to take part in any possible resistance activities, and to record her experiences in a book.

Savitri probably began writing *Gold in the Furnace* shortly after her return to Germany. The Introduction to *Gold* is dated 3 October 1948 and was completed in Alfeld an der Leine, about 60 kilometres south of Hanover. Savitri remained in Germany until 6 December 1948, when she returned to London to spend the Christmas holidays with friends.[1] We know that the first two chapters of *Gold*, "The Philosophy of the Swastika" and "Brief Days of Glory," were completed before or during her holiday, as Savitri prepared a typescript of them while in London. She then wrote out the beginning of Chapter 3, "Now, the Trial," by hand and appended it to the typescript.[2]

Savitri returned to Germany sometime after Christmas of 1948 and resumed her activities. On 12 February 1949, she completed Chapter 3 of *Gold* in a café in Bonn.[3] She began writing Chapter 4 in a café in Hanover the day before she departed for Cologne,[4] where she was arrested on the night of 20-21 February 1949.[5] The remaining chapters of *Gold*—the end of Chapter 4 and ten other chapters—were written in captivity, at great speed, in a blaze of inspiration: "I wrote feverishly every day. I felt inspired. And the days were long."[6]

Savitri was transferred to the Werl prison on 21 or 22 February 1949. Although her manuscripts had been confiscated by the police, she was given pen and paper upon her arrival so she could write letters.[7] Fearing the manuscript of *Gold* lost, she promptly tried to rewrite the Introduction, Chapters 1-3, and the beginning of Chapter 4.[8] By 14 March, when her manuscripts were returned to her, she had completed Chapter 4 and Chapter 5, "'De-Nazification.'" By 5 April, the day of her trial, she had completed Chapter 6, "Chambers of Hell," and had begun Chapter 7, "Plunder, Lies, and Shallowness." Thus she wrote or

---

[1] *Defiance*, 52. The friends were probably Muriel Gantry (1913-2000) and Veronica Vassar (d. 1972).

[2] *Defiance*, 200.

[3] *Defiance*, 85.

[4] *Defiance*, 116.

[5] Savitri Devi, *And Time Rolls On: The Savitri Devi Interviews*, ed. R.G. Fowler (Atlanta: Black Sun Publications, 2005), 53.

[6] *Defiance*, 530.

[7] *Defiance*, 114.

[8] In *Defiance* (94), she gives the date 21 February, but this does not seem to be consistent with the chronology of the book's narrative, which indicates a later day. In *And Time Rolls On* (61), she gives the date as 22 February, which makes more sense.

re-wrote six chapters and part of a seventh in about six weeks—up to page 118 in this edition.[1]

On 5 April 1949, Savitri was convicted of disseminating Nazi propaganda by a British military tribunal in Düsseldorf and sentenced to three years imprisonment. She was returned to Werl to serve out her sentence. A few days later she completed Chapter 7 and began work on Chapter 8, "A Peep into the Enemy's Camp."[2] By 13 May, or soon thereafter, Savitri had completed Chapter 8, had gone on to write three other chapters (Chapter 9, "The Élite of the World," Chapter 10, "Divine Vengance," and Chapter 11, "The Constructive Side"—up to page 222 in this edition) and to begin work on a fourth (Chapter 12, "The Holy Forest")—all in about five weeks.[3] Savitri was still working on Chapter 12 when on 30 May her cell was searched and her manuscripts confiscated. On 17 June, however, her manuscripts were returned to her. Although she was expressly forbidden to continue writing *Gold*, she completed the book on the sly, finishing Chapter 12 and going on to write Chapter 13, "Echoes from the Russian Zone," and Chapter 14, "Against Time." She recorded that the final chapter was "Finished in cell no. 49 of the Werl prison, on the 16th of July, 1949."[4]

Savitri's speed in writing *Gold* seems all the more remarkable in light of the fact that she was writing her *magnum opus*, *The Lightning and the Sun*, at the same time. She wrote the first chapter of *Lightning* on 9 April 1948 in Edinburgh while on tour with Ram Gopal.[5] She recorded that Chapter 3 of *Lightning* was completed in the railway station of Karlsruhe in Baden-Württemberg on 6 December 1948, the day she left Germany to spend the Christmas holidays in London.[6] Savitri mentions that on 8 April 1949 she decided to return to working on Chapter 4 of *Lightning*.[7] By the time her cell was searched and her manuscripts were seized on 30 May, Savitri had started writing Chapter 5 of *Lightning*. Although Savitri was forbidden to work on *Gold* after her manuscripts were returned to her on 17 June, that very day she was

---

[1] *Defiance*, 184. Savitri marked the point in Chapter 7 where she resumed work after her conviction with a footnote. See below, 118 n2.

[2] *Defiance*, 288.

[3] *Defiance*, 393.

[4] *Gold*, 288.

[5] Savitri Devi, *The Lightning and the Sun* (Calcutta: Savitri Devi Mukherjee, 1958), 19.

[6] *Lightning*, 55.

[7] *Defiance*, 276.

given a writing pad, pen, and ink to continue writing about Genghis Khan in *Lightning*; on 22 June she was given a copy book.[1] Amazingly, none of the British authorities who examined the early chapters of *Lightning* thought it sufficiently National Socialist in orientation or political in implication to consider the book dangerous.[2] After Savitri completed *Gold* on 16 July, she continued to work on Chapter 5 of *Lightning* until her release from prison on 18 August. At the end of Chapter 5, she records that it was "Written in Werl (Westphalia) in July and August, 1949."[3]

The manuscript of *Gold*, along with the manuscripts of *Lightning* and *Impeachment of Man*, narrowly escaped destruction after being confiscated during the aforementioned search of Savitri's cell on 30 May 1949. Although the authorities may have heard rumours that Savitri was continuing to write *Gold*, it is not among the stated reasons for the search. Instead, her cell was searched because Savitri had received forbidden visits from female prisoners convicted of war crimes; furthermore, as the holder of a British passport, Savitri was entitled to better food than the German prisoners, and she had shared her rations with the war criminals; moreover, once Savitri was locked up for National Socialist propaganda, she simply continued her efforts among the prisoners, talking to them and sharing the texts of her leaflets; Savitri also wore Indian earrings adorned with the swastika and showed them to fellow prisoners; she even kept a picture of Hitler in her cell.

On 3 June, Savitri had an interview with the Governor of Werl, Colonel Edward Vickers, who complained of three things: that she had a picture of Hitler in her cell, that she had a copy of *Das neue Soldaten-Liederbuch* (*The New Soldiers' Songbook*), vol. 3, the first song of which was "Wir fahren gegen Engelland" ("We are going [to War] against England"), and that she received visits from war criminals. It was Savitri who raised the topic of her manuscripts. Vickers told her they were in the hands of experts and that they would be destroyed if deemed subversive.[4] Vickers repeated the threat on 10 June, when he told Savitri, to her lasting joy and pride, that she was "the most objectionable type of Nazi" he had ever met.[5]

After three agonizing weeks of fear for her manuscripts, Savitri was

---

[1] *Defiance*, 527-28.
[2] *Defiance*, 527.
[3] *Lightning*, 86.
[4] *Defiance*, 467.
[5] *Defiance*, 514.

stunned to learn on 17 June[1] that all her seized property had been returned to her: her manuscripts, her National Socialist songbook, her personal copies of her propaganda leaflets, even her picture of Hitler.[2] Savitri never learned the reasons behind this decision. Perhaps the British authorities simply could not have been bothered to read her manuscripts. Perhaps they followed the recommendation of the prison doctor who examined Savitri and found that her ordeal was taking a toll on her health.[3] Whatever the proximate causes, Savitri believed she spied the hand of Providence at work behind them and gave thanks to the gods.

Savitri also made the best of her dark night of the soul. It wrung from her some of her deepest reflections and most inspired prose, namely Chapter 12 of *Defiance*, "The Way of Absolute Detachment." Here Savitri tries to reconcile herself to the possible destruction of her manuscripts and to justify going to any lengths to save them. To accomplish this, she appeals to the Bhagavad-Gita's doctrine of "karma yoga," which teaches that one who does the right thing, one's duty—detaching himself from all concern with positive or negative consequences and leaving all such concerns to the gods who look after the welfare of the world—can rest in consciousness of complete moral rectitude.

Aside from the temporary seizure of her manuscripts, Werl turned out to be an almost ideal place for Savitri to write. She had ample free time and few distractions. The women imprisoned for war crimes whom she met provided her with useful information. Above all, she enjoyed working and sleeping in peace and quiet, far removed from the maddening twenty-four hour din of Calcutta.[4] Having been arrested and convicted for Nazi propaganda, Savitri was, of course, forbidden to write it in jail. But most of the German members of the prison staff took a liking to her and either tolerated or actively assisted her writing. Furthermore, Savitri was not forbidden to write entirely. She could, for instance, write letters. So even if she were observed writing by someone unsympathetic to her, that alone would not raise suspicion. The authorities would have had actually to read what she had written, and no one in the Werl administration seemed inclined to do so. Before her trial, Savitri was not required to work; after her conviction, she was.

---

[1] There had already been a preliminary search on 26 May and a clandestine search on 27 May, thus her ordeal had lasted three weeks by 17 June.
[2] *Defiance*, 523-27.
[3] *Defiance*, 470-78.
[4] *Defiance*, 397, 452-53.

But a sympathetic German member of the prison staff gave her light duties so she would have time to continue writing.[1]

The lack of paper was a significant inconvenience, but Savitri was resourceful:

> I saved to the utmost the little paper I had. I would write upon the envelopes of the rare letters I received, or even upon the letters themselves, between the lines, or on the packing paper from the parcels that a kind friend occasionally sent me from England, so as to make the half a dozen sheets I had left last as long as I could. I wrote at first very faintly, with a black pencil. Then, again, upon the same paper, over the pale writing with more stress, so that, this time, only the second writing would show. Then, I used over that second writing an indelible pencil which Colonel Vickers had given me "to write letters," on the day following my arrival . . . . And whenever it was possible, I would write a fourth time over this third writing, with pen and ink. Each successive writing I copied, after correcting it, in the brown copy-book, with pen and ink.[2]

The lack of paper became even more acute after the search. Savitri was forbidden to continue work on *Gold*, and although she was given paper to continue writing *Lightning*, she could not use it for writing *Gold* because the pages had been counted, and she might have been asked to account for her use of each page. But again Savitri was resourceful:

> What I actually did was to write the rough text of my dangerous book . . . upon my wooden stool, with a piece of chalk that the searchers were kind enough to forget in a corner of my drawer; to correct it, wiping out with a damp cloth this sentence or that one, until I was satisfied with it; and then to copy it off with pen and ink, in tight writing, paragraph by paragraph, not upon my new writing pad nor in the copy-book . . . but at the back of the pages of the letters that I used to receive from Miss V [Veronica Vassar]. And that too, not in English, but in Bengali; and with many abbreviations and conventional signs of my own.[3]

After each letter was filled, Savitri returned it to its envelope and asked

---

[1] *Defiance*, 250.
[2] *Defiance*, 392.
[3] *Defiance*, 529.

to have it placed in storage until the day of her release. Once free, she needed only to translate the end of her book into English.

Another inconvenience was lack of access to reference materials. Savitri mentions this in the text of *Gold* itself.[1] Because of these limitations, *Gold* consists primarily of professions of faith and narratives of Savitri's and others' personal experiences, rather than rigorously documented philosophical and historical discussions of National Socialism, World War II, and the Allied occupation. Nevertheless, *Gold* does contain many quotations, and Chapters 7 and 11 in particular contain many footnotes. Thus it is tempting to conclude that these quotations and notes were added after *Gold* was completed, which belies Savitri's assertions that the book was composed entirely in prison.

Savitri did, however, have a remarkable memory. Even in old age, she was able to quote her favourite passages from Hitler's *Mein Kampf* from memory, including the page numbers. Her memory also suffices to account for her quotes from Racine's *Andromaque*, which she had committed to memory as a child, as well as her quotes from Leconte de Lisle, Victor Hugo, Akhnaton's hymns to the sun, Wulf Sörensen's *Die Stimme der Ahnen* (*The Voice of the Ancestors*, which she mistakenly believed to have been written by Heinrich Himmler), and other works. Furthermore, in *Defiance* we learn that Savitri had a number of books with her in prison: the Bhagavad-Gita, Gottfried Feder's *Das Programm der NSDAP* (*The Programme of the NSDAP*), H.R. Hall's *The Ancient History of the Near East*, Herbert H. Gowan's *An Outline History of Japan*, a *Mythology of Ancient Britain* (perhaps Charles L. Squire's *The Mythology of Ancient Britain and Ireland*), an *Art and Civilisation of Ancient America*, two books on Mongolian history[2] (Harold Lamb's *The March of the Barbarians*[3] and Ralph Fox's *Genghis Khan*[4]), and the aforementioned *New Soldiers' Songbook*. Moreover, Savitri mentions that she had copies of and extracts from the periodicals she cites in Chapter 7 with her in prison.[5] Finally, she mentions that the passages she quotes from Winston Churchill's *War Memoirs* in a footnote to Chapter 3[6] were copied from an issue of *Life* magazine given to her by a fellow prisoner.[7] So it is quite conceivable

---

[1] *Gold*, 182, 202.
[2] *Defiance*, 258.
[3] *Gold*, 196 n1.
[4] *Gold*, 283 n1.
[5] *Defiance*, 248.
[6] *Gold*, 20-21, n1.
[7] *Defiance*, 301.

that Savitri also had access to the other titles she quotes in *Gold* while in prison. Of course Savitri probably checked her citations from memory against the originals once she left prison, and she added at least two notes,[1] but her claim that *Gold* was written in prison is essentially true.

After her release from Werl on 18 August 1949, Savitri entered the French occupied zone to visit friends in Koblenz. On 21 August, she left Germany for France where she took up residence in her home town of Lyons. But instead of immediately publishing *Gold*, Savitri first wrote and published *Defiance*. It was Savitri's custom to write the Forewords to her books last. The Foreword to *Defiance* was written in Lyons on 29 August 1950.[2] *Defiance* was published in 1951 in Calcutta by Savitri's husband A.K. Mukherji. Savitri then turned her attention to *Gold* and *Lightning*. She recorded that chapters 6 and 7 of *Lightning* were written in Lyons in 1951 and 1952, but the book was not finished until 21 March 1956 in Hanover,[3] after many more adventures in Germany, some of which Savitri chronicled in *Pilgrimage* and *Long-Whiskers and the Two-Legged Goddess*.[4] The Foreword to *Gold* was written in Lyons on 21 August 1952. The book was published later that year in Calcutta by A.K. Mukherji.

On the Present Edition

The first edition of *Gold in the Furnace* contains many errors and stylistic inconsistencies. Savitri attributed these to the fact that the book was printed in India while she was in France, unable to oversee production. Page proofs were apparently sent to her, but she gives no indication they were ever received.[5] In truth, Savitri also needed the services of a good copy editor.

My goal as editor was to make the minimum number of editorial interventions necessary to bring *Gold* into accord with proper English and contemporary stylistic canons. Following Savitri's use of British English, I

---

[1] *Gold*, 56 n1, 118 n1,

[2] *Defiance*, vii.

[3] *Lightning*, 126.

[4] *Pilgrimage* (Calcutta: Savitri Devi Mukherji, 1958) was written in Emsdetten, Westphalia in 1953-54. The Introduction is dated 3 June 1953; the completion date of the book is 6 February 1954 (*Pilgrimage*, 8, 354). *Long-Whiskers and the Two-Legged Goddess, or the true story of a "most objectionable Nazi" and . . . half-a-dozen cats* (Calcutta: Savitri Devi Mukherji, 1965), was begun in Joda near Baramjamda in Orissa, India, in September 1957 and completed in Hanover on 10 July 1961 (*Long-Whiskers*, 136).

[5] *And Time Rolls On*, 68.

have corrected errors of spelling and grammar and made the style consistent throughout. I corrected a few "foreignisms": unidiomatic diction and syntax based on French and German, the languages that Savitri was using regularly while writing *Gold*. I corrected errors of diction, e.g., "enormity" where "enormousness" was meant, "ostensibly" where "ostensively" was meant, "specially" where "especially" was meant, etc. I strayed from my minimalist approach in Chapter 4, where I changed the tense of part of Savitri's account of her conversation with Sven Hedin to impart greater immediacy. I preserved Savitri's sometimes eccentric capitalization practices without trying to make them consistent.

The subtitle, "Experiences in Post-War Germany," does not appear in the first edition, but it translates the subtitle of the 1982 German translation of *Gold*, "Erlebnisse im Nachkriegsdeutschland." Since Savitri was in constant contact with the translator, Lotte Asmus, while the book was in preparation, it is reasonable to assume that Savitri approved of the subtitle.

Regarding punctuation and capitalization: Savitri did not merely use commas and semicolons to organize information on a page, but to indicate dramatic pauses in imaginary speech. She indicates quite a few pauses, which seems ironic to anyone who actually heard her speak, for she spoke quickly and without pause. Nevertheless, I have maintained her punctuation practices. There are six exceptions to this. First, I "updated" the use of hyphens, for example in "to-day" and "to-morrow." Second, I regularized the use of commas before conjunctions. Third, I removed a few commas that seemed to be obvious strays, conforming neither to accepted usage nor to Savitri's style. Fourth, I eliminated commas and, in a couple of cases, semicolons that were adjacent to dashes. Fifth, Savitri enclosed every instance of the word "de-Nazification" in "scare quotes." Although it pains my editorial conscience, I did not follow this practice when the repetition seemed tedious and excessive. Finally, there were several sentences that were difficult to read and understand because commas and semicolons had sprouted between virtually every word. I weeded out just enough punctuation to make these sentences readable.

I have translated all quotations in French and German or looked up existing translations. I have cited standard translations of French and German works, even where the translation is mine. Where possible, I have supplied complete citations for books and articles mentioned. Finally, where useful, I have provided editor's notes, which are clearly marked as such.

I encourage those who wish to check my editorial labours against the original to contact me at the Savitri Devi Archive (www.savitridevi.org), and I will provide them a photocopy of the first edition at cost or a PDF free of charge.

I judged a third edition of *Gold* necessary because of problems with the second edition, published by Historical Review Press, most notably the omission of two entire pages of text. I would have preferred the entire printing scrapped and a corrected version printed. That was not done, hence this third edition. In the end, it was all for the best, because preparing this new edition has given me the opportunity to discover and correct a number of my own editorial mistakes, thus bringing this edition into closer correspondence both with Savitri's original and my own editorial principles.

ACKNOWLEDGEMENTS

I wish to thank all who made this new edition of *Gold in the Furnace* possible: Colin Jordan for supplying a copy of *Gold* that had belonged to his ex-wife Françoise Dior, the copy that I scanned for this and the previous edition; Beryl Cheetham for supplying a copy of the dust jacket for *Gold* hand-painted for her by Savitri herself in 1961; Miriam Hirn for the cover photo and the 1948 photos of Savitri in Germany and Sweden; J. for the images of pages from Savitri's 1940-1950 passport; Fr. Genesthai for his advice on editorial matters; and John Morgan and D.A.R. Sokoll for carefully reading the page proofs. Special thanks are due Kevin Slaughter for recreating the original cover by Gabriella Anelauskaitė.

Beryl Cheetham was Savitri's friend for more than twenty years and was especially helpful to Savitri during the last year of her life, when, with failing health and fading eyesight, she travelled around France and Germany living on the charity of friends and comrades. Beryl's contributions to this new edition of *Gold* go beyond the back jacket/cover, for she has been indispensable to my research on Savitri Devi. Therefore, for her help to Savitri and to me, I wish to dedicate this new edition of *Gold* to her.

Savitri in Alfeld an der Leine, Lower Saxony, 5 December 1948

Foreword

In 1948, I was able to enter Germany for the second time thanks to the military permit granted to me by the *Bureau des Affaires Allemandes* (in Paris) on the ground that I was going there to gather the necessary information for writing a book. This book is none other than the present one (ironical as the fact might be, from the standpoint of the temporarily victorious Democracies). Its Introduction and three first chapters were already written when, on the 20th of February 1949, I was arrested on account of "Nazi propaganda," and the rest of it was entirely written in my cell in the Werl prison. It owes its publication, nay, its very survival as a manuscript, to a miracle, or rather, to a hardly believable series of miracles, of which I have related the extraordinary story in detail in another book of mine, *Defiance*,[1] written after my release.

All I wish to express here—four years after the actual writing of this book—is, once more, my boundless gratitude to the invisible Powers for having saved it as miraculously as if They had, indeed, pulled its pages, untouched, out of the fire. All I wish to express is my confidence in Their patient, passionless, impersonal Wisdom—in that Wisdom that uses everything for the greater glory of persecuted higher mankind and for the triumph of the Truth and Beauty it embodies. Those Forces which saved this book and brought it to light in spite of all, will bring my comrades and superiors back to power and, through them, save what is worth saving in the West, one day. Thus do I at least interpret the meaning of this miracle of Theirs in my favour.

Heil Hitler!
Savitri Devi Mukherji
Lyons (France)
21 August 1952

---

[1] Savitri Devi, *Defiance* (Calcutta: A.K. Mukherji, 1951).

Savitri's visa to pass through Denmark on "The Unforgettable Night" of 15-16 June 1948.

Introduction

"Age after age, when justice is crushed, when evil rules supreme, I come; again I take birth on earth to save the world."

—The Bhagavad-Gita[1]

"Ein ganzes Volk, eine ganze Nation fühlt sich heute stark und glücklich, weil in Ihnen diesem Volk nicht nur der Führer, weil in Ihnen diesem Volk auch der Retter erstanden ist."

—Hermann Göring[2]

Gods—*i.e.*, divinely inspired supermen—are not born on earth every day, nor every century. And when they do come, and live and act in their miraculous manner, not every man, not every nation recognises them. Blessed is the nation who follows to the bitter end the divine men born in her midst, and who, whether in victory or disaster, clings to their spirit! That nation will triumph over the forces of death, in the long run, and thrive in beauty, strength, and joy, while the rest of the ungrateful world lies in waste at her feet.

Thirty years ago, one could have believed that the days of the Gods were over forever; that the promise given to the world in the Book of books—the Bhagavad-Gita—was never again to be fulfilled; that mankind, day by day more degenerate, more bastardized, stupider, sicklier, uglier, had become incapable of producing an Individual worthy of carrying out a divine mission on an international scale. Both in the East and in the West, even the superior races were, or seemed to be, in full decay, nay, completely exhausted; nearing their end.

But the message of the triumph of life, over and over again—God's promise—can never fail. The words spoken by the world's eternal Sustainer, no one remembers when, in Kurukshetra:[3] "I come again . . . ," were not spoken in vain. They hold good for all times, and for all lands in which a truly noble race, however tired, however overwhelmed by the darkening shadow of death, is still alive enough to bear witness to

---

[1] The Bhagavad-Gita, 4:7-8

[2] "A whole people, a whole nation feels strong and fortunate today, for in you not only a leader but also a saviour has arisen" (Speech in Nuremberg, 15 September 1935) [Trans. by Ed.].

[3] The famous battlefield in ancient India, where the words in the Bhagavad-Gita were spoken.

their accomplishment; to marvel and to adore; and to rise at the bidding of the returning Saviour. "When justice is crushed, when evil rules supreme"—when all hope seems irretrievably lost—the Saviour is already there, waiting, unnoticed among the crowd; ready to reveal Himself.

At the close of the First World War, out of prostrate Germany, rose the Man destined to infuse a new strength and a new pride, to breathe a new joyful life, not only into his own people, but into the racial élite of the whole world; the greatest European of all times: Adolf Hitler. Alone, with no other riches but the love of his great heart, an indomitable will, and the intuition of things eternal; with no other strength but the compelling power of truth; with no other help but that of the invisible Gods, whose Chosen One he was, he accomplished what no man could have even dreamed. Not only did he raise Germany out of poverty, servitude, and demoralisation—out of the dust—once more to the rank of a great Power, but he made her the herald of a splendid idea of everlasting and universal scope. For a few brief years—until international Jewry succeeded in stirring against him the forces of the stupid majority of mankind—he was able to show the world the masterpiece of his creative genius: a super-civilisation, materially perfect, and, at the same time, inspired with a faith in the superior values of life, conscious of life's true purpose, as no other had yet ever been, even in Antiquity; the first step towards the New Order in Europe, forerunner of a new "age of truth" in the evolution of the world; that glory that was National Socialist Germany.

Had Germany emerged victorious from the Second World War, and imposed Hitler's dream upon the whole of the earthly sphere—or had there been no war, and had the Idea conquered ground slowly and steadily, through the sole strength of its appeal to the natural aristocracy of humanity—what a wonderful place this planet would have become, in less than a generation or two! We would then have witnessed the intelligent rule of the best, over a world organised according to that selfsame spirit in which the fair, strong and wise conquerors—the Aryans, or "noble ones"—organised India (that land of many races) in the far-gone days when the Nordic pride was still vivid in their hearts, along with the memory of their distant Arctic home.

We would have seen the natural hierarchy of human races—and individuals—part and parcel of the natural hierarchy of beings, ordained by the Sun, restored and maintained, stressed by law, exalted, in a reinstalled natural religion, wherever, in the words of the

Bhagavad-Gita, "the corruption of women has brought forth the confusion of castes"; a truly "new earth and new heaven"; the rebirth of the world under the Sign of the Sun.

Men were too stupid and too vulgar to feel the beauty of that dream. The world—the Aryan race itself, at large—refused the gift of Hitler's love and genius, and repaid him with the darkest ingratitude. Few of the great Ones have been so mercilessly vilified as he, by their worthless contemporaries. Not one has been so utterly misunderstood, so systematically betrayed, and, above all, so widely hated.

Now—outwardly at least—the agents of disintegration have had their way. Proud and beautiful National Socialist Germany lies in ruins; hundreds of Hitler's most active collaborators are dead; thousands are living, in captivity, a life worse than death. And the millions who acclaimed him only a few years ago with an enthusiasm amounting to adoration, are now silent. *"Es ist das Land der Angst"*—"this is the land of fear"—were the words addressed to me in Saarbrücken, in 1948, as the summary of the whole situation in occupied Germany. And no one knows where Hitler is, if still alive.

Yet, the National Socialist creed, based upon truths as old as the Sun, can never be blotted out. Living or dead, Adolf Hitler can never die. And sooner or later, his spirit must triumph.

This book is addressed to all his true followers, whether in or outside Germany; to all those who, in 1948, cling to the National Socialist ideals as steadfastly as they did in 1933 and in 1940.

But it is specially addressed to the German ones—to those who kept their faith in our Führer under the streams of fire and phosphorus poured down on them, from the Anglo-American planes, night after night, for five years; to those who continued to love and revere him in the midst of the atrocious post-war conditions imposed upon them by his enemies—under humiliations of all sorts; under persecution; and in hunger; in concentration camps, or in the bleak desolation of their ruined homes—in spite of all the frenzied attempts to "de-Nazify" them at all costs; to the men of gold and steel whom defeat could not dishearten, whom terror and torture could not subdue, whom money could not buy: the real Nazis, my comrades, my superiors—for I have not had the honour of suffering materially for our ideals, as they have— the only ones, among my contemporaries, for whom I would gladly die.

I thank all the friends who, in or outside this country, have helped me in my endeavour to prepare, along with them, the resurrection of our New Order.

I cannot also help thanking those of our enemies who, without knowing what they were doing, have so kindly made it possible for me to come to Germany. They too—for once—acted as instruments of those unseen Forces that are already clearing the way for the ultimate triumph of the Swastika.

Heil Hitler!
SAVITRI DEVI MUKHERJI
Alfeld an der Leine (Niedersachsen)
3 October 1948

Chapter 1

THE PHILOSOPHY OF THE SWASTIKA

"Thou hast set every man in his place. Thou hast made them different in form and in speech, and in the colour of their skins. As a divider, Thou hast divided the foreign people."

—Akhnaton[1]

"Out of the corruption of women proceeds the confusion of castes; out of the confusion of castes, the loss of memory; out of the loss of memory, the lack of understanding; and out of this, all evils."

—Bhagavad-Gita[2]

"Alle großen Kulturen der Vergangenheit gingen nur zugrunde, weil die ursprünglich schöpferische Rasse an Blutvergiftung abstarb."

—Adolf Hitler[3]

A Movement such as National Socialism, destined to appeal to millions, does not attract every one of its adherents for the same reasons. That matters little, as long as the Movement is triumphant. Then, the more the better. Even the fellow who joins the Party for the material advantages he hopes to get out of it, can be made use of. And his children, at any rate—provided they be of irreproachable blood— can be trained into better Nazis than himself.

But, those alone who uphold the National Socialist Idea for the sake of something vital and fundamental—those alone who found in it the perfect expression of their own life-long philosophy—can be expected to cling to it under all circumstances whatsoever. I do not say they are the only ones likely to cling to it. A sense of duty, a chivalrous feeling of obligation towards their glorious past, a consciousness of gratitude towards a régime that gave them great privileges as long as it lasted, can, of course, prompt thousands of others to remain faithful in the

---

[1] Longer Hymn to the Sun, circa 1,400 BC.
[2] Bhagavad-Gita, 1:41-42; based on Eugène Burnouf's nineteenth-century French translation—Ed.
[3] "All great cultures of the past perished only because the originally creative race died of blood poisoning" (*Mein Kampf*, I, xi, p. 316; cf. Mannheim, p. 289) [Trans. by Ed.].

midst of untold hardships. And those thousands are to be praised. Yet, no allegiance is worth that which is based upon the physical impossibility of betraying one's own self. "One cannot kill a *Weltanschauung*—an outlook on the universe; a philosophy—by force, but only through the aggressive impact of another *Weltanschauung*."[1] These are the very words of the Founder of National Socialism. And how true they ring today, after twenty-five years! The real Nazis—those who can (and will) resist, and defeat, in the end, the coalesced forces of a temporarily triumphant world—are those to whom not merely the political side of National Socialism, but the National Socialist conception of man and life is so natural that no other "*Weltanschauung*" can possibly appeal to them, however cleverly advertised it be, by people who pretend to know the art of advertising in and out.

* * *

The National Socialist conception of man and life is anything but "new." Its first exponents on this earth were probably the oldest seers of mankind, and the principles on which it is based are as ancient as life itself. Only the National Socialist movement is new. Not merely new, but unique of its kind. It is, in the whole evolution of the West, the sole systematic attempt to build a state—nay, to organise a continent—upon the frank acknowledgement of the everlasting laws that rule the growth of races and the creation of culture; the one rational effort to put a stop to the decay of a superior race and to the subsequent confusion. It is the movement "against Time" *par excellence*—the movement against the age-old downward trend of history—conscious of the one way out of the evils and ugliness of our degenerate epoch, back to the joy and glory of every great beginning, and boldly urging along that way the noblest people of the West.

But precisely in order to appreciate all its novelty, and all its beauty, one should bear in mind the eternity of the philosophy that lies behind it; of what I call the philosophy of the Swastika.

This is not the philosophy of any man. It is, in the clear consciousness of the really great Ones who are capable of feeling it—from the oldest Aryan lawgivers of Vedic and post-Vedic India, down

---

[1] This is a paraphrase of ideas expressed in *Mein Kampf* I, v, pp. 186-89; Mannheim, pp. 170-72.—Ed.

to Adolf Hitler today—the wisdom of the Cosmos, the philosophy of the Sun, Father-and-Mother of the earth.

For man is but a part of the Cosmos—"a solar product," as a brilliant English author put it![1] He cannot, with impunity, set up laws for himself, against those unwritten, everlasting laws that govern life as a whole. In particular, he cannot disregard the laws that regulate the art of breeding and the evolution of races, and expect to escape the consequences which automatically follow, sooner or later, that "sin against the will of the Creator"[2] and which are "physical and moral degeneracy."

The Christian philosophy—nay, the philosophy of all those international religions whose adherent "any person" can become, on a level of equality with all other adherents—puts stress upon the mind, the "soul," the "immaterial" side of man (supposed to be everlasting and all-precious) at the expense of that transient thing: the body. It forgets that, as the one vehicle of transmission of life, the body also partakes of divine everlastingness; that it is not merely the "temple of the Holy Ghost," but the creator of that consciousness which *is* the Holy Ghost, in the individual, in the individual's progeny, in the race at large.

The oldest religions in the world—none of which were "international," but all of which applied to the folk in the midst of whom they sprang the one, super-human wisdom—stressed the primary importance of the physical side of man; the holiness of the act of life; the duties and the responsibilities of the body not only towards the individual "soul" of which it may be considered as an instrument of development, but towards past and future generations; towards the race, that is to say, towards the Cosmos, of which the race is a part. They upheld the private cult of each man's ancestors and the public cult of each folk's heroes, and forbade objectionable marriages as a sin against the dead and against the unborn—against Life eternal. They admitted as a matter of course the fundamental inequality of human beings, rooted in imponderable causes; the inequality of human races, and the absolute differentiation of the sexes.

We have not copied the Ancients. No living thing is ever a "copy." And the National Socialist movement, if anything, is living; nay, is, in spite of the temporary triumph of its enemies, the one real force of life

---

[1] Norman Douglas, *How about Europe? Some Footnotes on East and West* (London: Chatto and Windus, 1930).

[2] *Mein Kampf*, I, xi, p. 314; cf. Mannheim, p. 286.

and resurrection in the half-dead world of today. No, we have not copied the Ancients. But we have, under the inspiration of that god among men—Adolf Hitler—become once more aware of the wisdom of all times without which life is bound to decay; of the wisdom, to the gradual forgetting of which is to be traced, from the dawn of history onwards, the increasing degeneracy of mankind and, in particular, the decline of the Aryan nations. We have become once more conscious of the fact that "only in pure blood does God abide."[1] And from the man-made religion and man-centred morality that had dominated Western consciousness for the last fifteen hundred years at least, we have come back to a life-centred religious outlook, to a morality based upon the inequality of rights and the diversity of duties among both individuals and races, and to a political conception proclaiming the right and the duty of the superior races—and of the superior personalities in every race—to rule. And we have set out to make this world first a safe place for the best—for the racial élite of mankind—and then a safe place for all the living, under the protection of the best.

* * *

This is so true that the intelligent and orthodox representatives of the one part of the world in which the aristocratic tradition of the Aryans, fossilised as it may have become in the course of centuries, was never submerged—Hindu India—have more than once judged National Socialism with a clearer insight than most Europeans outside Germany. It would astonish many German National Socialists to know what enthusiasm greeted the Führer's victories, in that distant land, during the recent war. There was, undoubtedly, a great deal of enmity towards British rule expressed in it. But there was in it also, something else, something deeper, much deeper. There was the expression of six thousand years of unflinching allegiance to the fair, strong, truly superior Race, the Aryans, or "noble ones," worshippers of the Sun and of the Northern Lights, who once brought the Vedas from their long-forsaken Arctic home,[2] and founded the civilisation which, to this day, in India, still bears their stamp; the recognition that the spirit of those ancient hallowed Aryans had at last awakened in their most genuine

---

[1] Wulf Sörensen [attributed to Heinrich Himmler], *Die Stimme der Ahnen. Eine Dichtung* (Magdeburg: Nordland, 1936), p. 36. [In English: *The Voice of the Ancestors: A Poetical Work by Wulf Sörensen*, trans. anonymous (Hammer, 1993), p. 39.—Ed.]

[2] Lokamanya Bal Gangadhar Tilak, *The Arctic Home in the Vedas: Being Also a New Key to the Interpretation of Many Vedic Texts and Legends* (Poona: Kesari, 1903).

modern descendants, in far-away Europe, and was triumphing.

India would soon no longer be "the last stronghold of Aryan culture," as some Hindu revivalists had called it. For Aryan culture would reconquer Europe under the rule of one of those men who appear once in the history of the world. But that Man's victory—the victory of the Aryan over the "*Mlechha*"[1]; of the ideal of racial hierarchy over that of democratic uniformity; of inspired leadership over the vanity of the obstinate herd—would be India's victory also, for the best of India's tradition was the age-old gift of that Man's eternal Race. And although not everyone could express this, many felt it, more or less dimly. Already more than one high-caste Hindu, aware of the real nature of the European conflict—not Germany versus England, but National Socialism versus all forms of democracy; the true Aryan outlook versus the Jewish—already more than one, I say, had acclaimed in the promoter of the western resurrection, Adolf Hitler, a "*devata*," *i.e.*, a "shining one," a being above mankind, and the modern incarnation of the ever-recurring Saviour. I have heard them say so, some of them in public.

But out of the hazy consciousness of the illiterate masses of India, sprang also, in those days, remarkable intuitions. I shall always remember a young servant—a boy of fifteen or so—telling me, in glorious '40: "I too, admire your Führer." And as I asked him if it were only because he was triumphant that he admired him, the boy replied: "Oh no! I admire him, and love him, because he is fighting to replace, in the West, the Bible by the Bhagavad-Gita." He had got that extraordinary piece of information from a talk in the Calcutta fish market. I was dumbfounded. For the information, though literally fanciful, was perfectly accurate in spirit.[2]

And I recalled in my mind the words of the old Sanskrit Scripture: "Out of the corruption of women proceeds the confusion of castes; out of the confusion of castes, the loss of memory; out of the loss of memory, the lack of understanding; and out of that, all evils," or, in modern language: out of indiscriminate breeding proceeds the mixture of unequal races (always to the detriment of the superior race); from that mixture, comes the loss of racial memory—the ignorance of who one's ancestors were, and of who one is one's self—and from that, the lack of understanding of one's rights and of one's duties—of one's

---

[1] The word used, in ancient Sanskrit Scriptures, to designate the inferior races.
[2] For a more complete telling of this story, see Savitri Devi, "Hitlerism and the Hindu World," *The National Socialist*, no. 2 (Fall 1980): 18-20.—Ed.

natural place in the world—and the consequence: "all evils," decay; death.

Yes, it was true that the "New Order in Europe" meant the restoration of the Aryan outlook expressed in this immemorial text, as opposed to all the religions and ideologies of equality; the triumph of the Philosophy of the Swastika over that of either the Cross or the Crescent or the Hammer and Sickle, and the end of that primordial cause of "all evils": shameful breeding. And it was true that Adolf Hitler was conducting the war to defend this New Order against the agents of disintegration who had planned to crush it. And it was true also, that, for centuries, no great man of action in the West or in the East had lived and struggled in absolute selflessness and detachment—actually according to the teaching of the Bhagavad-Gita—as he had. The marvel is that simple people, so far away, had found a forceful sentence to formulate that truth.

* * *

The central idea of National Socialism is that in the natural nobility of blood alone, source of the inherent qualities of the race, lies the secret of greatness. It is no use asking why one race is more gifted than another; why one has creative genius and others not. It is as silly as to wonder why a plane tree is not an oak tree. The Sun Himself, responsible for all differences among men as among other living species, has decreed from eternity which was to be, on this planet, the creative race *par excellence*. And that is why the immemorial solar Symbol—the Swastika—has become identified with the National Socialist Movement. Behind the will of Adolf Hitler, who decided that it should be so, was the divine will of the Sun.

It is, in particular, amazing, how historically sound are all Hitler's statements concerning the supremacy of the Aryans all over the world, throughout the ages—all the more so that, at the time he wrote his famous book, the Führer had seen nothing of the world outside Germany (save the battlefields of Ypres and other places where he had fought as a soldier during the First World War) and had never had the time to become a scholar.

He wrote from his heart. Yet, at the other end of the earth, outlandish monuments, raising their majestic lines out of coconut groves, under strange skies; hymns and poems in outlandish languages; atavistic memories and hallowed traditions of strange peoples—some, perhaps unknown to him in 1923—proclaim the truth of what he wrote.

Paintings and sculptures in South Indian temples, sacred dance dramas on the coast of Malabar; friezes upon the ruined walls of Angkor Wat; stories repeated to this day all over India, Java, Bali, perpetuate the glory of the fair Aryan hero, Rama, whose deeds once filled the East and the South with wonder and whom the descendants of the subjugated races still revere as a god. And as one recalls the inspiration behind those works of art and those traditions, one cannot but marvel at the exactitude of that bold summary of the evolution of mankind written by the modern champion of the Aryan race in the fortress of Landsberg am Lech: the eleventh chapter of the first part of *Mein Kampf*. Indeed, wherever one admires the tangible remnants of a great culture (provided one takes the trouble of going far enough back into the past) one finishes by tracing that culture to the glorious creative Race from the North to which belong both the fair warriors exalted in the Sanskrit epics (and portrayed in the technique of their Southern worshippers, on the walls of Dravidian temples and Cambodian palaces) and the author of *Mein Kampf* himself, and his beloved people.

The whole of Asia owes more or less its culture to the influence of Indian thought. And Indian thought—Sanskrit thought—is but the flower of the Aryan, or Nordic soul, in a tropical environment. And if, as some scholars believe, one can also prove that the same influences have given birth to the cultures of old America, to which the Swastika was also sacred—and that the same fact, namely "the gradual disappearance of the original creative race" through mixture of blood, has caused their downfall—then, one will only have proved how extraordinary Hitler's intuition of history is, and how solid is the rock on which he founded National Socialism.

* * *

Some have said that Adolf Hitler's greatness lies in the fact that he roused German patriotism as none had done before. Those who hate Germany—those who have, or think they have, some interest in trying to keep her down—hate him for that very reason. But in reality his greatness lies in far more than that. For the German patriotism which he roused is not the conventional patriotism that every European child is taught at school ever since there were separate states in Europe. It is a particular aspect of a broader and deeper—and more natural—feeling. It is the expression, in the German people—the first to have the privilege of regaining it in the West—of the world-wide Aryan consciousness, which is above frontiers; of the collective pride of all those who, however far they be living, now, from their original Nordic home, claim to belong to that truly noble and beautiful race to whom the world owes the best of its culture.

An upheaval such as no nation had yet experienced—an outburst of regained triumphant youth; a song of joy and freedom, on a scale of millions—was actually witnessed in Germany under the spell of Hitler's magnetic personality, and that, in spite of over fifteen hundred years of demoralizing influences. But there lies not the whole of the "German miracle." It lies also—it lies perhaps even more—in the fact that Aryans all over the world (few, admittedly, but the very best) hailed Hitler and Germany with him as the champion of their rights, as the Man and the country destined to fulfil, at last, their age-old aspirations. It lies in the fact that, during this war, Englishmen were happy to suffer in concentration camps in their own country for the National Socialist idea; that people of several foreign nations at war with Germany—including one or two Frenchmen[1]—have died for it; that, in far-away India, in 1942, some men and women were waiting with joy to see the German army march down from Russia through Afghanistan on the triumphal road the first Aryan conquerors had taken, six thousand years before—the Khyber Pass—and meet in Delhi its Japanese Allies; that, *after* this war, there remained (and still remains) a minority of non-German Aryans ready to face torture and death for the pleasure of defying the persecutors of National Socialism upon the very soil of occupied Germany.

This world-wide appeal of Adolf Hitler shows sufficiently that, although in its modern form it originated in Germany—and could not possibly have originated anywhere else—the National Socialist doctrine transcends Germany. As I have said, it is the everlasting truth about the laws of life and the evolution of human races, apprehended from the angle of the Nordic race.

That this Nordic race is a natural aristocracy, there is no doubt. First a physical aristocracy. To make sure of that, one need only look at its representatives, especially the purest Germanic types among the Germans and the Swedes, outwardly, perhaps, the finest men on earth. An aristocracy of character also, as a whole. One only has to live with Scandinavians, Germans, or *real* English people, after spending years amidst less pure Aryans, or totally different races, in order to find that out. An aristocracy of kindness, too—its most attractive sign of superiority. And this *is* a fact. The best proof of it is to be seen in the

---

[1] Such as Robert Brasillach, shot on 6 February 1945.

spontaneous sympathy which most pure-blooded Nordic children show towards animals, even before being taught to do so. Compare that with the spontaneous cruelty of the children of other races, with few exceptions! A five-year-old young German or young Englishman will stop to caress a cat, or offer something to eat to a dog in the street. A five-year-old child from the Mediterranean lands—or the Middle East—will throw a stone at the dog, pull the cat's tail, or do something worse, many a time. The indifference of the grownups to animal suffering, anywhere in the world save in the few lands where Nordic blood obviously prevails, is appalling enough, not to speak of the inborn nastiness of the majority of children.

That alone would be sufficient to confirm one's belief in the superiority of the pure Aryan, and to strengthen one's hopes that, after three or four generations of proper training—and enlightened breeding—the race could be made a race of supermen, creators of a new golden-age culture worthy of Nietzsche's dreams, worthy of Hitler's love. It would be enough to confirm one in one's conviction that the task which National Socialist Germany had undertaken—the systematic strengthening of the master race in Europe so that it might carry on an unparalleled super-civilisation—was, and still is, well worth its while.

* * *

That task was begun in Germany, as everyone knows, by the promulgation of a certain number of wholesome laws, intended to stop all objectionable breeding (and thereby to prevent the further physical and moral deterioration of the race), and by a wide-scale new education. When one remembers that Adolf Hitler took the government in hand in 1933, and that England, as a docile instrument of international Jewry, declared war on him in 1939, one can but marvel at the enormousness of what he accomplished within six years. No god could have done better in so short a time.

Yet, the measures actually taken would not have been sufficient to keep the people in the desired path for centuries without a new—or very old—religious outlook, expression of the reborn Nordic soul, coming into being and growing up side by side with the National State. The prominent men of the Movement—Adolf Hitler more than any other—were aware of this. And not merely theoreticians like Alfred Rosenberg,[1] and professors of the new thought like Ernst Bergmann[1]

---

[1] Author of the famous *Myth of the Twentieth Century, Der Mythus des 20.*

and others, but cool and practical-minded thinkers such as Dr. Goebbels,[2] have stressed over and over again the necessity of putting an end to the influence of the Christian Churches of every persuasion if National Socialism is to enjoy a lasting triumph.

Indeed the fact that, owing to the war against the foreign agents of Jewry, not enough attention could be paid to the struggle against the Churches and especially against the Catholic Church—that bitterest of all the opponents of National Socialism at home—that fact, I say, must be counted as one of the main causes of the loss of the war. The Churches have proved only too well, by their attitude towards defeated National Socialism after the war, what a responsibility they had in its defeat and what an amount of power they expected to enjoy upon its ruins.

But there is more than that in the instinctive dislike we all feel for them, to the extent we are conscious of what we stand for. The Churches, as temporal organisations, commercialised and power-grabbing, are bad enough. The Christian "*Weltanschauung*" itself is far worse an enemy of National Socialism. It is of no use trying to hide the fact in order "not to frighten" people: one *cannot be* at the same time a Nazi and a Christian of any description. It is nonsense to say one can. It is wasting time to point out concrete instances of men and women who actually are. Such people are either bad Christians or bad Nazis or both; sincere but illogical people, deceiving themselves, or clever rogues, trying to deceive others.

One only has to think five minutes to realise that a doctrine centred around race and personality cannot possibly go hand in hand with a teaching that proclaims all human souls equally precious in the eyes of a God who hates pride. The Churches would perhaps, one day, contemplate the possibility of compromising with us, if they judged it expedient. But there can be no compromise whatsoever between Christianity—or, by the way, between *any* man-centred religion of equality—and the Philosophy of the Swastika. If we are to triumph in the end, then, Christianity must go—whether that pleases or not all our friends who still today bear the stamp of a Christian upbringing. Christianity must go, so that the Nordic soul, which it crushed over a thousand years ago, might live and thrive once more in the strength and pride of its renewed youth; so that Germany, and all the countries in

---

Jahrhunderts (Munich: Hoheneichen, 1930).

[1] Professor at the University of Leipzig under the National Socialist régime, author of *Die 25 Thesen der deutschen Religion*.

[2] See the numerous passages of the Goebbels *Diaries* attacking the Churches.

which the Aryan blood is still alive, might evolve their own religious consciousness—the consciousness they *would have had* if Rome and Jerusalem had never interfered with them.

The religion of the reborn Aryans must naturally have much in common with that of the pre-Christian European North, and with that, of similar origin and spirit, kept alive to this day, in India, in the tradition of the Vedas. It must be, before all, the religion of a healthy, proud, and self-reliant people, accustomed to fight, ready to die, but, in the meantime, happy to live, and sure to live forever, in their undying race; a religion centred around the worship of Life and Light—around the cult of heroes, the cult of ancestors, and the cult of the Sun, source of all joy and power on earth. Indeed, it must be a religion of joy and of power—and of love also; not of that morbid love for sickly and sinful "mankind" at the expense of far more admirable Nature, but of love for all living beauty: for the woods and for the beasts; for healthy children; for one's faithful comrades in every field of activity; for one's leaders and one's gods; above all, for the supreme God, the Life force personified in the Sun, the "Heat-and-Light-within-the-Disk," to quote the expressive words of the greatest Sun-worshipper of Antiquity.[1] The religion of the regenerate Aryans must be one in which the Christian idea of "conception in sin" gives way to that of conception in honour and joy within the noble race, the only "sin" being (along with all forms of cowardice and faithlessness) the sin of shameful breeding—the deadly sin against the race.

The conflict between National Socialism and the Christian Churches in our times, is but an aspect of the age-long struggle between the creeds of Life which accept the natural hierarchy of human races—and individuals—no less than of animal species, and which treat man as a part and parcel of living Nature, and the man-centred creeds which deny the irreducible differences in quality between one human race and another while postulating, on the other hand, an artificial abyss between "mankind" as a whole and the rest of creation. The *par excellence* man-centred creed of today—Communism—is but the natural and logical outcome of Western Democracy based upon "the voice of the majority," as Adolf Hitler has himself pointed out a number of times. But Western Democracy, in its turn, is but the natural and logical outcome of centuries of Christian teaching. All Rousseau's sentimental twaddle and the subsequent nonsense about the "equal rights" of all human beings, to which the French Revolution owes its prestige both at

---

[1] King Akhnaton of Egypt, circa 1,400 BC.

home and abroad, would have been unthinkable in a Pagan Europe, unaffected from the start by the original Jewish twaddle about the equal rights of all human souls and the subsequent "dignity of all men" in the eyes of a man-loving God.

Those of us who fully realise this, and to whom what I have called the Philosophy of the Swastika—expression of their own deeper aspirations—is the only satisfactory one, can face with calm the present and the coming hardships. No democratic, humanitarian, or Christian propaganda, whether outspoken or in disguise, can alter *them*. They form that chosen minority of real Nazis around whom, one day—after the coming crash—the remnants of the undaunted Aryan race will gather to start a new historical cycle, under Hitler's undying inspiration.

Chapter 2

BRIEF DAYS OF GLORY

"Nirgends auf der Welt gibt es eine derart fanatische Liebe von Millionen Menschen zu einem . . ."

—Dr. Otto Dietrich[1]

"Deutschland, erwache!"

—Dietrich Eckart[2]

There was a time when the personality of Adolf Hitler dominated European consciousness; when his voice stirred millions; when he used to pass by, on solemn occasions, cheered by millions—the idol of the nation whom he had raised from the abyss to unparalleled greatness. There was a time when Germany was prosperous, strong, full of self-confidence; when her reborn people, well-fed, well-clothed, and well-housed, were happy to work together for a future in which they believed; when they *lived*, as they had yet never lived before, under the firm and wise rule of the Leader who loved them as no man ever had.

One can hardly believe it today. It all seems so unreal—like a wonderful story from another world. And yet, it is true. There really was such a time, and that, not long ago. Collective enthusiasm was then as general in Germany as fear and bitterness have become since. Military parades, youth demonstrations, and enormous mass gatherings were usual occurrences. One watched the Brown battalions march past one's house, and listened to the inspiring music of the Horst Wessel Song as a matter of course. One saw portraits of the Führer wherever one went. And one greeted one's colleagues in offices and factories, and one's friends in the street, in trams and buses, everywhere, with one's right arm outstretched and with the two magic words that expressed all one's love and reverence for the godlike Leader, all one's hopes, all one's dreams, all one's pride—all the joy of those splendid days: "Heil Hitler!"

The German ambassador had greeted the King of England—at that

---

[1] "Nowhere in the world is there such a fanatical love of millions of men for one."—Ed.

[2] "Germany, awake!"—Ed.

time, also Emperor of India—with those triumphant words and that gesture. England was amazed, but said nothing. Could say nothing, for there was nothing to be said. There was only a fact to be faced: the fact that Hitler ruled over eighty million people who adored him, and that, in those people, a new soul was rapidly taking birth—or rather, that the old, real, everlasting Aryan Soul was re-awakening in them. *"Deutschland, erwache!"*—"Germany, awake!" These words of the early poet of National Socialism had not only the honour of becoming one of the battle-cries of the Movement; not only were they written upon the standards of the Party formations, but they had rung through the hearts of the German people as a supernatural signal calling the dead to life. And Germany *had* awakened indeed.

And the people of the earth were watching her—some, already, with hateful envy, and fear; many with genuine admiration; some with love; with the certitude that Hitler's New Order was the first step towards the sort of world they had always wanted. Glorious days!

* * *

Without war, by the sole pressure of that strength that the certitude of her rights had given her, Germany had now taken back within her boundaries practically all the people of her blood. Saarland, Austria, and finally Sudetenland had become part and parcel of the Third Reich. Danzig, and the impossible "corridor" linking Poland to the sea through German territory, were soon to follow. But then England declared war on Germany.

Why war? To keep that German town, Danzig, from calling itself German? No. In England's eyes, at least, the town was not worth it. To "protect Poland," then? No, surely not, however much the hypocrites might say so, and however much the fools might believe it. Poland could well do without the impossible "corridor." And if she could not, who cared? No. War was waged upon Germany to crush Germany; not for any other reason. The unseen, all-powerful Jew, who governed—and still governs—England, had decided that Germany should be crushed, *had to be* crushed, because he hated her. And he hated her not because she had grown free, strong, and proud and was a "threat" to the peace of Europe (which she was not) but because she was National Socialist Germany, Hitler's Germany, the herald of the awakening of the Aryan soul all over the world, and a very positive threat to the continuation of the unseen rule of the Jew behind all so-called "national" governments.

But Germany was not easy to crush. She answered the attack of the Jew and of his allies by a series of victories which filled the world with amazement. Her onward march in all directions seemed irresistible. And one could believe, in the middle of 1942, that the New World Order, expansion of the New Order in Europe, was at hand. From the northernmost shores of Norway, facing the Pole, to the Libyan desert, and from the Atlantic to the Caucasus and the Volga, the Führer's word was now the law—while Germany's efficient and brave ally in the Far East, Japan, already mistress of the Pacific, of Indonesia, and practically the whole of Burma, was expected at any moment to thrust her armies across the Indian border and to capture Calcutta. There was yet no sign of ill-luck in Russia. And it was natural to expect that the German hosts would continue their triumphant march through that endless land and beyond; continue their march—the age-old march of the Aryans to the East and to the South—and meet their allies in imperial Delhi.

With profound sadness one looks back today to that great lost dream: the resounding of the Horst Wessel Song in the majestic rocky solitude of the Khyber Pass, the reception of Adolf Hitler—*Weltführer*—in the historic eastern capital. It was not impossible. At one time it even seemed—to the observer in India at least—the only logical conclusion of the Second World War. The tide of events had not yet turned in favour of the forces of disintegration. And few people, if any, even in Europe, even in apparently well-informed circles, could foretell that it was to turn so soon and so completely. These were still great days—days of confidence, days of hope; days in which, in spite of the immensity of the struggle, one felt strong and happy, wherever one happened to be; days in which one believed that all hardships, all sufferings would soon be forgotten in the joy and glory of "after victory."

* * *

But, for that very reason one did not know—one could not know—in those days, who was a true National Socialist and who was not: nor, in the wide world outside "the Party," who was a sincere believer in Hitler's ideology and a true friend of National Socialist Germany, and who was only pretending to be.

Up till 1942, the whole of Germany seemed to be heart and soul with the Führer. The whole of Europe obviously was not—since there was a war going on—but it appeared that, also in the occupied countries, a growing number of people were realising that the coming of the New Order was unavoidable and that the best they could do was to collaborate with victorious Germany. In Asia, with the sure, elemental perception of primitives or the superior intuition of highly evolved souls, increasing millions strongly felt the importance and the value that Hitler's victory would have for the whole world. They felt it would mean a better world from *their* point of view also—the end of long-detested dominations; the end of the rule of money; and also, in some cases, the triumph of the age-old ideas that they accepted as a matter of tradition; the triumph of a spirit familiar to them for millenniums. And they wanted it. If the war had ended in 1942 by the defeat both of Communist Russia and the Western Democracies, and the meeting of the Axis armies of East and West in Delhi, then not only would the whole of Germany have rejoiced, as one can well imagine, but the entire world (with the exception of the Jews and of a stubborn minority of Democrats and Marxists) would have burst into one immense cry of happiness: "Heil Hitler!" The magic words would have rung triumphantly from Iceland to Indonesia.

But one would never have known how far they came from every man's heart or were just an effect of mass suggestion. The weaklings and the hypocrites—the time-servers—would never have "changed their opinion"; the potential traitors, in Germany itself, would have remained loyal. The actual traitors would have taken good care to keep their fruitless underground activities forever unknown. Nay, more than one of those scoundrels would have been honoured—and remembered—as a prominent member of the ruling hierarchy and an organiser of the victory—for there were such ones even in the midst of the Nazi Party!

They began to reveal themselves as soon as the tide of events definitely took a bad turn. They ceased to take so much trouble to hide their shadowy doings, so much so that some of them got found out. One is only amazed at the fact that more of them were not found out sooner. A traitor of first magnitude like Admiral Wilhelm Canaris remained unsuspected in his high position as chief of German Intelligence until 1944. Even such a penetrating eye as that of Dr. Goebbels could not see through him. And had it not been for that monstrous conspiracy against the Führer's life, in July 1944, in which he took part, who knows if the man would ever have been discovered? Others were not until *after* the war—*after* the disaster, when it paid to tell the world that one was an enemy of National Socialism, and to prove it. If the war had been won, a fellow such as Hjalmar Schacht would still be seen in the solemn Party gatherings, wearing upon his arm the badge of the Swastika; standing by the genuine Nazis as though he were one of them. Now—in 1948—he has written his *Abrechnung mit Hitler*[1] and proved what a faithless man he is—and *was,* all those years.

There were thousands of creatures of that type, in the golden days. And there were millions of weak people, neither good nor bad, whose devotion to the Man they had so often frantically acclaimed was skin-deep and gave way under the hardships of "total war." But there were those, too, whose faith was unshakable, whose fortitude knew no limits; whose National Socialism was the outcome of thought and experience, rooted in the depth of life.

There was gold, base metal, and slime among the so-called National Socialists of the days of glory. Now, after all is lost, the slime has gone over to the Democracies' side—the right people in the right place. The base metal exists, but no longer counts; no longer claims to stand for any ideology. The gold alone is left—and is more plentiful in Germany, today, than the world imagines. It can also be found among the few—very few—foreign National Socialists who have remained faithful to Adolf Hitler and his ideals after Germany's defeat; among such men as Sven Hedin and a handful of others, less well-known, of different nationalities.

---

[1] Hjalmar Schacht, *Abrechnung mit Hitler* [*Settling Accounts with Hitler*] (Berlin: Michaelis, 1948)—Ed.

Chapter 3

Now, the Trial

"You will be tried like the gold in the fire."
—2 Esdras 16:73

"Wir sind das lautere Gold, das im Schmelztiegel auf die Probe gestellt ist. Laßt den Ofen flammen und brausen! Es gibt nichts, was imstande ist, uns zu zerstören!"
—From a Nazi leaflet distributed in occupied Germany in 1948[1]

One must have seen with one's own eyes the ruins of Germany, to believe the enormity of the hatred that laid that country waste. Surely London was bombed. So were other English and continental towns. War is war. But *this* bombing was something different. What the half a dozen apologetic air raids of the Japanese on Calcutta were to the London air raids, so were the latter, in their turn, compared with the hellish bombing of Germany by the Allied planes, in formations of hundreds at a time, night after night.

Broad, lurid streaks of phosphorus filled the sky. In their glaring white light, the outlines of a city could be seen for the last time. A few seconds later, the whole place was ablaze; a few hours later, it was a heap of ruins still on fire. The very earth, soaked in phosphorus, burnt on slowly, for days.

Not one, not ten or twenty, but *all* the German towns were submitted to that systematic destruction by the enemies of the New Order—"crusaders to Europe," as the American lot call themselves. That was to punish the German people for loving Adolf Hitler, their Leader, their Saviour, and their friend. That was also to punish Adolf Hitler for loving the German people and the Aryan race at large more than anything in the world; for having dared, for their sake, to challenge the might of the unseen Jew behind the screen of world politics. The rascals who planned and carried out that inhuman bomb-

---

[1] "We are the pure gold put to test in the furnace. Let the furnace blaze and roar! Nothing can destroy us."—From Savitri's own leaflet. For the full text, see p. 34 of this volume.—Ed.

ing knew that the surest way to torture him was to inflict that terror and that suffering upon his helpless people. They smashed Germany so that he might see it smashed. They burnt thousands of Germans alive—stuck in the boiling mud of the streets they had no time to cross, or roasted in the cellars where they flocked for shelter—so that the thought of their horrid deaths might haunt him day and night. They reduced the whole country to heaps of smoking ruins, so that he, poor great One, might suffer, even more than the men and women that the phosphorus bombs affected materially.

The most effective devastators of all times, the Assyrians in Antiquity and the Mongols in the Middle Ages, were pretty thorough in warfare; nearly as thorough, in fact, as the airmen who poured fire and brimstone over unfortunate Germany, only yesterday. But even *they* did not display such a fiendish will to exterminate a whole enemy population. The Mongols definitely spared, as potential concubines and slaves, the desirable women, the useful craftsmen, and the children not taller than the wheel of a cart. The airmen of the United Nations spared nobody. The only people who, in olden times, proved to be as enthusiastic mass murderers as they (to the extent the technique of ancient warfare permitted) are the Jews. One has but to re-read, in the Bible, the monotonous but instructive accounts of the conquest of Canaan by that self-styled "Chosen People"—accounts of unbiased Israelitish source, all of them—in order to understand what I mean. But even they never mingled, with their hatred towards a hostile nation, such stubborn, fanatical, and yet methodical hatred for one great Individual. That remained to be done, in this war, by the Aryans and semi-Aryans in the pay or under the influence of their modern descendants.

And who was that hated man, Adolf Hitler? Not only the first one who had striven to give back a collective consciousness and pride to the whole of the Aryan race, outside Germany as well as within; not only the one who, after doing all he possibly could to avoid war, had three times offered England an honourable peace; but the man who had spared the remnants of the fleeing British Army at Dunkirk, and refused to invade England and pursue his victory, still believing, in his loving heart, that England would understand the sincerity of his gesture, renounce her frenzied anti-German policy, and help him to build a beautiful world upon the ruins of the sole enemy of better mankind: the money power of the international Jew.

That is the one against whom they let loose all the savagery stored within them for centuries.

Today, as one walks through the bombed streets of Hamburg, Cologne, Koblenz, Berlin, or any German city; or even as one beholds, from the windows of a railway carriage, those miles and miles of ruins in whatever part of the country it be—charred walls of which the torn outlines stick out against the grey or blue sky, or the glow of sunset, as far as the eye can see; impossible piles of twisted iron, disjointed stones, and blocks of cement, heaped over endless waste spaces where life once flourished, where men once were happy; where the Führer held out his hand to little children less than five years ago—as one sees *that*, I say, and as one recalls in one's mind the inferno that preceded and caused such appalling devastation, one does not only think of the glorious pre-war days and feel: "That is what they did to kill new Germany!" One also evokes another, and quite different picture: the muddy beach of Dunkirk, and the pitiable survivors of the British Expeditionary Force gathered there, in the late spring of 1940, tattered and torn, wounded and hungry, but, above all, scared out of their wits like hunted animals; the roaring sea before them, the German divisions behind them, rain and lightning and the dark night all round them; awaiting in terror the only fate that seemed likely to befall them: death. It would have been so easy for the victorious German Army to step forth and kill them all off—and put an end to the war. Oh, so easy! But orders came from above, to the bewildered generals and the soldiers on their onward march; orders from that Man whom England was fighting, but who was not fighting England; from the generous, loving, trusting German Führer, who recognised no enemies in the misled Aryans who composed the bulk of the British Army: "Leave several kilometres between them and the German Army," in other words, "Spare them! Allow them to wait undisturbed for their ships, and to reach the coast of England safe and sound."[1] Whatever the German High Command

---

[1] Mr. Churchill, in his *War Memoirs*, gives a different explanation of these orders of the Führer to General Halder, Chief of the German General Staff. This is only to be expected. He writes: "He [Hitler] felt he could not sacrifice armoured formations uselessly, as they were essential to the second stage of the campaign. He believed, no doubt, that his air superiority would be sufficient to prevent a large-scale evacuation by sea. He therefore, according to Halder, sent a message to him through Brauchitsch, ordering 'the armoured formations to be stopped, the points even taken back.' Thus, says Halder, the way to Dunkirk was cleared for the British Army.

"Other German generals have told much the same story and have even suggested that Hitler's order was inspired by a political motive, to improve the chances of peace with England after France was beaten" (Winston Churchill, *War Memoirs*, Vol. II., *Their Finest Hour*).

The supposed "actual diary" of General Rundstedt's Headquarters "*written at the*

might have felt towards the defeated aggressor, orders were orders. The remnant of the British Expeditionary Force was allowed to live and go home; allowed to recover and fight again.

One remembers, I say, that episode of the Second World War as one beholds the ruins of all the German cities, the plight of men and women in the overcrowded areas still fit to live in, and all the misery, all the bitterness, consequent of that devilish bombing. Streams of fire, tons of phosphorus, relentlessly poured over his people for five years, these were England's thanks to Adolf Hitler for having shown mercy to her soldiers in his hour of victory. These were the thanks of the United States of America for his orders not to shoot the parachutists captured on German soil. These were the thanks of the unworthy Aryans both of Russia and of the West to the Man who loved them, as a race, and who had dreamed for them an era of glory and prosperity, side by side with his own people, in a world freed from the tyranny of the money system.

* * *

Under that continuous terror, the German people suffered, at first with the hope that the ordeal would soon be over, that victory was at hand; and then, more and more, as months passed and no sign of betterment appeared, with no hope. The traitors, as I remarked in the preceding chapter, became bolder and bolder. And disaffection grew among the ordinary folk who could not understand how anything— including unconditional surrender—could possibly be worse than what they were enduring.

---

time," on which Mr. Churchill bases his statement that the orders were given on the initiative of General Rundstedt, are very probably *not* "written at the time" at all, but after the war. I have come to this conclusion for the following reason.

On the 6th of April 1949, I was told by Colonel Edward Vickers, British Governor of the Werl prison where I was myself a political prisoner, that "political prisoners are the last ones to whom the British authorities would grant light in their cells after 8 p.m. and the facilities to write" (I had precisely asked for extra light, which I was not given). "But," added Colonel Vickers, "those who write things for us," who do "secret work in our interest, *are given every facility.*" On the other hand I was told by a responsible member of the British police in Düsseldorf, who intended to impress upon me how "good" and "lenient" the British are in Germany, that General Rundstedt was given in captivity all sorts of special advantages—not only light after time and the permission to write, but the permission to leave his prison on "parole" which is indeed much. I would not like to be unfair to anyone, especially not to a German general, but I cannot help wondering if the "diary" of his mentioned by Mr. Churchill is not another "secret work in the interest of the British" of the kind Colonel Vickers had in mind on the 6th of April 1949.

In May, 1945, when Germany did actually acknowledge defeat, very little seemed to remain of the splendid spirit that had lifted the country so high between the two World Wars, and in the early part of this war. From East and West, hostile armies every bit as greedy, brutal, and hateful as each other—every bit as "anti-Nazi," whether professing to uphold the Marxist ideology or the more hypocritical or sillier form of Democracy—rushed forth to occupy disarmed Germany. The bulk of the tortured Nation looked at them coming, with the tired resignation of those who have reached the limit of what it is possible to suffer.

The eastern gang raped all the women they could catch; stole everything they fancied; drove millions out of house and home in order to replace them by Russians, Poles, or Czechs. The western gang, while behaving with perhaps a little less savagery as regards women, was hardly better in other respects.

The French kicked people off the trains under the slightest pretext—I have seen one of them do it *now*, three years after the end of the war, and can well imagine them in 1945. They also stamped about the streets ostensively loaded with edibles, in front of the starving population. They brought their families over, to occupy the best remaining houses and to be fed and fattened at the expense of exhausted Germany. The British and the Americans did much the same. They gave people anything between fifteen minutes and an hour to leave their flats and go wherever they liked—wherever they could—when *they* wanted comfortable lodgings. Usually, they would turn the flats into pigsties in a couple of days, and carry off whatever objects they found desirable when they moved. They built a shockingly luxurious "victory club" in the midst of the ruins of Hamburg and, like the Russians, tore down all the likenesses of the Führer from public buildings, burnt all the National Socialist literature they could set hands upon, and pursued with systematic hatred all those whom they knew—or believed they knew—to be National Socialists.

Whatever might have been their professional efficiency, none of these were allowed to retain the positions they had formerly held. Most were not permitted to work at all. Thousands were arrested, imprisoned, savagely tortured, sent to concentration camps, or to their doom. Among these were Hitler's closest collaborators: the members of the National Socialist Government, the generals of the German Army, the leaders of the SS regiments and of the Youth Organisations—some of them, the finest characters of modern times. For weeks and weeks, months and months—in fact, for over a year and a half—the all-too-famous Trial of 1945-46, that most repulsive of all the parodies of justice staged by man since the dawn of history, dragged on. It ended, as everyone knows, by the ignominious hanging, in the slowest and cruellest possible way (each execution lasting about twenty-five minutes), of men whose only crime was to have done their duty without having succeeded in winning the war. And that atrocity took place in what was left of the old mediaeval city which, only a few years before, had been witnessing the glory of reborn Germany in the splendid pageantry of the annual Party rallies: Nuremberg.

When, between the two wars, a couple of Italian Communists, Sacco and Vanzetti, were tried and executed in the United States of America, a wave of indignation rose from the four corners of the earth. Placards were posted on all the walls, and public demonstrations were held in all the large towns of Europe to protest against the condemnation of the two martyrs of Marxism. In 1945, 1946, and 1947, no such feelings stirred God-forsaken Europe (or the God-forsaken world, at that) in favour of the twenty-one victims of the Nuremberg Trial, or of the thousands of other National Socialists labelled by their persecutors as major or minor "war criminals," and condemned as such by the bogus Allied tribunals in occupied Germany. No—even in the neutral illegality of the trials, in a few people's casual comments on current events and, perhaps, in one or two booklets—and those, worded as mildly as possible. And on the other hand, either the boisterous glee of triumphant savages at the sufferings inflicted on their captured enemies, or else the still more revolting smugness of self-righteous rogues and fools; the patronizing lectures of self-appointed reformers of mankind, hoping that after such historic "justice," the Germans would at last "learn their lesson," i.e., renounce National Socialism and toe the line with their victors' ideology like good little boys; talks on the wireless about the gradual return of the German people to the "ideals of Christian civilization," now that the Nazi "monsters" were dead.

How I remember that silly, vulgar, cruel, positively nauseating gloating of English-speaking apes of varied breeds over one of the greatest crimes of history, and that hypocrisy in addition to it all! Never, perhaps, could one feel more keenly what a curse the very existence of Christian civilization was. Pagans would not have disgraced themselves to that extent. *We* would certainly not have behaved in any like manner, had we won the war—we whose aim was to resurrect the proud Pagan spirit among the Aryans of the whole world. We might have crushed all opposition out of existence, but we would have neither made a farce of justice in order to condemn our enemies nor tried to convert them to our philosophy. Oh, no! For we know how to kill, and we know how to die; but we do not know how to lie in order to justify our actions in our own eyes and in other people's. Our only justification is the triumph of National Socialism—the organisation, now, on this earth, of a harmonious hierarchy of human races led by a race of real earthly gods. We need no other. Our enemies—with, I must say, the exception of the Communists, who are as thorough and sincere as ourselves in their way—persecute us in the name of "morals" in which they do not believe. We despise them from the bottom of our hearts. We despise them more than we can ever hate them. Maybe we lost this war; or, to be more accurate, weaklings and full-fledged traitors—*ersatz* Nazis and downright anti-Nazis—lost it for us. But we would prefer to perish forever, even in men's memories, having remained ourselves to the end, rather than to rule the world and resemble our victors. We would prefer to perish, and leave in the dark infinity of time, as a flash in the night, the unrecorded fact of our brief and beautiful passage, rather than to acquire a single one of their democratic "virtues."

* * *

But the National Socialist soul—the Aryan soul, quickened after nearly fifteen hundred years of slumber—is not prepared to die again. Purified by untold suffering, erect, invincible, it gleams—when one takes the trouble to appeal to it—in the eyes of every German worthy of the name; it expresses itself in silent gestures, in whispers; in a superhuman will to live and once more to conquer; in a splendid defiance of torture and death; a reaction to persecution which, even from the mere aesthetic point of view, has hardly any parallel in world history.

In 1945, torn and desolate Germany, overrun by hostile armies, plundered by rapacious occupants, insulted by a whole cowardly world, could do nothing, say nothing, hardly think anything. Like a boxer temporarily knocked out in the ring, she was stunned. Cases of mass suicide, as well as of large scale deportation to Siberia were reported from the Russian occupied areas, while hungry, completely destitute, packed like goods in cattle wagons (or worse), the whole German population of East Prussia and of Sudetenland—over 18 million people—uprooted by the Russians and by the Czechs, poured into western and southern Germany. All over the country, arson and outrage were taking place on a scale unheard of for centuries. The mere fact of a house being or having been occupied by Nazis was a sufficient excuse for all the criminal elements of the neighbourhood to rush to it for loot, knowing they could now do so with impunity. No man or woman known to be a sincere follower of Hitler was safe in the street or indoors. In a twinkling of an eye every external sign of the National Socialist régime was being effaced by the invaders aided by the Jews of Germany.[1] In offices, in cafés, in the ruined railway stations, in every public place, members of the occupying forces, with the help of the few rascals on the spot, were busy tearing down all likenesses of the Führer, with ferocious glee. Every blow they struck, every thrust of knife or sword into cardboard or wood, every tearing up of paper, every desecration of the reminders of the glorious days or of the holy sign of the Swastika, was to them a new assertion of their victory over National Socialism.

The sincere Nazi who happened to pass by, powerless—the one among thousands in whom hunger and hardships had not temporarily silenced all idealism, in those atrocious days—felt his eyes fill with tears and his heart with rage. He had already witnessed, that day, a dozen scenes of similar vulgarity, and many others before. He had seen, at the stalls, the headlines of the now Allied-controlled papers announcing the latest arrests of prominent National Socialists. He had heard the nearest "bunkers" in the countryside being blown up one after the other as detested remnants of the power of the Third Reich. He had seen the soldiers of the victorious democracies march up and down the streets and their officers walk in and out of the Club erected in haste in the midst of the ruins of his town. He knew that for months—perhaps for years—such scenes would be common occurrences, such news daily news, and such an atmosphere of persecution and depression, of fear and hate, the "normal" atmosphere of his proud Germany. He knew there was now no hope, no immediate future for all he loved and stood for. And he turned his head aside not to see the picture of Adolf Hitler trampled in the mud, and the repulsive glee on the faces of the victors of the day.

Still, whatever might have happened, whatever was yet to happen— whether National Socialism was one day to reassert itself or not—*he* would never, he *could* never withdraw his allegiance to the everlasting Idea on which the Führer had tried to build a truer civilisation and a more beautiful humanity. On the contrary, never had the greatest

---

[1] We are accused of having exterminated goodness knows how many "millions" of Jews. It is strange—to say the least—that so many were still living undisturbed in Germany at the time of the Capitulation.

European of all ages seemed so great to him, perhaps, as now, visualised from the depth of disaster, from the midst of persecution, and of worse than persecution; from the midst of the apparent apathy of his very own people, in whose millions five years of savage bombing and now hunger and destitution had killed all but the elementary animal reactions to food and warmth, every desire but the desire to be left in peace and to suffer a little less.

The faithful young man hastened home. He came to a block of houses in ruins, went down some steps, reached the only inhabitable room left in the surroundings: the cellar, in which he lived with a friend. The place had at least the advantage of being lonely—away from unwelcome onlookers and listeners ready to inform against any true National Socialist. He opened the door, and shut it carefully after him. Then, lifting his right arm—in May, 1945—he greeted his comrade as in the days in which they both marched side by side in the ranks of the Storm Troopers: "Heil Hitler!"

In the silence of the cold, damp, and desolate room, in which there was nothing to eat but a few boiled potatoes from the day before, the two mystic words of love, pride, and power resounded clear and triumphant. The comrade, rising to his feet and making the same gesture, repeated them in answer, now as *then*, now as always: "Heil Hitler!"

Hail, invincible Germany! Hail, undying Aryan youth, élite of the world whom the agents of the dark forces can starve and torture, but never subdue! That unobtrusive profession of faith of two unknown but real Nazis in 1945 is itself a victory.

It is not the only one.

In the winter of that same awful year 1945—or was it in the beginning of 1946? The eyewitness who reported the episode to me did not remember—a train passed through Saarbrücken, carrying off to different concentration camps in occupied Germany several thousand German prisoners of war whose sole crime was to belong to that élite of the National Socialist forces: the SS. The young men, squeezed against one another, had been standing for goodness knows how many hours in the dark freezing cattle wagons, without food, without water, without the most indispensable human commodities. They were going towards a destiny worse than death; towards the very chambers of hell—and they knew it. And yet, although no one could see them (for the wagons were completely closed save for a narrow slit at the top) one could hear them. They were singing—singing the glorious song of the SS legions in defiance of their horrid present conditions and of the still more horrid future awaiting them. As the train rolled past, well-known words reached the silent and sullen crowd gathered on the platform—an echo of the great days of National Socialism and, in the midst of Germany's martyrdom, the certitude of indestructible might and, already, the promise of the new rising, never mind when, and how: "If all become unfaithful, yet we remain faithful . . ."[1] Every bystander was moved to tears. And so was I, when now—nearly three years later—the fact was brought to my knowledge.

The train passed by and disappeared in the distance. One could no longer hear the song of the SS. But one knew the young warriors were still singing. And one remembered the words that sprang from their lips—the motto of their lives tomorrow, for months, perhaps for years, in hunger, fever, and agony; in torture at the hands of the cowardly Jew and of his agents, till the very minute of death: "Faithful as the German oak trees, as the moon and as the Sun."[2]

Where are they now, those fine young National Socialists, real men among apes, followers of a god among men? Dead, probably, by this time, most of them; or back from captivity with ruined health and apparently no future—crushed by the all-powerful machinery of "de-Nazification," that whole organisation set up in Germany by the sub-men to grind to dust all that is naturally strong and beautiful, alive, intelligent and proud, and worthy to rule; all that the worms cannot understand and therefore hate. That is, no doubt, the fate of the great number of them. But not of all. Thanks to the Aryan gods Who love and trust eternal Germany, some have miraculously retained their physical vitality along with their National Socialist ideals and, whether still in concentration camps or in their homes, are waiting to lead and conquer in the coming struggle. Heroes of that episode worthy of Antiquity which I have just related, or of other, equally moving incidents of which I have not heard, wherever they be, now, the undaunted survivors of our immortal SS—and SA—may the song that sprang from the wagons of captivity, in the station of Saarbrücken, on that bleak evening when all seemed lost, resound, one day, along the highways of Europe and Asia, accompanying their resumed onward march to the South, to the East, to the ends of the world! They deserve it. And we deserve it, all of us, far and near, who in secret action or in silent expectation remain faithful to our Führer and to our ideals among a majority that has lost faith.

---

[1] "Wenn alle untreu werden, so bleiben wir doch treu . . ."
[2] ". . . treu wie die deutschen Eichen, wie Mond und Sonnenschein!"

* * *

Majorities are always faithless. Majorities are composed of average men and women, neither good nor bad, for whom the security and comforts of everyday life and personal ties always come before great impersonal ideals such as ours. Majorities stand openly for great ideals, and proclaim their devotion to great leaders by word and deed, only when they feel they can safely do so without impairing their daily bread or disturbing their private lives. Even the best Aryan majority is not yet free from those weaknesses; and one can doubt whether it ever could have been—whether it ever can be—even after years of National Socialist training. And that is why, although centred *first* around race, our socio-political philosophy is not centred around race alone, but also around personality. Personality is always the privilege of a minority—all the more so that it is stronger and more conscious, more definite, and consequently more reliable.

And yet, in spite of this undeniable, universal fact, what astounds a foreign National Socialist today, in occupied Germany, is not to meet so few genuine German ones, but, on the contrary, to discover so many, often in the most unexpected circles; it is not to be forced to acknowledge, with disappointment, how similar the most consciously Aryan population in Europe is to any section of mankind considered *en masse,* despite twelve years of the National Socialist régime, but, on the contrary, to behold how different it remains, even after such a brief experience of the New Order as it had.

As I have already said, the desolate nation is—apparently—devoid of every external Nazi sign, picture, or book, and the German people are silent—casual, noncommittal—(at first sight at least) about all that is connected with National Socialism. They talk of everything but "that."

The foreigner who has come to "occupy" the land, or to buy and sell, or to send "interesting" articles to the democratic newspaper of which he is a correspondent—the unsympathetic outsider in whose eyes National Socialism is a curse, or all politics a matter of indifference—shrugs his shoulders and says: "Well, they are probably sick of the blessed 'régime'! Can't blame them, seeing the mess in which it landed them." Or else he mistakes the German people for a passive flock interested only in eating and drinking, daily work, material betterment; ready to follow anybody who will promise them these things—and keep his promise. "What do you think?" told me, in Paris, a Frenchman in high position who had spent three years in

Germany, "They followed Hitler because of what they got out of him: the opportunity to stuff themselves at the expense of other nations; to stamp about in jackboots and behave as bullies both at home and abroad. Not one of them cares two hoots for him now, save a handful of fanatics. They only grumble over the advantages they lost and await the new master who will again give them parades and plenty, whoever he be. That's the Germans!" I wanted to say: "Don't be so cocksure of it, my dear sir." But I had not come to discuss.

In other instances, the enemy settled here ever since the capitulation finds the Germans "sly" and "undignified in defeat," to quote the expression of an official in the French Zone to whom I paid a visit shortly after my arrival in the country. (One just has to keep in with the creatures, outwardly, however much one might detest them at heart. And all the more so, that one lives more dangerously.) "There are," said this man, "any number of Nazis about; and of the worst type. But they will never tell you so. You will never know what they really think. I have been three years in the country. I speak the language fluently. I have made friends with many people. But I only met one—one in all that time—who told me that he (or rather she, for it was a woman) still clung to National Socialism. And some say that I am lucky. They met none." "My dear sir"—I thought—"you are not 'lucky' at all. I have been only a week in the place, and I have already come across over fifty people, both men and women, who told me 'that,' or allowed me to guess it without difficulty. But I am not saying a word, lest you might suspect what sort of a customer I am myself, in such a case, and start investigating about me. No fear! I do not disturb the sleeping dog. You will not know me—or real Germany—until the liberation."

Now, in the meantime, the only outsider who can expect to know anything about real Germany is the genuine foreign National Socialist. And not the mere thinker at that; not the one who draws his conclusions in silence and waits philosophically for the next war to put things right. But the active one; the one who loves the Führer enough to take risks; who loves the German people enough to share with them the burden of hardships and persecution; the one who in his beautiful life of poverty, faith, and danger, has no protection but that of the immortal Gods, and theirs. Such a person has naturally a truer insight into the reactions of the Germans, today, than any other outsider, and even than many Germans themselves, for no one can possibly fear him. The downright enemies of the National Socialist régime—who would have had every reason to fear him a few years ago—know only too well that he can do no harm to them now, however much he might like to. (It is, on the contrary, they, who, if they find him out, and if they choose to do so, can do any amount of harm to him. But they express themselves frankly, imagining in their vanity that no outsider can still seriously support the régime they hate, after its defeat. The foreign Nazi scents the danger and takes good care they do not get to know him too well.) The bulk of the people who have "no politics" but who, in the present-day atmosphere of persecution, are afraid to say a single word in praise of "Hitler's times," give him their genuine opinion about all the prominent men of the New Order, as soon as they know for certain who he is. Sometimes, they even destroy some of his illusions without meaning to. But they surely trust him—precisely *because* he is a National Socialist.

And, above all, he (or she) is the only foreigner whom the genuine German National Socialists—those who, in these days of trial, not only retain the courage of their convictions but are ready to resume the struggle at the first opportunity—can, and do, trust implicitly.

And it is amazing, not merely how aware—how alive—but also how numerous these are among the outwardly silent, outwardly subdued—"selfish" and "devoid of all idealism"—average Germans. I once asked a man whom I know to be a Nazi of the purest quality, how many others there were "like himself" in the whole country. He answered with earnest pessimism: "Very few; perhaps two million; surely not more than three."—"Germany deserves to rule," I replied, "if she can still boast of three million such sons and daughters, now. It is a very high proportion." (And I am personally inclined to believe they are many more than three million.)

To feel the confidence of that proud élite of Europe (which is also the élite of the world) now, in 1948, when it knows it can trust nobody, is surely the most moving experience a foreign Nazi can have, in present-day Germany. To sit in some humble dwelling in the midst of a ruined town, or in a lonely place in the countryside, and to hear, with one's own ears, words of unshakable faith in our Führer and all he represents, from men and women who have acclaimed him in glory and stood by him in disaster, and suffered all manner of persecution at the hands of his enemies, during these three years; from men and women who have never, even outwardly, compromised with those who hate him, whatever their courage might have cost them materially, and who now, when all seems against us, are ready to fight again for the triumph of his great dreams; to experience the comradeship of such people, it is worth coming from the other end of the earth.

To admire in them the proud soul of everlasting Germany and to bring them, through one's devoted collaboration in hardships and danger, a foreshadowing of the future homage of the whole of Aryan mankind, which they so deserve, it is worth any sacrifice. To be worthy of them—to earn the right to think and say "we," and not "they," when referring to them—it is worth living with the knowledge that one's career might end, at any moment, in prison or in a concentration camp.

In the meantime, as long as one is still free, one has the pleasure of defying those who now hold Germany under their heel. One forces them to feel—to know—they cannot keep the country down for long. One teaches them that material power is something, no doubt, but not everything; that, as our Führer rightly said, "One cannot kill a *Weltanschauung* by force, but only through the aggressive impact of another *Weltanschauung*."[1]

* * *

Another *Weltanschauung*? Which one? What have our enemies to offer the world in the place of National Socialism which they are trying so hard to destroy as the purest expression, in our times, of a natural élite they detest? What have they, to build the future upon? Christianity, of which the world is already sick, anyhow? Or Democracy, that other large-scale farce?—"freedom of speech for everybody," save for those who think for themselves and love truth; "freedom of action for everybody," save the better men and women, those who would act as they think, if given power, and who think as we do; the systematic installation of the wrong people in the wrong places; the plunder of the nations' wealth by clever rascals; the rule of the scum? Or Communism—that most cunning of all mass delusions, that philosophy outwardly endowed with many characteristics of ours—and therefore, at first sight, attractive to sincere haters of capitalism—but devoid of the two fundamentals to which our creed owes its everlastingness: the acknowledgement of the natural hierarchy of races, and that of the importance of personality in history and in all walks of life?

Do they seriously expect anyone who has studied National Socialism—and *a fortiori* anyone who has lived it—to fancy one or the other of these snares of the human mind?

Christianity might still satisfy the blind, the old, the weak—people

---

[1] Cf. *Mein Kampf* I, v, p. 189; Mannheim, p. 172.

of the type of those kind and silly elderly virgins of Great Britain who, to this day, refuse to believe that their male compatriots used phosphorus bombs during this war, or mishandled German prisoners. Such naïve people, living in a fools' paradise, can spend their few last quiet days musing over the possibilities of what they call "esoteric" Christianity as opposed to the exoteric brand which has failed. But the world's millions have no time for that nonsense, whatever might be its next label. And the strong ones despise it. Democracy is doomed by the fact that the Democrats themselves know it is nothing but a pitiable show. And Communism—real Communism; not the diluted stuff for Western consumption—might well be the best ideology for Chinese coolies, for the lower castes of India (the former customers of the Christian missionaries, and the once easy converts to Islam) and for the lousy masses of North Africa and of the Near East. But not for the working men and women of the superior races, whether in the West *or* in the East—especially when these come to know all that the Founder of National Socialism has done for the labourers. And not for the thinking people in whom the Aryan consciousness has once been awakened—not for us. Never! Let the wave come! It might for a time subdue the whole of Europe, materially, and prolong our trial. But its impact will prove, ultimately, as powerless as that of the Democratic *Weltanschauung*. "Nothing can destroy that which is built in truth."[1] In these words, circulated throughout Germany in a Nazi leaflet in 1948, lies our confidence in the future. The truth behind our socio-political philosophy—along with the character of its faithful representatives, now, during the time of our trial—is the strongest guarantee that we can never be submerged.

Today, we suffer. And tomorrow, we might have to suffer still more. But we know it is not forever—perhaps even not for long. One day, those of us to whom it will be granted to witness and survive the coming crash, shall march through Europe in flames, once more singing the Horst Wessel Song—the avengers of their comrades' martyrdom, and of all the humiliations and all the cruelties inflicted upon us since 1945; and the conquerors of the day; the builders of future Aryandom upon the ruins of Christendom; the rulers of the new Golden Age.

---

[1] From Savitri's propaganda leaflet. For the full text, see p. 34 of this volume.—Ed.

Chapter 4

THE UNFORGETTABLE NIGHT

"When all is lost—when thou hast no possessions, no friends, no hope left—then I come, I, the Mother of the world."

—The Goddess Kali (according to Swami Vivekananda)

I was coming from Sweden, and going back to England through Germany and Belgium. The train was rolling on towards the German frontier, which I was to cross at Flensburg on the same day, the 15th of June, 1948, at about 6 p.m. All these years, I had lived six thousand miles away, in India. I had never *seen* Germany in the grand days of Hitler's power. Now, the Gods had ordained that I should have a glimpse of her ruins. Bitter irony of fate! "But there must be a meaning to it"; I thought, "All that the Gods do has a *meaning*."

I was travelling—officially—as a dresser in a theatrical company.[1] And I marvelled at the network of circumstances that had been preparing for me, of late, a new life. Never, perhaps, had I felt more grateful to the principal of the company[2] for having taken me to Sweden two months before. That trip had been for me the welcome awakening after a long nightmare. I had met in Stockholm an old friend: the sincerest, perhaps, and surely the most intelligent of all the English Nazis I happened to know; a fine character, and the one person to whom I had been able to open my heart in London when I first came there from India, in that wretched year 1946.[3] We had talked again, and he had managed to convince me that things were now a little less awful, from our point of view. And through that friend, I had soon met others, Swedish Nazis, magnificent men and women of the purest Nordic stock, faithful to our eternal ideals; real Pagans according to my heart. And through these—and through the will of the Gods—I had had the honour of meeting one of the great men of the New Order, the famous explorer and the Führer's friend: Sven Hedin, aged eighty-three, looking forty-five, and speaking as only everlasting youth can express

---

[1] The dance company of Ram Gopal (1912-2003)—Ed.
[2] Ram Gopal—Ed.
[3] Elwyn Wright—Ed.

itself. I had had a four-hour interview with him on that memorable Sunday, the 6th of June. "Have confidence in the future," had he told me, among other things: "There are millions like you in darkest Europe. Trust them as you would trust yourself." And as I had recalled our irreparable losses, in particular, the death of the martyrs of Nuremberg, he had replied: "Germany has other such men, of whom you never heard." And as I had pointed out that one Man, at least—namely the Führer himself—must be looked upon as irreplaceable, he had told me: "Do not be so sure of his death. Several versions of it were published, none of which is convincing."—"So," I said, "perhaps . . ." I was too moved to finish my sentence. "Yes, perhaps . . . ," replied Sven Hedin. He said no more. But I understood.

After three years of despair and disgust, I felt an inexpressible happiness fill my breast. I had known from that minute that a new life had begun for me; that all was *not* finished—that all was perhaps just beginning. I then told Sven Hedin what I intended to do during this first journey of mine through Germany. He had not discouraged me but only told me that "times were not yet ripe," and tried to make me realise how risky my project was. Several young Swedes who had indulged in similar activities had never come back or been heard of again. Still I said, "I shall try." The pleasure of defying those who had set out to destroy the National Socialist Idea was something too tempting for me to resist.

So I spent two nights copying on separate papers, five hundred times, in my own handwriting—for I knew nobody in Sweden who could print such literature—the following words in German:

Men and women of Germany,

In the midst of untold hardships and suffering, hold fast to our glorious National Socialist faith, and resist! Defy our persecutors! Defy the people, defy the forces that are working to 'de-Nazify' the German nation and the world at large!

Nothing can destroy that which is built in truth. We are the pure gold put to test in the furnace. Let the furnace blaze and roar! Nothing can destroy us. One day we shall rise and triumph again. Hope and wait! Heil Hitler!

And now I was sitting in a corner of the railway carriage, with my precious papers in my pockets and in my luggage; waiting to throw them out of the windows of the train at every station we passed through, as soon as we reached Germany. I was sitting and thinking of the glorious past, so recent, and of the wretched present—and of the future, for now I knew we had a future.

The train rolled on. I was not the only one to think of these things. There were in the same compartment as myself three Indian girls— three dancers of the company with which I was travelling—and also two Jewesses. One of the Indians, a Maharashtrian of the warrior caste, started relating how, in Stockholm, she had read, in an American magazine, an article discussing the question of whether Adolf Hitler is alive or dead; and she added: "How I do wish he is alive! For the good of the whole world, such a man should live!" My first impulse was to press the girl in my arms for having said that. My second one was to reply that "such men always live," but this ugly world of knaves and fools is unworthy of them. I refrained from both these forms of self-expression and merely gave the girl a sympathetic smile. With five hundred leaflets in my pockets, I could not afford to attract further attention to myself. But I thought: "Even a twenty year old girl from the other end of the world finds it impossible to feel herself nearing the German frontier without thinking of our Führer." And I recalled in my mind the words heard long ago, in the days of glory: "Adolf Hitler is Germany; Germany is Adolf Hitler." These words still express the truth. They always will. And I thought: "Just as, today, this daughter of the southernmost Aryans, so, for endless centuries to come, the whole world will identify, in its consciousness, Hitler and Germany and National Socialism—as one cannot help identifying to this day the Islamic civilisation, Arabia, and the Prophet of Islam." Once more, I marvelled how broad and how eternal National Socialism is.

But the two Israelites present did not allow me for long to think in peace. "How dare you?" exclaimed one of them, turning to the highcaste Hindu; while the other sprang up like a wounded snake from the place where she was reclining and thrust herself at the girl: "Yes, indeed," said she, "how dare you praise such a man?—Hitler, of all people! What do *you* know about him? You should learn before you speak . . ." Her eyes flashed. And she spat out, against the Germans in general and against the Führer himself, the vilest, the most nauseating tirade I had ever heard since the gloating of one of her racial sisters over the Nuremberg Trial in a London boarding house in 1946.

The world accuses us of cruelty. *I* am supposed to be "cruel," and— if given power—would surely be more merciless to our enemies than any other National Socialist whom I personally know. And yet even I have never said—never thought—that I would "be delighted to see" any man, any devil, "torn in two." I have not said that of the rascals who conducted the Nuremberg trial; nor of those who organised the bombing of Germany to the finish. Can a Jewess hate our Führer more than I hate those people? No. But what the world miscalls our "cruelty" is just ruthlessness—the earnest and frank use of violence whenever it is necessary. The really cruel ones are the Jews. And that is why the fate of any of us in their hands is incomparably worse than the fate of any Jew in our power.

I shuddered as I heard that young daughter of Zion speak. Nobody yet had ever, in my presence, uttered a word against Adolf Hitler without my replying vehemently. But now, though burning with indignation, I was mute and motionless. I had those precious leaflets with me. I thought of the godlike Man for the sake of whom the German people are so dear to me. Was I to defend him against that tapeworm of a woman, and create a row, and get discovered, and become useless—or distribute my message of pride and hope to the people he so loved? I held my peace. But I gave the woman such a glance of hatred that she recoiled—and was never again to address a word to me. And I rose from my place and went and wept in the one place in which, even in a train, one is always sure to be alone.

* * *

The train rolled on towards the German border. There were some difficulties awaiting me at Flensburg. I was asked to get out of the train to be questioned on the platform by a man—visibly a Jew—to whom the stage manager of my employer's company, also a Jew, was already talking. I possess a pair of Indian earrings in the shape of swastikas. I had them on; and intended to wear them right through German territory, in sheer defiance of all "de-Nazification" schemes. I threw a shawl over my head (there was no time to do anything else) and came out. The man on the platform, I was told, was "a member of the police."

"Are you Mrs. Mukherji?" said he, as he greeted me.

"Yes, I am."

"Well," he continued, "There are rumours about you. Can you tell me how far they are justified?"

"What rumours?" said I.

"You surely know."

"I do not. I have not the faintest idea. People say so many things."

"Some say you are a Nazi. Are you really?"

"Does it matter what one is, in a land to which you are supposed to have brought 'freedom'—so you say?" I replied ironically.

"It does," said the man. "We don't welcome people likely to make the already difficult task of the Occupying Powers still more difficult."

"I don't see how anyone could display such might from behind the windows of the Nord Express," I answered—wishing all the time *I* could.

I had hardly finished saying these words when one of the youngsters of the company, who knew I was wearing my lovely and dangerous earrings, pulled the shawl off my head from behind, "for a joke" he later explained. The "joke" could have proved a tragic one. But the boy did not know—nobody knew—what I was carrying with me and what I was intending to do. The hallowed Symbol of the Sun gleamed on each side of my face in that first German frontier station, now in June, 1948, as it did in the streets of Calcutta in glorious '40.

"I see it is useless talking to you any longer, Mrs. Mukherji," said the man to me. "You'd better stay off the train. We shall search your luggage."

"You can," I replied, with outward calm. But I ran to the principal of the company, who was taking a stroll, and took him aside at the other end of the platform.

"You must help me to get on that train again at once, without them searching my things," said I.

"Why? What has happened?"

I explained what had happened, and the principal promised he would try to help me.

I could not tell what he said to the official or semi-official "member of the police" who had questioned me. He probably pointed out to him that no person seriously intending to indulge in Nazi underground activities would be such a fool as to advertise herself beforehand by wearing a pair of golden swastikas. And the argument, apparently, proved convincing. My very stupidity saved me. My luggage was not searched. At last the train moved on. "The Gods still love us," thought I, as I rolled triumphantly into German territory.

* * *

Right and left the land stretched out, green and smiling, in all the glory of its summer garb—"as beautiful," thought I, "as when 'he' ruled over it."

I stood in the corridor, with as many of my leaflets as my pockets and handbag could carry—some concealed in packets of ten or twenty cigarettes or in small parcels of sugar, coffee, cheese, or butter (whatever I could buy in Sweden), others placed in envelopes, others just loose. The railway ran parallel to a road. Walking along the road were a woman and a child. I waved to them, and threw a little packet of sugar out of the window—a packet with a leaflet in it, naturally. The woman picked it up and thanked me. I was already far away. By the side of a small station through which we passed without stopping, was a café. A youngster and a girl were seated at one of the tables, out of doors, drinking beer. I threw them a packet of cigarettes also containing a leaflet. The packet fell a little further from the table than I thought it would. The young man got up to take it, and smiled at me while I leaned out of the window to catch a glimpse of him. He was a fine young man: tall, well-built, blond, with bright eyes. The girl—a graceful and slim maiden with golden locks—had also got up and was standing at his side. She too, was smiling, glad to have the cigarettes.

As the train carried me further and further away out of their sight, I imagined them opening the packet, finding the paper, unfolding it. I imagined their eyes sparkling as they saw at the top—once more after three dark years—the unexpected Sign of the Sun, and as they read the words written for them from the depth of my heart: "Hold fast to our glorious National Socialist faith, and resist! . . . One day, we shall rise and triumph again."

They had thought they had got twenty cigarettes and lo, they had got *that* along with them: a message of hope. I was happy. The idea did not enter my head that the message was perhaps wasted on them; that, after all, they might not necessarily be Nazis. I took it for granted that they were, at heart. However much this may seem childish, nay, foolish, utterly out of keeping with the seriousness of what I was doing, they struck me as too beautiful to be anything else.

* * *

And on I went, through the lovely countryside, my head at the open window. Whenever we passed through a station, or whenever I saw anybody within my reach—workmen on the side of the railway, people walking along a road or waiting at a level crossing for our train to pass—I threw out some small parcel and a handful of loose leaflets. The faces of which I caught a glimpse were haggard and tired but dignified faces; faces of men and women who, obviously, had not had enough to eat for a long time, but whom an iron will kept alive and whom an invincible pride kept unsubdued. I admired them.

A little before we reached Hamburg, I thrust from the toilet window over a hundred of my leaflets onto the crowded platform of some station through which we passed, and then came back into the corridor. The train was rushing on at full speed. I had no time to see what happened. "But surely," I thought, "some of my papers must have fallen in good hands." Then it struck me that some, also, being so light, might well have flown back into the train. I knew that the Jew B.T.,[1] the stage manager of the company, was sitting in a railway carriage nearer the end of the train than mine. And I shuddered at the idea of *him* suddenly seeing one fly in from the window and fall upon his lap. "Oh, dear!" said I to myself, "I must be more careful henceforth!"

The Sun had already gone down, and we were running through the suburbs of Hamburg. For the first time, I beheld what I was soon to see every day: the ruins of Germany. Black against the pale green and golden sky—the afterglow of the late summer sunset—I saw no end of shattered walls; of heaps of wreckage; of blocks of iron and stone out of the midst of which emerged, now and then, the skeleton of what had once been a boiler, or a wagon, or an oil tank; no end of long dark streets in which no life was left. The whole place looked like an immense excavation field.

Tears came to my eyes, not because these were the ruins of *a* once prosperous town, the lamentable remnants of happy homes and useful human industries, but because they were the ruins of our New Order; all that was—materially—left of that super-civilisation in the making which I so admired. Far in the distance, I noticed the steeple of a church standing, untouched, above the general desolation—like a symbol of the victory of the Cross over the Swastika. And I hated the sight of it.

Once more, as in the last days of the war and in the months that followed, I experienced for a while the feeling of despair. In my mind, I recalled those darkest days: my departure from Calcutta already at the close of 1944—when one knew what the end would be—not to hear, not to read, and, if possible, not to think about the war; not to be told *when* National Socialist Germany would capitulate; and then, my wanderings from place to place, from temple to temple, all over central, western, and southern India, without my being able to draw my attention away from the one fact: the impending disaster. I saw myself again in a train on my way to Tiruchendur, at the extreme south of the Indian peninsula. A man holding a newspaper in English was sitting

---

[1] Ben Topf—Ed.

opposite me. And I could not help reading the headlines in big letters: "Berlin is an inferno." It was in April, 1945, a day or two after the Führer's birthday. The man had looked up at me as he had seen me reacting and had said: "Well, we are safe out here, anyhow!" And I had replied: "It is all right for you, but I wish I were not safe. I wish I were there." And before he had had the time to overcome his astonishment and ask me why, I had gotten up and gone out into the corridor, and there, easily abstracting myself from my tropical surroundings, I had thought of that inferno—as far as one *can* think of such a thing without having seen it. And I had pictured to myself the Man against and around whom raged the fury of a world possessed by demons, the Man who had striven for peace and on whom three continents were waging war: my beloved Führer—in the midst of the noise of exploding bombs and of crumbling buildings, his stern and beautiful face lighted up, now and then, by the sudden glow of new fires started in the vicinity. And I had felt all the more tormented in my security far away, because I could not look up to that tragic face in the hour of ruin and tell my betrayed Leader: "The East and West may turn against you now, but I am with you forever!" And I recalled, after that, my return to Bengal in July, 1945; the news: Germany divided into four "zones"; and then, the three long, gloomy years that had followed, until I had found in Sweden a new ray of hope.

I was thinking of all this as the train halted in Hamburg station, along the one remaining platform of the twenty-eight the station once possessed.

* * *

I soon noticed a gathering before one of the windows of our train—the window of a compartment nearer the end than the one I occupied. People were rushing forward, pushing one another, struggling with one another for something at their feet on the platform. Then, for a minute, all was calm again—all eyes were once more gazing at the window in expectation until, at last, the desired thing fell, and all again rushed to pick it up. The thing was a cigarette—a single one.

I walked down the corridor to the carriage from which it had dropped. It was the one occupied by the stage manager of the company, the Jew whom I mentioned. And there I actually saw Israel B.T. standing at the window, gloating over the ruins of Hamburg and of all Germany at the top of his voice—saying he was sorry an atom bomb had not been dropped on each town—and throwing onto the platform *one* cigarette at a time (only one) just to have the pleasure of seeing twenty people rush forth to pick it up. Twenty people who less than ten years—less than five years—ago, had acclaimed the Führer at the height of his glory with their right arm outstretched and the cries of "Sieg Heil!"; twenty people who had fought for the triumph of the Aryan Ideology and for the overlordship of the Aryan race in this world, were now, after three years of systematic starvation, oppression, and demoralisation, fighting for a cigarette thrown to them—like a dry bone to a pack of hungry dogs—by a fat, ugly, mean, cruel, gloating Jew! My heart ached with shame and indignation. I wanted to get down from the train, to rush to the ones on the platform—to my Führer's people; to *my* people—and tell them: "Don't pick up that thing! It is the gift of mockery. Don't!"

But the train had already started moving on. I turned to Israel B.T. with cold, contained rage: "If you must see people fight for your damned cigarettes, you could at least throw out a packet of twenty—something worth having." I loathed the spiteful, cowardly creature from the depth of my heart, but I just could not keep silent. The Jew looked around at me and said: "I keep my cigarettes for Englishmen, and would advise you to do the same, if you have any."

"Mr. B.T.," I replied, "what have *you* in common with England and Englishmen? As for advice, let me tell you straightaway that I take none from my racial inferiors."

It was the first time I ever had shown the creature my National Socialist feelings in all their glaring nakedness! He was taken aback. "What is the matter with you?" he said. He did not know me enough—yet—to understand at once.

"What is the matter with me?" I repeated, "Nothing. We are in Germany. That's all."

The train moved forth between further expanses covered with ruins. Yes, we *were* in Germany.

* * *

It was now dark. A bright starry night, and that desolation—those endless charred and blasted walls, and those emaciated, stern, and dignified faces—beneath the splendour of the heavens; and I, still standing in the corridor with a new supply of leaflets in my pockets. "Why had I not come years before, during our great days?" I was thinking. "Why had I not stood, I too, along those now devastated streets and cried out 'Sieg Heil!' at the passage of the one Man of my times whom I revered as a god? Why had it been my destiny to spend all those years six thousand miles away from Europe and to come *now*—now that proud Germany lay in the dust?"

Tears filled my eyes as I gazed at the deep sparkling sky, and then at the rare lights scattered here and there in what was left of that immense city: Hamburg. The dark infinity above reminded me of one of the many names of the immemorial Mother Goddess, in Sanskrit, the sacred language which the Aryans once brought to India: *Shyama*—the Dark Blue One; Goddess of indestructible life, Goddess of death and destruction; lover and avenger; Energy of the Universe. And I recalled the words which the Mother Goddess Herself is said to have addressed to a Hindu sage: "When all is lost—when thou hast no possessions, no friends, no hope left—then I come, I, the Mother of the world." And I remembered that, to the Hindu mind, the universal Mother lives in every woman. "In me, also," I thought; "I too have come when all is lost, when all is in ruins; when all is dead, save the invincible Nordic soul, in Hitler's people. Is that why I have come so late?—to speak to the German soul for fifteen hours from the corridor of the Nord Express?"

We passed through a station. More leaflets flew out of the window, written by me, thrown by me—"written and thrown by the Gods *through* me," I felt. We rushed through another station. I repeated the gesture.

I was alone in the corridor save for a young man standing there—a handsome blond with a frank, trustful face. I had sworn to myself not to touch food or drink of any sort and not to sleep as long as I was in Germany—a manner of self-imposed penance for not having come before, and a symbolical expression of solidarity with the starving and the homeless among my Führer's people.

I continued to distribute my leaflets. Save for two papers concealed, one in a packet of sugar, and the other in a small tin of butter, I had now only loose messages left. Each time we stopped, I expected the police to come, the train to be searched, and me found out and arrested. I knew I was doing something risky and had not for one moment hoped to get away with it. When, on the morning before, I had seen the Baltic Sea gleam in the sunshine, and watched the seagulls come and go in the bright sky, I had felt convinced that these were my last hours of liberty. I was prepared for the worst. But nothing happened.

The young blond I have mentioned did not seem to be watching me or even to have noticed what I was doing. Yet, I thought I had better try to find out who he was and what views he held . . . "in case." I went up to him, and we started talking. He was a Dane, he told me. I had met in Iceland, over a year before, a couple of Danes who were convinced Nazis. But I knew, of course, that a very great number were not. I asked this one the testing question which, generally, no European whose country was recently under National Socialist rule can answer without revealing his tendencies: "How did you fare with the Germans, during the war? Badly?" He smiled and replied: "Better than since they left." I thought for a minute that he had guessed his answer would please me. But no. That could not have been. It was not written on my face that I am a National Socialist. And also, I was then dressed in the Indian style, in a "sari," as I always had been, for years, before I came to live in occupied Germany. And few people knew what a response Hitler's message had found in the hearts of some of the "southernmost Aryans." The young man was probably sincere. And I felt I could talk a little freely to him. I told him how the sight of the ruins shattered me to the depth, and how I was in sympathy with Germany in her martyrdom.

"Yes," he said, "I see you throw cigarettes and food to these people."

"And better than that," I suddenly replied, as though something had prompted me to betray myself—or as though I were sure the young Northerner would not betray me.

"What do you mean by 'better than that'? What is better than food for the starving?" said he.

"Hope," I replied, "the certitude of a future. But don't ask me for further explanations."

"I shall not. I think I understand you *now*," he said. "And you have all my sympathy," he added in a voice that seemed sincere. "But may I ask you only one question: you are not yourself a German, are you?"

"I am not."

"Then, what is your nationality?"

"Indo-European," I replied. And I felt my face brighten. In a flash, I imagined on the map of the world the immense stretch of land from Norway to India on which, from time immemorial, the different nations of my race created cultures. And as the young Dane seemed puzzled, I explained: "Yes," said I, "I *have* no other nationality. Half Greek and half English, brought up in France, and wedded to a Brahmin from far-away Bengal, what country can I claim as mine? None. But I can claim a race—a race that stands above conventional boundaries. Fifteen years ago, to someone who asked me whether I gave my allegiance to Greece or to India, I answered: "To neither—or to both along with many other lands. I feel myself an Aryan, first and last. And I am proud to be one."

I did not add: "And I love this land, Germany, as the hallowed cradle of National Socialism; the country that staked its all so that the whole of the Aryan race might stand together, in its regained ancestral pride; Hitler's country." But the young man understood; "I know," he told me; "and I repeat: you have all my sympathy. I shall not betray you."

I was now sure he would not. He talked a little longer to me and then withdrew into his compartment. I soon was alone, awake in the sleeping train rushing on at full speed in the night through Germany. We halted at Bremen and at other stations. But, in order to avoid getting found out, I threw out my leaflets, as much as possible, at small stations through which we passed without stopping, whenever I saw people on the platforms. Every time the train stopped, I thought I might have been detected; I expected to be asked to get down and follow some man in uniform to the nearest police station. But nothing happened. Of all those who had picked up my message dropped from the windows of the Nord Express, none had yet been willing to betray me.

* * *

The train halted at Duisburg, and although it must have been about 3:30 a.m., there were plenty of people on the platform. To throw out a handful of leaflets was out of the question. The train was stopping. I would have been seen and arrested at once, without any profit to anybody. But I had an idea: I stuffed the pockets of one of my coats with leaflets, folded the coat in four carefully, and, as soon as the train began to move once more, threw the bundle out of the window. Someone, I thought would be glad to wear it the following winter. (It was a good coat, given to me in Iceland.) In the meantime, whoever picked it up would find in the pockets enough Nazi propaganda for himself and all his friends.

The train moved on . . . but stopped again. Had I been discovered, this time? I experienced that same uneasy feeling of danger which I had known so often since my narrow escape at the frontier station. Then, I noticed two men in railway uniforms get into the train by one of the doors that opened into the corridor where I was standing. One of them was carrying my coat. The uneasy feeling left me all of a sudden, as by miracle, and was replaced by absolute calm. I now was sure I was going to be caught. I watched the two men walk toward me, as the train started once more.

They greeted me and asked me whether I spoke German.

"A little," said I.

"You come from India?" asked again the same man, noticing the white cotton "sari" in which I was draped.

"Yes."

"And you threw that coat out of the window?"

"Yes. It is my coat. I hoped someone among the people would pick it up."

"But there are papers in the pockets of that coat—very dangerous papers. Did you know of them?"

"Yes," said I, calmly, I would nearly say casually—my fear had completely vanished—"I wrote them myself."

"So you know what you are doing, then?"

"Certainly."

"In that case, why do you do it?"

"Because, for the last twenty years, I have loved and admired Adolf Hitler and the German people."

I was happy—oh, so happy!—thus to express my faith in the superman whom the world has misunderstood, and hated, and rejected. I was not sorry to lose my freedom for the pleasure of bearing witness to his glory, now, in 1948.

"You can go and report me, if you like," I added, almost triumphantly, looking straight into the faces of the two bewildered men.

But neither of them showed the slightest desire to report me. On the contrary, the one who had spoken to me, now gazed at me for a second or two, visibly moved. He then held out his hand to me and said, "We thank you, in the name of all Germany." The other man shook hands with me too. I repeated to them the words I had written in my leaflets: "We shall rise and conquer once more!" And, lifting my right arm, I saluted them as one would have in the glorious years: "Heil Hitler!" They dared not repeat the now forbidden words. But they returned the gesture. The man holding my coat gave it back to me: "Throw it out in some small station in which the train does not stop," he whispered. "It is no use taking unnecessary risks." I followed his advice. The coat—and the papers it contained—must have been found at daybreak, lying on the lonely platform of some station of which I do not know the name, between Duisburg and Düsseldorf. The two men had long got down from the train.

The name of Düsseldorf reminded me of the early days of the National Socialist struggle, of the days when the French occupied the Ruhr after the First World War. It also reminded me of one of the Führer's speeches there, on the 15th of June, 1926, and I recalled a sentence from that speech: "God, in His mercy, has made us a marvellous gift: the hatred of our enemies whom we hate in return with all our hearts." "Yes," I thought, "whoever cannot thus hate, is also incapable of loving ardently." I loved. And I also hated. And for the thousandth time, I realised all that I had lost for never having seen the Führer with my own eyes. Oh, why had I come so late, to behold nothing but ruins? I did not know that, in less than a year's time, I should have the honour of being tried before a Control Commission Court in that same town—Düsseldorf—for having indulged in "Nazi propaganda."

In the meantime, the words of the unknown railway employee filled my consciousness: "We thank you, in the name of all Germany." Was it to hear these words addressed to me that I had come from so far? And was it to deserve the love of my Führer's faithful ones—now, in the days of trial, when only the faithful ones remained—that I had come so late?

* * *

The train rolled on. I was still there in the corridor, standing in the same place. I was neither tired nor sleepy, although this was the third night I was spending awake. The thrill of danger and my devotion to our Führer sustained me. And the memory of those glorious, unexpected words addressed to me by one of the thousands who still love him—and the first German in the country who had spoken to me—filled me with joy and pride. I would soon be out of Germany now. But I longed to come back—although I could not imagine *how*—to come back, and begin again.

We reached Cologne—another ruined city. In the bright morning sunshine, this time, I saw once more those same endless rows of burnt and shattered houses, those deserted streets. The sight was perhaps even more heartrending than in the subdued light of evening. The wounds of the martyred town gaped in all their horror, calling for vengeance.

I saw people pass in the streets below the level of the railway—those same worn and dignified faces I had noticed all over Germany. When we came to a bridge built above a street, I threw out my last leaflets and my last parcel—some sugar (and, naturally, a leaflet) wrapped up in green paper. The train halted on the bridge, and I watched people pick up my message. They had a look at the papers, saw the swastika at the top, and quickly put them in their pockets; such literature was not to be read in public. For a long time the green parcel lay in the middle of the street. Then, a young man on a bicycle stopped and picked it up. He felt the parcel. Lumps of sugar—or perhaps sweets—something fit to eat, anyhow. He put it in the basket fixed to his bicycle and disappeared.

I imagined him reaching his home—some cellar, or some narrow rooms in a half-destroyed house—and opening it; seeing the old sacred Sign of the Sun, which is also the sign of National Socialism, at the top of the paper; reading the writing. He would show it to his friends. And when his friends would ask him where he had got it, he would say: "From nowhere. It dropped from heaven into the street. The Gods sent it." Yes, the Gods. And the words of hope would travel from one end of the country to the other.

The train moved backwards. Had someone at last betrayed me, and was I going to be asked to get down? No. I was not to be arrested till several months later, in this very station of Cologne, but through my own abysmal stupidity, not through the betrayal of any German. The train was only changing lines. As we passed before a ruined house of which the ground floor alone was inhabited, I saw before the door a plate out of which a stray cat was eating something—some black bread soaked in water, probably; all that the poor people could spare for it. And I was deeply moved by that kind attention to dumb animals on the part of starving people, in the midst of a town in ruins.

The train started to move again, slowly. For a while, I went back to my carriage where I found two of the Indian girls alone. The Jewesses were not there—thank goodness! I stood at the window, gazing at what was left of Cologne. Then, turning to the girl from the warrior caste—the one who had said, the evening before, that she would like to feel that Hitler were alive—I said to her, in Bengali: "Look! Look what they did to beautiful Germany—to my Führer's Land!" And I burst into tears. Then, I remembered the splendid starry sky I had seen all night from the windows of the corridor. And I remembered the Dark Blue Goddess, the Mother of Destruction, Whose presence I had felt that night. In faraway India, during the war, I had visited her temples and offered her wreaths of blood-red jaba flowers for Hitler's victory. The implacable Force had not answered my prayer. But I knew that the ways of the Gods are inscrutable. I now turned my face to the sky, as though the Dark Blue One had been there, invisible, but all-pervading—and irresistible—standing above the ruins. "*Kali Ma,*" I cried, again in Bengali, "*Pratishod kara!*"—"Mother Kali, avenge!"

The Hindu girl saw how moved I was, and heard my appeal to heaven. She looked up to me from her corner and said: "Savitri, believe me, I understand you. The way these people treated Germany is disgraceful."

* * *

Aix-la-Chapelle,[1] another city in ruins. Our train stopped again. It must have been, by now, nine o'clock in the morning. A woman came to sweep the train, a woman with a kind, sympathetic face. Seeing me alone and willing to talk, she talked to me. She showed me the ruins one could see from the train and told me the whole country was in the same state. "*Alles kaputt,*" she said.

"*Jawohl; alles kaputt.*" I repeated—all lies in the dust. "But that is not the end. The great days will come back, believe me," said I, with the accent of sincerity. I had no leaflets left to give her. But I knew their contents by heart. I told her what I had written: "We are the pure gold put to test in the furnace. Let the furnace blaze and roar! Nothing can destroy us. One day, we shall rise and conquer again. Hope and wait." She looked at me, bewildered, hardly daring to believe that she really heard my words. "Who are you?" she asked me. "An Aryan from the other end of the world," I answered. "One day, the whole race will look up to the German people as I do today." And I added in a whisper, as she pressed my hands in hers, "Heil Hitler!"

She looked at me once more. Her tired face now shone. "Yes," she said, "he loved us—the poor; the working people; the real German nation. Nobody ever loved us as 'he' did. Do you believe 'he' is still alive?" she added. I was not yet sure of it. I said: "He can never die." Some people were coming. We parted.

The two Jewesses were walking up the corridor with the stage manager. The female who had spoken like a devil from hell on the evening before did not address a word to me—the Gods be praised! But the other one burst out at me in anger. She felt she could say what she pleased to the dresser.

"Where were you all night?" she asked me.

"Standing in the corridor."

"Why weren't you in your place in the compartment?"

---

[1] Aachen—Ed.

"I wanted fresh air. And whose business is it, anyhow, whether I care to sit or stand?"

"Fresh air, my foot!" she exclaimed. "You were feeding your bloody Germans all night. Don't we know."

"*Feeding* them, only," thought I. So they did *not* know the whole truth after all. "Can't I feed whom I please with my own money?" I replied. "Again, what business have you to pry into my affairs?"

But the stage manager stepped into the row. "The Germans!" said he. "You should go and live with them, if you find them so wonderful: live on boiled potatoes in some cellar, like they do, and see how you like it!"

My eyes flashed, and my heart beat in anticipation of the beautiful life that I so wanted to be mine. Without understanding what he had said, the Jew had expressed my most ardent, my dearest desire. "Gods in heaven," I thought with a longing smile, "help me to come back, and live among my Führer's people." But the Jew was not shutting his mouth. My silence, and possibly the happy expression on my face, irritated him.

"You should be ashamed of yourself," he continued. "You should think of the British soldiers who lost their lives in this country before you go giving butter and cigarettes to these people."

"Mr. Israel B.T.," I replied, stressing that word *Israel* that used to precede all Jews' names officially under the National Socialist régime—"Mr. Israel B.T., I happen to be half-British. And my other half is at least European. You are neither British (save by a misuse of the word) nor European."

"A bloody Nazi, that's what *you* are!" the Jewess now shouted at me, as loudly as she could, so that all the English-speaking people in the carriage could hear.

My face beamed. "The highest praise given me in public ever since I left India," I wanted to say. But I held my peace. We were still in Germany. There was no purpose in further irritating those angry dogs, and calling for unnecessary trouble. I needed my freedom to come back—and begin again.

The row subsided, as rows always do. I was once more standing at the window alone, my head against the wind. My task was done—for the time being. I looked back to those fifteen intense hours across Germany. I thought of those famishing people, living among ruins. Five hundred of them had got my message. Any of these could easily have taken the paper to the police, and said that it dropped from the Nord Express, and with the reward given him, bought enough black market food to stuff himself for a month. The Nord Express would have been stopped, and searched, and I arrested. But no; of five hundred Germans taken at random along a route of four hundred miles or more, not one had wished to betray the holy sign of the Swastika—not for money, not for food, not for milk for their children. I admired these people, even more than I had in glorious '40. "My Führer's people," I thought, "I'll come back to you somehow. I wish to share your martyrdom, and fight at your side in these dark days. And wait with you for the second dawn of National Socialism."

* * *

I crossed the Belgium frontier without difficulty. The train now carried me on towards Ostend, towards the sea.

Still standing in the corridor, I was singing an Indian hymn to Shiva, the Creator and Destroyer—the very hymn I had sung, over a year before, in Iceland, on the slopes of burning Mount Hekla, when I had faced in the night the majesty of the volcano in full eruption. At regular intervals, mighty subterranean roarings then answered my song. Now, I felt as though the noise of the redeeming war—the voice of that irresistible coming Vengeance that I had invoked—was answering me. Out of further ruins—the ruins of the whole world this time—the people who had not betrayed me, Hitler's beloved people, would one day rise again, the Voice said.

On the evening of that day, the 16th of June, 1948, I was back in London. A few weeks later, the Gods had granted me my wish. I was again in Germany, having entered the French Zone with over six thousand more leaflets—printed ones; and larger ones too—also written by me. My new life, or rather the period which stands as the culmination of my whole life, had begun.

Savitri with unidentified friends (the man may be Elwyn Wright), Stockholm, May 1948

Chapter 5

"De-Nazification"

"Woe to him who assails thee!
Thy City endures,
But he who assails thee falls.
The sun of him who loves thee not goes down, O Amon!"

—From a hymn to Amon[1]

"Jeder Versuch, eine Weltanschauung mit Machtmitteln zu bekämpfen, scheitert am Ende, solange nicht der Kampf die Form des Angriffs für eine neue geistige Einstellung erhält."

—Adolf Hitler[2]

In all times—ever since the primaeval Golden Age in which the right conception of life and the right religion of truth prevailed all over the world—there have been great struggles of ideas, religious wars under one form or another. One of the oldest known is the struggle between the perennial Solar religion reorganised as a State cult by the Pharaoh Akhnaton, and the Egyptian religion of Amon, in the fourteenth century before Christ. This war—World War number two—was also a religious war (along with an economic one, as are necessarily all wars planned and waged by plutocratic States). It was fought as bitterly as any religious war of old can have been. And it presented the same phenomenon of a minority of people (on each side) standing against the country to which they were expected to belong, for the Ideology dear to their hearts—in England, and even in France (which is still more remarkable), a National Socialist minority which longed for Germany's victory because Germany was fighting for the Aryan cause (just as there were, in sixteenth century England, Catholics who desired the victory of Spain because Spain represented the cause of the Roman Church); and, on the other hand, a minority of German

---

[1] From a hymn to Amon written after the overthrow of the Religion of the Disk (14th century BC) and preserved on an ostrakon in the British Museum.

[2] "Every attempt to fight a worldview by means of force will fail in the end, unless the struggle takes the form of the attack of a new spiritual attitude" (*Mein Kampf*, I, v, p. 189; cf. Mannheim, p. 172) [Trans. by Ed.].

Democrats and Communists who desired—and helped to bring about—the victory of the United Nations. Ideologies have always soared, and always will soar, above frontiers.

But there ends all the analogy between this recent conflict of ideas and the other European ones, whether in the Middle Ages or in Modern times. This conflict of the two allied forms of Democracy versus National Socialism has nothing in common, fundamentally, with any ideological war among Christians. It is, on the contrary, after many, many years, the first phase of the resumed struggle between the very spirit of Christianity and that of undying Heathendom; between the cult of suffering humanity and the joyous, ever-young, and pitiless philosophy of the Sun; the man-centred conception of the world and the life-centred; between the age-old international spirit of Jewry (which asserted itself in turns in Christianity, in Social Democracy, and in Communism) and the Aryan spirit; the national spirit, identified, not with the superstition of frontiers but with the religion of Race, i.e., with the Religion of Life in all peoples of Indo-European stock—something far more full of meaning than any quarrel about two conflicting interpretations of the same foreign Bible.

And while the minorities which, on both sides, stood for their faith against their country in the religious wars among Christians can be, and should be, accused of treason from a national point of view, the Aryan minorities who, in England, in Norway, in Holland, in France, and elsewhere, worked for the victory of Germany during this war, can certainly not be. For they set up, above the conventional conception of nationhood, not a still more flimsy conception of the Unknown, but the positive, the natural, the living reality of the Race, apart from which nationhood itself loses all its substance. From the strict, but enlightened, national point of view, no less than from the broader racial standpoint, the traitors, in every Aryan nation, were not they, but the ill-advised majority who believed, and the criminal leaders who carried on, the anti-German propaganda—the people who waged war against the champions of their own cause, the defenders of their own race, thus willingly or unwillingly playing into the game of the alien Jew. As for the anti-Nazis of German blood, they are, of course, the most unpardonable of all the traitors who worked against their race in this war, all the more so that they had every opportunity of knowing and of understanding (if only they cared to) the real nature of the issue at stake.

Now that this first phase of the renewed age-old struggle has ended with our disaster, it was only to be expected that the victorious supporters of both forms of Democracy would try to wipe out every trace of us, and to prevent us from rising again. And they *are* trying; in fact, trying hard. There has never been, in the history of the world, such a desperate attempt to crush any ideology—save, perhaps, 3300 years ago, the persecution of the Religion of the Disk under Tutankhamon, and especially under Horemheb, in Egypt. "Woe to thy enemies, O Amon," intoned the priests of the Egyptian god in Karnak, as they solemnly cursed the memory of the inspired King, Akhnaton, Living-in-Truth, "Woe to thy enemies, O Amon! Thy City endures, but he who assailed thee falls!" And the Man who had stood for the Philosophy of the Sun against the philosophy of vested interests, was henceforth known as "that heretic" or "that criminal," until, within a few years, his following had ceased to exist, and his very name was utterly forgotten.

The one modern counterpart of that most radical, most systematic and merciless of all persecutions in Antiquity (including the better known and more spectacular ones of the early Christians under several Roman emperors) is the persecution of our *Weltanschauung* in present-day occupied Germany: "*Entnazifizierung*," as they call it—"de-Nazification."

But in spite of the parallelism,[1] the result might not be exactly the same. For although National Socialism itself is undoubtedly the modern expression of the self-same perennial Philosophy of Life and Light; and although its enemies are the self-same slaves of the perennial money power, in modern European garb, its persecuted supporters—the undaunted Nazis of 1948 and 1949; the real ones—are of an entirely different mettle than the time-serving adherents of the ancient solar state cult of Tell-el-Amarna[2]; as far above them, in fact, as pure gold is above clay (and bad quality clay at that).

* * *

There is one way of thoroughly getting rid of an Ideology, namely, to kill off *all* its supporters, and to bring up the new generation in the admiration and reverence of a rival Ideology. And even then, one is never quite sure that the condemned *Weltanschauung* will not one day

---

[1] Remarkably enough, both persecuted régimes—Akhnaton's ideal state dominated by the Religion of the Disk, in ancient Egypt, and Adolf Hitler's New Order in modern Germany—lasted about 12 years: 1377-1365 BC, and 1933-1945 AD.

[2] "His Majesty has doubled to me his gifts in gold and silver. My Lord, how beneficent is thy Teaching of Life!" (Inscription in the tomb of Ay at Tell-el-Amarna).

spring up again, from no one knows where. With unsurpassed ruthlessness, the first Shoguns of the Togukawa Dynasty practically succeeded in uprooting Christianity from seventeenth-century Japan. Yet, nothing could prevent *some* Japanese from taking an interest in that religion in the twentieth century. And long before, Charlemagne had done his best to blot out Heathendom in ninth-century Germany—and had succeeded, with all the display of barbarity one knows. Yet he could not—nobody could—prevent the awakening of the spirit of eternal Germanic Heathendom in National Socialism, in our times.

But people who set out to kill ideas are, in general, nowhere near as thorough as either the Saxon slayer, in the West, or iron-handed Iyeyasu and Iyemitsu, in the Far East. First of all, because the opposite idea in the name of which they act does not, as a rule, mean all that much to them. Secondly, because, in their unqualifiable vanity, they seldom realise that philosophies, religions, socio-political systems which *they* dislike, might have supporters to whom they are dearer than anything in the world—far dearer than anything which they (the persecutors) profess to love is to them. In all such cases, the attempt to uproot the idea misses its aim, however horrible a form it might occasionally take.

Apart from that, as I have said before, the success—or failure—of persecution does not depend upon the quality of the persecutors alone. It depends as much—and, in most cases, still more—upon the courage, the tenacity, the single-mindedness of the persecuted; upon their power of dissimulation, also: their capacity to lie brazenly to their enemies while remaining, at heart, loyal to themselves and to their ideals—which, in times of emergency, is also a virtue.

The people who establish statistics about the progress of de-Nazification in Germany since 1945, and the people who study them—and especially those who conduct the whole show—have a tendency to forget these truths of all times.

* * *

Ever since the enemies of the New Order have acquired mastery over German territory, National Socialism has been systematically persecuted in its homeland, both by the Russians, in the name of Communism, and by the Western Allies, in the name of Democracy; more radically, perhaps, by the Russians, only because (give the devil his due!) the latter, being themselves more earnest about their own hateful *Weltanschauung* than the Westerners about their principles, take us—their only irreducible opponents—more seriously.

The aim of both gangs is to suppress our philosophy as a living force. Their methods are also, fundamentally, the same; the methods of anyone who ever attempted to blot out an ideology in any epoch; the exploitation of fear and need—terror and bribery—also the exploitation of ignorance and weakness—"persuasion," applied to those who happen to be too young or too ill-informed, or too congenitally stupid to be able to form an opinion of their own.

As everyone knows, the first step of the new masters of Germany was to send to their doom, as "war criminals," as many of us as had played—in the National Socialist organisation, or in the struggle against Jewry, or simply on the battlefield, in the defence of Germany—a part too prominent to be quickly forgotten. Former ministers of state, *Gauleiter*, generals, governors of countries occupied by Germany during the war, people who had done nothing more than their duty, thoroughly and selflessly, as one should, were hanged, or sentenced to long terms of imprisonment (often to imprisonment for life) by tribunals pretending to deal out "justice" while being, in reality, but the instruments of a vengeance that had not the guts to call itself such; the vengeance of hypocrites and cowards, mean and cruel as cowards are bound to be.

The same sort of "justice" was exercised in the Russian Zone, with the only difference, perhaps, that there it was not disguised under such a thick layer of humanitarian nonsense. It was summary, brutal, passionately destructive—the glaringly barbaric vengeance wrought by highly organised primitives on their overpowered superiors. It was openly dealt out to us because we were Nazis—and not, outwardly, because we had "sinned" against "mankind" but, in reality, because we were Nazis. Those Germans who had held any sort of position in the National Socialist hierarchy, and who were not lucky enough to be killed outright, were deported no one knows where: to places beyond the Ural Mountains; to slave camps in the heart of High Asia—out of touch with the rest of the world—to toil for the rest of their lives under the whip.

That would not de-Nazify them—any more than the humiliations, the hardships, the ill-treatment inflicted upon their comrades in the Western Zones would the latter. But it would keep them out of the way—for a long time at least; the Russians hope "forever." Along with the measures applied in the Western Zones, it would help to de-Nazify Germany and the world by keeping less important people away from the influence of the "dangerous" ones. So our persecutors think.

* * *

Apart from brutal force, the advocates of de-Nazification use another weapon: economic pressure. They first do all they possibly can to deprive people, known as or supposed to be National Socialists, of the means of earning a living. And then, more and more, they offer new jobs to people with a National Socialist past who are willing to be de-Nazified. They even offer to reinstall them in their former posts, in the rare cases in which these have not already been given to notorious anti-Nazis as a reward for their war-time treacheries.

To be de-Nazified consists in going through the proceedings of a de-Nazification court and in paying a sum of money, after which one is looked upon—by the occupation authorities—as though one had never been a Nazi. Needless to say that, in the three Western Zones, all people who, thanks to some exceptional luck, have been allowed to retain a post in spite of their former connection with the National Socialist Party, are *compelled* to undergo that formality if they care at all to remain in office. In the Eastern Zone, I am told, no such a show is put up, for the simple reason that there *are* no persons in office who ever were, at one time or another in their lives, even distantly connected with National Socialism.[1]

Sometimes, the penalty for having been a member of the NSDAP—or just somebody sincerely interested in social welfare, who took a more or less active part in the truly admirable work sponsored by the Party in that field—does not go so far as losing one's job, but consists in a degradation in one's professional hierarchy, and in a subsequent reduction of salary, regardless of years of honest and efficient service. This is—among thousands of others—the case of Fräulein W, a woman with thirty-four years of service to her credit in an office of the German Railway, somewhere in the now denominated "French" Zone. She has been brought down to the rank of a beginner, with a pay of 116 marks a month instead of the 360 marks she formerly earned. And why? Just for having attended women's meetings during the grand days, and for having devoted a little of her time to the babies of her country. And I would not even call the lady a National Socialist—not by any stretch of the imagination! She is far too much of a pious Christian to deserve that glorious title.

Entnazifizierung—de-Nazification—has upon the lives of totally

---

[1] This was true in 1948 and 1949, when this book was written. It is no longer true in 1951.

unconcerned people, in Germany, unexpected bearings. It has been, for instance, ever since it was imposed, the cause of a disastrous lowering of the level of education. As soon as the Occupying Powers took over the country, all schoolmasters who were listed as Nazis or reported as such, were turned out of employ (and not permitted to work at all in their own line) unless they could prove that they had been "forced" to join the Party while being, at heart, as anti-Nazi as the Occupying Powers themselves. But, with very few exceptions, *all* schoolmasters of any worth *were* convinced National Socialists. As a consequence, all of a sudden, there were practically no schoolmasters left in Germany. For the whole year following the capitulation, the schools and colleges were shut. The Occupying Powers did not care. Why should they? The children and the young people were the sufferers. And they were only Germans—the heirs of that New Order that the United Nations so much wanted to crush. A year without schooling would do them good—until the Occupying Powers would be ready to stuff them with their new democratic propaganda.

After that, up to the end of 1947—in some places up to 1948—the children were granted an hour or two of schooling *a week* (a few new schoolmasters had somehow been secured; and some of the old ones, whose past was not too damnable in the eyes of the Occupying Powers, had been after consideration allowed to remain). At the end of 1948, and in 1949—four years after the capitulation—school-going children between six and thirteen in the British Zone (in the region of Hanover) enjoy still only an hour or so of schooling a day. That is the negative side of Germany's "re-education"—*Entnazifizierung*.

Another aspect of the same is the prevention—according to Article 7 of Law 8 of the Occupation Statute—of any attempt to keep alive "the military and the Nazi spirit" in occupied Germany. I was myself arrested in Cologne, on the 20th of February 1949, for violating this regulation; and this chapter, as well as the end of the former one, was written in prison while awaiting my trial. In fact, ever since my entry into Germany, I had been doing nothing else but "Nazi propaganda," and not merely under the crude form which, in the end, caused my arrest. This crude form consisted in distributing leaflets and sticking up posters bearing the sacred sign of the Swastika and calling the German people to remain firm in our National Socialist faith—firm in the certitude that they are the first Aryans re-awakened to racial consciousness and racial pride, and that they deserve freedom, plenty, and power; firm in the certitude that the agents of the forces of death cannot keep them down forever. I had stuck up several such posters in a town of the French Zone on the 30th of January—the sixteenth anniversary of the day National Socialism rose to power—and a few days later, I had been distributing similar leaflets in Cologne. *That* constitutes a crime—for which the maximum penalty is death—in the eyes of those who, so they say, fought six years to secure, all over the world, and especially in Germany, the "freedom of the individual"!

Yes, the "freedom of the individual" . . . unless he (or she) be a Nazi—that is how they should have put it, to be honest. But we all knew all the time what the slogan really meant. And many Germans who, perchance, did not know, then, have surely learnt since 1945.

Any form of self-expression, any form of art or literature which reveals more or less obviously "Nazi tendencies"; any philosophy which might pass for a new—or an older—edition of ours, and especially which justifies whatever we have done in the past and are likely to do in the future; anything of that description, I say, is anathema in the eyes both of Democrats and Communists; of those who are bent on de-Nazifying Germany and the world—*if they can,* that is to say.

The ban on National Socialist literature is not even restricted to Germany. Although there are no *laws* actually forbidding one to do so, it is, in fact, practically impossible to publish anywhere even plain historical truth showing, without comments, the excellence of the National Socialist régime, or the soundness of its basic principles, or the greatness of its immortal Founder, let alone books in which personal devotion to Adolf Hitler and to the Nazi cause is expressed with the warmth of sincerity. (I do not expect this present book ever to see the light, unless radical changes take place in the world.)

Nor is the ban *in* Germany restricted to National Socialist literature. It extends to books that have nothing whatsoever to do with politics or even philosophy; to books of travel and exploration, written *before* the National Socialist Movement was ever heard of, if these happen to be written by someone who is well-known as a Nazi. Sven Hedin's books, for instance—written as early as 1908, about Tibet and the Himalayas—come under the ban. No new edition of them can be printed in Germany today. Sven Hedin told me so himself on the 6th of June 1948. Given this, one understands how the books of Friedrich Nietzsche—the spiritual father of National Socialism—are nearly as difficult to find in the country as pictures of the Führer (unless, of course, one knows where to look for them). And I was told that, a year or two at least after the capitulation, Wagner's music was "dangerous" to play . . . for the simple fact that the Führer admires it![1] That is the stuff they call "*Entnazifizierung.*" Pretty significant, anyhow, as an index of the quality of that world that turned against its Saviour.

* * *

But the attempt to make people forget us has also its positive aspect. The Occupying Powers in Germany do not use force alone. They use persuasion too. They *try* to. In the schools and colleges they have taken over—i.e., which they have given over to Germans who hate all that we stand for—they do their best to tell the young that all we did at the time we were in power was wrong; that the principles from which our Ideology draws its strength are false—"unscientific," "not in keeping with facts," etc. . . ; that our scale of values is wrong—"inhuman"; contrary to the morality of "decent" people, etc. The Churches—the arch-enemies of National Socialism—help this propaganda as much as they possibly can, by harping upon the Christian values as opposed to our essentially Heathen ones. More doubt is stirred in the minds and consciences of young Germans, once wholeheartedly devoted to National Socialism, by the Christian preachers than by all the official "democratic" propaganda in the three Zones rolled in one.

Also, a number of books criticizing the Führer's policy—or the Führer himself—from varied standpoints, are exhibited in the bookshops. Their sale is sponsored by the Occupying Powers. And not only here, in Germany, but all over the world, publications attacking in more or less all civilised languages, the philosophy of the National Socialist régime, or its relations abroad, or its conduct at home—or all three—are printed freely, nay encouraged, under local governments directly or indirectly indebted to Jewish money, while the tale of the other side—the tale of *our* grievances against those who, not content with having ruined a whole continent in order to crush us, have been persecuting and slandering us for the last four years—is not given a chance to reach the ears of the thinking people, let alone to move the feelings of the unthinking but kind-hearted masses.

Our enemies have decided that the world must remain in ignorance of all that we really stand for; in ignorance of all the good we have actually done; in ignorance of all the beauty we have created. Its

---

[1] In January 1949, the world-famous German pianist Walter Gieseking was not allowed to play in the USA on the ground that he had been the "musical ambassador" of the Third Reich.

labourers must not realise all that our Hitler did for the health and happiness of the German labourers, nor its mothers, all that he did for the German children, lest they might love him. Its "intelligentsia" must learn to consider as masterpieces the products of decadent art which we condemned—only because *we* condemned them—and ignore the work of such an artist as Arno Breker, which expresses, in all its splendour, the very soul of National Socialism. Its millions of East and West must look upon the opponents whom we fought and overcame as heroes and martyrs—only because *we* fought them—and remain in ignorance of our heroes and of our martyrs. Yes, of us Nazis, the world must remember nothing but a series of horrors—the exaggerated picture of the violences we *had to* resort to in order to surmount the obstacles which those very same people, who now accuse us, had put in our way; and the wholesale lies added to it by those who hate us or believe they have some interest in slandering us. *That* is de-Nazification on the broadest possible scale—that concoction of cleverly presented half-truths and downright lies, coupled with complete silence about all facts that proclaim the glory of National Socialism louder than anything or anyone can preach against it.

Is that the weapon with which they hope to *kill* our *Weltanschauung*? Lies never kill truth—not in the long run. And not even in the short run, if the champions of truth can help it.

* * *

I have already said: after that of National Socialism, now, the most thorough persecution of truth in history is perhaps the persecution of the Religion of the Disk under the Pharaoh Horemheb, in ancient Egypt. Within a few years, not a trace of that beautiful cult of Solar Energy, and of King Akhnaton himself (its Founder)—not a sign of his brief passage upon this earth—was left. And for thirty-three solid centuries, not a man in the whole world even knew of his existence—let alone of his philosophy. The triumph of the priests of Amon seemed complete. And yet! In spite of all their curses and of all their glaring success—in spite of that endless period of 3300 years during which nothing challenged their victory—could they keep the truth from coming to light, one day? Could they keep a humble peasant woman from discovering, by accident, the famous Tell-el-Amarna tablets in 1887 AD? Could they keep Sir Flinders Petrie and his successors from excavating the site of Akhnaton's destroyed capital? And, in lands of which they did not then suspect the existence, in languages which were not yet spoken in their days, could they keep men and women of our times from reading the translation of what remains of his hymns to the Sun, and from marvelling both at the literary beauty of those songs and at the accuracy of the eternal ideas which they reveal?

In a like manner, even if the agents of the dark forces could crush us out of existence, still they could not blot out the everlasting truth on which our socio-political Ideology is founded. Even if, by killing us all, they could de-Nazify the earth in its length and breadth, still they could not keep Life from evolving, now and always, on this and on all planets in space, according to those self-same iron laws regulating the rise and downfall of races, which Adolf Hitler recognised and stressed in his speeches, in his writings, in his whole career; still they could not de-Nazify the Gods.

But can they even de-Nazify Germany—as the priests of Amon (like they, worshippers of vested interests in their days) swept the Religion of the Disk out of Eighteenth Dynasty Egypt? That is already too great a task for their ability. Not that *they* lack the cunning—the methodical art of threat, and blackmail and bribery; the capacity to exploit the worst side of humanity hidden in most men—nor the hatred that once distinguished the ancient sacerdotal gang. But *we* are not the light-minded courtiers of Tell-el-Amarna. We are prepared to resist all attempts to destroy our spirit, with the same enthusiastic fortitude as that displayed by the early Christians in the defence of a *Weltanschauung* less beautiful and less eternal than ours. Thousands of us have proved it, during these last four years. Thousands more will prove it in the near future—until at last we win.

* * *

The whole apparatus of de-Nazification is powerless against those of us who, whatever their official status in life, admit no ties—no allegiance to anyone, save to Adolf Hitler; no personal love, save for him and for his other followers; no interest, save that of the Movement, that of the Idea for which he stands. Such ones are free, even behind bars. Such ones are strong, even when their bodies are broken. They stand beyond the reach of threat and bribery. But they are the minority among a minority—naturally. Pure gold always is.

But even the great number of our comrades, the average Nazis (to use together two words that strike me as incompatible), the men and women who share our philosophy but who happen to have personal ties as well, defy, in a different way, the "cultural" schemes and the "re-education" programme of the Occupying Powers.

I do not say that they put up a very glorious show. Anything but that! They fill out the forms stating that they have ceased to believe in Hitler's ideals, and sign them; they go through the formality of de-Nazification in all its humiliating details, and pay the sum of money they are asked (twenty marks at least) and come home with some kind of written attestation that they are no longer to be considered as National Socialists; especially, no longer to be submitted to the restrictions that had hindered them (and their families) economically, up to that day. But all this does not keep them from being just as good Nazis as before. And how they laugh at the whole process of *Entnazifizierung*! "*Dieses Affenspiel*"—"that monkey play"—that is what they call it. That is, in fact, what we all call it. If only the representatives of the Occupying Powers could see and hear us laugh when we are among ourselves! It would do them good. It would destroy some of their silliest illusions and strike a blow at their vanity; it would teach them how contemptuous the whole country feels about their precious "de-Nazification" effort. It would show them how lightly we consider all that they take such pains to quack at us, and force them at last to realise that, save of course for the cash they get out of it, the whole business *is* just what we call it: a monkey play.

But perhaps they love the cash so much that even that knowledge would not induce them to stop the nonsense.

I have told some of them myself what we think of them and their de-Nazification—not in the hope that they would put an end to it a day earlier, but merely for the pleasure of hurting that insufferable vanity of theirs. The trouble is that vanity refuses to admit facts that might hurt it and also that I cannot afford to risk harming our friends by exhibiting too precise facts, for the sterile satisfaction of wounding our enemies' vanity. If I were not pledged to silence by the very nature of my connection with the people concerned, I could have told the bloated political reformers of a few cases of which any single one would be enough to shake a Democrat's faith in de-Nazification. The case of Fräulein S, for instance.[1]

Fräulein S is a most sympathetic young National Socialist of under thirty, employed by the French Military Government, somewhere in the

---

[1] All the people I mention in this book are living people whom I actually know. I refrain from writing their full names and particulars for *their* safety's sake, as one can easily understand. And the initials by which I designate them, here as well as in other chapters, are not necessarily their real initials. [In every case that can be checked against Savitri's letters, interviews, and other writings, she does use real initials.—Ed.]

French Zone. I met her in a railway station, a day or two after my second entry into Germany, and have learnt to love her more and more ever since. Her first words to me, after I had told her I was intending to write a book about present-day Germany, were: "Don't believe all 'those people' will tell you about us, Germans. See and judge us for yourself. That is my only request." I! Fancy me believing anything of what the enemies of the New Order would tell me about Hitler's people! But how could the girl guess?

I looked up at her with the grieved face of one who feels accused of a thing he would never dream of doing. "You do not know who I am," I said; "otherwise you would never tell me that."

We were standing amidst ruins. In the girl's tall, athletic figure, in her healthy face, in the metallic gloss of her ash-blond hair in the morning sunshine, I saw the symbol of Germany's invincible vitality. I recalled in my mind the sight of the whole country laid waste by the Allied bombs and thought, "Mortar and stone. That can be rebuilt. As long as this magnificent youth is alive, nothing matters really." Against the background of the torn and gaping buildings, I imagined a procession of new Storm Troopers, in the resurrected National Socialist State—the irresistible future—and I smiled. Was Fräulein S to be the leader of a hundred younger Hitler Maidens in those days of my dream? I wished she would be. And then I at last asked the girl: "Have you kept the ideals that once inspired you, here in Germany?"

She seemed a little surprised at my question; and a little uneasy.

"Do you mean 'those' ideals?" she said, referring to those that no foreigner in Germany today professes to admire.

"Yes," I replied; "I mean the National Socialist ideals."

"Some of us still adhere to them in the secrecy of their hearts," she said.

"Do *you*?" asked I. "Whatever you might say, you have nothing to fear from me."

She hesitated a second, and then probably reflected that I would not have spoken so openly, had I been some "*agent provocateur.*" She replied firmly: "I do." My face brightened, and I took her hands in mine.

"Come and have a cup of coffee with me," I said, "and I shall tell you who I am and why I came."

We went to a café, and there, in a corner, after half an hour's conversation, I gave her a handful of my leaflets.

"You wrote these?" she asked me, as she read one, carefully hiding the Swastika printed at the top.

"Yes. I."

"And you managed to cross the border with them?"

"Yes, with over six thousand. I was lucky."

"And what if you had been caught?"

"I was prepared for the worst. It is the only thing I can do, now, in '48, for my Führer and for you, his people, whom I love."

The girl was gazing at one intently. She got up. "Come," she said, "come to my home. You are the first foreign Nazi I have ever met. But please, for heaven's sake, not a word of politics to my old parents!"

"Why? Are they against us?"

"Goodness no! On the contrary. But they would be scared at the thought of what might happen to me if I associate with you. And I wish to associate with you, now that I know. I shall do all that is in my power to help you—or rather to help Germany through you, her faithful friend. I am so glad I met you!"

On the way to her house, she told me that her old father and mother were dependent upon her for their livelihood. She had a good job in an office of the French Military Government.

"Why *you,* with those people?" I asked her.

"We have to live," she replied, "and jobs are not easy to get. Moreover, is it not preferable that I should have the post, rather than some anti-Nazi?"

I agreed that it was. Still, I felt a little uneasy, being by nature an uncompromising person, and being also a newcomer in occupied Germany.

"Do 'they' know your views?" I asked.

"I should think not! Why should they, anyhow? I told them the ordinary tale: that I was 'forced' into the Party 'as nearly everyone was.' And the fools believed it. They will believe anything that tends to point out that their so-called insight into German affairs is correct. And who cares, after all, what they believe? All I want is well-paid work to keep my house going. Those people think they have 'converted' me. I think I am exploiting them."

I could not help admitting that there was much to be said in support of the girl's attitude. What else *could* she do, without causing her parents to suffer?

We became good friends. And on several occasions Fräulein S helped me substantially, actually taking serious risks—endangering herself *and* her parents—for the sake of the National Socialist cause. That alone, in my eyes, proves that she is genuine. Nobody would have done what she did without being sincerely devoted to our Ideology.

Yet, only a month or two before my arrest, the girl informed me that she was to be de-Nazified. I was grieved to hear of it. I took it as a matter of personal shame. To me, the idea of a comrade going through *that* humiliating process, was nearly as unbearable as that of a younger sister being outraged by some undesirable man.

"Why?" said I. *"Must* you really do it?'

"I have to," she replied, "or else, abandon my parents to starve. I have no choice. It is a part of the routine. *All* former Party members who are now in service of the French military government must go through that formality or give up their jobs."

And she told me of the questions she would have to answer in writing, stating that she no longer adhered to our socio-political principles and our philosophy of life—she, Fräulein S, of all people!

"I know," she added, "how much the whole business disgusts you. It does me, too, believe me. It means writing and signing a heap of blatant lies. But what else can one do in the circumstance?"

"What would happen if one boldly wrote the truth?" I asked, knowing all the time what the answer would be.

"One would just be turned out of one's post without being allowed to hold another in one's own line; and one would be replaced by a person willing to lie—or by some real anti-Nazi, which would be still worse."

She paused for a second. "I know how the disgraceful show disgusts you," she repeated. "But *you* are free. You can afford to be truthful. You can afford to be defiant. Nobody is depending on you for his or her livelihood. Nobody will suffer with you, if you suffer. So you can do what you feel—what we all feel—to be right. I cannot. Very few of us can. This is the tragedy of the matter: we are given the choice to lie or to die. That is Democracy, as you know yourself."

"I hate from the depth of my heart those who place such a choice before you and thousands of others," I said. And I meant it. And I mean it.

Fräulein S looked at me with a sympathetic smile. "We all do," she said. "But we must not take them and their mad regulations too seriously. They will not be here forever, anyhow. Germany cannot be kept down indefinitely; you know that as well as anybody. And who will care for their blasted "de-Nazification" once they are gone? In the meantime, we have to submit—outwardly; to play the game with them, the monkeys' game, *"Affenspiel"*; *"cette singerie,"* she added in French. "That is indeed the right name for it in all languages."

For all I know, the person who thus spoke less than two months ago is de-Nazified by now. And the authorities in charge of the "re-education" of the Germans believe that they have won a victory—made an extra convert to their detested Democracy—while in reality they have only added a little more bitterness to the bitterness already prevailing throughout the country, and earned a little more contempt from one extra individual.

The story of Fräulein S is by no means unique. It is the story of practically every de-Nazified German, man or woman. I have related it from the beginning and in detail, only to show that one should not hasten to brand as "turncoats" the great bulk of those Germans who consent to play the confounded comedy imposed upon them as an alternative to starvation.

* * *

The only cases—rare, I hope—in which de-Nazification results in no bitterness are those of people who never were National Socialists, although they might have been, at one time, outwardly, members of the NSDAP.

For long years, I was simple enough not to believe in the existence of such creatures. I well knew—from my own experience and from that of a few other non-German Aryans wholeheartedly sharing Adolf Hitler's ideals—that it was possible to be a Nazi without being a Party member. But I had to come to Germany in order to believe that the reverse was also possible, namely that people could be—and far too often were—Party members without being Nazis. (It appears to me, now, that it was much too easy to become a Party member. And all those time-servers, pretending to be National Socialists only because it then paid to pass off for one, have played no small part in the disaster of 1945. Out of their ranks sprang the least detectable, and therefore the most dangerous, of the traitors who brought about Germany's ruin, and postponed the triumph of National Socialism in the world.)

Such people can get de-Nazified without qualms of conscience. And tomorrow, they can turn to Communism or to anything else that "pays." They are of no use to any party; of no help to any cause. Let them go over to the democrats! A little scum more or less in that gang will not make much difference. It is also safer for them than becoming Communists. There, they would perhaps not be given a chance to turn their coats once more. The leaders of our bitterest opponents purge their party. Our generous Führer had too much confidence in the Germans who came to him; he loved them too much, to suspect treason. He did not purge his Party as often and as drastically as safety demanded. Now, the Gods are purging it for him. And the various forms of pressure exercised upon us by the machinery of de-Nazification are, along with other, less ludicrous means of persecution, a detail in the implacable scheme of the Gods.

After these atrocious years, never must the old Party rise again *as* it was. No. The surviving followers of Adolf Hitler must emerge out of the trial reduced in numbers, no doubt, but purified, strengthened in quality; comprising only the hundred percent genuine National Socialists and not a single one of the others. That is the will of the Gods. And that is the one great lesson of a defeat brought about by long-drawn treachery. And the one great hope, the one glorious promise that brightens our lives in these days of humiliation.

In the meantime, what really matters is not to accept or to refuse to be de-Nazified on paper; to lie to our oppressors and laugh at them, or to defy them openly. What really matters is, whether in mockery or in defiance of the organised anti-Nazi forces, to remain equally firm in our principles, equally faithful to our Führer, equally impervious to all obvious or subtle anti-Nazi influences, until the day dawns for us to rise and conquer once more.

Chapter 6

CHAMBERS OF HELL

"They shall lay hands on you and persecute you, deliver you up to the synagogues and into prisons, being brought before kings and rulers for My name's sake."
— The Gospel according to Luke 21:12

"Alle Verfolgungen der Bewegung und ihrer einzelnen Führer, alle Lästerungen and Verleumdungen vermochten ihr nichts anzuhaben."

—Adolf Hitler[1]

The relentless persecution of National Socialism in occupied Germany since 1945 is characterised, above all, by the hatred with which it is pursued—hatred of our philosophy of life, no doubt, *and* also hatred of our persons. This is a trait which, if not entirely new, had not, at least for centuries, distinguished an ideological struggle.

Much is made, in usual European histories, of the persecution of the early Christians by the Roman authorities, for the Western world is—or was, for a very long time—a Christian world. But, whatever else they might have done, the Roman authorities did not *hate* the obstinate men and women whom they sent to death in the circuses. They rather despised them; looked upon them as strange fanatics. They could not understand why the customary lip-homage to the divinity of the Emperor constituted such a crime in their eyes. When they had them tortured, it was to extract from them some confession or some denunciation, not for the sheer pleasure of applying torture.

The men of the Holy Inquisition did not hate the "heretics" whom they handed over to the "secular arm" to be burnt at the stake. On the contrary, they loved them—in their strange, very strange way. They loved their souls, in Christ and in the holy Church, as it was their duty, and hoped till the end for their conversion, and prayed for God's grace to enlighten them, while the bodies were burning.

---

[1] "All persecutions of the movement and its individual leaders, all vilifications and slanders, were powerless to harm it" (*Mein Kampf*, Conclusion, p. 782; cf. Mannheim, p. 688) [Trans. by Ed.].

The furious reformers of the French Revolution killed off their opponents by the thousands, after a rapid trial or no trial at all, without bothering to torture or to humiliate them, save in a few special cases. They too, did not hate them. They only wanted to get rid of them.

And we, National Socialists—we whom the whole world accuses of all possible and impossible crimes, now that we are no longer in power—we never hated anyone in our grand days. We were ruthless, yes; we had to be. But we never were cruel, whatever the liars might say. We killed, if we were forced to, but with detachment, and as quickly and cleanly as possible. We never inflicted pain, unless it was absolutely necessary, for State reasons. And then we never considered it a pleasant necessity.

Our persecutors have, countless times, inflicted pain upon us, without it being in any way a State necessity from their point of view. They have starved us, beaten us, tortured us, and compelled us, at the point of their bayonets, to undergo the worst possible humiliations, for the sheer delight of knowing that we felt the hunger, the pain, and the insults, and that we suffered—we the strong and the proud; the hated Nazis—for the sheer delight of feeling that we were now in their power, and that any ill-treatment could henceforth be meted out to us with impunity. Maybe, they have treated *me* a little better—either because I happen to possess a British-Indian passport, or because their democratic conceit does not allow them, even now, to realise how deeply and passionately Nazi I am; or because they know I can speak, and are afraid of what I might say, when free once more, and wish to placate me beforehand. But rest assured, my kind and considerate British custodians, that any amount of exceptional treatment with which you may favour *me*, now—and for which, I suppose, I should be grateful—will never induce me to forget what I know of the martyrdom of my comrades and of my superiors, at your hands and those of your allies; and never lessen the bitterness of my resentment; and never silence my call for retribution.

* * *

Why has such savage hatred been stirred against us—nay, systematically cultivated, all these years? For two main reasons: because we endeavoured to free the Aryan world from the yoke of international Jewry, and because we claim to have, as Aryans and as National Socialists, greater duties, greater responsibilities, and greater rights than other human beings, whether these be members of the lower races, forever our inferiors whatever they do, or Aryans like ourselves, but not yet racially conscious. It is that which the world takes as a personal insult and will not forgive us. For this is a Jew-ridden world; and, in the West at least, to a very great extent, a bastardised world—thanks to a religion that has never raised an objection to unwholesome marriages, provided they be blessed by the Church. And the half-Jew, the quarter-Jew, the one-eighth Jew—the fellow who, more often than not, has Jewish blood without knowing it—sides irresistibly with the anti-Aryan forces against us. "Blood is thicker than water"—in most cases.

And many pure-blooded Aryans also side against us—alas!—and against the vital interests of their own race, thanks to the unnatural, anti-racial outlook which they have acquired from a Christian, Democratic, or Marxist education, and from the Jewish press and literature, and learnt to hold as natural and commendable. They might not be fundamentally cruel—real Aryans seldom are—but they add their voice to the clamours of the Jewish and Judaised portion of mankind. They put their fine inborn qualities to the service of the ideologies of disintegration, thus indirectly helping our persecutors. And sometimes they too torture and insult us—their blood brothers and natural friends—shame on them! The Englishmen and Americans who organised the phosphorus warfare against Germany—and still less the airmen who carried it out—were not all half-Jews or quarter-Jews. Nor were all those who staged the Nuremberg mockery show; nor all those who tortured our unfortunate SS boys, or stuck the points of their bayonets into the flesh of captured Nazi women. Nor had all the Russians who committed similar atrocities upon us the excuse of being half-Mongolians. But they were all prompted by some outlook, some doctrine, or some ideology of Jewish import. The Jew was, and still is, at the root of that untold hatred with which half the world or more has been pursuing us already before and during the war, and more than ever since 1945—since it became profitable as well as fashionable to be our enemy. It is the Jew's own hatred. That is why it is so bitter and so cruel.

* * *

In the spring of 1945, on German soil overrun from all sides by invading armies; and already before that, in every country formerly occupied by Germany, as soon as it was clear that Germany could no longer hold out against the combined pressure of East and West, began, in all its horror, that long-drawn trail of unheard-of brutalities: the persecution of National Socialism.

At first, it took the form of a general outburst of mass violence—of looting of Nazi property, of murder and outrage—seasoned with varied individual atrocities, from the beating to death of wounded or tired German soldiers unable to leave the accursed country in time (as happened over and over again in France) to the tearing to pieces or burning alive of local National Socialists, Germans or "collaborators" of other nationalities, as in Poland and Czechoslovakia, the two countries in Europe who, in hatred of us and in barbarity, managed to outdo even France—which is indeed an achievement! Then, it became more and more official, organised, backed by military authority, and was finally sanctioned by law, at first in the trials of the so-called "war criminals" and then, in a less spectacular form, in the Occupation Statute.

I have already written in this book—and elsewhere[1]—what I think of the bogus tribunals set up in occupied Germany by Germany's victors, to judge and condemn as "war criminals," and hang, transport, or imprison all National Socialists who formerly held any high position in the country. I shall not repeat here how repulsive is the very idea of that so-called "justice," put forward by people whom their own conduct towards Germany alone, during and after the war, would reduce to silence, if they had any shame at all; by people who, after the atrocities which they tolerate or support, both in their colonies and at home, on men[2] and beasts,[3] as a matter of course, should refrain from censuring the Chinese, Assyrian, and Carthaginian horrors of old, let alone our clumsy, amateurish acts of violence. What I only wish to denounce—apart from the vile hypocrisy that underlies *all* those trials of so-called "war criminals"—is the cruelty which inspired every one of their proceedings, from the arrest of the accused to the final sealing of their fate at the end of a rope or in a prison cell.

I have never had the honour of meeting any of the Twenty-one[4] sentenced at Nuremberg on the 15th of October 1946. Only through other people have I heard of the physical and moral tortures and daily

---

[1] In my book *The Lightning and the Sun* (yet unpublished), ch. 1. [The book was published in 1958: Savitri Devi, *The Lightning and the Sun* (Calcutta: Savitri Devi Mukherjee, 1958)—Ed.]

[2] One-third of the population of Bengal—15,000,000 people—were starved to death or permanently injured in their health through the effect of prolonged hunger, from April to December 1943, as *all* the rice had been requisitioned to supply the British and American troops fighting in Burma.

[3] Over one million innocent animals are vivisected yearly, in Great Britain alone.

[4] Ten were actually hanged; three put an end to their own lives; seven others are in prison to this day. Hjalmar Schacht alone was acquitted.

humiliations to which they were submitted to the very end. The one episode which Montgomery Belgion—an Englishman and an anti-Nazi—reports in his book *Epitaph on Nuremberg*,[1] about the treatment inflicted upon one of the men on trial, during his imprisonment, is revolting enough to brand Germany's victors forever with the mark of infamy. Julius Streicher, says he, had asked for some water to drink. A number of rascals among his custodians—doubtless mostly Jews—all spat in a basin, and then, forcing open the unfortunate man's mouth with crooks, one of them poured the spittle into it, while the others held him down as still as they could. They then mocked him saying that, if the beverage were not to his taste, he could drink the contents of the lavatory.

However much a Jew might hate the former *Gauleiter* of Franconia and editor of *Der Stürmer*—one of the greatest fighters in the struggle against the Jewish yoke—still nothing can justify such behaviour as this. Nothing can even explain it, save a mean, cowardly, typically Jewish hatred. A man might wish to kill the sworn enemy of his race. And surely Julius Streicher himself had wasted no superfluous pity upon the Jews. But it takes a worm, with a dirty, perverted imagination, to think of such a revenge as *this*.

Perhaps less mean and dirty in itself, but proceeding, nevertheless, from the same sickening cruelty, is the final scene of that darkest drama of our times: the hanging of the Ten martyrs. The executioner had been specially flown over from America. One can well imagine what sort of a man he was: one of the same type as those American airmen who were heard in a train, in England, laughing and joking about the "grand fires" they had lit in their trip "over" Germany; a fellow who detested Nazis without even knowing why—because it was the thing everybody did, in Roosevelt's silly USA—and who enjoyed torturing. The creature did his job only as such a one as he could do it: he hanged his victims as slowly as he could, and made them suffer as much as it was possible. Each execution took about half an hour, and the photographs of the martyrs' dead bodies—which were published[2]—reveal an unusually painful agony.

However, I repeat, I have not come in contact with *any* of the Twenty-one, during or immediately after their trial—save, perhaps, with one, but in such an extraordinary manner that, were I to mention

---

[1] Montgomery Belgion, *Epitaph on Nuremberg: A Letter Intended to Have Been Sent to a Friend Temporarily Abroad* (London: Falcon Press, 1946)—Ed.

[2] In several English and American magazines.

it, nobody would believe me save those who have themselves some knowledge of that extension of Nature which we miscall the "supernatural."[1]

But on the other hand—thanks to the immortal Gods and to the British authorities of the Occupation—I have had the honour of speaking to more than one of the so-called "war criminals" imprisoned here, with me, at Werl, in Westphalia. Along with its many obvious drawbacks, prison life has some advantages of which the greatest, to me, is, undoubtedly, the opportunity of obtaining first-hand information (nowhere else available) about those facts that constitute, in themselves, the best impeachment of our persecutors. I thus improved my knowledge about that all-too-famous item of anti-Nazi propaganda: the German concentration camps under our régime, and about the equally all-too-famous trials of so-called "war criminals" connected with them.

* * *

Belsen—to take one instance among many—*was not* the place of horror that the average uncritical swallower of propaganda imagines. That, I knew, before coming here. And—although I did not need to be convinced even then—this was told to me in France, in 1946, by the first honest anti-Nazi whom I met there, a Frenchman who had himself been interned three years in the ill-fated concentration camp. Only such internees as deliberately rebelled against the discipline, "*les récalcitrants*," were, said he, roughly brought to order. The others, the great majority, were kindly treated. And this is all the more to the credit of the staff that the number of people in charge of the place was, in proportion to the number of internees, amazingly small. (Twenty-nine women *only* were responsible, at least during the last weeks of the war, for the good management of the whole female section of Belsen, comprising about 30,000 internees. With so much to do they could be excused even if they had, at times, lost their temper.)

It is only in early April 1945, that Belsen started to become a place of hunger both for the internees *and* for the staff, not through any fault or neglect on the part of the staff or of the German food-supply, but through the sole action of the Allied Nations themselves—through the

---

[1] Savitri is referring to her dream, on the night of Hermann Göring's death, of visiting him in his cell and giving him a cyanide capsule, a dream that Sven Hedin suggested may have been a case of "astral projection." For the full story, see Savitri Devi, *And Time Rolls On: The Savitri Devi Interviews*, ed. R.G. Fowler (Atlanta, Georgia: Black Sun Publications, 2005), pp. 43-44—Ed.

ceaseless bombardment by the Anglo-American planes, which had completely disorganised all transport services in Germany and which had, in particular, smashed to pieces whole trains carrying provisions and medical aid to the camp. The vanguard of the invading troops—in this instance, British—found the camp in a state of famine. And instead of blaming themselves and the RAF and the war in general, they immediately threw the whole burden of responsibility upon the unfortunate German staff. It was so easy! The men and women in charge of the camp were, of course, all out-and-out National Socialists—the men all members of the SS. What a lovely opportunity to inflict upon them all manner of torture with the blunt excuse of dealing out "justice," and then, either to hang them as "major war criminals" or else to let them rot in prison any number of years, so that the world might never hear what *they* have to say! But truth will come out, sooner or later. It cannot be suppressed forever. It cannot be suppressed even for long without, one day, suddenly bursting forth in a murderous explosion. The gullible people of all countries have heard enough of "Nazi atrocities," real or faked. The Gods have sent me here so that I might supply them—at last—with a little first-hand information about anti-Nazi ones—only too real—and British ones in this particular instance no less than Jewish ones under British supervision, if that can add to their interest.

I shudder when I recall the horror of the scene described to me by Frau E,[1] one of the main persons sentenced to long terms of imprisonment by the British judge in that iniquitous "Belsen trial"—the scene of the arrest of the German staff of the camp.

Twenty-five of the women who, at first, had left the camp with one of the SS men in command and had gone to Neuegamme, were treacherously told by the Allied military authorities that they could safely come back to Belsen; moreover, that they were to resume their posts there, and to run the place under Allied supervision. They came back in confidence, only to find themselves immediately surrounded by a crowd of yelling men, with drawn bayonets. Huddled against one another in terror, they saw the narrowing circle move towards them from all sides, nearer and nearer, until the cold, sharp points of steel touched them, scratched them, were thrust an inch or two into the flesh of some of them. They saw the ugly, evil glee on the grinning faces of the Jews and degraded Aryans who accompanied them and helped them in this cowards' enterprise. For along with the regular British soldiery,

---

[1] Hertha Ehlert—Ed.

the Allied military authorities had sent and were still sending to Belsen, as to every other place in which prominent National Socialists were captured, motor-lorries full of frenzied Israelites. It was to these that Adolf Hitler's unfortunate followers were to be specially delivered.

The women were completely stripped and, not only submitted to the most minute and insulting examination in the midst of coarse jeers, but threatened or wounded with bayonet thrusts without even the slightest pretext, or dragged aside by their hair and beaten on the head and on the body with the thick end of the military policemen's guns, until some of them were unconscious. Needless to say, everything they possessed—clothes, jewellery, money, books, family photographs, and other property—was taken away from them and never given back to this very day. (Frau E was thus robbed of 12,000 marks—the whole amount of her savings from several years of honest hard work—by the British Occupation authorities.) The internees, now set free—and stuffed with white bread, butter, meat, eggs, and jam until half of them burst of indigestion—were given most of the valuables belonging to the German staff. The new masters of Germany, Jews and non-Jews, stole the rest.

Then, the women were hurled into the mortuary of the camp, a small, cold, and dark room, with a stone floor, and locked in. They were given nothing to lie upon, not even straw, and were not allowed more than one blanket for every four of them. The room contained nothing but an empty pail in one corner, and had no ventilation. The long day dragged on. No food and no water were brought to the prisoners. Now and then, from outside, a sharp, thin shriek, or a loud howl—a distant or nearby cry of pain—reached their ears. They half guessed what was going on from one end of the camp to the other. But they were locked in. And had they not been, still they could have done nothing. The whole place—nay, the whole of Germany—was now in the hands of the Jews and of their vile satellites. There was nothing one could do, save to suffer in silence, and hope that one day one's comrades would be avenged.

A long sleepless night followed that atrocious day. And a new morning dawned. Still no one came to unlock the cell. Still no food and no water were brought to the helpless women. The day wore on, as slowly and as horribly as the one before. The same shrieks of pain were heard. Sometimes they seemed as though they came from very near; sometimes they seemed to come from far away. And still the door remained closed. And still not a scrap of bread to eat; not a drop of water to drink—or to wash in. The pail in the corner was now overflowing and useless. And the whole room was filled with its stench.

The night came, and slowly passed also. The third day dawned. And still no one came to open the door; to remove the pail; and to bring food and water—water especially. Weakened by hunger, their throats parched with thirst, sleepless, and more and more dirty—now sitting and lying in their own filth—the helpless women began to give way to despair. Were they all going to be left to die in that horrid room, that chamber of hell if ever there was one? Perhaps. One can expect anything from Jews newly come to power.

But the Jews—and their satellites—wanted a more long-drawn revenge; a revenge that would last years.

Another night dragged on. Then came the morning of the fourth day, and a part of the fourth day itself. At last the door opened. The women were given some food and some water. But only because they had to be kept alive in order that their martyrdom might continue.

* * *

Through the famine conditions that had prevailed ever since the destruction of means of transport by the Allies themselves, as I have said, many of the internees were already in a hopeless state of health before the Allied forces set foot in the camp. Most of these died. Many more—who might have been saved, had they been fed gradually, at first on light food—were killed through sudden over-eating, thanks to the senseless kindness of their "liberators." Plenty of dead bodies were lying about, without mentioning those of the SS warders, whom the British military policemen had tortured and done to death.

The German women, hardly able to stand on their legs after their three days confinement—and several of them wounded by bayonet thrusts—were made to run, at the point of the bayonets, and ordered to bury the corpses; which they did all day, and the following days.

Along with the dead bodies of internees, the women recognised those of a number of their own comrades, the warders of the camp, all bearing horrible wounds, some with entrails drawn out. The sharp shrieks and howlings of pain heard during those three days, became more and more understandable. Moreover, these were not the last victims of the invaders' brutality within the camp area. Frau E and Frau B,[1] who both lived through all that I have just tried to describe from

---

[1] Herta Bothe, according to Goodrick-Clarke (*Hitler's Priestess*, 143).—Ed.

their accounts, were the actual eyewitnesses of further nightmare scenes. They saw men wearing the uniform of the British Military Police overwhelm more of the surviving SS warders in struggles of several against one. They saw them knock them down on the floor or upon the heaps of dead bodies, kick them in the face and beat them with the thick end of their rifles till their heads were battered in; or rip open their bellies with bayonets and draw out their intestines while the martyrs were still alive, howling with pain. The ones in British uniform seemed to enjoy the cries, and the groans of agony. For who were those men, still in power but a few days before, now shrieking in pools of blood, disfigured, dismembered, torn to pieces—and mocked? Nazis. In the eyes of the vile Jew, and of those degenerate Aryans—traitors to their own race and a disgrace to mankind—who had accepted to side with him, no torture was vile enough for them.

Frau E could not retain her tears as she related to me those scenes of horror that haunt her to this day—that now haunt me, although I have not seen them myself; that will haunt me all my life.

I looked up to heaven—to that eternal blue heaven that contains the Dance of the Spheres, perennial illustration of the merciless Laws that compel the effect to follow the cause. And from the very depth of my heart—with tears in my eyes, I too—I repeated the prayer that had sprung from my lips at my first sight of the ruins of Germany; my answer to all the cruelties committed against those and other National Socialists, my comrades, my friends, the only people I love in this despicable humanity of today: "Avenge them, irresistible Force Who never forgives! Mother of Destruction, avenge them!"

After they had, under the brutal supervision of the Military Police, buried as many of the dead bodies as they could, the German women were sent back to the narrow room—the former mortuary—that they occupied as a common prison cell. The place stank. The overflowing pail was still there. And for many days more the prisoners were neither allowed to empty it and put it back, nor given another one for the same use, nor given a drop of water. They could neither wash themselves nor wash their clothes. Their hands, reeking with the stench of corpses after each day's servitude, they could wash, if they cared to, only in their own urine. And with those hands they had to eat!

Any human beings—any animals, including pigs—would have suffered the utmost, if forced to live under such conditions. For all the living abhor the smell of death even more than that of excreta. But if one bears in mind that these prisoners were Germans and National

Socialists—i.e., women belonging to one of the cleanest nations on earth, and women whose very philosophy of life stresses, more than any other in the West,[1] the care of bodily purity—then one will realise how this life must have been, all the more, a torture to them.

When at last all the dead bodies were buried, the prisoners were made to clean the lavatories. It was pointed out to them—deliberately, so that they might feel the humiliation all the more—that these were used by the numerous Jews, now masters of the camp. Under the threat of bayonets—as always—the proud Nazi women were ordered to remove the filth with their own hands. Then, and then only, were they allowed to clean their own awful cell, which by this time had become a cesspool.

* * *

After all that unforgettable horror and humiliation, at last, came the trial of the prisoners—a disgraceful piece of iniquity like the rest of those trials of so-called "war criminals."

Of the 30,000 female internees of Belsen, over half were Jewesses. Out of these were selected the "witnesses" for the prosecution—such "witnesses" that were ready to swear anything in order to have the hated Nazis condemned; such "witnesses" that wanted them to be condemned not because they had done this or that, but only because they were Nazis, and therefore hated. Jews related to or acquainted with the internees were also brought in. And they, too, swore falsehoods.

Frau E, Frau B, Frau H[2]—the most kindly, the sweetest women; persons one cannot know without loving them—were condemned to long terms of imprisonment for "deliberately ill-treating" internees. A Jewess whom Frau E had once slapped—and that, not without reason, for she had caught the woman stealing—reported that the accused had made it a habit of beating her. This Jewess—as the other "witnesses" in the disgraceful trial—was not even present at the time the trial took place. All the former internees had been sent abroad by plane by the Allied authorities themselves. The accused were condemned on the sole strength of what the "witnesses" had said before their departure! Democratic justice.

Frau E had been in service at Belsen since the 13th of February,

---

[1] At least since the days of ancient Greece.
[2] Anna Hempel or Irene Haschke, according to Goodrick-Clarke (*Hitler's Priestess*, 143).—Ed.

1945—i.e., for about nine weeks only. Before that, ever since 1935, she had helped to run the female section of four other camps, and had been, for a time, at the head of one. It is strange, to say the least, that no complaints were ever heard—even from Jewesses—about her behaviour there. As for Frau B, she had not even slapped anybody; and yet the most disgraceful type of anti-Nazi propaganda was circulated around her name, she being characterised as a "blond beast" and so forth. For nothing! For being *in* Belsen, as a member of the staff, at the time the Allied bombing had severed all connection of the place with the outside world; and, as Frau E and Frau H, for being a Nazi—a real, sincere one. Democratic justice, I repeat; Jewish justice, for the whole prosecution was a Jewish show. Even the interpreters who translated the answers of the accused from German into English (for the trial, as all similar ones, was conducted in English) were Jews. Of the accused, very few, if any—none among the women—knew English.

From what I hear about unfortunate Irma Grese from women who worked with her, lived with her, knew her personally, she too was no more guilty of all the so-called "crimes" attributed to her, than Frau E was, herself, of "ill-treating" the internees. She was described to me as "a lovely girl." But like the others, she was there at the time. And like them, she was a National Socialist. And the Jews who accused her, perhaps hated her all the more for being young and pretty. So they succeeded in getting her hanged—as they very nearly succeeded in getting Frau E hanged, so Frau E herself told me.

And what can be said of the women "war criminals," of whom I have now the honour of knowing a few, can doubtless be said also about the men, far more numerous, of whom I cannot meet here even one. Every "war criminal" case, from that of Hermann Göring, one of the finest characters of modern Europe, down to that of any rank and file SS man accused of "brutality," constitutes a shocking piece of iniquity, hatred, and hypocrisy, on the part of the anti-Nazi powers. The suffering inflicted is *always* either gratuitously imposed, or else, entirely out of proportion with the actual deed of which it is supposed to be a "punishment" and—what is more—outrageously out of keeping with punishments dealt out by British and other Courts for real offences; it is, also, in revolting contrast with the complete impunity that all actual war criminals have enjoyed whenever they happened to be neither Germans nor National Socialists. Frau E was sentenced, in 1945, by British judges, to fifteen years' imprisonment, in fact, for slapping a thief. Frau B and Frau H were sentenced each to ten years for nothing more grievous. In 1943, a butcher from Calcutta, named

Mahavir Kaliar, was sentenced, also by Britishers, to *one month* imprisonment only, for flaying two goats alive. But goats are not Jews, although they feel pain. And the criminal was an Indian Untouchable—anything but an Aryan and, *a fortiori,* anything but a Nazi. And those Britishers themselves, and those American "crusaders to Europe" who, through their phosphorus bombing, caused thousands of Germans to be burnt to death, like living torches, their feet stuck in boiling asphalt, those, I say, never stood before any Court of justice at all. How could they? They were fighting in order to deliver the world—including England and America—into the hands of Israel, forever.

* * *

But, numerous as they might be, the so-called "war criminals" are but a very small section of the sum total of Germans condemned by our enemies to suffer for the sole reason of their being National Socialists. Moreover, some sort of a charge, however fanciful, was cooked up, some sort of an excuse, however blunt, invented, in order to arrest and try those men and women who came under what is known as "category I." The much more numerous political prisoners who came under "category II," were not even arrested under the pretence of any charge other than that of having held some responsible post in the National Socialist Party organisation. Anybody who had enjoyed the slightest authority in "Hitler's days"—an ordinary *Zellenleiter*[1]—could come under that category, provided he had shown, in the discharge of his duties, sufficient zeal to win for himself the hatred of the local Jews (if any) and of the less detectable treacherous German elements. Often, even that was not necessary. The military authorities of the Occupation would just round up all "dangerous"—i.e., prominent—Nazis they could set hands upon, in a given area.

These people have suffered no less (if not, often, even more) than the so-called "war criminals" themselves, for the cause of the Swastika. Many are still detained in concentration camps without their families knowing, to this day, whether they are alive or dead. (I know the authorities deny this fact. I know they even deny the existence of concentration camps in post-war Germany. But I happen to have met relatives and friends of National Socialists who were never heard of since their arrest in 1945 or 1946—and not merely in the Russian Zone, but in the other three as well. And they have no reason to hide the truth

---

[1] Cell leader—Ed.

from me, while the authorities have.) Other political prisoners have been set free, but, many of them, in such a state that it seems impossible for them ever to regain their former health and strength. I have met many such ones, day-to-day martyrs of the National Socialist faith for the rest of their lives. And I have had the honour of spending a few days in the company of one, amidst friends. His name is Herr H.[1] I shall say something of the deep impression he left upon me, in one of the following chapters. Presently, I shall only repeat the tale of awe which I heard from his lips; the tale of the chambers of hell where he spent nearly three years, a captive of those who hate us. What prompts me to speak of his experience rather than of similar ones of other faithful Germans is, first, that I know this man personally, and also that I look upon him as one of the finest National Socialists whom I have ever met—which is saying a lot.

Herr H had been *Ortsgruppenleiter*[2] in a town of the present-day French Zone, ever since 1932. He was arrested by the new masters of Germany—namely the Americans—at the end of May, 1945, for no other reason than that he was well-known as a genuine Nazi. He had never used his power to harm anyone, and there were no grievances against him.

He was first taken to Diez and there, locked up with thirty other people in a tiny room for two days and two nights, without food or drink or . . . any indispensable commodity; without sufficient space to sit down, let alone to lie down. The prisoners, tightly squeezed against one another all the time, were forced to sleep (if they could) and also to give way to the necessities of nature, in that standing position. And they did not know, of course, for how long they would be left to rot in that room.

After forty-eight hours, however, they were brought out, and taken, in cattle wagons, to Schwarzenborn near Treysa, in the Rothar Mountain Range. There had been gathered in a concentration camp, nine or ten thousand National Socialists prominent not only on account of their position in the Party organisation, but also by their status in life, their family, their intellectual or professional achievements. Prince August-Wilhelm of Prussia, and the Prince of Waldeck, and many other members of the old German aristocracy were there; and the rank and file prisoners were no common men. (Herr H himself is a very well-known architect.) About two hundred women were there also, some of them

---

[1] Friedrich Horn—Ed.
[2] Local Group Leader—Ed.

expecting children that were eventually born during their internment.

The men were lodged in what had once been the stables of the German cavalry. Three men were made to live, day and night, in the space originally destined to accommodate one horse. They lay upon straw, with no blankets; and they were given, for their daily ablutions, not separate jugs and washstands, not even a common tap of running water (which they could have used in turn), but a long and narrow common trough in which about a hundred of them were forced to wash themselves all together in the same water, like cattle. They were divided into sections of five hundred without any communication between one another. And for the ablutions of each section, the trough was refilled perhaps three or four times.

They were put on a diet of systematic starvation; half a plate of thin, watery soup, and two or three hard biscuits about five inches long by two and a half inches wide *per day*; and then—after two or three months or so—one extra slice of bread which was given to them, not by the Americans (who ran the camp) but by the German population of the neighbourhood. Five per cent of the internees died of hunger during the first fortnight. And that proportion increased, as time went on. Herr H—a tall, strong man, with an immense store of vitality—lost forty-five pounds during the first month. However, the Americans decided to give the helpless prisoners a cup of coffee at midday, and an extra slice of bread.

Then came Christmas 1945, that most lamentable Christmas, perhaps, in the whole of German history. The Americans, and especially the Jews among them, knew what the immemorial Winter Solstice Festival, now disguised as the conventional birthday of Jesus Christ, has always meant and still means to the Germans. It would have been a miracle if they had not thought of being cruel to the Nazi inmates of their concentration camps on that occasion. And they did think of it. The ration of the prisoners on Christmas Eve and Christmas Day consisted of half a plate of watery soup *only*—without even any dry biscuits or bread at all, this time, let alone cakes or oranges or any niceties of the kind. Half a plate of thin, watery, tasteless soup, and nothing else—not a kind word from anybody; not a line from their families, for they were allowed neither to write nor to receive letters, and their families and friends did not even know where they were!

The Germans employed in the kitchen, however, managed to put aside six cakes for the internees, out of those they were allowed for themselves. And such was the fear the Americans inspired, that the servants hid those cakes . . . in the lavatory, in order not to be found out.

By the end of December, Herr H, who had now lost sixty-five pounds, was no longer able to stand on his legs. He was sent to the hospital attached to the camp.

* * *

But one should not imagine that American brutality consisted merely in keeping the prisoners on a famine diet that was hardly believable, and under the hellish conditions I have just tried to describe from Herr H's account. It extended to every dealing of the conquerors and "reformers" of Germany with the hated Nazis. It found expression in the collective punishments they imposed upon the latter, without any grounds, and in the impunity that the warders enjoyed, whatever they might choose to do.

Herr H told me, for instance, that the whole camp had once gone without any food or water at all for a whole day, just because a photo camera belonging to an American was missing. The object was found the next day in the pocket of another American, who had stolen it. Still, no extra food was given to the internees as compensation. Another time, an American guard, posted near the place where the prisoners used to go to have their meagre meals, fired for no reason whatsoever—just "for fun"—at one of the Germans quietly eating. The man was killed on the spot. He was an out-and-out good man, Herr H told me, and the father of six children. The guard was never even reprimanded, let alone punished. And these are the people who at Nuremberg assumed the rôle of judges; the people who, to this day, along with their allies, persecute National Socialism in the name of a so-called "more humane" outlook on life!—The vile hypocrites!

In February 1946, Herr H was sent to another concentration camp, in Darmstadt. Although he and several of the other internees sent with him were still ill, they were made to travel in cattle wagons without heating and without even straw to lie upon. And, on their arrival, the sick were not sent to hospital but straight to the cells, with the others.

The cells contained nothing but bed frames and had neither light nor heating. The mattresses that should have been on the bed frames had been thrown out of doors in the snow, and were covered with ice. They were brought in. The ice slowly melted. And it is on those wet, cold mattresses that the men—including the sick—were forced to lie. Twenty-five shared the same cell as Herr H.

Herr H was for two days and two nights shut in that cell, and then was again taken to hospital, where he remained three months. His body, once as strong as iron, had become so exhausted by hunger and hardships that his heart was hardly beating at all. To this day, he suffers from periodical fainting fits, and his pulse, which I have myself felt, is slow beyond belief. And there is no hope for him ever to recover. His health is irretrievably lost.

One remembers, perhaps, how cold the winter of 1946-47 was all over Europe, and particularly in North and Middle Europe. In Darmstadt, where 40,000 political prisoners were interned, the temperature within the cells was 25 degrees centigrade below the freezing point. And the cells, I repeat, were not heated.

And Darmstadt, and Schwarzenborn, were by no means isolated instances of places deserving, in occupied Germany, the name of extermination camps. There were others—there *are* others, to this day—run with equally Democratic zeal. In such a camp, at Bad Herstfeld, political prisoners captured immediately after the capitulation were made to sleep upon the bare earth, without a roof over their heads whether in fine weather or in the rain, for weeks altogether, with hardly any food. They were forced to walk between double rows of soldiers, to be beaten by each one until they were unconscious—or dead. Camp 2288, run by the British, near Brussels, also in 1945, and containing 40,000 prisoners, was of the same description, from what a British officer, Mr. R, who was there, told me himself.[1] Dachau, once, under National Socialist rule, a camp for men mostly convicted for unnatural sexual offences, and world-famous on account of the repeated mendacious allusions to it in the anti-Nazi press and propaganda literature, was taken over by the Allies in 1945. They continued to use it as a concentration camp, with the difference that the internees were no longer sexual perverts, but just Nazis, and preferably men belonging to the Waffen SS. Many of these were afterwards sent to Darmstadt where Herr H met them. And he repeated to me something of the long tale of horror which he had heard from them, and which several of them, whom I had the honour of meeting myself, later on, confirmed.

Dachau, *after* the Allies had taken it over, became a place of torture—not merely of hunger, and cold, and hardships of all sorts, but of deliberate infliction of pain with all the repulsive apparatus attached to it; a chamber of Hell in the fullest sense of the word. And in that hell, the fiends were the Jews, mostly political culprits who had gotten into trouble for their shadowy activities under the National Socialist

---

[1] Mr. R was relieved of his post and forced to leave for having protested.

régime, and who were out for an easy and cowardly revenge. All men to appear before Allied tribunals as "war criminals" were selected on the denunciation of Jews, and submitted to torture without any proof of the soundness of the charges brought against them. The tortures varied according to the amount and quality of imagination that the Jews possessed. Many of the victims were forced to lean in a row against a wall, with their feet a yard or so from it, and then struck on the legs with a rod, as hard as possible, so that they fell flat upon their faces, bleeding, and their teeth were knocked out. Others had their fingernails pulled out; or were hung up for any length of time or whirled around the room by a thin, strong rope, or a chain, fixed to their virile organs. The Allies themselves admit it. In his memorandum to the American War Minister Kenneth Royall, the American judge E. Lewy Van Roden states that the men who appeared before the American Military Tribunal at Dachau, charged with "war crimes," were submitted to all sorts of tortures. "They were kicked, their teeth were knocked out, their jaws broken; they were put to solitary confinement, tortured with burning sticks of wood, starved, threatened with reprisals on their families, and given false hopes of release, in order to extract confessions from them."[1]

In Darmstadt and in Schwarzenborn, under the slightest pretexts, the internees were often condemned to remain stark naked in a freezing cold cell for a whole month, being allowed one blanket at night only.

Such is the treatment inflicted upon my comrades in the post-war anti-Nazi concentration camps under Allied management, by those darling Jews whom the whole world has been taught to look upon as the innocent and lovable victims of our "monstrous" régime, and to pity, and to champion, but, in reality, all the time—unknowingly—to obey implicitly as a slave.

* * *

Herr H, to whom I owe the above information and a great deal more, was at last released in December, 1947, after spending nearly three years in hell.[2]

It is difficult to say how many thousands of other National

---

[1] This appeared in the *Rheinisch-Pfälzische Rundschau*, a democratic paper of Bad Kreuznach, on 31 December 1948. It was reproduced in French in the *Revue de la Presse Rhénane et Allemande*, vol. 4, no. 1, which was kindly given to me by the French authorities in Koblenz.

[2] He died on the 12th of December, 1949.

Socialists, once as healthy and able as he, have, like him, become physical wrecks in the same and in other extermination camps all over occupied Germany, and further east, in the unknown penal settlements of the Soviet Union, from which none have come back. It is difficult to say how many thousands have died. In particular, it is difficult to give a picture of that darkest and grimmest of all the varied aspects of the persecution of National Socialism: the martyrdom of the SS men. None is grim enough to be accurate.

Whether in occupied Germany, in Russia, or in other countries, it is this splendid élite of the National Socialist forces that has decidedly suffered the most—as could be expected.

France is one of the countries where the young SS men, easy to recognise, were deliberately subjected to the greatest hardships: made to lie for weeks upon the cold, damp earth; starved; beaten; tortured. Many were sent to slave labour camps in the French (or Belgian) equatorial colonies, that they might die there of exhaustion coupled with malnutrition, ill-treatment, and tropical diseases. I met one—Herr W[1]—who, in 1945, after his capture by the French, was sent from Marseilles to Sidi-bel-Abbes with 18,000 others, and from there, through the Sahara Desert under the escort of half-wild Moroccan auxiliaries, to the Belgian Congo. These Africans, alone with the unarmed prisoners in the burning solitude, made it a pastime of firing at them under the slightest pretexts or even under no pretext at all. The French had perhaps taught them to look upon Nazis as the natural enemies of all dark-skinned people—as British propaganda has quite a number of silly Indians. And that, along with an inborn propensity to murder, possibly prompted them. Many of the prisoners who were not killed off in this fashion died nevertheless on the way of malignant fevers. They had no medicine, no opportunity for medical aid whatsoever; no care, save from their comrades.

In the Congo, they were parked in a camp, also entirely under the supervision of wild North African and Negro troops, and made to work like slaves in the lead mines twelve hours a day—from dawn to sunset—with water up to their waists and hardly anything to eat. They were not allowed to write or to receive any letters, not allowed to have any books that would have helped to make their lives less wearisome, less gloomy, less desperate, in that hell in which they remained three long years!

Of those 18,000 men who had sailed from Marseilles in 1945, only

---

[1] Gerhard Waßner, the young man whose indiscretion led to Savitri's arrest—Ed.

4,800 lived to see the shores of Europe again in 1948; to see Germany in ruins, but also, perhaps—may all the Gods hear me!—to see their comrades and themselves avenged sooner than our enemies expect.

* * *

Yes, avenged, a hundredfold—not by the human agents, whoever these be who will, one day or the other, again plunge Europe and the whole world in streams of blood; but by the merciless unseen forces in whose play all human agents are but instruments; by the terror which our enemies have brought upon themselves every time they have hurt or insulted one of us. For there exists a Justice, immanent in the very nature of things; an unavoidable Law of action and reaction which measures the punishment to the enormity of the sin, and the enormity of the sin to the greatness of that against which and the value of those against whom it is committed.

I have seen the East and the West—visited fifteen countries; spent equally long years of my life in the Near East and in India. And, with the varied memories of those vast and varied lands forever vivid in my mind—the one advantage my strange destiny has given me over most other National Socialists—I say from the depth of my heart: I know nothing, in the modern world, as beautiful as the Nazi youth. Nothing. There are exceptional individuals everywhere among the Aryan and—in the Far East—among some of the non-Aryan races. There are still in India a few real Brahmins who would be fit to represent our mankind at its best before the inhabitants of another planet. But nowhere can one find a *collectivity* of human beings comparable with this physical and moral élite of Germany: tall, strong, handsome—looking, outwardly, like Baldur the Fair, the best of the Nordic Gods—truthful, reliable, self-confident, brave, and loving; kind to creatures; pious towards Nature; Heathen, in the highest sense of the word; devoted to one another and devoted heart and soul to that living god of our times, Adolf Hitler, and to the everlasting ideal of perfection which he embodies.

There is no forgiveness for people who have deliberately harmed such men as these; no forgiveness for people who have starved them, scourged them, disembowelled them, rejoicing in their groans of agony; who have thrown them alive into the chambers of hell. There is no forgiveness either for those who have treated likewise the elder National Socialists, the teachers, the inspirers, the creators of that godlike youth; the fathers and mothers of that unparalleled élite. With passionless exactitude, with smiling detachment, that impersonal, all-pervading Justice of which I spoke will grind them to death. And no amount of money or skill can save them.

And what if the irresistible wave of destruction overtakes us, also?

Were this just another struggle of material forces it probably would. But this is not. This is, as I have said already, the modern phase of the eternal struggle between the unseen Forces of Life and Light and the equally unseen Forces of death; between the world's will to live, expressed in the will of its élite to thrive and rule, and the world's age-old sickness—its tendency towards disintegration, expressed in the will of the parasites, of the weaklings, of the sub-men—of the multifarious scum—to destroy the natural élite and come to the top in its place. And in this, the all-important, the real struggle, we have already won the battle. However much we might appear, at present, powerless and hopeless, utterly crushed, we have already conquered on the invisible plane. We have kept our spirit. Kept it, not in victory—that is easy; that, any worthless fighters can do—but in the very abyss of disaster, humiliation, and agony; in the monotonous routine of prison life, day after day, month after month, for already four years, like Frau E and the other so-called "war criminals" who were not hanged; or like Herr H in the freezing cold cells of the anti-Nazi extermination camps (the proper ones to deserve that name) with nothing to eat; or in torture chambers; or, like Herr W and his comrades, under the Negro's whip, in slave labour settlements in the burning heart of Africa; or, as thousands, to this day, in the midst of similar hardships in mines in the Ural Mountains, in Siberia, no one knows where.

After he had told me that he and the other SS men, prisoners in the same camp, were not allowed to have any books, Herr W added: "But I managed all the same to keep *this*." And he produced from his pocket a tiny volume. I read upon the cover *Selected Thoughts of Friedrich Nietzsche*. And Herr W said again: "A few golden words of the author of *The Will to Power*; that is what sustained me all through these hellish years."

"Yes, words of pride and of power, not words of consolation," thought I.

And, recalling all that the young man had suffered, I was overwhelmed by a feeling of religious elation, as before the rising Sun—the daily victory of Light over darkness. I hailed in my heart that victory of the Nazi spirit, that triumph of everlasting youth—the assertion of that power of the world's natural élite, that nothing and no one can ever break.

Chapter 7

PLUNDER, LIES, AND SHALLOWNESS

"... man stirbt nicht für Geschäfte, sondern nur für Ideale."

—Adolf Hitler[1]

The object of the far-sighted international Jew, when he prompted England to declare war on Germany on the 3rd of September 1939, was to crush National Socialism. Germany, to him, meant nothing else but the cradle and the stronghold of that extremely dangerous socio-political philosophy. Germany *without* National Socialism was no match for him, however powerful she might become. That, the Jew knew. Centuries of experience had taught him—only too well—that there is nothing so easy to exploit as pure Aryans, so long as they are not racially conscious. "The purer, the stupider," thought he, taking—as he would!—the inborn magnanimity of the Aryan for dullness of intellect. He was not afraid of them; not as long as they were kept asleep. But the dangerous philosophy had already awakened most of them in Germany. And it was beginning to awaken them in other countries too; to stir the whole of the Aryan race. It therefore had to be crushed, so that the Jew might continue to thrive as the masterful parasite of Europe and America; the lord of the whole world through his control of the international money system.

The Jew's attack on Germany—already before the war, through propaganda—had no other meaning.

But the purpose of the short-sighted Aryan of England and elsewhere in accepting to become the Jew's allies against the champions of his own race, was quite different. Either he was a sentimental idiot galloping off to deliver the Israelitish darlings from the clutches of the Nazi "monsters," or else . . . he was just jealous of the prosperity of his German brothers, jealous of their productive factories, of their reorganised army; of their growing influence; of their splendid "*Autobahnen*"; of their clean, spacious, sunny workmen's houses with modern kitchens and geraniums on the windowsills; of

---

[1] ". . . one does not die for business, but only for Ideals" (*Mein Kampf*, I, iv, pp. 167-68; cf. Mannheim, p. 152) [Trans. by Ed.].

their gardens full of healthy children; of their youth parades and inspiring Party rallies; jealous of their joy and vitality—of the fact that *they* had somebody to look up to and love, and something to live for, while the rest of Europe and the greatest part of the world had nothing. And he hated the fortunate Germans and the superman who had brought them such prosperity and such happiness.

And, also, he was, himself, out for plunder. For the Jew had forgotten to tell him that *that* was *his* department and that, even if his ally did grab some little profit out of Germany's defeat, the main profit—the permanent profit—could only flow, ultimately, into the pockets of "God's own people"; that *they* were to exploit not only Germany, but England and America as well—the whole world—upon the ruins of the hated Nazi system. They, and no others. Had the English and even the French Aryan realised that, perhaps he would not have fought his German brothers with so much readiness. Unless, of course, in him, the hatred bred by jealousy was greater even than the instinct of self-preservation and—widely speaking—tomfoolery over the precious Jews of Central Europe, greater than everything.

* * *

Some of those who fought Germany during the war are less stupid and more cynical than others.

I was introduced to such a one—a Frenchman who now occupies in Saarland an important post in one of the German factories that the French have taken "under control" and who, during the war, played an active part in the French *"résistance."* The man professes to detest Democracy, being a monarchist; and he certainly nourishes no illusions about Christianity and the Christian Churches. As for the Jews, he expressed his opinion about them to me in a joke: "Those were surely no gas chambers which your pals used in Germany," he told me. "They must have been . . . incubators. Why, one has never seen so many 'Yids' all about the place as since the end of the war!"[1]

I burst out laughing, for the joke is an excellent one. But I was astounded to hear it from a *résistant*. True, this man was as polite as if he had come straight out of the seventeenth century; and the common acquaintance through whom I had met him had introduced me as "a red-hot Nazi." Still, I could not help thinking that this was going a little too far out of his way to please a lady.

---

[1] A French composer of songs was the first man to make that joke public.

"But, apart from any joke," said I—after I had finished laughing—"if you really do feel as you say about Democracy and about the Jews, then why on earth did you fight *us* during the war, like an idiot?"

"We never fought National Socialism," replied the man, to my further astonishment, "We only told the fools that we did—to make them join us."

"What did you fight, then?"

"Germany."

"After 1933," said I, "one cannot separate Germany from National Socialism."

"Perhaps. And I am sorry for that. For in that case, National Socialism had to pay the penalty for being German."

"I fail to understand," said I. "The National Socialist outlook on life transcends Germany and transcends our times. It is—or should be—the outlook of every Aryan conscious of his natural privileges and proud of his race. If one realises this, one cannot fight the Man who has given his nation such an outlook; nor that nation, which is his and which he loves. Adolf Hitler has made Germany a sacred land in the eyes of every worthy Aryan in the world. If, as you say, you do not hate our philosophy, how could you raise your hand against Germany?"

"Because she was too prosperous and too powerful, and consequently too arrogant," said the Frenchman; "because her industries were far ahead of ours; her people healthier, stronger, more disciplined, more warrior-like, and more prolific than ours, and simply had to be our masters—unless we crushed them in time; because her armies had overrun France and were overrunning the whole of Europe; because, in the united Europe that she was about to lead and control permanently, we French people would only have had a third rate place."

I looked at the man in surprise. He had given me the right account of France's war aims, the account which, in fact, any German would have given me. "*Au moins,*" said I, quoting Racine, "voilà un aveu dépouillé *d'artifice!*"[1] So you would have liked the leadership of Europe for yourselves, is it not so?"

"We wanted, first, our country for ourselves," replied the Frenchman.

"But in reality, you gave it to the Jews, as you yourself admit. Was not a united Europe thriving under Hitler's strong protection far better than that—even if you people did not occupy in it the first place? Have

---

[1] "*At least,* here is a confession stripped *of artifice!*" This is a paraphrase of a line spoken by Hermione in Act IV, Scene 5 of Jean Racine's *Andromaque.*—Ed.

you the first place now? Can you expect to have it tomorrow? Can you expect ever to have it? Can England herself expect ever to have it again? I hope not!—were it only as a divine punishment for rising against the inspired Leader of our age, mean, short-sighted fools you all are, the whole continent!" said I, retrospectively indignant at the idea of that collective madness that the Second World War represents in my eyes.

The answer that came to me was so utterly cynical in its simplicity that it sounded childish—embarrassing in the mouth of a man of forty-five: "Hitler was not French," said the Frenchman.

Yes, thought I, and not English either, but profoundly, passionately German. And it is because you narrow-minded and narrow-hearted people could not forgive him for loving his Germany so; because you could not forgive him for being a part and parcel of his own people at the same time as one of the greatest Aryans of all ages, you turned against him! You preferred to ruin your respective countries yourselves, rather than to see a German save them. You gave them over to the Jews, who hate you, rather than see him, who loved you, rise to the leadership of a regenerated West; rather than renounce, for his sake your petty, selfish claims, your dreams of separate security—each obsolete State behind its obsolete narrow boundaries—your silly belief, as Englishmen, Frenchmen, Poles, Norwegians, Russians, Greeks, that your separate existence as administrative units is worth more than the creation of a higher humanity, Aryan in both the senses of that ancient word: in the sense of "Nordic" and in the sense of "noble."

Criminal, unpardonable fools!

"I admired him," continued the Frenchman, speaking of the Führer. "I still admire him. No sensible person can help admiring him. But I could not follow him; not after the war broke out; not at the cost of my country's independence. Had he been French, I would have followed him blindly wherever he led me."

I suddenly recalled my happy home in Calcutta sometime at the close of 1940, when Greece had just stepped into the war. My husband came to me and said: "The Greeks are now routing the Italians, but sooner or later the German army will have to intervene. Mussolini is the Führer's ally and has to be supported. Maybe the struggle will be a bitter one. Maybe the whole country will be smashed. If so . . . will *you* still be on our side?"

I had looked up to him, rather surprised that he had so little confidence in me as to ask such a question.

"Naturally, I shall," I said. "Why do you ask me? Why do you doubt it? Am I not as devoted to the Führer as anyone can be?" And I had explained my attitude: "Whatever the men at the head of the present Greek Government might say or do, is it not true that National Socialism has brought to life once more—and how brilliantly!—those eternal Aryan ideals of perfection (beginning with physical perfection) that have been the ideals of Greece ever since the Aryan race settled there—ever since the victory of Hyperborean Apollo over the Python, to express history in terms of mythology? Rest assured, I shall never sacrifice the eternal to the transient, the racial values to the narrowly, conventionally national ones; the Aryan, to the narrowly Greek, or narrowly English; or narrowly Indian. I shall always be on our side— on the Führer's side—whatever might happen."

My husband—that son of the oldest Aryan aristocracy of the Far South which the caste system has kept aloof and pure—was pleased and said: "I know. I only asked to see what you would answer."

I related this episode to the Frenchman.

"You are Indo-European," he replied. "I am just French."

"Unless you and your compatriots and the British and all other Aryans can sincerely feel themselves Indo-Europeans—Aryans— before anything else," said I, "and accept the New Order as it is, you will have to sink down into slow decay, become Judaised, become bastardised, disappear. The truly Indo-European socio-political philosophy, National Socialism, is the only force that could and still can save what is worth saving in France as in other Aryan countries. But, of course, you can choose decay. You have, in fact, chosen decay."

"Perhaps you are right," he admitted at last. "But you must agree that it is hard on us to have to choose, as you say, German supremacy or the Jewish yoke . . . while your German pals only have to prefer their own domination to that of the Jews in order to be perfect National Socialists."

"You have to agree," said I, "that they *are* purer Aryans than yourselves, as a whole. No man with eyes to see can deny it. And they are the Führer's people, too."

"I admit that my outlook is, philosophically speaking, neither as consistent nor, especially, as disinterested as yours," declared the man at last. I laughed.

"That is a fine thing indeed for a former French *résistant* to tell a Nazi in 1949," said I; "is it not?"

* * *

I asked this man, who seemed so willing to tell the truth, what he thought of the dismantling of the German factories. "It is an excellent thing," he replied.

"What?"

"Surely," said the Frenchman. "The more factories are dismantled, here in Germany, the more German industry is crippled by us, the more the production of French industry increases in proportion, and the more French goods get a chance to flood the world market, in the place of German ones. Each one of the other occupants argues, on his own behalf, the same as we do—although you might not find many people in high position to tell you so as frankly and bluntly as I have."

"And you call that fair, in Democratic circles?"

"That is business," replied the Frenchman. "Business is never fair. Business means to make money at the expense of one's rivals, that is all. But, of course, one cannot *tell* that to the fools, or else they would no longer be willing to play the game. To them, one speaks of 'Democracy'—just to give them an illusion to stick up for, while, in reality, they help the capitalists of their country to become rich. One speaks of 'fighting the fascist beast'—so that one might canalise their stupid fury against one's rivals of dangerously prosperous countries. Business . . . War itself is nothing but that."

I was disgusted. For I knew the man spoke the truth.

"And you like that sort of thing?" I asked, without caring to hide my contempt.

"Whether one likes it or not, that sort of thing is the world—at least as it has become today," replied the Frenchman.

"*Your* world; that degenerate, ugly, venal world which we fought to destroy," said I; "not *ours!*"

And I recalled and quoted those words of the Führer: "Men do not die for business; they die for ideals." "We National Socialists die for ideals," I stressed; "those who fought us, fought only for business, you admit it yourself; and for other people's business at that; for the business of your capitalists, who deceived them. How wonderful! We have every reason to hate the Jews. They are the natural enemies of all that we stand for. But you? Why should *you* dislike them—if you really do, as you say? Have you not much in common with them, in spite of your different blood? Are they not also just 'businessmen,' like yourselves?"

"They are our rivals in business," said the Frenchman.

"To us, they are the parasites sapping the life-blood of the finest race on earth," said I. "Our grievances are different, as are also our ideals."

And I took leave of the Frenchman after thanking him for the light he had thrown (supposing that I needed any) upon the true mentality of those who, at present, occupy Germany and persecute National Socialism.

* * *

Indeed, "business"—a polite word for plunder, in this particular case—is the keynote of the Allied Occupation in Germany, and the secret that lies behind and explains, directly or indirectly, all the objectionable steps taken by the foreign Powers, from the brutal confiscation of individual German property to the recent Ruhr Statute.

The cost of the Occupation alone, steadily increasing since 1945, absorbed, in the British Zone, one third of the total amount of taxes paid by the German people in 1947, and over forty per cent after the Currency Reform of 1948, according to the memorandum which Dr. Weitz submitted to the Military Government in December 1948.[1] And this large-scale robbery is by no means restricted to this Zone. The French Occupation costs, proportionately, even more, as the number of occupants (and of occupants' families) settled in Germany is far greater in comparison with the number of Germans inhabiting the Zone. According to a declaration of General Hepp, head of the Information Department of the French Military Government in Baden-Baden, at a Press Conference in December 1948,[2] there were still, at that date, 22,263 houses entirely requisitioned and 25,475 partly requisitioned in the French Zone. And in Baden-Baden alone, where "the occupying power has taken possession of practically all the main hotels,"[3] German enterprise, both private and municipal, has incurred a loss of over twenty million Reichmarks, in spite of the compensations given (of which the greatest part was lost through the Currency Reform of 1948[4]).

And all this is practically nothing compared to other forms of wholesale, systematic plunder to which the Allies of both East and

---

[1] See the *Neue Volkszeitung* (Dortmund), 13 December 1948.
[2] Reported in the *Allgemeine Zeitung* (Mainz), 23 December 1948.
[3] See *Badische Neueste Nachrichten* (Karlsruhe), 29 December 1948.
[4] *Ibid*, quoted in *Revue de la Presse Rhénane et Allemande*, vol. 3, no. 52.

West have submitted Germany ever since they set foot in the country: the dismantling of an enormous number of factories; the confiscation or "control" of those factories which were not dismantled, as well as of such private or public enterprises on which depends the whole economic life of the country (such as the shipping concerns on the upper Rhine[1]); the seizure of German goods under one pretext or another; the shameful policy of deforestation; and, at the close of the year 1948, the Ruhr Statute.

The guiding spirit at the back of those confiscations, "controls," seizures, etc., on the part of the occupying Powers, is a mystery to nobody. They all aim at keeping Germany forever under the economic domination of her victors of 1945. The German newspapers, however, do not dare criticise too openly the robberies of the Military Government of the Zone in which they are printed. For obvious reasons, the impeachment of the occupant of one Zone is only to be found in the papers of another one. And even so (save in the case of Russian controlled papers criticizing the Western Allies' policy, or of the Western Zone papers criticizing the Russians), it is always a very mild and polite impeachment, springing from an alleged desire to see "truly Democratic principles" govern the life of the country. (The papers, despite the so-called "freedom" granted to them, must show that they have "learnt their lesson," or else . . . they would be suppressed at once—and prosecuted for "attempting to keep the Nazi spirit alive" under the same Article 7 of Law 8 of the Occupation Statute under which I am, myself, imprisoned here.)

Thus, for instance, in its issue of the 24th of December 1948, the *Main-Post* of Würzburg (American Zone) criticises the seizure by the French of a number of shipping enterprises on the Upper Rhine and of the property of many industrial concerns, some of which have their headquarters in the British and American Zones.[2] This step "puts Württemberg and a great part of Bavaria at the mercy of the sweet will of French shipping companies for their coal supply."[3] And the factories that turn out fireproof bricks—an article of primary necessity in the setting up of blast furnaces—"are now compelled to export their

---

[1] See the *Main-Post* (Würzburg), 24 December 1948.

[2] The newspaper names a few of the well-known concerns effected—Franz Haniel, Duisburg-Ruhrort; Rhenania-Rheinschiffahrt, Homburg; Harpener Berghau, Abt. Schiffahrt; Linden-Reederei, Duisburg-Ruhrort; Klöckner Werke, and the Reemtsma cigarette works.

[3] *Main-Post* (Würzburg), 24 December 1948, quoted in *Revue de la Presse Rhénane et Allemande*, vol. 3, no. 52.

products to Lorraine, thus encouraging competition to the disadvantage of the German industry of the Ruhr."[1] Moreover, states the same paper, this step had been prepared carefully ever since the time of the capitulation. From that time,

> French shipping companies had taken possession of the equipment and ships of the left bank of the Rhine. A "German Shipping Bureau" with headquarters at Mainz, was authorised to requisition the ships and to transfer them to French purchasers. The French- privileged companies, at the time of the Currency Reform, exchanged their capital at the rate of 10 Reichmarks for 8 Deutschmarks, thus realising their present capital of 12.8 million Deutschmarks. The whole coal supply of Pfalz and Württemberg is in the hands of the "Union Charbonnière" which exerts a growing pressure upon the further Bavarian country. The company is now trying to acquire vast grounds at Karlsruhe and at Heilbronn.[2]

The suppression of the great industrial "cartels" had no other aim but to break the economic power that Germany still possesses, and to forward the interests of the rival French coal mining and iron and steel industries; "to fasten the grip of France upon the economy of the whole country lying between the Rhine, the Main, the Meuse, and the Mosel," as the above quoted paper puts it.

And this is only one instance among many. The Berlin paper *Tagesspiegel*, licensed by the Americans, criticises the grabbing policy of the French in no less clear although courteous terms, in its first page article of the 21st of December 1948.[3] It would be easy, but tedious, to give a long list of German papers of the British and American Zones that do the same. As for the German papers of Berlin and of the whole Eastern Zone, licensed by the Russians, they do not hesitate to accuse the Western Allies of turning Germany into a "colonial country" and to characterise—and rightly so—the entire Occupation Statute of West Germany as a device to enslave the German people permanently.[4] Naturally, they forget to speak—or rather are not allowed to speak—of the no less systematic and wholesale plunder of German property by the Russians, and of all the Russian regulations that constitute a no less

---

[1] *Ibid.*
[2] *Ibid.*
[3] Quoted in *Revue de la Presse Rhénane et Allemande*, vol. 3, no. 52.
[4] *Tägliche Rundschau* (Berlin), 23 December 1948.

complete enslavement of the German people in the Eastern Zone, let alone of the vast portions of territory from which the German population has been entirely removed.

* * *

But the two forms of robbery that have surely been the most bitterly resented by the Germans ever since the beginning of the Occupation and that, to this day, every German cannot but take as open acts of hostility, are the dismantling of the factories and the large-scale deforestation of the country.

One must know something of the German labourer's high standard of technical education and of his genuine interest and pride in his daily work, to realise what an amount of bitterness the Allies are storing against themselves in the hearts of millions of Germans, through that mean policy of thieves which they have pursued since 1945, and are still pursuing, in all the Zones. Even if their orders to remove piece by piece, or to destroy, thousands and thousands of valuable machines, were actuated by the sole desire for "security," i.e., by the sole fear of seeing a powerful, warrior-like Germany rise again in amazingly short a time out of the utter ruin of today, still I would characterise their policy as criminal. For what right have they, anyhow, to try to keep down a great nation forever, just because it has more potentialities for military efficiency than they? Who are they, that they alone in the world should be armed and ready for war, and others, by no means their inferiors, should yield to them? But that is not even the case. The attitude of the victors, in this matter of plunder, as in the others, is inspired by "a policy of economic competition,"[1] to quote the words of another German paper, written precisely in connection with the dismantling of a factory. This is so true that not merely armament factories, but many others, of which the production is entirely affected to peaceful aims—such as the firm Hellige, Morat, and Company of Freiburg, specializing in manufacturing medical and physiological instruments—were also dismantled.

On the other hand, the German people—now powerless to act, but not powerless to think and feel—and especially the workmen attached to the factories that are to be dismantled, witness the proceedings with healthy, concentrated bitterness. Over and over again, cases have occurred in which the workmen appointed to take part in the

---

[1] *Handelsblatt* (Düsseldorf), 2nd week of January 1949.

dismantling categorically refused to pull down, piece by piece, the machines that had been in their hands, for so long, instruments of prosperity. Recently—in January, 1949—the 11,000 workmen of the Bochumer Verein factory (which the British insisted on dismantling) sent a telegram to the President of the USA, Mr. Truman, stating that "they would not take part in the destruction of their instruments of labour, even under military pressure." The further wording of the telegram is full of significance: "One cannot ask us to demolish our own house, and to give bricks and old iron to feed our increasing population. No true German will dirty his fingers by contributing to the destruction of our factory."[1]

Proud and sensible words, that were not "nothing but words"; for, a week or so later, began before the British Military tribunal of Bochum, the trial of several workmen of the Sulzbach concern, from Essen, who had refused to take part in the dismantling of the Bochumer Verein factory.[2]

One can imagine the feelings of these men, tried for not agreeing to lend a hand to the systematic ruin of their country's economy imposed, under threat of arms, by rapacious foreign capitalists. As millions of workmen all over Germany, they must have looked back, within their hearts, to those glorious days in which they acclaimed the Führer—the maker of Germany's prosperity—and in which the Führer held out his hand to them, individually, and to their happy children. And if, among them, several had not, in those days, wholeheartedly supported the National Socialist New Order; if, during the war, some had allowed themselves to be deceived by anti-Nazi propaganda, and had expected out of Democracy some greater good than that which our loving Hitler could give them, how they must have regretted their folly!

The destruction of Germany's splendid forests is something even more tragic than the dismantling of her factories. However precious might be highly perfected machines, living trees are still more so. And they—the outcome of Nature's patient fecundity, not of man's skill—cannot be replaced in a couple of years even with the help of any amount of money. I have, years ago, expressed in another book what I think of deforestation in itself, apart from any utilitarian consideration from man's point of view.[3] To the extent one does not resort to it

---

[1] Quoted in *Revue de la Presse Rhénane et Allemande*, vol. 4, no. 2.
[2] *Allgemeine Zeitung* (Mainz), 17 January 1949.
[3] *Impeachment of Man*, ch. 9, "The Rights of Plants." The book is still unpublished. [*Impeachment* was written in 1945-46 and finally published in 1959: *Impeachment of Man* (Calcutta: Savitri Devi Mukherji, 1959).—Ed.].

extremely cautiously and sparingly (replacing every tree one fells) and then too, only when one is absolutely compelled to, by some vital necessity, to that extent, I say, I look upon it—whenever and wherever it be—as a crime against the divine beauty and majesty of Nature. Here, in Germany, now, it takes on a still more sinister character. It is not merely the repetition of the stupid sacrilege which countless generations of men have committed every time they have cut down trees for some petty human purpose "not worth it"; for some temporary convenience or satisfaction, without realising what they were doing. It is a deliberate sacrilege, coupled with inexcusable robbery, on a scale that one has seldom seen; a double insult to Nature Herself and to the German people who, in the West at least—and more so after that admirable National Socialist education which the younger ones have received—are perhaps the nation that understands and loves Nature the best; the nation among which the old Aryan cult of the Tree has left the strongest roots.

One needs no tedious statistics to become convinced of the enormity of the disaster. One only has to take a trip through the Black Forest—to travel, for instance, from Baden-Baden down to Titisee—and to use one's own eyes. In a number of places, along the main road, one beholds, right and left, for miles and miles, nothing but empty expanses in which appear stumps of felled trees—thousands of them. That is what the French call *"des coupes à blanc"*[1]—cutting down of a portion of forest until there is not one tree left; until the once thick, living patch of vegetation is reduced to *a blank*. In any of those *"coupes à blanc"* one can walk for hours without seeing a standing tree. And it is not true that such devastation can only be found on the border of the main road going south. There are also plenty of "blanks" in the interior of the Black Forest. The contrast with the luxuriant green portions that have not yet been touched, makes the sight of the cut down areas even more heartrending.

One recalls the first verse of a fairly well-known French poem: *"Les Turcs ont passe la; tout est ruine et deuil."*[2] But no; here it is not the Turks; it is only the French themselves—and the British in the British Zone, where the great sacred forest, the Hartz, has suffered no less than the Black Forest in Southwest Germany; and the Americans, and the

---

[1] Clear-cutting—Ed.

[2] "The Turks have passed through; all is ruin and mourning" (From "L'Enfant" ["The Child"] in Victor Hugo's collection of poems entitled *Les Orientales* [Paris, 1829]) [Trans. by Ed.].

Russians, who have wrought equal devastation all over the country, from East Prussia, now a desert, down to the ruined cities of central Germany and of the Danubian region. The Turks would not have done the job so thoroughly.

And it is not only the Black Forest and the Hartz, and the forests of North Germany. Wherever one goes, one is bound to see hilltops on which nothing is left of the once glorious green mantle of living woods. The extensive patches of forest that can still be seen, and that one imagines prolonged over the horrid "blanks," help one to realise (if one has not actually seen it) how beautiful Germany was before the disaster of 1945. The Allies are simply disfiguring the land for the sake of their petty profits; perhaps also for the pleasure of disfiguring it—they are mean enough for that.

Wherever one goes, one is bound to see, also, travelling along the railway lines, or waiting in the stations to move on behind another engine, wagons and wagons of wood; whole tree-trunks, heaped upon one another horizontally, or relatively small pieces of wood placed vertically one by the side of the other. And it is not once, it is not twice, it is not "often"; it is every day, and at every time of the day or night. It looks as though the trees of Germany—those trees that the German people love so much and of which they were so proud—are *all* being deliberately cut down and carried away.

The German people can say nothing and can do nothing about it, as much as the daily sight of that systematic plunder and ruin of their country fills them with legitimate indignation. They only know that they have lost the war, and are now disarmed, and cannot rearm themselves as long as the Occupying Powers hold the land. They have lost the war, not through their own fault—most of them have been loyal and enduring, and have done their duty well—but through the fault of the anti-Nazi traitors who helped the coalesced forces of East and West to crush the National Socialist State. And because they are vanquished they must suffer, they, and the very land itself. *Vae victis!*[1]

And yet . . . as one walks about in those devastated, those massacred forest areas—those "blanks" where not a tree is left standing—one sees that there are already green leaves appearing on the sides of many of the stumps; new, tender shoots, springing up from between the roots; new trees growing between the old ones in the bright sunshine, from nowhere—from the bosom of the invincible earth.

One remembers the fresh green grass, or the creepers with pink and

---

[1] Woe to the conquered.—Ed.

white flowers that one sees so often in the cracks of burnt and blasted walls, in the ruins of all the German towns. Here, as there, life continues. No Occupying Power can kill it. Here, as there, patient Nature reasserts herself, after the work of death wrought by the little men, agents of the death forces. And in the German people themselves, too, the will to live—which is the beginning of life—and the will to conquer—which is the beginning of victory—bursts forth already, in the midst of the bitterness of defeat.

Under a show of resignation; under apparent adhesion to the professed principles of the victors; under de-Nazification reluctantly and only outwardly accepted for practical purposes, the soul of Hitler's people watches and waits!

"We are waiting for the spark," said to me, in October 1948, one of the sincerest National Socialists I know in Saarland.

* * *

That readiness, that expectation, that impatience under the yoke, was manifested recently in the unanimous reaction of the Germans against the Ruhr Statute—the latest device to secure for the Occupying Powers the maximum opportunity of permanent plunder, and to keep Germany down forever.

What does the Ruhr Statute amount to? All Germans know, only too well. Yet, it is perhaps worthwhile repeating it here, for those readers of the far-flung English-speaking world, if any, who might have forgotten it by the time this book sees the light—if ever it does. It was decided by the Western Allies, in December 1948, in London, that

> an international body in which the Germans, when they once more have a Government, will be represented by three delegates, as also France, the USA, Great Britain, and the Benelux, will supervise the *distribution* of coal, coke, and steel, of which a part will be used for home consumption while the rest will be exported. That body . . . will have, in addition, the right to examine the *commercial utilisation* of these products. And when the Occupation ends, it will possibly take over the power lying at present with the military governors, in connection with the eviction of former Nazis, the interdiction to reconstitute cartels, and the management of the industries.[1]

---

[1] *Journal de Genève*, 1st week of January, 1949, quoted in *Revue de la Presse*

Side by side with the international authority, of which the function is essentially economic, will be set up an Allied body of "military security," "which will see to it that the disarmament and demilitarisation (of Germany) are maintained. It will be the duty of that body to enforce the interdictions and limitations that are to be imposed upon German industry."[1] The Office of Military Security is to be constituted in a near future, probably at Koblenz or at Bad Ems. The International Committee for the Ruhr will only really come into function after the end of the Military Occupation.

One has no need to be a politician to see at once that this new dictate is anything but "a solution that allows the reconstruction of Germany while giving legitimate guarantees to her neighbours."[2] One has even no need to be more than moderately intelligent to see that it is no step towards a "peaceful and friendly" collaboration between the countries of Western Europe. It is an outrageous document, sealing (in the minds of the Allies, forever) the relegation of Germany not merely to the rank of a third-rate power, but to that of an actual colony of the Western Democracies; to that of a State in which the very standard of life of the people would no longer depend upon their own efficiency or their own social laws, but rather "upon the vote of the competitors of the German economy."[3]

Three main features of the Ruhr Statute cannot but strike one's attention: first, it *limits* the production of coal and steel in the main German industrial area and controls the use to which these goods are to be put at home *and* abroad; second, through the Office of Military Security, it aims at suppressing every possibility of a new rise of the National Socialist spirit, i.e., at keeping Germany, politically also, under control; and third, both these outrages to the German nation are to be made permanent. (At least that is what the Allies want.) To us, the first feature constitutes no less than the *official* sanction of organised plunder on behalf of the Western victors of 1945; the second and the third are attempts to avoid the possibility of the plunder being one day put to an end.

Not only is the production of steel in the Ruhr never to exceed 10.7 million tons a year, but, in addition to that, according to article 14 of the Ruhr Statute (to take only one instance), the new international

---

Rhénane et Allemande, vol. 4, no. 1.

[1] *Le Monde*, 1st week of January 1949, quoted in *Revue de la Presse Rhénane et Allemande*, vol. 4, no. 1.

[2] *Bulletin de la Semaine*, *Revue de la Presse Rhénane et Allemande*, vol. 4, no. 1.

[3] Professor Ludwig Erhard, *Der Spiegel* (Hanover), 8 January 1949.

authority is to distribute among the different purchasing countries the output of about 7,000 German enterprises.

> The Ruhr furnishes the raw material for 80 percent of German exports. The new international authority is given the power not merely to fix the minimum quantities of coal, coke, and steel to be absorbed by German industry, but also to determine *the nature* of Germany's exports, which allows it, for example, as regards steel, to eliminate at one stroke all German exportation of dentistry appliances, a rich line that would bring in currency. Provided they agree, the representatives of the Western powers are therefore practically in a position to strangle any line of German exports that would risk becoming a danger to their own economy. Along with this power of control over the German exports, the international authority can also stop arbitrarily all commercial transactions between Germany and the Scandinavian countries, Spain, Italy, and the Southeast of Europe. The Western Allies can therefore also use the Ruhr exports as a means of very effective pressure in matters of foreign politics.[1]

And, in order to make that total and permanent dependence still more secure, the German concerns would have to send periodical accounts of their activity to the international authority, while the representatives of the latter would have free access to all the factories!

If that is not carefully planned plunder, then I ask: What is?

Of course—as always, with Western Democrats—it is plunder under the cover of some excuse. (They have not even the guts to be thieves frankly and boldly). The excuse is the same old one—that wearisome, sickening one that has saturated Allied speeches, Allied discussions, and the European press, ever since the end of the First World War: France's security. Strangle, shackle, weaken, keep down the naturally strong—the healthy, the pure-blooded, the martial, the fit to live and fit to rule—so that those born tired might at last feel "secure"; stifle the representatives of a more virile humanity, so that a few quaint flowers of decadence might bloom at ease, amidst the many weeds of mediocrity, in the thick and soft manure of undisturbed corruption! That is the whole spirit, the whole justification of Democracy, and the secret of its appeal both to the degenerate Aryans of the West and to so many "intellectuals" of the inferior races who, all

---

[1] *Der Spiegel* (Hanover), 8 January 1949.

over the world, re-chew and re-swallow with delight, like docile camels, their equalitarian teachings and their anti-Nazi slogans! That is also the real meaning of French security in this connection; that and nothing else.[1]

But security is only an excuse. The true motive behind the Ruhr Statute in 1949, is the self-same one which lay behind the Occupation of the Ruhr by the French in 1923—plunder; in Democratic language, "business." The Democrats say so themselves, when they leave off talking propaganda. The Parisian bulletin on economic affairs, *L'Echo de la Finance*, puts it indeed very nicely: "It is especially our former enemies' industrial possibilities that make us feel uneasy. If tomorrow the German steel industry were to oust us from the European market, it would no longer be possible for us to secure for ourselves the currency which, however, we absolutely need. It is not in the military field but in the field of economy that we shall have, henceforth, to measure our strength with our enemies of yesterday."[2] This is spoken clearly enough. It is addressed to businessmen, not to sentimental fools.

Is it any wonder if a German paper calls the Ruhr Statute, "a realisation of the Monnet plan which provides for a transplantation of the steel production from the Ruhr into Lorraine,"[3] and, if even a Social-Democratic paper such as the *Telegraf*, from Berlin, writes that "the control foreseen for the Ruhr will discourage and discredit the Democratic forces of Germany, and will again render 'radical' the broad layers of the German people"?[4] Is it any wonder that the nefarious plot was denounced officially by the directing Committee of the Social-Democratic Party itself as a "temporary solution for the abolition of which" that party will "fight with all its strength"?

And if that outrage on the part of the Allied Western Democracies can force even the leaders of the SPD to remember that they are Germans, then I leave one to imagine what its effect must be upon that great section of the German people—and that intelligent and faithful

---

[1] It is interesting to note here what *Der Abend*, a Berlin paper licensed by the Americans, says in this connection, in the 1st week of January 1949: "One always speaks of French security, but one forgets that, within the last three hundred years, the French frontiers have advanced more and more towards the east. And who speaks of the security of Germany? Growing generations and generations not yet born are sacrificed to the French Security complex."

[2] Quoted in *Revue de la Presse Rhénane et Allemande*, vol. 4, no. 2.

[3] *Westdeutsche Zeitung* (Düsseldorf), quoted in *Revue de la Presse Rhénane et Allemande*, vol. 4, no. 1.

[4] Quoted in *Revue de la Presse Rhénane et Allemande*, vol. 4, no. 1.

Aryan minority outside Germany—silent since 1945: the National Socialists.

* * *

As I have pointed out above, the plan for permanent plunder is completed, or rather buttressed, by a plan for the further persecution and permanent annihilation of National Socialism.

But one should have no illusions about the true motives that inspire this plan—or, by the way, that underlie the whole persecution of our *Weltanschauung* since and already before 1945. They are by no means humanitarian, as simple people believe. They are commercial. They have very little or nothing to do with the way we might have treated the poor darling Jews. On the other hand, they have a lot to do with the way National Socialism pulled Germany out of political and economic servitude after the First World War, and made her the leading Power in Europe. Had the hated Nazis not accomplished *that* miracle, under the leadership of Adolf Hitler; had they not, out of the hungry, disarmed, demoralised Germany of 1920, made the Greater Germany of 1940—prosperous, victorious, irresistible—then, it would not matter how many worthless parasites were gassed. The clever businessmen of the soft-hearted Democracies would not care; and the sentimental fools who provide the rank and file of the anti-Nazi forces, would not know. The press, the wireless, and the films, would never have told them.

The unpardonable crime of National Socialism, in the eyes of its foreign persecutors, is to have made Germany great. And the one feeling that actuated all the steps taken to crush it by the present-day masters of the unfortunate land, is fear—the fear lest, out of this abyss of ruin and desolation, again Greater Germany might rise, to the music of the Horst Wessel Song. They know it can. They know it will, sooner or later. Still, they do all that is in their power to prevent it, so that they might continue to plunder the land a little longer. That is the secret of all their arrangements for the permanent disarmament of Germany, for permanent Allied control and permanent eviction of National Socialists from all posts of importance.

The Jews really hate us for *all* we stand for. They are the ones who hate us for the most natural, the most vital reasons; and who therefore hate us the most. They are the ones who hate us personally, individually; who are capable of any atrocity upon any one of us. That is the reason why they are used by Germany's enemies as our direct persecutors—as false witnesses in the trials of so-called "war criminals"; as torturers in the anti-Nazi extermination camps. No one could do those jobs as well as them.

The Communists—when they are not also Jews—hate us for our philosophy, but without that deadly physical element that makes hatred irreducible. They hate us like Christians hate Pagans (or used to hate them, when there still were Christians), not like mice hate cats. The average anti-Nazis of the West hate us without knowing why; because they have read, printed in black and white, a hundred thousand times, that we are "monsters," so it must be true.

The clever people who have a word to say in the persecution of National Socialism in occupied Germany only hate us because our philosophy is indissolubly linked with Germany's greatness. In reality, it is Germany they hate—Germany, the least Judaised among the great Aryan nations of the West, and their natural leader; in the meantime (even in defeat!), their dreaded competitor.

They always reproach Germany with nurturing a "dangerous nationalism." What about *their* nationalism resting, not upon the right of a healthy people to seek more living space, but upon the claims of an objectionable confraternity of businessmen to fill their pockets? Nay, what about their chauvinism—a better name for it—regularly and piously fed by the money of the international Jew? For behind the patriotic French, British, American competitors of Germany in the struggle for industrial, commercial, and ultimately political supremacy; behind those who hate and persecute National Socialism as Germany's guiding force on the way to greatness, there stands—again!—the international Jew who hates Germany both because of her technical efficiency *and* her racial consciousness; both as a businessman *and* as a Jew. The bitterest, most consistent, and most powerful anti-Nazi of all, he is the one who uses the patriotic fears and the commercial greed of the Aryans against National Socialism, as those Aryan renegades themselves, who control occupied Germany, use in their turn the hatred and cruelty and anti-Nazi fanaticism of the rank and file Jews to break at least the bodies of "dangerous" German Nazis, knowing all the time that they can never break their spirit.

* * *

More than any others, those large-scale thieves now busy making Western Europe a safe place for themselves, are also liars. They do not say: "We are thieves"—who does?—And if they sometimes admit it to one another, or to people whom they think they need not fear—as that

Frenchman did, whose conversation with myself I reported at the beginning of this chapter—they cannot possibly admit it before the world, for that would deprive them of the support of the simpletons, who, in modern Democracies, have one vote each like any man or woman, and who are millions. As things stand, the simpletons condone such robbery as goes on in occupied Germany. They call it a "guarantee of security," of "peace," of "justice," echoing the voice of their morning paper, which, in its turn, echoes the interests of the capitalists who hope to edify their country's permanent prosperity—and first of all their own—upon Germany's permanent impoverishment. They must continue to call it so. Therefore excuses must be found to justify both the plunder itself, and the indispensable persecution of National Socialism, without which it could not last six months.

The better organised the plunder, the cleverer the lies that serve to excuse it.

I have already said what I think—what every National Socialist thinks—of the Western Democracies' insistence upon the limitation of Germany's industrial output, for the sake of the "security" of Europe, and especially of France. Another mild word for theft, in Democratic jargon applied to German affairs, is "restitution," "justice." This is particularly true in the case of all property sold to National Socialists by Jews who left Germany under the Nazi régime. The people who acquired the property have paid for it—not always as high a price as the Jews would have liked, admittedly, but they paid. Now, many of the Jews have come back. And the Allied military authorities, their humble servants, force the new owners to return, without compensation, the houses, land, or other property for which they had given money. That is called "restitution." The same applies to a great number of objects acquired by Germany in occupied countries during the war, whether they were taken as spoils of war (without hypocritical excuses) or paid for. According to French official information, objects worth two hundred million dollars (eight milliards[1] of francs, at the rate of exchange in 1938, forty-two milliards of francs now, or a hundred and twenty milliards, if one takes into account the proportion in which prices have risen in France) were returned to their former owners, in France alone, up till June 1948, naturally without compensation to whoever was in possession of them in Germany.[2] Also "restitution."

---

[1] A milliard is one thousand million, in American terms, one billion.—Ed.

[2] *Wirtschaftszeitung* (Stuttgart), 8 January 1949, quoted in *Revue de la Presse Rhénane et Allemande*, vol. 4, no. 2.

But there are far lovelier excuses than these; for example the explanations kindly given to me by one of the high officials of the "Bureau de l'Information" at Baden-Baden, during my first interview with him on the 9th of October 1948. The reckless massacre of the Black Forest? Just a very unpleasant necessity!—Not merely a necessity from the standpoint of the Frenchmen's pockets; not merely a "just" compensation for damages caused in France during four years of German Occupation, but a necessity in the interest of the trees themselves! A disease—so the Frenchman told me—had attacked a certain number of trees, in different areas of the West. And those trees and the trees around them were cut down . . . to prevent the disease from spreading. In other words, the French have perpetrated the mass felling of those trees of which one can see the thousands of stumps in now completely blank areas, all along one's way through the Black Forest, only in order to "save" Germany's glorious living ornament! How kind of them indeed! But it is strange, to say the least, that such "kindness" was necessary in *all* the great forests of the country, and also that the rapidly spreading disease only made its appearance after the Occupying Powers had settled in.

As for the commentaries of this same Frenchman on the dismantling of the German factories, they surpass in crooked ingenuity anything that I have heard before or since. Undoubtedly, France and her Allies had dismantled numberless factories for the sake of their "security" and also in order to carry off very useful machinery as a contribution to "war reparations." But . . . the Germans did not really resent it. At least, the German industrialists did not. On the contrary, in the secret of their hearts, they were only too glad to get rid of their old machines, hoping to replace them as soon as they could by more up-to-date ones! The resentment of the people? The refusal of the workmen to help to dismantle their factories? That was all due to "a pernicious propaganda."

Needless to say, in addition to this, every time they possibly can, the Military Governments of the Occupying Powers publish denials of the little information given in the German papers about their confiscations, their Occupation expenses, and other forms of plunder. But the figures which even *they* admit are impressive enough.[1]

---

[1] For instance, the French military government has denied having confiscated more than 300,000 tons of ships on the Upper Rhine (*Allgemeine Zeitung* [Mainz], 30 December 1948).

Also General Bishop has denied the figures quoted by Dr. Weitz regarding the Occupation expenses in the British Zone. Still he admits that the Occupation expenses amount to one fifth of the total expenses in the budget for the year 1 April 1947 to 31

* * *

Along with the lies intended to justify Allied plunder in occupied Germany there are those still greater lies, half-truths, and total suppressions of truth, intended to provide a convenient excuse for the persecution of National Socialism.

The main idea behind them all is to make us Nazis appear as monsters of fanaticism and cruelty in the eyes of the whole world. To attain that result, the first step of our enemies is to show—or try to show—that *they* are, and have always been (even in war time) and cannot but be—being Democrats—well-balanced, kindly people, incapable of such atrocities as ours; "decent" people. They therefore have to suppress all facts that would prove the contrary—and how glaringly! So, to begin with, not a word must ever be said or written— and not a word *is* ever said, if they can help it—about *their* atrocities; not a word about all that went on in the torture chambers of Ham Common, a few miles from London, during the war, and in similar ones in other places, in all Democratic countries as well as in Soviet Russia; not a word, either, about the manifold horrors perpetrated upon Germans, also during the war, by that scum of the earth which composed, by the admission of many honest Frenchmen themselves, the bulk of the French *"résistance"*; not a word for instance, about the rascals who, having caught hold of twelve German officers and tied them up, slowly pressed them to death between the iron teeth of an enormous winepress in a village of the centre of France named Oradour; not a word about the cruelties of all description committed upon Nazis, mostly by Jews, under British, American, or French supervision, after the war, in the anti-Nazi extermination camps of West Germany, or by the Russians, in East Germany and farther East; not a word about Darmstadt and Schwarzenborn, and Herstfeld, and Dachau *after* it was taken over by the Allies; nor about Galgenberg, near Bad Kreuznach, nor about camp 2288 near Brussels, and other places of hunger and ill-treatment under Allied management, both in and outside Germany, after the capitulation. Woe to him who dares to throw some light upon such facts! The British officer who reported to me the horror of the hunger camp 2288, was forced to resign his post

---

March 1948, and that excludes all expenses in connection with reparations, compensation, disarmament, prisoners of war, and displaced persons (*Rheinische Zeitung*, 3 January 1949, quoted in *Revue de la Presse Rhénane et Allemande*, vol. 4, no. 1). [The French official's name is Rudolf Grassot. See Chapter 8, pp. 130-36.— Ed.]

and turned out of occupied territory for having had the honesty to point out the same to the competent authorities.

The next step is to harp upon whatever violence we might have resorted to, whether in war or in peace time; to exaggerate it, naturally; and to forget to mention the outrages in punishment or in reprisal by which it was permitted and is justified.

The shooting of hostages, in countries occupied by Germany during the war, is one of the familiar themes of anti-Nazi propaganda. The "poor" hostages had not *done* the deed for which they were shot. Admittedly. But why was the deed done? Why was, for instance, some perfectly harmless German soldier suddenly shot dead, no one knew by whom, while peacefully taking a stroll in a public garden after sunset? Was *that* fair? And if that was fair—if that was "war"—then why had not the fellow who did it the courage to come forward and give himself up rather than allow a dozen "innocents" to be shot in his place? And who were those "innocents"? Men whom the Germans picked up at random, in the streets? No—save in a few extreme cases in which repeated aggression on the part of the population had exasperated the local German authorities—but people collected from the prisons where they were already detained on account of their proved anti-Nazi activities. Was it not just natural that such ones should suffer, in that circumstance, for the acts of hostility committed by their comrades, when these comrades were not themselves prepared to suffer for their own deeds?

As far as I know, there have been, in present-day occupied Germany, no similar acts of hostility against the members of the Allied occupying forces. But had there been, would not the Military Government of whichever Occupying Power have killed any number of hostages in order to reassert its authority?

There were sometimes reprisals ordered by the Germans in occupied countries. But why were they ordered? I shall be content with recalling one sole instance—sufficiently eloquent in itself to need no comment—that of the "wiping out" of the village of Oradour, in the centre of France, an episode which has been exploited *ad nauseam* by the enemies of National Socialism, all over the world, as a major "Nazi atrocity." (I first heard of it in India; then I saw the "ruins of Oradour" on the screen, in Iceland, among the *"actualités"*[1] projected before the main film, at a cinema show of the Alliance Française, in 1947. But I had already been told in 1946, in France, by a Frenchman, of the real

---

[1] Newsreels—Ed.

atrocity that had been perpetrated in the broadly advertised village.) I have mentioned it above: twelve German officers had been slowly pressed to death in an enormous winepress, to the devilish glee of some two or three hundred bystanders. Their legs were crushed first, as they were erect, and some were still alive when the steel teeth, closing in on the upper part of their bodies, at last put an end to their martyrdom. And those twelve men had not even been specially selected for such a horrid fate because of something that they had done to the inhabitants of the place or to other French people. They were tortured for no other reason save that they were officers in the German army—"hated Nazis." Is it a wonder that the village was "wiped out" after *that*? It would have been a disgrace had it not been. One knows of the terrible reprisals of the British against the Indians for excesses committed during the Indian Independence War of 1857, or even far more recently, during the disturbances of the last twenty years. Had the Indians treated not twelve officers, but one single British soldier, as the French treated those innocent Germans, it is not only a village but a whole province that the British army would have "wiped out."

* * *

But certainly the most popular of all those biased accusations brought against us National Socialists, is that of having "persecuted the Jews." Those "poor Jews," all as innocent as lambs, all benefactors of humanity, kind, honest, gifted, disinterested people—God's own people; what more can they be?—were the defenceless victims of us "inhuman monsters!" Around that lie (for it *is* a lie) a worldwide anti-Nazi propaganda has relentlessly worked with such skill that it succeeded in turning against us not only millions of simple folk indifferent to "politics," but also a very great number of the earlier admirers of our régime, in all countries outside Germany. The fact that the lie is a partial truth (like all or most of the greatest lies are) made its success all the more rapid and all the more persistent.

There is no doubt that we fought and are still fighting Jewry. And fighting Jewry and "persecuting the Jews" look much the same. Nevertheless, they *are not* the same. We have fought and are still fighting Jewry in self-defence; nay, in defence of the whole of Aryan mankind. It is not true that we hate Jews "for no reason at all," or out of mean commercial jealousy (as quite a number of anti-Nazis do) or on account of their "talents." No. Had the Jews remained in their place, and lived an honest national life in a land of their own, like other races (or even in other people's land, if they were able to conquer it in fair battle; most races have sought new homes at one time or the other of their history) then, I say, there would have been no mention of them in National Socialist literature. There is no mention of Arabs, although racially, the Arabs and the Jews are both Semites. But the former are warriors, the latter parasites, and, what is more, parasites of this continent. It is because the Jews are dangerous and, apparently, congenital parasites—for they have never been anything else ever since they existed—that there arises, sooner or later, a "Jewish question" wherever they settle. It is for that reason that, sooner or later, whether in ancient Egypt or in modern Germany, steps have to be taken against them in defence of the race, or races, at the expense of which they live and thrive. It is for that reason that, as champions of Aryan humanity, we have put such stress upon the struggle to liberate Germany and all Aryan nations from the subtle Jewish yoke. That is not "persecuting the Jews." That is just defending the Aryan people, in their own home, against the pernicious infiltration of a parasitic, alien race. We were— and are—bound to be ruthless in this struggle. One always is, when one is defending one's life. And this is the struggle in which the very survival of the Aryan race is at stake. Yet, as I have already said, though we might have been ruthless, we were never cruel. The accusation, brought against us all over the world, of deliberately inflicting pain upon Jews for no other reason than they were born Jews, is a blatant lie.

Many—in fact, far *too* many—Jews were living free and prosperous under the Third Reich. And those who left Germany, left— unfortunately—with all their property. I have met such ones in London. They used their property to stir up hatred against National Socialist Germany in foreign lands. Now that they have nothing to fear, they boast of it. Those who remained free in Germany were, after a time, made to wear a yellow "star of Israel," so that one might at first sight characterise them as Jews, even if there were any doubt about it from their appearance. Why do so many of them seem to find that regulation outrageous? I do not know. They should have been glad to wear their own star. Or are they themselves, at heart, conscious of their natural inferiority and ashamed of being Jews? One would think so. *I* would only be too glad if our enemies, now in power, were to ask me to wear a swastika. In fact, I bitterly resent their not allowing me to wear one openly, at least here in Germany.

The Jews who were interned in concentration camps were all there for something more than for merely being born Jews. Like the

Germans, or Poles, or Czechs interned with them, they all had, in some way or another, acted or propagandised against the National Socialist régime. They were treated as any irreducibly hostile elements—whether or not actual conspirators—would be under a strong and earnest Government that knows what it wants and with what mission it came to power. They were deliberately standing in the way of the creation of that glorious resuscitated Aryandom that we were—and are—striving for, at the cost of immense sacrifices. Were we to pat them on the back and set them free, and tell them: "Work against us as much as you please, old fellows; we don't mind"? In a thousand years' time, in a racially conscious world in which responsible, enlightened breeding coupled with the complementary system of education would have made practically all men and women accept National Socialism as a matter of course; when this present struggle, visualised in its historical aloofness, would have appeared as the heroic foundation of the established civilisation, then, perhaps, we might have done so. But *not now*; not within the first decade after coming to power; nor within the second, nor the third, nor even the tenth. We could not afford it. No young Movement can afford to tolerate opposition. It is, for it, a matter of life or death.

But I repeat: though ruthless, we were not cruel. There may have been, here and there, cases of individual brutality. Who denies it? Any party that counts its members by hundreds of thousands is bound to include some people who happen to be brutal by nature. But, if so, in the present instance, these people were brutal *in spite of* being Nazis, *not* because they were Nazis as our enemies pretend. And any gratuitous act of brutality on their part, whenever detected, was severely punished. That was told to me, among others, by a woman who held an important post in the management of five concentration camps in turn under the Third Reich, and who therefore should know what she is talking about; a woman, moreover, who, knowing fully well how little I really care, at heart, to what extent such acts took place and how far they were discouraged, had no reason whatsoever to hide the truth from me.[1] And if I repeat, here, what I know to be true, it is by no means in order to excuse my superiors in the eyes of the Democrats. Our right to rule rests upon physical and moral strength alone—upon racial and personal value—not upon "whitewash." No. If I repeat what I know to be true, it is only because it is true. Indeed, we do not care what the Democrats and Communists—and the vast non-political

---

[1] Hertha Ehlert—Ed.

majority of mankind—think of us. But on the other hand, we expose the lies that form the kernel of all popular anti-Nazi propaganda on the sole ground that they are lies.

We do not deny that there were gas chambers in *some* of the German concentration camps, under the Third Reich. They might have been an unpleasant necessity, and an unaesthetic one; instruments of execution are never pleasant or pretty. Yet, they were a necessity. But first, the people who met their death in them were all sentenced for some serious offence for which that particular penalty was foreseen; they were not "innocent" people, guilty only of being Jews (otherwise there would not have been a Jew left in the whole country in 1945, and goodness knows how many thousands there still were). Second, while the soft-hearted Democrats purposely prolonged the agony of the martyrs of Nuremberg for half an hour—and think nothing of it—an execution in a gas chamber took not more than fifteen or at the most twenty minutes, and sometimes less. And the condemned were unconscious long before that time was over. The information was given me by a comrade who had himself acquired it from repeated personal experience. Finally, there were extremely few gas chambers in Germany. There were five in Auschwitz; there was one in Lublin. But there were none in Ravensbrück until November 1944, when one was built. There were none at Krakow, none at Belsen, none at Buchenwald, although these were important camps. There were none in a dozen of the other camps, equally important, and none in the minor camps, while the gullible victims of anti-Nazi propaganda willingly imagine one in every place of internment.

Along with the gas chambers, the next things to become world-famous thanks to our enemies' lies are the crematoria. Cremation—the age-old typically Aryan form of disposal of dead bodies—was encouraged by the National Socialist State all over Germany, for everybody, not merely for the inmates of the concentration camps. And there were—and there are still—crematoria everywhere, as there are in England, in many places. There only were special crematoria attached to concentration camps in case a sufficient number of probable executions would render them necessary. In Auschwitz, there were five; in Lublin one. There was not one in any of the camps in which there were no gas chambers. And—what our enemies always omit to say—wherever they did exist, crematoria were for the dead, *never for the living*. To assert that internees condemned to death were thrown alive into the furnace is the most shameful lie—and our enemies know it as well as we do. Nobody, Jew or non-Jew, was ever burnt alive by order of any National Socialist authority. That is the sort of thing the Christian churches once did (and would probably do again, were they to enjoy the same unlimited power as they did in the sixteenth century). Whatever our enemies may say, it is not like us to indulge in such atrocities. And those who have purposely cooked up and circulated that lie all over the world in order to discredit National Socialism; those who, at least for the time being, have won a war with such weapons, are vile cowards, all the more criminal if they have not even the excuse of being Jews. I repeat: had any subordinate put a live Jew into the fire, he would have acted upon his own initiative and *not* under orders and, when detected, would have been punished with utter severity. *I know* it from people who have worked for years in more than one concentration camp, and who are more than sufficiently sure of my unshakable loyalty to our system to tell *me* the truth, whatever it be.

But why waste one's time to prove the fundamental dishonesty of all this anti-Nazi propaganda, when one or two eloquent facts would suffice?

I was shown in January 1949, in an issue of the American illustrated magazine *Look*, an article relating the supposed life of Frau Ilse Koch, the woman accused of having had lampshades made out of the skin of dead internees from German concentration camps. Even if this were true, by the way, I fail to see why it should be looked upon as such a "crime," and punished with life-long imprisonment. The alleged internees were, after all, dead; and they were not killed for the sheer purpose of having their skins. But *is* it even true? The American paper showed photographs of tattooed skins supposed to be those out of which Frau Koch had had her lampshades made. Many of those skins were decorated with pictures of women wearing hats. Strangely enough—to say the least—*all* those hats were in the fashion of the 1920s! The people from whom the skins were supposed to have been taken all died between 1940 and 1945. I repeat: it is strange. And the whole story looks like a cleverly plotted propaganda tale. But it is difficult—very difficult—to work out a tissue of lies so cleverly that some detail does not, sooner or later, betray the nature of the whole scheme.

This appears even more glaringly in the instance of the faked film supposed to represent the "horrors" of the German camp of Buchenwald. In Kassel—where every adult German was forced to see the famous film—"a doctor from Göttingen, watching the film, saw himself on the screen, looking after the victims. *He had never been to Buchenwald*, and could not recall the incident in which he figured. So he took a colleague to see the film, to help clear up the mystery. The latter suddenly recognised the incident. It was part of a film taken after the raid of the 13th of February 1945 on Dresden, where in fact the doctor had been working."[1] This was reported in the *Catholic Herald* of the 29th of October 1948. Now, whatever one might say for or against the Catholics, one thing is certain: nobody can accuse *them* of being pro-Nazi. On the contrary; as I have said in the beginning of this book, they are, along with the Communists, the bitterest and most consistent enemies of National Socialism, and therefore have no interest whatsoever in exposing our enemies' lies. If still they expose them, and as strongly as one can see in the above report, it must be that really they exceed the limits of accepted dishonesty.

But the bitterest and most shocking irony of all, perhaps, in the concoction of lies just mentioned, is that the non-existing "Nazi atrocities" in the faked film were made up out of scenes from that perfectly real atrocity of the Allies themselves: a savage air-raid by British and American bombers upon a town crowded with refugees for whom there were no adequate shelters; a raid during which 27,000 people were killed, and over 30,000 injured, according to official figures.[2] If that is not an insult to the most elementary decency, then what is?

The only explanation is that, in the eyes of the Allies, nothing was horrid enough to advertise us as "monsters." The Jewish and Assyrian atrocities of old, unfortunately for them, could not be filmed. Failing that, the second best could only be their own latest performances in Germany.

Many other similar lies can be pointed out, such as, for instance, that well-known accusation brought against us of being the authors of the famous mass-execution of Poles in Katyn. We believe the Russians are the authors of it. The point has already been the object of endless controversies and, after the glaring proofs of Democratic dishonesty which I have just quoted, it is hardly necessary to repeat, here, the arguments in support of our thesis. Personally, I do not think it matters much who did what. The Democrats have thrown the blame of the "Katyn massacre" on us only because the Russians—of whom they are *now* afraid—were, *then*, their "gallant allies." "Gallant allies" must

---

[1] *Catholic Herald*, 29 October 1948.
[2] I say "according to official figures," for in reality nearly 500,000 German civilians were killed in that abominable air raid.

never commit "mass murders," or even resort to mass executions. At least, never officially. And when they do, then they must be white-washed . . . always at the expense of the enemy. Shivering and shaking in their shoes at the news of the advance of the "Russian roller," were those very same Western Democrats, our persecutors of today, to seek our help tomorrow, the world would at once witness the practical implications of that truth. The "Katyn massacre" would become a Russian atrocity overnight.[1] And any other of our alleged "horrors" would quickly be attributed to its real authors or else either dismissed or "white-washed."

. . . Until, of course, we ceased to consider such an unnatural alliance as this expedient and therefore worth prolonging.

* * *

Slander is our enemies' main weapon. And their main allies, human weakness and human stupidity. Without those, they would have achieved nothing—not even with the help of all the Jewish money in the world. Money can only buy weaklings and fools. They would have achieved nothing through that "humanity" of which they boast so loudly. For it does not exist. What the Euro-American Democrats would like people to take for "humanity" in their dealings with their opponents—and in particular with us—is just shallowness. They are not as ruthless as we, not because they are "better" than we (they are far worse), but because they do not believe in that which they profess to stand for, as we do in our eternal *Weltanschauung*. Nine times out of ten their alleged Christianity is but the cult of vested interests—"business" again—and their Democracy is bunkum ten times out of ten.

They have now sentenced me.[2] And they tell me that, had I been tried in the Russian Zone instead of in the British, I would have got thirty years' hard labour in Siberia instead of three years' imprisonment at Werl. Do I not know it? And had I been called upon in a Nazi state to pass judgement in the counterpart of my own case (supposing I were a judge), it is not three years nor thirty that I would have given anyone

---

[1] Now—in 1952, three years after this book was written—a Commission is investigating on behalf of the "free Democratic nations" into the Katyn case, in order to prove that "the Russians did it" (now that they would like us to join them against them, against their former "gallant allies" the Russians).

[2] This—and the rest of the book—was written in Werl *after* my trial in 1949. The beginning of the chapter and chapters 4-6 were written there during the time I was "on remand."

guilty of having distributed 10,000 anti-Nazi leaflets and of having stuck up posters in prominent places against all I love. *I* would have given him (or her) a death sentence straight away—especially if the person were a sincere idealist like me and had spoken in Court as clearly and fearlessly as I have. For such people are the only *real* enemies of any cause that stands in the way of theirs. *I* take them seriously. *I* know they should be taken seriously. I know it, being one such person myself. The Communists know it, for they too, however misled, are at least earnest. The Democrats do not know it; will never know it; cannot know it—cannot realise it—for they are *not* earnest. To them, the system of ideas and values in the name of which they persecute us is just "politics," and "politics" are a separate department of life—not *life*. To us, the system of ideas and values for the sake of which we are persecuted is life; our whole life; ourselves and more than ourselves. It is the greater life of the Race, nay, the greater life of endless Creation, which gives ours its meaning. And the Man who embodies it—our beloved, our revered Führer, living or dead—to us is a living man; an everlasting Man, not merely a "politician," not merely the head of a party, not merely the founder of a faith, but the exponent in our times of the eternal Religion of Life, more specially on the socio-political plane but also on all planes. For *that* and for *him,* no sacrifice is too great, no action too drastic. Nothing and no one that is an obstacle to its and to his triumph can be too ruthlessly removed. We are therefore not afraid to suffer. Nor do we hesitate to inflict suffering—if it be necessary.

The Communists, strange as this might seem to us, feel about Marxism somewhat like we do about our *Weltanschauung*. They know what they want. (I speak, of course, of the intelligent ones.) Every time I met one, and especially a German (I have never met a real Russian one), I have respected his sincerity and consistency, and regretted that those fine qualities were not put to the service of a better cause; of *our* cause, in fact. I hated him, perhaps—for, the greater his personal value, the greater the loss and also the danger that he represents from our standpoint. But I took him seriously. And he took me seriously, knowing fully well what he could expect from me under different circumstances. The Democrats never take us seriously until we actually hit them on the head. That is the whole secret of their pretended "leniency" and "humanity." They believe it is possible—even relatively easy—to de-Nazify us. And they try—in many cases, admittedly, using methods of intimidation, but in many cases also using the subtle bribery of "kind treatment." It takes, with people who, like them, are not earnest; with people whose political life is nothing but an advantageous "career" or an exciting show. It does not take with us. We see through it. If we are not taken seriously, we can only feel insulted—or amused, according to our mood—until the time comes for us to demonstrate by our actions how foolish our enemies were to imagine they could induce us to forget or to forgive.

* * *

I was arrested here, in Western Germany, after indulging in National Socialist propaganda, undisturbed, for over eight months. And had it not been for the clumsiness of a young German[1] with whom I had been seen (and whose arrest, consequently, caused mine) I probably would still be free. They tell me that, in the Russian Zone, under similar circumstances, I would not have remained free for eight days. And I believe it. Again, not because the Democrats are "more humane" than the Communists, but just because they are more shallow. Politics do not mean, to them, all that they mean to our real enemies, and to ourselves.

One of the very few out-and-out anti-Nazis whom I met in Germany was a man—a German—travelling in the same railway compartment as myself between Baden-Baden and another place in the French Zone. The train halted several hours in Baden-Oos. Being practically alone and having nothing else to do, we talked. The man, who had nothing to fear from me under the protection of the French Military Government, was frank enough to tell me, after two hours' conversation, that I reminded him of the "worst type" of Nazis of whom he "hated the sight" in the days of our power. "I have spoken too much to the wrong person," thought I. But I remained calm and replied that, if the ideology which means everything to me was really as repellent to him as he said, the best thing he could do *now* was to go and report me. I even added that I would surely consider it my duty to report him, if ever I met him again in a future National Socialist Europe.

The man's answer was eminently democratic. Admittedly, said he, he disliked that "arrogant and aggressive" racism of mine; admittedly, he could not understand how any foreigner could "idolise such a man" as Adolf Hitler; yet, in his eyes, each person was "entitled to hold the views he or she liked." Moreover, he "could not be bothered" to miss his connection for the pleasure of getting a "harmless fanatic" into

---

[1] Gerhard Waßner—Ed.

trouble. *That* was the true explanation of his not running to denounce me, in spite of all the hatred he professed for my views; *that* and not "humanity." The fellow did not hate me enough to go out of his way for the pleasure of harming me. He did not hate me enough because he did not take me seriously. He could take none of us seriously, now that we no longer have the power to get him or his precious family into trouble. He did not love his own ideology enough to take *it* seriously; otherwise, he would have thought it was worthwhile to miss a train in order to defend it against any sincere enemy, however "harmless." The few Communists whom I have met would have reported me, under a Communist Order, to the Communist authorities. But they hate the Western form of Democracy nearly as much as we do. They had a reason not to interfere with me in the Western Zones; an ideological reason, not a personal one.

* * *

This fundamental shallowness of the Democrats makes the persecution of National Socialism at their hands none the less thorough, but all the more hateful. It is not—as in the Russian Zone—the persecution of a faith in the name of another faith; of truth, in the name of a sincere illusion. It is the persecution of the eternal Religion of Life in its modern form, for the sake of nothing else but vested interests of the lowest order; business interests.

Of course, behind those business interests, there is far more. There is the irresistible tendency of a degenerate world towards its doom; the frenzied rush to death of Judaised Europe, at an accelerated speed. We who have long overcome in ourselves that general human tendency; we, the children of Light and Life—the regenerate—joyfully holding out against the current of time, our eyes fixed, beyond the ruins of today and of tomorrow, upon the glory of the new Beginning; we, I say, the only ones in the world who stand in the way of the death forces and defy them, we must be crushed, if the death forces are to triumph forever. And *that* is the real reason why persecution has been waged upon us from all sides on their behalf. But in the East, those unseen forces have chosen as their vehicle a false Ideology sufficiently deceitful to impress, along with the unthinking masses, quite a number of the best men and women. In the West, they knew, so to speak, that allegiance to vested interests on the part of the clever few, coupled with selfishness, chauvinism, moral cowardice, squeamishness, and gullibility on the part of the many, were enough to inspire and sustain, for any length of time, the persecution of our everlasting Idea.

But ultimately, nothing can prevent the triumph of life. Nothing can alter the iron laws that regulate the succession of cycles in time, bringing back an era of resurrection after the worst era of disintegration.

One day, with the help of all the Gods—I hope—we shall see to it that the Democrats and even the Communists bitterly regret not having killed more of us. In the meantime, the fact that our enemies' shallowness has kept some of the most ardent ones of us alive, in spite of their defiant boldness, is a sign from the Gods; a sign that National Socialism is to live, and to become, once more in a relatively near future, *the* ruling force of the Aryan world.

Chapter 8

A Peep into the Enemy's Camp

"Jede Halbheit ist das sichtbare Zeichen des inneren Verfalls, dem der äußere Zusammenbruch früher oder später folgen muß und wird."

—Adolf Hitler[1]

One of my earliest contacts with the representatives of the Occupying Powers in Germany was, naturally, at the technical frontier that separates Saarland from the French Zone. There I had a glimpse of the puerile arrogance with which one of the most conceited nations in Europe lords it today in a part of unfortunate Germany.

I crossed that frontier at Saarhölzbach on the 11th of September 1948, at about nine in the morning. It was a bright sunny day. I lined up with the other passengers for the control of my passport and the examination of my luggage, not without a little anxiety, for I had with me, among other things, an extremely heavy trunk containing, concealed between books, six thousand National Socialist leaflets—or, to be more accurate, six thousand minus the few dozen I had already distributed in Saarland. I had written them myself, in Sweden, and had them printed in England. It would not do, now, for "them" to find "those," I thought, as a man helped me push the trunk in front of the customs officer. I was prepared for the worst. Yet, if I were destined one day to "get caught" I hoped it would be *after* I had finished distributing my papers, not *before*. For a moment, I withdrew myself, mentally, from the surroundings, and thought of our beloved Führer. And also of the invisible Gods who had, up till then, helped me to do my best for our ideals and at last brought me to Germany. If such was their will, they would also help me cross the border unscathed. If not, I would at least show our enemies that there are still National Socialists worthy of the name, even among the non-German Aryans. And I thought of all those who have suffered and died for our cause. Would I ever have the honour of suffering too? Of dying? I wished I had. But

---

[1] "Every half-measure is a visible sign of inner decay which must and will be followed sooner or later by outward collapse" (*Mein Kampf*, I, x, pp. 268-69; cf. Mannheim, p. 246) [Trans. by Ed.].

not yet; not until I had distributed all my leaflets, stuck up all my posters; done all I could.

I was pulled out of my inner world by loud shouting. It was the French customs Officer who had lost his temper with some German traveller whose turn was just before mine. I shall never know why the man had suddenly become so angry. But I shall always remember the tone of his voice and the expression of his face. He was spouting out a series of abuse in bad German. His face was congested; his mouth was twisted. However hard he might have tried, he did not look a bit like a military officer in a conquered land. He looked, rather, like a clumsy and overgrown schoolboy attempting, in a game, to play the part of a policeman. The German passenger, nearly twice as tall as he, was gazing at him in silence, inwardly no doubt with contempt. At last, the officer's vocabulary of abuse was exhausted; he pushed the passenger's open attaché case violently along the table and, pointing to the exit, cried out in French at the top of his voice: "*Foutez-moi le camp!*"[1] My turn was next.

I speak perfect French, having been brought up in France. I handed over to the officer a letter from the French "Office of German Affairs" (Bureau des Affaires Allemandes) in Paris, stating that I was the authoress of several books on "historical and philosophical subjects"— which is true; that I had come to Germany "in order to gather the necessary information for writing a book about that country"—which was partly true—and finally asking "the French and Allied Military authorities" to be kind enough to provide me "with every help within their power." I had obtained that precious letter through a French woman who had once sat at school in the same class as I, and who, since then, had become the wife of one of General De Gaulle's prominent collaborators and worked in London, during the war, in the "free French" information service.[2] Both she and her husband knew the official in whose power it was to grant me a military permit to Germany. The woman had not seen me for nearly thirty years, and she did not ask me what views I held, nor what I had done in India during the war. She remembered that I had always been, even in my childhood, "an out-and-out 'Pagan,'" and told me so. But it did not occur to her that "an out-and-out Pagan" in the modern world can hardly be anything else but a National Socialist. The official had seen me five

---

[1] Bugger off!—Ed.
[2] Jacques and Georgette Soustelle—Ed.

minutes and asked me nothing at all, so that I had not even needed to lie in order to obtain that unexpected *sauf-conduit*[1] to occupied Germany.

The face of the enraged customs officer softened at once.

"So you know Monsieur S, you say?"

"Yes. I was at school with his wife, years and years ago . . ."

"Oh, well, in that case . . . it's all right. Tell me all the same what you have in there," he said, pointing to one of my travelling bags.

"A few edibles; three kilos of sugar, five kilos of coffee . . ."

"Much more than one is allowed, you know. But it does not matter, since you know Monsieur S."

"And what have you got in there?"

"There," in an iron box, I had all my jewellery: lovely massive gold necklaces and armlets and earrings from India. I intended to sell them in Germany in order to live and carry on my National Socialist activities, or else—if I came across any serious Nazi underground organisation—to give them, for the same purpose. But intentions cannot be seen; papers can. I thought it good policy to distract the attention of the officer on this box. He would perhaps forget to examine the heavy trunk too thoroughly. So I opened the jewel box, and showed some of its contents. I was wearing my golden swastika earrings—under a scarf tied over my head. So they were not to be found in the box.

The officer marvelled at the exotic ornaments. In a minute, the whole customs office was around me, handling the glittering things.

"It is a treasure that you are carrying about with you!" said the officer: "Are you not afraid it might get stolen? There are plenty of thieves in this famishing country, you know!"

I thought within my heart: "They could have betrayed me for money, on the 15th of June, and they did not." But naturally, I *said* nothing. The police stepped in, wishing to see the Indian jewels. "Dear me! That would be worth something, in Paris!" said a police officer. "Why do you take all that with you?"

"I know nobody with whom I could leave it."

"And what about a bank?"

"Well," said I with a smile, "the truth is that I do like to wear those things sometimes, when I put on my Indian dress."

The policemen laughed. "Women are all alike," exclaimed one of them. And the chief police officer put an end to the exhibition by

---

[1] Safe conduct—Ed.

telling me that I was free to take the jewels into Germany. The trunk full of dangerous leaflets was completely forgotten. It is I who reminded the customs officer of its existence. He made an effort to lift it.

"It is damned heavy! What have you got in it?"

"Books."

"Books are indeed heavy things. Well, open it, will you? We cannot let you pass without even opening it," said he.

I opened the trunk with perfect assurance and calm. I now knew it would pass. The men were thinking only of the Indian jewels. The customs officer took a glance at it; picked out a book or two. "All in English?" he asked me.

"Some also in French," I replied, showing him a volume of poems by Leconte de Lisle, "one or two in German—a grammar, a dictionary, easy story books—and a few in Greek."

He laughed. "Greek! Oh, dear! That is too learned for me." And at last he uttered the words I was longing to hear, the words that were to enable me to continue in the "Zones" of occupied Germany the happy and dangerous life of which I had had, already, a taste in Saarland. "You can pass," said he.

And I sat once more in the train bound for Treves, with the jewellery that would now help me to live, and to move about, and with the leaflets written from the depth of my heart for the German people.

I sat in a compartment alone—there were relatively few passengers that day—and the train moved on in the beautiful valley of the Saar. Under the bright sunshine, both sides of the winding river, I could see nothing but green meadows and wooded hills. The train was making a terrific noise as it rushed along. And, with my head at the window, against the wind—like on my unforgettable first journey—I really felt, this time, that, notwithstanding my personal insignificance, I was entering Germany as a liberator. At least as a forerunner and as a sign of the coming liberation. Had I not put all I had and all I was to the service of the forces that are to free not merely my German comrades but the Aryan race at large, and the Aryan soul? "One day," thought I, "in many, many years to come, I shall remember this life, now beginning for me, and feel, with happiness and pride: 'I too had a place in the glorious Nazi "underground" during those darkest days.'"

And I felt elated at the thought that the Gods had willed me to do this. And, gazing at the lovely German land spread before me, I sang the Horst Wessel Song with something of the conquering joy of 1940.

The train was making too much noise for it to be heard in the next compartment.

* * *

Some time after this, I was going to Treves from a village named Wiltingen where I had spent a few days.

In occupied Germany, every train comprises several carriages reserved not only "for the troops of occupation," as stated on a notice hanging outside, but also for any person travelling with an Allied passport, and, an equal or often a smaller number of other carriages in which the Germans are allowed to travel. The former—the occupation ones—are warm and comfortable. And as there are relatively few people travelling with Allied passports, they are not crowded. No German is permitted to use them. That is a regulation of the Allied Military authorities. The other carriages—in which people holding Allied passports *can* travel, of course, if they wish to, but in which the Germans are forced to travel whether they wish to or not, if they must travel at all—are neither warm nor comfortable. They are—or were, until very recently—not lighted at night. And naturally, as they are very few, they are overcrowded. Needless to say, I never used the "occupation carriages" as a matter of principle. (I never took advantage of any privilege that my British-Indian passport could grant me, unless I could share it with at least some Germans of my persuasion.) But, on that day, the signal for the train to move had already been given when I reached the platform. I had no choice. I stepped into the first carriage before me. It happened to be an occupation carriage. And it also happened that some fifteen or twenty Germans who could not guess that I held a British-Indian passport and who somehow felt that I could not possibly belong to the "personnel" of the Occupation, seeing me get into it, stepped in too.

At the next station, a French officer came along, red with fury from the start: "What are you people doing here? This is an occupation carriage. This is not your place!" he shouted. "Your papers! Show your papers!" The terrorised folk started showing their "*Ausweis*."[1] Not one, naturally, had an Allied passport, except me. But this was not written upon my face. I was sitting in a corner with my luggage (including my heavy trunk full of Nazi propaganda tracts) at my side, and slightly smiling. I suppose my hardly perceptible smile infuriated the fellow all the more, for he turned to me and thundered: "And you! Your papers, I say! Have you not heard? Are you deaf?" This was all said in German, with the most shocking French accent.

---

[1] Identification papers—Ed.

"I am showing you my papers," I replied, in faultless French.

My accent must have impressed the man.

"But you are not French!" he exclaimed. "Or are you? You don't look it."

"I was born in France," said I; "That is all."

That simple assertion seemed to pour oil upon the fire of the man's fury. He flared up.

"And you went and married one of those . . . *sales Boches*"[1] (sic) he retorted. "In that case, you have no right to be here. Clear out!"

"I am sorry to disappoint you, sir," said I—and a triumphant irony rang in my voice—"but the man who gave me his name is 'only' a Brahmin from faraway India." And I produced my passport.

The Frenchman glanced at the cover, and his face changed. A passport issued in Calcutta in the days when India was still a British colony—that was enough to tame a foaming French officer in occupied Germany! "My Führer's people, how long will these rats rule over you?" I thought. The Frenchman was all honey. He did not even open the British-Indian passport. The sight of the cover was sufficient. "Quite all right! Quite all right!" said he. "Naturally, *you* can stay here. Why did you not tell me at once?"

"I wanted to show you my passport," I replied. "And it was at the bottom of my handbag."

"Quite all right! Quite all right! Don't bother to move."

The train slowed down its speed as we were entering another station. The Frenchman suddenly forgot that he had just been overwhelmed by the reflected prestige of an ex-colony of his country's allies. He only remembered that he was there to make as many Germans as possible feel the pressure of his unexpected and undeserved power. He turned to the other passengers. "Get out!" he shouted, "Get out!" He caught a man by the collar of his jacket and, opening the door, actually pushed him out before the train had stopped. Then—as at last it did stop—he pushed out half a dozen women who, in his estimation, were not getting down quickly enough. He kicked out what little luggage they had, and also kicked out a young boy about twelve or thirteen. The bulk of the passengers rushed to the other exit, and got down as speedily as they could. The frenzied man could not be at both doors at the same time.

Then, the railway employee on duty—who should have seen to it that these passengers did not enter the occupation carriage—was called

---

[1] Dirty Krauts—Ed.

in, reprimanded in the most abusive language, and told he would be dismissed for his carelessness. He wished to say something. The Frenchman cut his speech short: "Shut up, I tell you! And get out!" He spoke to him as though he were a dog—or worse. He spoke to them all—and treated them all—as though they were worse than dogs. Harmless people; peaceable people—far less aggressive than myself, the whole lot of them! Sitting, immune, in my corner, I mused over the injustice—and irony—of the scene I had witnessed. "Yes, peaceable people," thought I. "Not one of them is travelling with six thousand Nazi leaflets. But also, not one has a British-Indian passport!"

Alone with the Frenchman, I pretended to be sleepy, so that he might not talk to me. I did not wish to address a word to him—if I could help it—after the way he had behaved with the Germans. But we reached Treves, and I made ready to get down. The officer was getting down too, apparently. He remembered that I was a lady and not a German; nor in sympathy with the Germans—at least *he* thought, mistaking, as most people do, the average probability for the living individual reality.

"May I carry some of your luggage for you, Madam?" he asked me, as the train halted in the main station of Treves.

"How kind of you, Monsieur," I replied. "I am really grateful. In fact, I have here a trunk that is a little heavy. If only you were so amiable as to carry *that* for me, I would consider it a great favour."

He lifted the trunk and joined me, with it, on the platform.

"Gosh! It is heavy!" he said, "What have you got in there? Lead?"

"Books."

"Where are you going? To the waiting room?"

"To the cloakroom."

Along platform number one of the main station of Treves, and past those walls that the Allied bombs have reduced to a heap of ruins, straight to the cloakroom walked that French officer—that man whom I had heard and seen abusing and mishandling Germans, only half an hour before; that living embodiment of all that the word *"Besatzung"*—occupation—means to proud Germany. On he walked, ahead of me, carrying . . . my trunk stuffed with Nazi propaganda! That was something worth seeing indeed!

"*Merci Monsieur; merci infiniment*," said I, with a smile, to the oppressor of my Führer's people, when I reached the cloakroom and parted from the man forever.

* * *

On the 9th of October 1948, I paid a visit to a Frenchman in high position, Monsieur G,[1] whose address in Baden-Baden had been given to me by the Paris official who had granted me my pass to Germany. "The more one indulges in forbidden political activities, the more one should remain on 'friendly' terms with the established authorities," my wise husband once said shortly after the outbreak of the war. And I remembered the advice. I had therefore not come to discuss, still less, openly, to defy; but to hear, and to judge in silence—as far as possible.

This man had been in Germany ever since 1945, and before that had taken an active part in the French *résistance*. I had been in this country a little more than a month, and all through the war, nay for many years before the war, I had been living in India, officially "unconnected" with and outwardly "non-interested" in European affairs. It was easy for me, on account of these circumstances, to play the part of the ignorant in search of enlightenment. And I knew that, provided I had enough mastery over myself to conceal my natural Nazi feelings whatever the Frenchman might say, my acting would be welcome, for it would flatter the man's vanity both as a Frenchman and as a high official of the "Information Department" in occupied Germany.

Monsieur G, knowing nothing about me save what was stated in the letter from the "Office for German Affairs" (which, naturally, I showed him) received me with great amiability. He asked me a few questions about my projected book on Germany. "From what I understand," said he, after a while, "it is the German people—the German soul—that interest you, rather than the political or economical aspects of the 'German question.'"

"Surely; economics can only come second, or even third; factors of ethics and race come first," I replied. And I suddenly realised that I had been quoting *Mein Kampf* without meaning to.[2] But Monsieur G—who did not know the book by heart; who, as thousands of notorious anti-Nazis, had possibly never even read it—did not notice that the words were not mine.

"But the Germans are not really one race," he answered. "They have only tried to make us believe that they are, and failed. And as for ethics, National Socialism has deprived them of the little they had. You cannot imagine what a monstrous influence it has had on them. It has killed in them the sense of humanity. We are trying to re-educate them. But it is difficult, very difficult."

---

[1] Rudolf Grassot—Ed.
[2] *Mein Kampf*, I, x, p. 247; cf. Mannheim, pp. 226-27.

My spontaneous answer would have been: "I do hope it is impossible!" But again, I had not come to discuss. I had come to *see* one of our persecutors, as he is; as they all are. I acted up to my rôle. "But," said I—to see what the man would answer—"many Germans are Christians. And one cannot be a Christian and a National Socialist. At least I, who have studied logic under Professor Goblot,[1] cannot understand how one possibly could."

"*You* cannot; nor can I," replied Monsieur G. "But the Germans seem to. Their logic is different from other people's. You don't know them yet. You probably find them all charming. They are, at first sight. But wait till you know them. Wait till you know the Nazis—if you are clever enough to spot them out; for nobody will tell you that he or she is one."

"Have you not found any praiseworthy qualities at all in the Germans, including the National Socialists?" said I. "They are hard-working, clean, and courageous; one has to admit that. And,"—I added—"should I speak of *that*? Is it a general trait? Or did it strike me only because I have been but a few days here, and because I have come from India where the contrary has so often and so painfully impressed me? They seem to me to be kind to animals. Shall I tell you of a scene I witnessed in a village of the Saar?"

"Do."

"Well, I was stopping, waiting for a bus to another village. Nearby, I saw a man trying to bring a horse and cart out of some waste land on the border of the main road. The cart was loaded with earth. The horse tried as hard as he could to pull it. But he could not. It was too heavy. The man coaxed him, encouraged him. *He did not beat him.* The animal tried again, twice, without any result. In India—in southern Europe, why speak of the distant East?—the driver would have lost his temper, and started whipping and kicking his beast. This man did not. He merely allowed about one third of the earth to drop from the cart; he coaxed the horse again, patted him on the neck. And the animal gave a jerk, and came forth drawing the cart behind him. I could not say what were that man's politics, if any. But he was a German. And I have seen many other similar instances of kindness to beasts since I have come here. Only in England, and in the North of Europe, have I seen the same. The people, there, are of the same stock—which is perhaps an explanation."

"As for that," said Monsieur G, "I entirely agree with you; they *are*

---

[1] At the University of Lyons from 1924 to 1927.

kind to animals. And the Nazis more than the others. They were taught to be, under the Hitler régime. They were trained to love living creatures, trees, flowers, everything in Nature, and, at the same time, encouraged to be merciless towards their political opponents. Do you know," he pursued after a pause, "that in that world-famous place of untold horrors, Buchenwald, they had beautiful flowerbeds? And, hung up in the trees, wooden shelters in which the birds could find food and protection against the bitter wind in wintertime? *That*, along with their gas chambers and their crematoria! That is the Nazi logic."

I said nothing. For the only thing I could think of in answer to this tirade was: "I thank you, Monsieur, for your information about the flowerbeds and the bird shelters at Buchenwald. You have made me feel sorry that I cannot congratulate the governor of the place." And to say that, would have been to step out of my *incognito*.

Monsieur G continued: "I say 'the Nazi logic,' for it *is* a logic in its own way, but a logic that baffles us; that baffles all decent people. It is the logic of a nation in which, as I told you before, all sense of human rights has been killed; a frightful logic.[1] Those people's whole mental outlook was guided, dominated by one principle, namely that everything else must be subordinated to the triumph of National Socialism. They crushed all opposition. But, at the same time, they used their opponents to the utmost. To make them work to their maximum capacity, in concentration camps, was not sufficient. They had to use them even dead. They made soap with their fat; strong ropes with the women's hair; lampshades with their skins. Nothing was to be wasted. And those same people were against cruelty to animals. Those same people made the use of steel traps illegal; ordered that even pigs were not to be killed for food save in one second, by an automatic pistol. Can you understand such logic? I am sure our few French National Socialists would not have followed it to the end, had they seen it at work. But the Germans did. Because the German soul is fundamentally made up of contrasts and contradictions. Show that, in your book, and you will be telling the truth."

"I am not a German," thought I; "and yet that absolute logic, which frightens this fellow so much, is mine, nevertheless; has been mine all my life. To me, innocent animals are far more lovable than one's human opponents. Undoubtedly! Does this Frenchman imagine that he is going to stir my sympathy for those who fought us or betrayed us, for the sole reason that they have two legs and no tails? No fear! The

---

[1] "*Une logique effroyable*," are the exact words of Monsieur G.

fellow does not know me." That is what I thought. But naturally I did not say it. To the best of my ability I remained expressionless, and prepared my answer.

I knew that half the accusations against us (of which Monsieur G had only repeated a few) are groundless. But had they all been buttressed by facts, I could not have cared less. I surely could not—and cannot—understand why so many consider it a crime to make use of people's hair (or skin) once they are dead. In my eyes, one can only object to such a thing on purely sentimental grounds, namely, in the case of one's friends, not of one's opponents; not of people who are out to destroy all one loves. And to raise such points against a régime that has done so much, on the other hand, not only for animals, as Monsieur G admitted, but also for the best among living people, seems to me utterly absurd; mad—all the more shocking that, in those very countries in which anti-Nazi propaganda has been the most successful, countless horrors are tolerated, nay, encouraged, even in peace time, provided they be performed in the name of some real or supposed interest of "mankind" upon innocent beasts instead of upon dangerous human beings. I did not wish to discuss the truth or falsity of Monsieur G's statements about our doings, for I knew that this could only raise his suspicion. But I felt I could not remain silent about *that* inconsistency, *that* contradiction—for it surely is one—and I spoke. "Are not contrasts and contradictions the characteristics of average human nature?" said I cautiously.

I was going to say more, but Monsieur G interrupted me with vehemence: "That may well be. But no civilised people have ever committed such atrocities as those Nazis," he exclaimed, "not in our times, at least; and not in Europe."

"People who practice vivisection under the cover of the law in nearly all so-called civilised countries of the world, in Europe and elsewhere, and in our times, commit far worse atrocities," said I, risking at last to be found out. I am not made for a diplomatic career, and could not stand the conversation any longer.

"But that is on animals," retorted Monsieur G, "We make a difference between them and human beings. Don't you?"

"I am not a Christian," I replied; "and I love all life that is beautiful." I did not add: "And I make a difference—and a very great one—between human beings who hate all that I love, and others." I thought I had already spoken too much, and was inwardly reproaching myself with my lack of suppleness. But Monsieur G did not seem to notice, or even to suspect, the source from which my answer had sprung.

"I too, am no Christian," said he; "but I believe in humanity. And I know you do too, at heart."

I wanted to reply: "Do you, really?" But I thought it wiser to say nothing.

* * *

I have already reported some of the fanciful arguments which Monsieur G put forward to justify in my eyes the plunder policy of the Allies in occupied Germany.[1] They rank among the most remarkable lies I have ever heard. But Monsieur G—that kind Monsieur G, who "believes in humanity"—said something more to me; something that will remain engraved within my heart as long as I live. He spoke to me of one of the unknown thousands who died for the National Socialist Idea; of one whom he had known, at least a few hours, and in the murder of whom I feel sure he played a part.

He was speaking of what he called the "contrasts" of the German soul—his favourite theme. He had told me that, in 1945, he had met some Germans who appeared to him to have "little dignity in defeat." "But," he added, "while I was in the *résistance*, during the war, I have seen a few of them die; all real, hundred percent Nazis. And those, I cannot help admiring. I have never seen anybody show such fortitude as they in suffering, nor such calm and fearlessness in front of death."

I felt an icy sensation run along my spine and all through my body. I kept in my breath, and listened. This was the story of my own comrades—of those who had loved our Hitler as I do, and who had had the honour of dying for him, which I had not had. And one of our persecutors was telling it to me, as an eyewitness, if not . . . something more; something worse—without knowing who I was.

"Yes," continued Monsieur G, wrapped up in his own recollections, and not noticing how moved I was, "yes; and there is one among them all, whom I can never forget; a boy of eighteen, a mere lad, but a lad whom we were forced to respect, we hardened men of the *maquis*.[2] We caught him in France, never mind where. He was to be executed the next day. A tall, particularly handsome German type; the best specimen

---

[1] In Chapter 7, p. 109.

[2] Literally a thick and intricate wood in Corsica to which men pursued by the regular police fled for safety. During the 1939-45 war, another name for the French anti-Nazi underground organisation.

of Hitler youth one can imagine. I could have felt sorry for him, had I not known who he was. But I knew. And had I not been quite sure, my night long conversation with him would have been more than sufficient to convince me that he was a full-fledged Nazi. He had behaved as they all did: ruthlessly, without the slightest regard for human life. But he believed in what he did. He had a purpose, and ideals, and was perfectly sincere. He knew he was to die in a few hours' time. Yet, during that night, he explained to me his whole philosophy with the earnestness and the happiness of absolute faith, thinking perhaps that, one day, I might remember what he said and admit he was right. You know the philosophy; I do not need to tell you. He believed in what they all did—in what they all still do, at heart: in the God-ordained superiority of the Aryan and the divine mission of the German nation; in the prophetic rôle of Hitler in world history. There was beauty, there was greatness in what he said, even if it were but a misconception, for *he* was beautiful from every point of view. Beautiful and strong; absolutely sincere, and absolutely fearless.

"He was shot the next morning. I have never seen anyone look so happy as that boy walking to the spot of execution. He refused to be tied or blindfolded; stood against the pole of his own accord; lifted his right arm in the ritual gesture which you can guess, and died in a cry of triumph; 'Heil Hitler!'"

"And it is you, you yourself who killed him! I would bet anything that it is you—you swine, you devil!" These were the only words I could have said—shouted—had I not known that, to speak thus to Monsieur G was to ruin all the possibilities I had to work for the National Socialist Idea in occupied Germany. But knowing this, I said nothing. For the sake of the unknown thousands for the love of whom I had come, I had no right to be rash. Yet, I was moved to my depths. Every one of the Frenchman's words had gone through me like a knife. I now loathed the creature, for I felt sure that he had been more than a mere eyewitness to this murder. And the handsome, sincere, and fearless young Nazi, I loved, as though he had been my son. I felt proud of him; and at the same time aggrieved, as one is for a loss that is irreparable. Those large thoughtful blue eyes that shone as the young man spoke of our great ideals; those eyes that had looked straight into the faces of the men who shot him, without a shadow of hatred or fear, would never see the Sun again . . .

Controlling the tears that I felt welling up into my eyes, I asked Monsieur G: "Could you tell me the name of that young German, and where exactly, and in what year he was shot?"

The Frenchman seemed a little surprised. "Why do you wish to know all those details?" said he. "I only told you of this episode in order to illustrate what I had tried to explain previously concerning the contrasts of the German soul."

"That's just it," I replied. "I was thinking of putting it in my book, as it is so illustrative. And I was going to ask you if I could not quote your name, both in connection with this episode and with what you said of the 'appalling logic.'"

"Oh, you can mention me with regard to the 'appalling logic' as much as you like. But not with regard to this. No please; on no account. Those were very tragic times and . . . I think it is better if my name does not appear."

"Could you not tell me, at least, who shot that young man?"

"I am sorry," replied Monsieur G, "but I cannot answer that question. Moreover, I cannot understand what interest all this has for you."

I felt more and more convinced that he had done the deed himself, or that he was, anyhow, one of those who did it. I got up and took leave of the Frenchman, on the pretext of an appointment that I would miss if I did not go at once.

But the thought of that young hero pursued me. I imagined him telling me, from beyond the gates of eternity: "Why are you so grieved because of me? Did I not die the very sort of death you envy? And am I not happy, by the side of Leo Schlageter and of Horst Wessel, forever?"

I remembered it was the 9th of October 1948, exactly forty-one years after the day Horst Wessel was born.

And I recalled in my heart those two lines of the immortal Song:

Comrades whom the Red Front and the Reaction have shot,
March in spirit with us, within our ranks!

* * *

I met a few other specimens of the Allied forces in occupied Germany: one or two more Frenchmen in Baden-Baden and in Koblenz, and a handful of Britishers before and during my trial. The Frenchmen, who did not know who I was, were either typical representatives of France's official opinion like Monsieur G, or else, equally mediocre but less conscious Democrats: people who really did not care two hoots what happened to the world as long as they, and their wives and children, were all right and could get meat and wine every day and enjoy a cinema show once a week. These only hated war because it upset their insignificant little lives, and also because, one must admit, it is a dangerous game. They were "against Nazism" only because they had been taught that it was "the cause of the war." In fact, they did not care for any "ism." They cared for themselves, and felt uneasy in the presence of anyone who cared for something greater. Such people always do.

The Britishers with whom I came in touch—Military Intelligence officers, police officers, one or two members of the English governing staff of this prison, and the policewoman in whose charge I was on every one of my journeys between Werl and Düsseldorf—all knew who I was. I could therefore speak freely to them. I asked practically the same question to all: "You say you fought six years to make the world a safe place for the free expression of the individual—'freedom of conscience' as you call it. You fought us—you say—because we refuse to admit that the law should express the will of a majority of individuals won over by free propaganda. Why then do you deny *us*, now, the right to propagate our views, nay, the right to express ourselves as National Socialists? Why do you persecute us?"

The answer of *all* of them has been printed in a letter addressed to the editor of the *Observer* by E.I. Watkin, and published in that paper on the 27th of February 1949: "Experience of National Socialism and Communism should have taught us that toleration, if it is not to stultify itself, must have a limit. We cannot tolerate *the dangerously intolerant*."[1]

The intelligent Frenchmen (like the one whose talk I reported in the beginning of a former chapter[2]) admit that "business"—that is to say, plunder—is the ultimate motive behind their whole disgusting policy in Germany. And the British would doubtless admit the same, had they the moral courage and intellectual honesty to do so. But the sincere and courageous ones among them are either fools, misled by the press and the radio, or (in those rare instances in which they happen to be intelligent) National Socialists, ex-internees of Brixton or of the Isle of Man under "18B," not to be found in present-day Germany. The intelligent ones are, generally, neither courageous nor sincere. They are congenitally prudish, congenitally squeamish, and, if moral cowardice

---

[1] This letter to the editor is entitled "Cromwell's religion."
[2] In Chapter 7, pp. 90-95.

and hypocrisy can he cultivated, their whole education has helped to give those vices a foremost place in their psychological makeup. *They* will never call a spade a spade, even among themselves. They have grown so accustomed to a scale of spurious values, to moderation and "decency" through falsity, that they believe their own lies. And that is, partly, the secret of their diplomatic successes in war and peace. That is also the secret of their hold upon the mind of the average coward. Moderation; "decency"; toleration of all but the "dangerously" intolerant—of all but the sincere, the bold, the strong; of all but those who prefer healthy violence to diplomacy; who despise diplomacy, even when compelled to use it; the average coward relishes such an attitude and therefore likes *them.*

They—and the Americans, with whom I have not come into contact but who, I am told, are even more bent on "de-Nazification" than they are—have not come here for plunder. They do not persecute us because they know that, in our hands, a free and racially conscious Germany would not take more than a couple of years to rise once more, *on the material plane also,* to the leadership of the Aryan world. Oh, no! They do not want the material leadership of the world for themselves, those broad-minded, humane, peace-loving British and American Democrats—so they say. They persecute us for philosophical reasons: because we are prepared to enforce our scale of values—which is the complete denial of theirs—by violence, while they, old, sickly, decadent people, have nothing to enforce, save rules destined to protect, forever, the worthless lives and silly amusements of a more and more ape-like majority, as well as the profits of the "decent" capitalists with Christian ideals of charity and a deep-rooted horror for eternal truths expressed in new, living words.

There is, undoubtedly, a far more impressive connection between our enemies' economic greed and fears, and their "philosophical" dislike of National Socialism, than one suspects at first sight. But it is not, perhaps, the simple causal connection one expects. The Democrats' "philosophical" objection to our Ideology, and their alleged horror of our methods (as of those of the Communists, who, as I said before, are also earnest people) are perhaps not so much an excuse for their plunder policy, as the insatiable material greed behind that policy is a consequence of the whole mentality of the decadent West, embodied in Democracy. In other words, the Democrats want a free hand to exploit the world, and hate all possible competitors, because they have nothing nobler, nothing more lovable to live for than their pockets. And they are so "tolerant" not out of a generous comprehension of every point of view (for, in such a case, they would tolerate us too) but out of indifference towards anything that does not threaten the cherished security of their little lives—the material security, no doubt; but the moral security *also*; the comfortable feeling that all is well with the established Judeo-Christian tradition of degenerate Europe.

They speak of us and of the Communists in the same breath, however fundamentally opposite our two philosophies be, however contrary be our basic aspirations. They are hypnotised by one fact, namely that we and our bitterest enemies both know what we want and believe in what we preach; that we are both prepared to use any methods which are expedient, any means that lead to triumph; in one word, that we and they are equally intolerant.

All living *Weltanschauungen* are equally "intolerant."[1] Christianity was, when it was alive. The Greek religion of old, in its narrow, ritualistic aspect, was not—so they say. But even if this be true, the real racial and national *Weltanschauung* at the back of the public cult—the Hellenic edition of our broader Aryan philosophy, expressed in the proud words: "*Pas men Ellen, Barbaros*" ("Every man who is not a Hellene, is a Barbarian") could not have been more radical, more intolerant. As our Führer has rightly said: "The greatness of any active organisation which is the embodiment of an idea, lies in the spirit of religious fanaticism and intolerance in which it attacks all others, being convinced that it alone is right."[2] But the Democrats are old and sick and tired—decadent, as I said before. At heart, they are afraid of any people bearing, like we, that glaring sign of youth: intolerance—precisely because it is a sign of youth. They envy us that faith and devotion that fills us, that once filled the early Christians, *their* forerunners, and that they know *they* will never have again. And they fear us, and they hate us because we are young; because we are the embodiment of Aryan vitality, the everlasting Youth of the Race. For they know, as everyone else, that youth is to take the place of decrepit old age; that the living are to take the place of the dying and of the dead.

* * *

---

[1] Except if—like Buddhism—they be aimed exclusively at drawing man out of the bondage of time.

[2] *Mein Kampf*, I, xii, p. 385; cf. Mannheim, p. 351.

The attitude of the few French and British people whom I met in occupied Germany, to us and our way of life, is essentially the same as that of most anti-Nazi specimens one comes across in France or in England. Only a little more cynical, perhaps—or else, still more hypocritical—in the case of the clever ones; and, if possible, still stupider, in the case of the average. For one does not remain in the service of the Allies in that oppressed land, unless one is brazenly selfish and cynical, congenitally dishonest, or incurably stupid. Any person who does not possess one of these three qualifications—or two; or all three—becomes disgusted of the Allies' doings and resigns, or is forced to resign, within a remarkably short time.

As a rule, I do not discuss with anti-Nazis if I can help it. I only wait for the time and opportunity to silence their quack[1] by force. Yet, from the few I came in contact with, out of policy or out of compulsion—useful members of the British and American forces in India during the war; useful officials, in or outside Germany after the war, and, last but not least, people who cross-examined me during or before my trial—from all those, I say, the impression I received confirms entirely that which written Democratic propaganda had made upon me long before: those self-styled champions of "humanity" and "decency" have no philosophy whatsoever. Their stubborn enmity towards us; their blind hatred of all we stand for; even their pretended horror of our uncompromising methods, all spring from the same source: fear, and bitter envy—the envy of the mental (or physical) cripple at the sight of us, healthy Heathens, in whose world he knows he would have no place; the envy of the *blasé,* pitiable product of decay, at the sight of the rising Youth of the Race in whose heart, in spite of material disaster, confidence still abides and love can still work wonders; the envy of the weakling and of the coward, too cautious to be radical, too squeamish to face facts, too shaky to walk more than half way along the path of resurrection, at the sight of those who, in one frantic leap, have thrown themselves into the struggle for the survival of Aryan mankind with Hitler's immortal words "Future or ruin!" as their battle cry; that envy, and . . . the fear of coming death.

Those are not our final enemies. However much they might hate us and persecute us, the real, the final issue does not lie between us and them—any more than it does between them and their "gallant allies" of yesterday, the Communists. The ultimate issue lies between us and the

---

[1] Savitri seems to be (mis)using the English word "quack" as a synonym for the German word "*Quackelei,*" i.e., silly talk, nonsense, prattle.—Ed.

Communists. For they alone profess the Democratic principles without being impaired by that insurmountable shallowness of the Western Democrats; by that mania for "moderation" and "decency"; that unhealthy admiration for half measures. Their *Weltanschauung* is diametrically opposed to ours; but it is a *Weltanschauung*—not just an excuse for dabbling in politics without any serious inconvenience to one's physical comforts and moral and intellectual slumber. It is Democracy, nay, it is Christianity—that oldest successful snare held out to the Aryan world by the ubiquitous Jew—carried to the limits of its logical implications. (The attitude of the Communist *State* to the Christian *Churches,* as temporal organisations, lessens in no way the importance of that philosophical fact.) It is more than the artificial creation of the brains of idle, decadent Aryans under the influence of Jewish thought. It is the brutal, physical impact of an immense portion of the multifarious non-Aryan world, coalesced in aggressive hatred against us, its natural betters, and against that outward expression of our legitimate consciousness of superiority: racial pride.

The unpardonable crime of the democrats is to have strengthened *that*, by fighting us for their petty ends.

May they suffer—and die—for that crime!

Chapter 9

THE ÉLITE OF THE WORLD

"Der Stärkere hat zu herrschen und sich nicht mit dem Schwächeren zu verschmelzen, und so die eigene Größe zu opfern. Nur der geborene Schwächling kann dies als grausam empfinden, dafür aber ist er auch nur ein schwacher und beschränkter Mensch; denn würde dieses Gesetz nicht herrschen, wäre ja jede vorstellbare Höherentwicklung aller organischen Lebewesen undenkbar."

—Adolf Hitler[1]

Somebody once asked me what had attracted me to National Socialism. I replied without a shadow of hesitation: "Its beauty."

And today, after many years; after the test of disaster and persecution has reduced our number, but strengthened our faith; today, from the narrow prison cell to which our enemies have confined me—like thousands of my betters—while the free, sunny world blooms and smiles far and wide in the glory of spring, I am happy to repeat those words. For, strange as they might have seemed to my anti-Nazi interlocutor of long ago (who gazed at me in amazement, as though this was the last statement he had expected in answer to his question); strange as they might appear to all those who do not realise the full meaning of what we stand for, or who are too coarse to feel the appeal of an eminently aristocratic philosophy such as ours, they are true, and could not be more so. I know nothing in our times and, since a very remote antiquity, nothing in the past, also, which can be compared for beauty with the life and personality of Adolf Hitler, with the history of his struggle, or with the National Socialist *Weltanschauung* itself.

Many a time, in this book and elsewhere, I have stressed the truth of the National Socialist doctrine, the unquestionable facts that underlie it, the natural laws, older than the world, on which it rests. But aesthetic perfection is the glorious tangible sign of absolute truth. Even before I

---

[1] "The stronger must prevail over and not merge with the weaker and thus sacrifice his own greatness. Only the born weakling can feel aversion to this, but after all he is a weak and limited man; for if this law did not prevail, any conceivable higher development of all organic life forms would be inconceivable" (*Mein Kampf*, I, xi, p. 312; cf. Mannheim, 285) [Trans. by Ed.].

fully realised how sound and everlasting Hitler's ideas are, his sociopolitical system appealed, in me, to the artist. And I know of no other system—nay, apart from the immemorial cult of the Sun which I profess, I know of no religion—capable of appealing in like manner to me or to anyone else who, like me, is first and foremost a lover of beauty, and especially of visible beauty; a lover of this earth and of this life, here and now; a worshipper of the body in all its strength, grace, and vitality; a worshipper of Nature in her merciless majesty; a real Heathen.

Two words appear over and over again as a *Leitmotiv* in the few splendid pages that Heinrich Himmler has devoted to our philosophy under the pen name of Wulf Sörensen: "*Wir Heiden*"—we Heathens.[1] They provide the key to our whole outlook. For not only I, but every true National Socialist is a Heathen at heart. And—which is more—every true Aryan Heathen of our tines is bound to be a National Socialist. (If inhibited by "humanitarian" reservations, he or she is no true Heathen.)

One does not *become* a National Socialist. One only discovers, sooner or later, that one has always been one—that, by nature, one could not possibly be anything else. For this is not a mere political label; not an "opinion" that one can accept or dismiss according to circumstances, but a faith, involving one's whole being, physical and psychological, mental and spiritual: "not a new election cry, but a new conception of the world"[2]—a way of life—as our Führer himself has said.

And it is, essentially, the way of life of those in whose eyes the value of man, which lies in his all-round beauty—in his faithfulness to Nature, that calls on him to *surmount* humanity—is far more important than that "individual happiness" of which the "bourgeois" make such a fuss; more particularly, it is the way of life of those whose personal happiness is inseparable from the awareness of their rights and duties as Aryans, *i.e.*, of their value in the natural hierarchy of human beings.

* * *

... The axe has mutilated the forests,
The slave crawls and prays, where swords once clattered;

---

[1] *Die Stimme der Ahnen*, a small book of only 37 pages.
[2] *Mein Kampf*, II, i, p. 409; cf. Mannheim, p. 373.

And all the Gods of Erinn have departed. . . .[1]

Thirty years ago, I read for the first time that concise and pathetic description of the twilight of European Heathendom, which a French poet has put into the mouth of an old Irish bard. And I sobbed desperately because I—in 1919—could do nothing to bring back the proud and beautiful Gods of bygone days. From my earliest childhood, I had always been a bitter rebel against the Christian values; a soul to whom the Christian ethics had never meant anything but silliness or perversity—or "pose"; to whom the Christian message meant nothing. And I loved the Gods of the ancient North, as well as those of Greece and of the Aryan East, with passionate, nostalgic love. And I kept within my heart the healthy, warrior-like ideal that they embodied, while despising the dreary humanity in the midst of which I lived—that humanity that tried, through the teaching of Christianity or of the principles of the French Revolution, to impose its wretchedness and sickly benevolence upon me.

I was not, then, aware of the dawning of National Socialism in Germany, only a few hundred miles away from my native town. I did not know I was destined, one day, to hail in that inspired Movement the long-delayed awakening of the Aryan Gods within the consciousness of the undying Race that had once created them. I only began to take a serious interest in it ten years later. And yet, at heart, I was already a National Socialist. And my continual conflict with the world around me and both its Christian "humanitarian" and Democratic values—its man-centred, equalitarian values—was nothing else but the conflict of the new Movement itself with those same values, those same traditions, those same principles, outcome of centuries of decay; with that same ugly world, boasting of its incurable sickness and hypocrisy under the name of "moral progress."

Oh, if only I had known that, in 1919! I could have done nothing, for I was a mere thirteen year old girl. But I would have dried my tears, and looked with hope and confidence to the slowly rising Leader beyond the Rhine and to his handful of followers. Instead of mourning for a past that would never come back, I would have sought in the living present and in the future that eternal beauty for which I was

---

[1] ". . . la hache a mutilé les bois,
L'esclave rampe et prie, où chantaient les épées,
Et tous les Dieux d'Erinn sont parties á la fois."
—Leconte de Lisle, "Le Barde de Temrah," *Poèmes Barbares* [*Barbaric Poems*] (Paris: Alphonse Lemerre, n.d.), p. 70.

craving, and spared myself ten years' more bitterness.

* * *

As I have said before, National Socialism is not merely the one modern "ism" which is anything but modern; the only political Ideology which is infinitely more than political. It is the only system concerned with social questions and government, with economic and territorial problems, national welfare and international relations, in our times—and perhaps in all times—to which a man or woman who is first and last a lover of beauty and nothing else, can be wholeheartedly attracted; *should,* indeed, be wholeheartedly attracted.

No out-and-out lover of beauty can help feeling bitter, at times, if not utterly dejected, in a world in which, roughly speaking, everything is beautiful and lovable save his own species. And such seemed to be our world, until very recently; until, in fact, out of the hopeless general slush of slowly decaying humanity, new Germany rose, as by miracle, under the leadership of Adolf Hitler, a living picture of what the whole Aryan race—the world's natural élite—*could* re-become, if only it were willing to follow its true friend and Saviour. And, what is more, for the last four years already, the reborn Nation has stood the terrible test of disaster. She suffered; and there were times when one could believe she had reached the limit beyond which no human beings could keep faith in themselves and in their destiny. And yet, invasion, prolonged occupation, with all its demoralising consequences, hunger, humiliation, de-Nazification: she stood it all and did not lose faith. And the worthy ones among her martyred people are, more than ever, today, a splendid example of what the Aryan race can be, when invigorated anew with the sound doctrine of pure blood and legitimate racial pride. More than ever, the lover of beauty cannot but admire them, and feel happy to have at last found a land where the unchanging beauty of Nature outside man is equalled by the superhuman, all-round beauty of a small section of mankind; a land where a few hundreds of thousands if not a few millions of men and women fulfil the purpose of their race—which is to create a "supermankind"—as surely and as simply as the beautiful beasts of the forest, or the trees, or the distant stars in heaven fulfil theirs.

National Socialism has performed that miracle. That new Germany, that stands today erect in the midst of her appalling ruins, a thing of indestructible beauty forever, is entirely Adolf Hitler's handiwork; the product of that love that led him to the intuitive knowledge of a few eternal truths and to the ruthless application of that knowledge to the complete remoulding of a whole nation. And the miracle is unique. For nothing, save the short-lived application of the Nazi Ideology to government and education, seems ever to have arrested man's unavoidable decadence, even for a while, let alone to have raised a superior race, once more, towards its forgotten perfection, against the all-powerful current of time. So much so that, if the Western world is one day to rise again, it will have to date its resurrection from the birth of the National Socialist Movement, or at least from the 30th of January 1933, the day Hitler came to power. And if it is never to rise, still it will remain true that the only way to resurrection was once opened to it by our Führer.

How is it so? And how is it that so many other political, social, and religious changes have taken place, in this and other continents, without leaving a trace, save upon the externals of life? The answer is simple. The other political movements, even the great religions ancient and modern, have all accepted as a matter of course—or tried to conceal— the tragic fact of man's *physical* decay, as though nothing indeed could be done about it, and have striven to cultivate man's personality, to raise man's ethical or spiritual level, or even his mere material standard of life *in spite of* that fact—which is absurd.

All recipes for the moral, intellectual, spiritual, or merely social development of a physically decaying humanity are humbug. Like other "quack" remedies, they are, at the most, fit to fill the pockets or to advertise the otherwise worthless names of those who put them forward. If physical decay be irredeemable; if race, even when slightly weakened or vulgarised, can never be restored—if even a little poison can never be eliminated from the racial body—then there is only one solution to the human problem: extinction; only one ideal to be upheld, with utmost vigour: the monastic ideal; only one request to be made, or rather only one order to be given to men and women before they sink to the level of perverse apes: "Cease breeding, and leave this planet as soon as possible!—Die in dignity, while you still perhaps retain enough of your ancestral nobility to feel that death imposes itself as the only tolerable future; death, rather than endless degradation."

If not—if there *is* hope for man—then salvation should be sought not in the social, economic, moral, or spiritual uplift of the degenerate *as they are,* but first and foremost in an arrest of degeneracy; in a return to health, without which there is no morality, no spirituality, no beauty, nothing worth living for. It should be sought in a world-wide policy of systematic healthy birth and healthy life but, before all, in a policy of healthy birth and life applied to the natural leading race of the world, the Aryan, of which the decay, if definitive, would mean the greatest disaster from the human point of view. Our Führer has expressed all this far better than I or anyone else can do, in that magnificent Chapter 11 of the first part of *Mein Kampf*, which contains the kernel of our eternal philosophy. With the stirring eloquence of clear, objective truth allied to unshakable conviction, he has advocated that ruthless policy of purification and strengthening of the Aryan race—that regulation of man's sexual life with a view to the birth of healthy children of pure blood—which it is the glory of the National Socialist régime to have carried out. It is the only sensible policy, in alternative to that of systematic extinction. And it is the only policy that can—that must—result in the re-creation of a humanity which the out-and-out artist can admire and love without reservations.

* * *

There is a curious and, in my eyes, a very significant fact in religious history—a fact which nobody, up till now, as far as I know, seems to have noticed. Of the two great religions of India, Brahminism and Buddhism—the two typical products of the Aryan mind in a tropical environment—the former is nothing else but the eternal creed of blood purity and racial hierarchy—*our* creed—applied to a land of many races; and the latter is the most pitilessly consistent religion of extinction that man has ever conceived at the sight of irredeemable decay.

And while, in spite of all attempts to suppress it, from without, or to mar it from within, the race policy embodied in the immemorial caste system, has preserved in India, to this day, an extremely small, indeed, but still worthy blood aristocracy—the southernmost and easternmost outpost of Aryan humanity in the world—the policy of extinction has failed lamentably. For alone, or nearly alone, those individuals of the superior races who adhered to it, carried it out to its end, with all the courage and thoroughness natural to them.[1] To the millions of *Untermenschen* who gradually came to be labelled Buddhists, in the length and breadth of Asia, the great religion of non-violence and chastity soon meant nothing but a mere ritual, and a mythology,

---

[1] It is remarkable that, while most of the first converts to Christianity were slaves or Jews—the non-Aryan, and the least Aryan elements of the Roman world—the first and best converts to Buddhism were Indians of the Brahmin or Kshatriya castes—Aryans.

without any bearing upon their lives. No philosophy can teach the *Untermenschen* to stop breeding. Wherever their number should be kept down, it is the business of sterilisation, not of religion, to see to it. The countless multitude and the poor quality of the professed followers of the most logical religion of extinction in the world, today, after two thousand five hundred years, proves this only too well. The main result of the preaching of a philosophy of extinction on a worldwide scale, would be to reduce in number the superior races, making place for the unrestricted increase of the inferior ones, and their mastery over the whole earth; in other words, to lower the human level and to create, not nothingness, but ugliness; not a world in which beautiful wild beasts would prowl alone in the re-grown forests, over the dust of forgotten towns, but . . . Chinese slums and Indian "bustees."

The philosophy of extinction can therefore only express the individual attitude of those men and women who have lost all hope in life's possibilities and all interest in material man. It is merely the outcome of one's personal determination not to contribute to the continuation of a doomed world, not to allow one's own blood to lose itself into the general stream of decay. It provides no practical solution for the human problem which is, ultimately, the problem of the survival of the superior races. And the struggle for the maintenance or restoration of pure blood—our struggle—remains the only course.

As far as I know, this course has been seriously taken only twice in the long history of our race: in ancient India, some six thousand years ago, when the newly settled Aryan invaders from the North, bearers of a culture entirely different from that of the civilised natives, first became aware of the dangers of blood contamination and invented the caste system, or—if it already existed, as some scholars think—remoulded it upon a racial basis,[1] in order to keep themselves pure and worthy of their recently acquired overlordship of the southern subcontinent; and in our times in National Socialist Germany. In the first instance, it resulted in the extraordinary preservation of Aryan blood and culture in an immense tropical land—nearly as large as Europe—densely inhabited by four hundred million people of different non-Aryan stocks, from the most primitive Negroid[2] or Mongoloid tribes[3] to the highly evolved Dravidians. In the second instance, out of

---

[1] The Sanskrit words for "caste" are *varna* (colour) and *jati* (race).

[2] Properly speaking, there are no Negroid aborigines in India, but there are Australoids who look "Negroid" in a looser sense of the term.—Ed.

[3] Such as the Veddas of Ceylon, the Santals of Chota Nagpur, the Nagas, Kashias, Kukis, Mishmis, Abors, and other hill tribes of Assam.

the desperate Germany of the 1920s, it raised a fully conscious aristocracy of blood, the world's real élite, which even a second disaster of far greater magnitude than the first, was unable to subdue or to demoralise.

The former, however, is no mean achievement in world history. And one must, perhaps, have lived in a land of many races—and especially in times like ours, when equalitarian teachings have infected the whole of the earth—to realise to its full the greatness of National Socialism. To most Europeans, still devoid of racial consciousness, the eleventh chapter of *Mein Kampf* (if they have read it at all) means nothing but an expression of "Hitler's prejudices." To most of us, it means hardly more than beautiful, uplifting pages, of which the truth can be proved only in the antagonism of Aryan and Jew. To me, it means that, no doubt, and much more. It evokes memories of the few and far apart tropical outposts of the Aryan race; outlandish scenes: a simple and spotlessly clean whitewashed room in a thatched cottage in some village of Bengal (or of South India, where the contrast between Aryan and non-Aryan is still more glaring) and in that room, a white clad man, one of the few Brahmins of the village, hardly darker—and sometimes fairer—than an Italian or many Frenchmen, with generally brown, but sometimes grey or greyish-blue eyes, and the self-same features as any pure Aryan of Europe. And that man quotes to me verses from the Rig-Veda, from the songs that the Aryan bards once sang to the glory of the Gods of Light and Life, the "Shining Ones," already before the race came to India; the songs in which allusions are made to those wonders of the still cherished distant Arctic Home, the Northern Lights.[1] And the modern language he speaks (if in Bengal) is a neo-Sanskrit language, closely related, through its roots, to German and English, Greek and Latin—an Aryan language. And the rites of his religion are those of the hallowed Northerners, and the legitimate pride that he feels as a Brahmin—a member of India's highest caste—is *their* racial pride, surviving in the midst of a foreign environment, through the narrow but uninterrupted stream of pure blood, for six thousand years. And I recall, also, the foreign environment, all round the peaceful cottage: the darker men and women of varied racial types, with features entirely different from those of the Brahmin, going along the dusty, burning hot road, with burdens upon their heads or working in the rice fields; or collecting the village refuse—the multifarious levels of hierarchised mankind, from the honoured castes immediately below the Brahmins,

---

[1] See the aforementioned *The Arctic Home in the Vedas*, by Lokamanya Tilak.

down to the meanest "untouchables"; levels that do not correspond to different shades of wealth, but *only* to a greater or lesser proportion of real or supposed Aryan blood (of which the lower castes are entirely devoid).

The culture reflected in the songs of the Rig-Veda, and in the warrior-like philosophy of the Bhagavad-Gita, which the Brahmin has kept alive, is the only ancient Aryan culture that has resisted victoriously, to this day, the impact of both Christianity and Islam, *i.e.*, the two great religions of human equality, sprung from Judaism. The Aryan who brought it to the tropics kept it, nay, stamped it upon the multitudes of India forever, first because he kept himself—kept his blood—pure against all odds, threatening with the severest penalty— not loss of life, but loss of caste, with all that this means in India— anyone who would become guilty of the sin of interbreeding. And to the extent to which he failed to avoid that deadly sin, the culture has become "fossilised," to repeat an expression used by the Führer in the eleventh chapter of *Mein Kampf*; stultified; for all practical purposes dead.

During my numerous years in India, how many times have I not remembered whole passages of Hitler's famous book, at the sight of the living realities resulting from the existence of an Aryan minority amongst a teeming non-Aryan population; at the sight of that traditional reverence of the non-Aryan for the Aryan in the old caste ridden land— reverence expressed in the small things of daily life and in the very spirit of current language: in the fact, for instance, that relatively fair skin is a very great qualification in a marriageable Indian girl of *any* caste; or that, in all the languages of India, the words *arya* and *anarya* have both a racial *and* a moral connotation, *arya* meaning "noble" and *anarya*, "ignoble," "infamous."

How many times have I not marvelled at the worship of the deified Aryan hero, Rama, by India's multitudes of *all* races, to this day! And, standing against a stone pillar, in one of the gorgeous temples of the far South, in the midst of the smoke of incense and the outlandish music of drums and flutes, how many times have I not shut my eyes, and let my thoughts wander back to distant Europe where Adolf Hitler had risen to power and was building up a new civilisation upon the age-old idea of Aryan supremacy! I watched the graceful Indian women walk along the endless pillared corridors, bearing offerings in large brass plates, their black hair adorned with jasmine flowers. Would the golden-haired daughters of the North learn again one day to worship Aryan Gods? All my life I had longed that they would. Anyhow, they were already learning again to revere in themselves and in their handsome, pure-blooded countrymen, the impersonal divinity of the Race. And that was the main thing. The rest would come afterwards.

* * *

The second historic achievement of the undying *Weltanschauung* of racial purity, namely the creation of new Germany—or rather the formation of the kernel of new "Aryandom"—is perhaps even greater than the first. Greater, I say, for it is more difficult to revive the spirit of a people after a pernicious foreign system of religious beliefs, philosophy, and ethics, has marred it for over one and a half millenniums, than to keep it alive in the midst of foreign multitudes that have accepted, or at least that respect, nay, reverence, the values that *it* has created. Greater, also, for that miracle has been realised through the genius and superhuman willpower, and love, of *one* Man—Adolf Hitler.

It is true that, even in its well-known political form, National Socialism is older than most people think; that, as early as 1904—when Hitler was yet only fifteen—Hans Krebs had gathered the best Germanic elements of what the Western Democracies have later christened Czechoslovakia into a party forwarding the same immediate aims, and bearing the same name as the immortal NSDAP, into which it finally merged. But it is and will remain Hitler's everlasting glory to have stressed before the modern Aryan world the philosophical and—I am tempted to say, however strange that might seem at first to many—the religious contents of National Socialism; to have conceived and proclaimed the *Weltanschauung* of pure blood not merely from the point of view of tragic emergency, but from that of eternity. And that is why we hail in him the inspired promoter of the Western resurrection, nay, the Saviour of the whole Aryan race. Other German patriots with a right vision of the same political realities, have founded parties. He has created the youth of new Germany; awakened the best elements in the country to a new consciousness; made Germany worthy, in fact, to take the lead of the Aryan world—worthier than ever, now, inasmuch as she has remained faithful to him and his principles all through these years of persecution. Above all, he has forced the most racially conscious among the foreign Aryans to welcome Germany's leadership, nay, to desire it, and—if they are consistently sincere—to fight for it; as I have once already said before, he has made Germany a holy land in their eyes. Apart from a very few within the National Socialist minority, the

Germans themselves do not seem to realise this sufficiently.

I have mentioned the splendid youth of new Germany. All great movements put stress upon the training of youth. "Catch them young," say the Jesuits. National Socialism has not merely "caught them young," but has striven to create them; to prepare them, not only from childhood, or from birth, but from the very moment of conception, to be the embodiment of the highest idea of all-round manly perfection— of physical health and beauty; of moral health and beauty; of character; of sound and clear intelligence, firmly linked up with the whole of life; *the* human élite, from every point of view. No other Movement has harped with such insistence upon the fact that all education is a sheer waste of time without the primary physical foundation of a noble body, and that nobility is God-ordained, not man-made, residing as it does in one's descent not necessarily from a titled ancestor, but surely from healthy ascendants of unmixed Aryan stock. No political movement, and hardly any religion—save the ancient Aryan religion still alive in India—has ever taught its followers so emphatically that the act of life, far from being an amusement, is an all-important, an extremely serious thing; a holy rite, in which two individuals become the actual link between the whole past of the race and its future, priest and priestess of Everlasting Life; an act which the strong, the healthy, the worthy, the men and women without blemish should alone be allowed to perform, if it is not to become a mockery and a blasphemy.

To have dared to stress this truth, and, which is more, to have dared to have enforced laws taking it fully into account, in a world that had forgotten it for the last two thousand years; to have had the courage to proclaim that the union in beauty of two young and healthy people of pure blood, whether sanctioned by a ceremony or not, is something commendable, while the marriage of an Aryan to a man or woman of another race or the union of two people of any race (including pure Aryans) if one or both be unhealthy, *is* a crime, however much the Christian or any other equalitarian, individualistic, and otherworldly faith might condone it; to have emphasised this as a guiding principle in the government of a great state, encouraging the sterilisation of the unfit, the painless elimination of the dregs of humanity, and strongly forbidding all shameful unions whether on grounds of health or of race, that, I say, is something for which a sane world should be everlastingly grateful to National Socialism. The universal blame which, on the contrary, we got for upholding those measures and the conception of life at the back of them, only proves to what a degree of degradation the whole world—and indeed the Aryan race—has sunk, under the long-drawn influence of such a man-centred creed as Christianity and of the ideologies of "liberty" and equality that in fact prolong its spirit, even if they pretend to stand against it, as some of them do. It only proves the enormity of the physical as well as moral decay of the Western world—for only sickly people can sincerely object to drastic measures for the restoration of the health of their own race.

This reminds me of the words addressed to me in 1946, by one of the finest Englishmen I know, a sincere National Socialist who had then just been released after six years' internment under the 18B Act.[1] "What can one expect of those millions of imbeciles?" the gentleman said, speaking of the majority of his countrymen. "Who are they, that they could act or think differently? The products of a drunken Saturday night's lust, most of them; and the remainder a bastardised lot, intermixed with Jews. What can one expect? If one really wants an élite, one has to breed it systematically, as they did in Germany."

Yes, when most men of our times speak of an "élite" they mean what they call a "moral" or "intellectual" élite. We mean an all-round one—and first and foremost a physical one. We *know* that there is no such thing as a "moral" or "intellectual" élite which is not at the same time physical.

There are, doubtless, exceptional individuals who are not physically sound and strong but who, in other ways, might be useful, very useful even, if they possess the right spirit, which is that of sacrifice for something greater than themselves. But these should remain exceptions, and never be allowed to mar the healthy average bulk of the community. In particular, they should never be allowed to breed, however clever or virtuous they might be, if they have not a perfectly healthy body or if they are not racially pure.

Had there been no war, or had this war not been lost, the National Socialist régime would be lasting still, unhindered since 1933 and extended by now to the whole of Europe. One can hardly imagine what a beautiful world would have evolved out of the West which we know after fifty, after a hundred years, of such a régime, provided our Führer's successors abided strictly and firmly by the principles laid down by him. Out of the new policy of sex with a view to natural nobility of birth—blood purity, health and strength—would have

---

[1] Defence Regulation 18B was an "emergency decree" in England sanctioning from the beginning of the war onwards the arrest and internment of anyone suspected of sympathy for National Socialism or "Fascism." [The internee is probably Elwyn Wright.—Ed.]

emerged generations embodying more and more Nietzsche's ideal of the Superman; human beings, but with Olympian bodies, and a mentality as far above that of the average man of today as the latter is supposed to be above that of the chimpanzee; the human species in its original perfection or—I am tempted to say—a new species; a species of living gods on earth.

Was not that glorious result well worth securing, be it through a certain amount of ruthlessness at the early stages of the struggle? To us, it was; to us, it is. And we are ready to resume the same course, at the next opportunity, for the sake of the same ideal.

Whatever our Führer achieved in Germany, he brought about not in fifty years, but in *six*—from 1933 to 1939 (when the war interrupted all constructive planning). Time was too short for one to see the consequences of the policy of healthy, noble breeding pursued by him so consistently. One could only see the effect of the National Socialist teaching upon the people already born—and, most of them, well out of childhood—at the time Adolf Hitler came to power. But that alone was something to marvel at. That alone was already the promising beginning of a new world—the formation of a *real* élite.

It will always remain my one great regret in life, that I did not come back to Europe in time to see the parades of the Hitler Youth through the streets of the German towns, and to be present at the great yearly Party Rallies—at that of Nuremberg, for instance, in September 1935—and to *live* in the uplifting atmosphere of the glorious days. I have only seen pictures of those days. But I know people who have lived through them. I have spoken to men who were between fifteen and twenty-five at the time, and who, themselves, have stood by the Party Standards on solemn occasions, and have greeted the Führer walking past between two delirious multitudes; men who still now, would give anything, do anything, to bring National Socialism back to power. And I have conversed with their faithful elders too, who were at the time between thirty and forty, or even more. The fact that they have all kept their convictions to this day proves that these were no mere product of youthful enthusiasm, or of "mass suggestion," as our enemies pretend, but the outcome of something deeper. It proves that one can rely upon those followers of Adolf Hitler. Personally I have *never* and *nowhere* met such fine people, both physically and from the standpoint of character. They are the true élite of the world, and curious, incredible perhaps, as this might seem to many of my readers, an outwardly recognizable élite, in most cases.

I have often remembered, in their presence, those words—worthy of an ancient Greek—addressed to me somewhere in Saarland, by an SS man, in 1948: "The first duty of a Nazi is to be beautiful." Strange words, at first hearing, but how true, when one starts to think of all they imply! For no human being, man or woman, can really be "beautiful" without health and strength; and these stand in the background of most of the virtues expected in one who shares our Ideology. I never met *one* representative of Germany's faithful National Socialist minority who did not come up to a fairly high standard of manly beauty. And I met many whose appearance reminded one of the Greek gods of old, or—to stick to our times—of the statues of Arno Breker, full of strength, poise, and unaffected grace. I realised how completely that great sculptor's whole creation expresses the new world that was taking shape all round him, with its new aspirations, its new soul; how, for example, his "Herald" is really the Herald of our New Order, projection, in immortal bronze, of Germany's living youth.

That youth has not died. It has only ripened, during these four atrocious years; more than ever, it has become hardened, self-possessed, invincible. And it has, perhaps, grown still more contemptuous of its inferiors—of that enormous majority of mankind (including millions of Aryans) who had not the inclination, or the brains to think for itself and to admit that we "were right" but preferred to swallow whatever propaganda against us the Jews or their agents dished out to it, in the press and on the wireless, and in cinema shows, and to bring upon itself the chaos that everyone knows. The National Socialist minority watches and waits, in dignified silence, knowing that it will rise and rule once more, when the time comes.

Strictly speaking, it is not their physical appearance *only* that points out its representatives to the attention of the careful observer sitting, for instance, on the opposite bench in a café or in a waiting room. It is the radiance of their personality; the stamp of their worth, as superior men and women, upon their faces; the shine of intelligence and courage in their eyes. And that is true of their elder ones as well as those who were mere adolescents in 1933, and who went through the splendid physical training of new Germany. As I have said before, now that it no longer pays to call oneself a Nazi, those who have remained faithful to our ideals, firm and confident and ready, are those alone whose lifelong aspirations, whose whole personal philosophy could not possibly be anything else but ours: the morally no less than physically healthy, the strong and consistent, the fearless—the very best of the land. And, along with health and race, it is those qualities of character that give their faces such beauty and that make one feel, in their circle, that one is in the presence of men far above the rest of men. In the days National Socialism was triumphant, quite a number of Germans, even in high positions, did not reach that level—otherwise, all would have gone well, and the war would never have been lost. Now, those alone who *are* at that level remain, ready to form, tomorrow, the real, the invincible Party, worthy to govern the whole earth under Hitler's leadership, forever.

* * *

I owe some of the most beautiful of all my memories to my short experience in the National Socialist struggle just slowly beginning again. And these are memories of the people with whom I came in touch; people of all social conditions—students, shopkeepers, workmen, men of liberal professions—and of all levels of education in the narrowly bookish sense of the word, but who form, in my eyes, a real aristocracy; the natural aristocracy of blood and of character, destined (I hope) to supersede the artificial aristocracy of money, position, or learning in our new world. How I love them!

We understood one another, whatever our level of education, first because the things we had to say were not, in general, to be found in books, and then, because there were a few basic books which we all had read. We did not necessarily agree on every minor point, nor was each one of us the replica of all the others—as so many of the Communists are, from what I know at least of the non-Russian ones—for he thought for himself; nor had we all come to National Socialism for the same main reasons; each one of us put stress on that which, in the *Weltanschauung* or its application, seemed to him the most attractive. But we agreed in all that is essential and, as I have said already, we all were—we all *are*—Heathens at heart, the whole lot of us, the faithful few. (There were, once, quite a number of inconsistent people who believed they could be both true Christians and Nazis at the same time. Defeat—and the subsequent intensive propaganda on the part of the Churches—has mightily helped such ones to recognise the incompatibility of the two philosophies as they stand, and to make up their minds. Had our *Weltanschauung* remained triumphant without a break, it never would have occurred to them how inconsistent they were—or how "wrong" we are, from a Christian point of view!)

I remember—with that nostalgia one feels at the thought of one's own lost possibilities—a remarkable young German of twenty-three or twenty-four, a student of physics whom I met in the train a month or so before my arrest. I admired the logic, knowledge, and self-assurance with which he was discussing with another student some point about alternating currents, and I stepped into the conversation after asking to be excused for doing so. (I was myself, once, a science student as well as a student of the arts.) We soon discussed other things than electricity, and I met the young man again, and came to know him better. He is a serious youngster, of few words but much thought and intense feelings, and a fine National Socialist, with all the virtues that such praise implies. I met his mother, a most lovable German woman also sharing our ideals, and I envied her for having given such a son to the Movement. His name is Herr F.

We were once walking down a steep road, leading from his house to the Rhine, and a great part of the town stretched before us. "You should have seen this place in 'our days,'" the young man said to me. (The greater part of the town is now in ruins.)

"Yes," I replied, "everything was beautiful 'then'; was it not?"

"It was. And then we had something to live for. We were happy."

He told me how, being then only eighteen, he had won the first prize in a fencing competition extending to the whole *Kreis*,[1] in 1943. "But sports were not merely sports, for us. They were a part of a broader and higher training, of our training as Germans and as Aryans. Competing with one another in strength, skill, and endurance; working hard and well; going on picnics in the countryside, a hundred together, or more, and watching the Sun rise over the hills and woods of our Fatherland; marching through the streets and singing our beautiful manly songs, we were becoming a new people," he said, "and we knew it; we felt it. We were so happy! Then the disaster came, and all seemed lost irretrievably . . . It was not our fault. Had it depended upon us, the young generation, the Führer would have been world-Führer long ago. But there were traitors among the elder generation."

"I know only too well. But you don't believe that everything *is* irretrievably lost, do you?"

"Goodness no! No force on earth can kill a healthy nation determined to live."

And his dark eyes flashed as he spoke. I stretched out my hand to him and said: "I wish every German, nay, every Aryan, would speak as you do."

"More than you seem to think, do," he replied.

I asked him what most of his fellow students felt about the two

---

[1] District.

dangers, Democracy and Communism.

"Who believes seriously in either?" he answered. "The only supporters of the former are those who draw or hope to draw some profit from the occupation—the good-for-nothing people, and those whom we chastised in our time and who now want an excuse to get back at us. The only supporters of the latter are those who have never lived in the Russian Zone."

Herr F *had* lived in the Russian Zone up till recently. We decided that he would help me to cross the border clandestinely with a friend of his, and to pay a visit to the Eastern part of Germany. On my return, he would introduce me to a group of students with our views, and we could perhaps—cautiously—"start something."

I was arrested before those grand projects could materialise.

I remember an elderly saleswoman, Fräulein E—who looks much younger than her age—and whom I also met during a journey. A very expressive face, showing great determination and great kindness (which are seldom found together) and thoughtfulness, also. Pale blue eyes, that can be extremely cold and distant, or brighten up into a flash of sunshine—according to what Fräulein E hears or says, or thinks about. She walked a few steps with me, as we both came out of a railway station somewhere in the French Zone. When I told her I was in Germany to write a book, she stopped and gazed at me.

"And you intend to write the truth?" she asked.

"Certainly."

"Well, in that case . . ." she said, and broke off abruptly.

"What, 'in that case'?" asked I.

She looked at me intently. "I know I should not tell you this," she continued; "After all, I have only just met you. I don't know who you are. It might be very foolish on my part—and dangerous for me—to speak. But you look as though you can be trusted. I have been in trade all my life and know faces. Well, I tell you: in your book . . . don't write about things of which you are not perfectly sure . . . don't be unfair to National Socialism."

I felt my face brighten. But I tried to control myself. "What prompts you to tell me that?" I asked. "Do you imagine I intend to be unfair to anything or anyone?"

"No," she said. "But many people are unfair without meaning to be, swayed as they are by various prejudices. And so much mud has already been thrown at us—so much!—by all the writers of the world! I only wished to tell you, you being a foreigner, 'don't throw any more.'"

I admired the woman's fearlessness—for she did not know me yet. She had only seen my British-Indian passport when I had shown it to an inspector in the train.

"Are you a National Socialist?" I asked her. And she is the only person in Germany to whom I ever put that question in such a point-blank form. Her courageous talk had authorised me to do so. Her answer was no less bold. "Yes, I am," she said.

"And so am I," I replied. "Don't fear that *I* might be impressed by lies against the Führer or against us; I have heard heaps, up till now, and spit at those who tell them. My book shall be the impeachment of our enemies." I was moved beyond words as I spoke.

"Can I really believe you?" said Fräulein E, amazed and stopping and looking at me once more. "You, a foreigner, *now*—when all the world is against us!"

"I have no time for that world of monkeys and its supposed 'opinion,'" I replied. "I know my words are difficult to believe. But you might believe my writing."

And pulling one of my leaflets out of a roll, I took her to a lonely corner in the ruins (we were in a town where there are plenty such corners) and showed it to her. "I wrote it," I said.

She believed me at last, and was visibly moved as she took my hands and told me: "I am happy to have met you, happier than I can say. But, my poor dear child, how dare you go about with all that dangerous stuff?"

"No German has betrayed me yet."

"No true German ever will," she answered. "But still, be careful. 'They' might find you out all the same. 'They' are probably watching you all the time. Anyhow, it is no use thinking of it beforehand. Come now, and I shall take you to some good friends of mine. *They* will be glad to make your acquaintance."

"Tell me something about the great days," said I, as we walked along a half-destroyed avenue. "I wish I had come then."

"You would have been happy in Germany, then. You cannot imagine how lovely it was. Now, look at what 'they' have done—our Christian-like enemies; those who came to 'reform' us, to 're-educate' us as they say." And she pointed to one of the streets in which (as in more than one other street of the same town) not a single house is left erect. "Look at that!" said she. "But revenge will come, one day. And then Germany will rise once more out of her ruins and the great days will come back!"

Once more, for the millionth time, I admired the invincible Nazi spirit.

The woman showed me the ruins of what had once been her shop, at the corner of a main avenue opposite a church. The sight of the church reminded her of a man and of an incident. But before telling me about it, she asked me whether I were a Christian.

"I? Goodness no! I know there is nothing so opposed to ours as the Christian philosophy, and I look upon the church as our greatest enemy."

"How right you are! *I* have always said that too, although many disagreed with me. Then I shall tell you of my friend W, who was a clergyman, but a very peculiar one—a clergyman, and a fighter for the Movement at the same time, if you can picture such a combination of opposites; a man who would throw a priest's robe over his brown uniform (jack boots and pistol and all) and run to church just in time to deliver a short address. The address was always thoroughly National Socialist in spirit, the word 'amen' at the end being practically the only thing in it that indicated that it was delivered from a pulpit. One day, what happened? Another preacher was speaking from the pulpit and my friend W—without his pious disguise, this time—was among the congregation. The preacher, who was a real Christian, not just someone trying to prepare the church-going crowds for the new times, started making certain hints against the régime. My friend W took a writing pad and a fountain pen which he always kept at hand, and noted carefully whatever the man said. Then, he waited for him at the church door, and stopped him on his way out.

"'You made such and such a statement?' said he.

"'*Jawohl*, I did.'

"'You implied that the policy of our Government is "nefarious"? See, I took down such and such words that you uttered.'

"'I admit I did. But . . .'

"'There is no "but." Did you, or not?'

"'I did.'

"'And the "undesirable people" to whom you alluded without daring to be too clear, were, I suppose, the Führer and his collaborators?'

"'*Jawohl*, they were, if you must know!'

"'Good! . . . So that's what you are—you swine!'

"And my friend W gave the fellow a slap that could be heard from the other side of the street. And then another. And another—'paff! puff!'—and several more until finally he sent him rolling in the dust with a kick in the pants: 'That will teach you, saying things against the Führer, you good for nothing rascal!'"

I burst out laughing, unable to stop for a minute or two. I had not laughed so wholeheartedly for a very long time. "Splendid!" I exclaimed; "Could not be more splendid! Gosh, I wish I had seen *that*! In what year was it?"

"In 1942, if I remember well."

"I was in Calcutta. I know I missed a lot. But *that*! That alone would have been worth the voyage. I would have enjoyed myself! How did the people take it?"

"The people who were just coming out of church you mean? Why, they enjoyed themselves too. Half of them were laughing as boisterously as you are now after all these years. I stepped in from the street, and went and congratulated my old friend: 'Well done, Herr W!' said I. 'That will teach him a lesson. One can't let those treacherous fellows go about quacking whatever nonsense they please, especially while we are fighting a war,' I said. They all agreed."

"And where is Herr W now? Could I see him?" I asked. "I would love to meet him."

"'They' took him off to a concentration camp in 1945. Since then nobody knows where he is."

A shadow passed over my face. I thought of that frank advocate of violence in the service of our ideals, spending four years in one of those chambers of hell of which I have tried to give a glimpse in a previous chapter. Four years! And for what? For being what he is—what we all are—a man who had the courage to repudiate once for all the false values that have been forced upon the nobler races of Europe as their "standards of morality" for nearly 1,500 years, and to speak and to act according to the standards of the strong; for being a Heathen in a Christian world. And once more I felt how powerful are the forces against us. And once more I was aware how bitterly I hate them.

I know the story of Herr W is not one that will endear us to our enemies. Most of these will find the incident of the clergyman "horrible"—and find me no less "horrible" for enjoying it. But who cares what they might think? As in the first, so in this second phase of the struggle also, we are not fighting to win their approval, but to reduce them, one day, to submission. I have told the story only in order to show what an abyss gapes between us and the Christian world; to illustrate the clean, brutal frankness of our attitude compared with that of the "decent" people. None of these would have chastised an opponent in broad daylight, before everybody, as Herr W did. No. *They* would have remained content with being "shocked," and would have kept silent—even if in power. They would first have made the opponent's life a misery and then, at the first opportunity, handed him over to hostile authorities, for far worse a treatment than a few slaps and a kick in the pants. That is, in fact, the very way they have behaved towards Herr W himself. I recalled the words of Friedrich Nietzsche on a different subject: "Christianity has not killed Eros"—the god of physical love—"it has only given him poison"—defiled love.[1] One could also say about violence: Christianity has not killed physical violence; it has only defiled it—made it indirect, and cowardly, and shameful.

And what powerful, elemental instinct has it *not* defiled, I would like to know?

* * *

Fräulein E took me to a confectioner's kept by the Ms—good friends of hers—and introduced me: "You come back at six o'clock, when the shop is closed, and we'll have a talk. Too many eyes are looking, and too many ears listening, during working hours. Be here exactly in time, and we will be waiting for you," they told me. I was in time, and remained there the whole evening.

I remember the conversation. And I remember the fine faces of that man and woman who were speaking to me, and the clearness, the assurance, the conviction—and the intelligence—with which they spoke, knowing thoroughly what they were talking about, and their awareness of the eternity of our Idea. "How can these people 'change' us, 're-educate' us, as they pretend?" said Herr M, referring to the Democrats. "How can they, now that the Führer has given us something to live for, which is at the same time eternal and understandable; something, the truth of which we need no longer 'believe' but can *see*, in all its glowing clearness, with our own eyes? Every turn of events, since 1945, is showing more and more how right we were—how right we *are*, absolutely, everlastingly—be it about the Jewish question, the racial principle, the right of the fittest to rule, or any other point. More Germans admit that we are right, now—in the secrecy of their hearts—than perhaps ever did before. But it is refreshing to know that at least *some* foreigners also continue to uphold the Idea, in spite of our defeat."

"All Aryans should. But when all Germans did not, from the beginning, although they were told the truth, nay, although they had the privilege of having the Führer in their midst, what can one expect of

---

[1] In *Beyond Good and Evil*, §168.

other Aryans, fed on the lies of the Jewish press?"

"That is true enough."

We talked for long hours. And for the thousandth time I compared in my mind this aristocracy of pure blood, which is at the same time an élite of character *and* intelligence—a real élite—with the usually-called "intelligentsia," those idle traders in empty phrases, hair-splitters, reciters of other people's prose, whom I know too well. "What a difference!" I thought.

Herr M introduced me to two people who rank among those who ever made the deepest impression upon me: a middle-aged man, formerly an *Ortsgruppenleiter*[1] and now a martyr of our cause, Herr H,[2] of whom I already spoke a little in another chapter,[3] and a woman in her forties, Fräulein B, also one of the finest National Socialists I know. I was their guest for a couple of days.

I have hardly ever seen even a *genuine* Indian yogi's face as supremely beautiful as that of Herr H—calm; radiating light and strength; loving, in an impersonal manner; all-knowing; a face that looks beyond the stupidity and ugliness of this present day world, not to a dream, not to "an" ideal, but to an unshakable certitude—to Reality; that expresses the clear, almost physical awareness of truth, without hatred, without regret, without fear.

His regular features are those of the purest Aryan. Herr H could hardly have been more handsome even as a young man. But it is not the features alone, it is the features *and* the invisible beaming of that face that cannot fail to impress anyone who is slightly sensitive to the mute language of the man that *is*, as distinct from the man that seems. When I stepped into the room, I immediately felt in the presence of someone by far my superior, as I probably would have before a genuine contemplative saint. I knew from Herr M that Herr H had spent three years in one, or rather in two, of the worst anti-Nazi concentration camps that are to be found in occupied Germany. I knew that he had, there, become a physical wreck. And I was astounded not to read in his face the slightest bitterness, let alone hatred. And when I told him how I felt about the martyrdom of Germany in general, and the persecution of such people as himself in particular, and begged him to tell me something of his experience of the chambers of hell, for my book, he

---

[1] Local group leader—Ed.
[2] Friedrich Horn—Ed.
[3] In Chapter 4, pp. 81-85.

replied that "thousands of others had suffered even much more" than he.

"It is a pity Herr So-and-so is not here," he said. "He is one of those unfortunate SS men who fell into the hands of the Allies in 1945, and was interned for months in Dachau. *He* could tell you something, if you care to gather firsthand information about the atrocities of the Democrats. I shall introduce you to him, when you come back." But I myself fell into the hands of our enemies before I had the time to "come back."

Herr H, who is an architect by profession, showed me some beautiful sketches that he had drawn from life, in the camps where he was a prisoner. One was drawn on a rough piece of yellow paper, with bits of half-burnt coal from the kitchen fire. "We were not given any paper or pencils, in the beginning," he explained to me. And yet the sketch, representing the stables where the internees were accommodated in Schwarzenborn, was executed in a masterly manner. I admired the detached mind—the mind of the real artist—that had guided the hand, in such surroundings, and on the famine diet of which I spoke in former pages. But what I admired the most in Herr H was his serenity; not the serenity of the indifferent or of otherworldly people, but that of a man whose clear vision can discern, under all the horror of darkest Europe, today and yesterday—under that very horror which has crushed his own body, ruined *him*, personally, forever—the irresistible action and reaction of superhuman unseen forces, bound to bring about, sooner or later, the New Order for which we stand; the serenity of a Heathen warrior, who is a sage at the same time.

I have always been convinced that National Socialism is far more able to fulfil the higher aspirations of the Western élite than the ill-adapted religion, imported from Palestine, which Europe has foolishly accepted centuries ago. If there ever was a living proof of that fact, it is Herr H himself.

On the wall, I saw the portrait of an exceedingly handsome youth. Herr H watched me admiring it. It looked like him. It could have been him when he was twenty-five. "You see there my only child," he told me.

"How beautiful he is!" I could not help saying.

"His manly soul was as beautiful as his face," replied the father. "The typical youth of our new Germany. He is dead, now. Died for Germany and for the Idea," he added calmly, and proudly.

And Fräulein B, a faithful old friend of Herr H who was also present, praised the young man in her turn. She had known him well.

So Herr H was all alone. Not only his health, but his only son, too, he had lost for the sake of the great impersonal idea of Greater Germany and of resurrected Aryandom. Alone, and living most precariously in one narrow room with a friend, in the midst of a city in ruins. And, by order of the kind-hearted champions of Democracy and "humanity," not allowed to work as an architect, or to hold any other employment. (His friend was supporting him, with great difficulty.) And yet, he could remain serene and confident, knowing that we *are* right, and that he has done his utmost for the eternal cause of Truth and for that of better mankind—serene and confident, without the help of any supernatural hopes or consolations; without anything to sustain him, but his faith in the immutable Laws of Life, in the divine mission of his country, in Adolf Hitler, the Führer of the Aryan world for all times to come, whether his people, *now*, be defeated or not. Verses of the Bhagavad-Gita—that age-old masterpiece of the Aryan genius—came back to my memory: "Thy business is with the action alone, never with its fruits. So let not the fruits of action be thy motive,"[1] and, "without attachment, constantly perform that action which is duty, for by performing action without attachment, man verily reacheth the Supreme,"[2] and, "the wise should act without attachment, desiring nothing but the welfare of the world."[3] And side by side, I recalled the golden words written in the same spirit by our Führer—the words which I was destined, two months later, to quote before my judges, at Düsseldorf: "Our thoughts and actions must not be determined by the approval or condemnation of our epoch, but only by our firm adhesion to a Truth that we recognise."[4]

I told Herr H and Fräulein B what I was thinking.

"Yes," said Herr H, "the old and the new expressions of it are bound to be alike, for the truth upon which our *Weltanschauung* is built, is everlasting." He went to a corner of the room, and started displacing a number of things in order to get out and show me the copy of *Mein Kampf* which he kept hidden there. While he was doing this, Fräulein B showed me a lovely portrait of the Führer carved out in a pendant of transparent, glass-like material. I took the little object piously in my hand, and gazed at it. I know the price of such remembrances of the

---

[1] Bhagavad-Gita, 2:47.
[2] *Ibid*, 3:19.
[3] *Ibid*, 3:25.
[4] ". . . unser Denken und Handeln soll keineswegs von Beifall oder Ablehnung unserer Zeit bestimmt werden, sondern von der Verpflichtung an eine Wahrheit, die wir erkannten" (*Mein Kampf*, II, ii, p. 435; cf. Mannheim, p. 394).

glorious times, in Germany today. They are nowhere to be found, save in the possession of people who appreciate them. I was therefore all the more touched when Fräulein B told me, "It is yours; you can keep it." I was overjoyed at the idea of keeping it. But I guessed she had only that one. "And still you give it to me," I said, "although you met me but an hour ago!"

"You are worthy of it," she replied; "that, I know."

"May I never fail to remain so, forever and ever!" said I, as I pressed the portrait to my lips, as a sacred thing.

I thanked Fräulein B from the bottom of my heart for her present, and for the spontaneous confidence she had shown me.

"What makes you think so highly of me?" I could not help asking her, after a while. She replied: "The fact that you too are a born Heathen, like Herr H and like myself." And she uttered the self-same words which I had so many times uttered in the course of these twenty years; the self-same words which I have repeated in this book because I am more and more convinced of their truth: "Only a thorough Aryan Heathen can make a real National Socialist."

I wore the pendant ever since, and am wearing it now, in prison.[1]

We spent the remainder of the day commenting upon some of the most beautiful passages of *Mein Kampf*—of which Herr H had produced his hidden copy—and I tried to show how amazingly true the main thesis of the book (the racial thesis) appears to me in the light of the little history of the wide world, ancient and modern, which I happen to know. But it is my interpretation of Christianity as "the subtlest Jewish snare ever held out to the Aryan" which bound me the most tightly to Fräulein B.

"Do you know," said she, "that even as a child I refused to sing the church hymns that alluded to Jehovah or to Israel, on the ground that I was a German and wanted no foreign religion forced upon me? How I understand your nostalgia for the Olympian Gods as well as for your mother's old Norse ones! How I do!"

"I am glad you do," I replied. "Only other National Socialists like ourselves have ever understood how important a part that yearning has played in my whole evolution. But fancy that the exact opposite of our attitude is to be found among some European Aryans! Have you heard of a religious sect in England whose members style themselves as 'British Israelites'?"

---

[1] The pendant was later discovered and destroyed while Savitri was imprisoned at Werl (*Defiance*, p. 548).—Ed.

"No."

"Well, such a sect exists. The adherents, mind you, are *not* Jews—although some, of course, might be mixed. But I know of some who are thoroughbred Englishmen—Celts and Anglo-Saxons; Aryans. Only they try to prove—by the most spurious arguments—that they and the whole English nation are descended from some 'lost tribe' of Israel. Pure-blooded Aryans trying to make out that they are Jews; wanting to be Jews! Have you ever heard of such disgraceful nonsense as that?"

"Well," put in Herr H, "they have been taught for over 1,500 years that the Jews are 'God's chosen people.' Can you blame them? As you say yourself, the original crime lies in the adoption of Christianity."

"The one before the last of the *Twenty-Five Points*," said I, "although it states that the Party as such stands for 'a positive Christianity,' advocates 'liberty for all religious denominations in the state, *so long as they are not a danger to it, and do not militate against the moral feelings of the Germanic race.*" Alfred Rosenberg has tried to explain what 'positive' Christianity means, and it appears to me that he has just reduced it to that basic commonsense morality which any Aryan can accept. But few people seem to be fully aware of all that is implied in the two reservations mentioned in that Point Twenty-Four: 'any religion . . . *so far as* it is not a danger to the state and does not militate against the moral feelings of the Germanic race.' Is *any* religion that allows marriage between its adherents *irrespective* of race, compatible with the existence of a State run according to National Socialist standards? And can one say that a religion that teaches that man is born in sin, and that exalts meekness and unending forgiveness as virtues, does not 'militate against the moral feelings' of any healthy race, let alone of the Germanic one? I wish to goodness I had been here in the great days; I would have stressed this point before those who were the most conscious of all the mischief Christianity has wrought in the world, and who happened to be at the same time in the Führer's entourage. I would have tried, at least."

"And they would have understood you, no doubt, and agreed with you wholeheartedly," said Herr H. "But they could have done nothing about it *yet*: the time was not ripe. As for the Party as such standing for 'a positive Christianity' which, as you say, Rosenberg took so much trouble to explain, the best explanation for it is just that it *was not* possible to put it otherwise in February 1920. There was plenty of all-important work awaiting us, which could well be done whatever people chose to think about religion. To attract public attention upon the enormousness of our revolution in the religious and philosophical domain *also* would have been disastrous at that stage of the struggle. It would have stirred doubts and caused trouble. But after victory was secured and our régime solidly established, we would have gradually brought up the new generations to think for themselves and to realise how incompatible Christianity is, as it stands, with our ideals. However, we lost the war, and thus have to wait still a little longer for this awakening. But it will come, be sure of that. It will come, for our Führer has not come in vain."

Reluctantly, after two days, I took leave of these new friends. I did not know that I was not to see them again for a long time. We greeted each other: "Heil Hitler!"

"By the way," said Fräulein B, "do you know how one is to say *that* in public without being detected?"

"Yes, I do," I replied. And I repeated the formula which *means* the same to all those of us who use it, but s*ounds* just empty nonsense to the uninitiated that might be listening.

"So you know it too."

"Who does not? Fräulein E told me, thinking she was telling me something new. But someone else had already told me last year. I am longing to see those days when we shall be free to greet one another as we please, in public as well as among ourselves."

"Yes; so am I. And those days will come; our intensity of purpose will bring them back—our selfless action, guided by a one-pointed will. For the time, let us wait. Heil Hitler!"

"Heil Hitler!"

* * *

I could speak of other representatives of that Aryan élite in which I salute the forerunner of a higher—healthier, stronger, better, more beautiful—mankind, and the hope of the world. For I have met many more in the course of these few months. And I have come in contact with one or two here, in this prison, among the political prisoners—in spite of all efforts on the part of the authorities to keep me apart from them—and . . . strange as this might seem, among the members of the German staff also. (These are not "supposed" to have anything in common with our Ideology. But many more people share it than the authorities think, among those who are the least expected to.) However, the few instances which I gave, especially the two last ones, are enough to illustrate what I mean by an all-round *élite*.

Almost the only Aryans today within the pale of the Indian caste system, the Brahmins, are styled by the members of the other castes as "*bhu-deva*," or "gods on earth." Some of them, but extremely few, are worthy of that title. It is here, in ruined Germany, among the genuine National Socialists of the dark days of trial, that I have met men and women who are, in the full sense of these words, glowing instances of the eternal greatness of *the* master race—living "gods on earth."

I have often tried to imagine what our world would look like if National Socialism, rising again, were not only to hold its own in Europe but to dominate the whole planet, for centuries. Along with an absolute separation of races, there would be an accepted racial hierarchy, the purest Aryans being naturally at the top, in other words a "caste system" extending to the whole of mankind—"each man in his place" according to the divine decree of Nature, the will of the Sun, to quote one of the oldest hymns that can be ascribed to any individual author with certainty[1]; something like that which we see in India to this day, but on a far wider scale and—if Germans or any other Northern Europeans are to manage the world—something infinitely better organised. And no more of those international religions of equality but a worldwide return to the different national heathendoms with, at the most, above them all—uniting not merely all human beings, but all life, each creature at its level—the worship of the Life force embodied in the Sun. How I would welcome such a world! And when I recall that splendid German National Socialist minority which I love and admire, I cannot help wishing, from the bottom of my heart, to see it one day rule the earth in its length and breadth. More than ever now, it is worthy to rule. More than ever now it is worthy to be called, by the rest of mankind, a minority of "*bhu-deva*"—"gods on earth."

---

[1] The Longer Hymn to the Sun by Pharaoh Akhnaton of Egypt, circa 1,400 BC.

Chapter 10

Divine Vengeance

"Figure-toi Pyrrhus, les yeux étincelants,
Entrant à la lueur de nos palais brûlants,
Sur tous mes frères morts se faisant un passage,
Et de sang tout convert, échauffant le carnage.
Songe aux cris des vainqueurs; songs aux cris des mourants,
Dans la flamme étouffés, sous le fer expirants."

—Jean Racine[1]

"Was folgte, waren entsetzliche Tage und noch bösere Nächte—ich wußte, daß alles verloren war. Auf die Gnade des Feindes zu hoffen konnten höchstens Narren fertigbringen oder—Lügner and Verbrecher. In diesen Nächten wuchs mir der Haß, der Haß gegen die Urheber dieser Tat."

—Adolf Hitler[2]

It was in Bonn on the Rhine, hardly more than a week before my arrest.

I had walked into a café to have a cup of hot coffee, and especially to find a relatively peaceful corner in which I could sit and write, undisturbed as long as the owner of the place would allow me to stay. And there, I made the acquaintance of a comrade unlike most of those whom I had met up till then, in Germany or elsewhere; of an awe-inspiring elemental force in human garb—a typical beer hall "tough."

He was sitting at a table drinking with another man. I could not help

---

[1] "Imagine Pyrrhus, with his flashing eyes
Bright in the blazing of our royal halls,
Hacking his way over my brother's bodies,
Bloody himself, cheering bloodshed on;
Imagine all the clamour—victor's cries
And cries of those that died, by flame, by sword."

(Jean Racine, *Andromaque*, Act III, Scene 8, in *Four Greek Plays: Andromanche, Iphigenia, Phaedra, Athaliah*, trans. R.C. Knight [Cambridge: Cambridge University Press, 1982], p. 34.)

[2] "There followed terrible days and even worse nights—I knew that all was lost. Only consummate fools could manage to hope for the mercy of the enemy—or liars and criminals. In these nights hatred grew in me, hatred for the perpetrators of this deed." (*Mein Kampf*, I, vii, p. 225; cf. Mannheim, p. 206) [Trans. by Ed.].

noticing him as I walked in. He looked like one of Hermann's warriors disguised in shabby modern workman's clothes. His head and shoulders were those of an aurochs of the Germanic forests of old. In his pale, greyish-blue eyes shining under bushy eyebrows; in his broad forehead; in his red square face, in his thick mouth, half-hidden under a fiery blond moustache, and in his powerful chin there was strength, and will, and thoughtfulness too, no doubt. But not the will and thoughtfulness of "a" man—of an *individual*; rather those of a whole multitude just awakening to consciousness; of a mighty, primitive, silent, invincible multitude of which he was the mouthpiece.

The other man, with more regular features but a far less expressive face; better dressed, and less boisterous—less "barbaric"—looked, by his side, like an individual; an average individual of the dying world of today. In this rough one, lived the soul of the ancient Hercynian Forest, and the soul of the happy German factories of the days of resurrection; "the old and the new," I thought; "the Germany that never died."

I much wished to talk to the man. But, of course, I did not. I only sat as near as I could to his table instead of taking a place in the corner. I ordered a coffee, took out my things, and started scribbling the beginning of a paragraph. It is the man who talked to me—as though his instinct had told him he should.

"Writing your school task, Madam?" he called out to me after a while, over the heads of half a dozen other customers. I looked up and smiled.

"I am too old to write school tasks; am I not?" said I, jokingly.

"Then, it must be love letters," replied the man. I laughed, this time, wholeheartedly.

"Goodness no!" said I. "I never wrote love letters. It is only a book."

"Oh, oh, a book! What sort of a book?"

And without giving me time to answer, he asked again: "Do you mind if we come and sit at your table?"

"Surely not. You are both welcome."

So the two men got up, took their beer with them, and sat by me. As they were coming, I could see that the one who had spoken to me was as tall as I had presumed. But one of his legs was maimed. The aurochs was a wounded one. And there was, to me, something heartrending in the sight of that huge strong body that had been broken.

"What are you drinking with us? A glass of beer?" said the man, as he and his companion sat down.

"With thanks."

"And now," he continued, "tell us what your book is about."

"Germany today," I replied.

At once the expression changed on the rough, red, square face. In the man's eyes, I read an earnestness that had not been there before.

"Were you here in the beautiful time—before the war?" he asked me.

"Alas no. I wish I had been," said I. "But I was not."

"If you have never seen *those* grand days, then you cannot realise all the difference with now. And you cannot write about present day Germany."

The man was probably right, I thought. And once more, as I recalled in a flash those glories that I have not seen, my heart ached with a feeling of inexpiable guilt. Once more, the knife had been thrust into the old wound. Yes, why had I come so late?

I looked at the man sadly and said: "It is true that I was not here then. I have never seen either the magnificent yearly Party rallies, or the parades of the Hitler Youth through the streets; nor have I heard the Führer's own voice address the German people (save on the wireless). All these years, I was ten thousand kilometres away—in India. But I have studied the Movement as much as one can from far. And I also had, directly, ample news from here that most people were not lucky enough to have. My husband was the owner and editor of the only National Socialist periodical in India, *The New Mercury*, a fortnightly publication to which every German in the country was to subscribe, by order of the German Consulate in Calcutta. The magazine was banned as early as 1937." (I could say that much without betraying anybody's secrets or my own; for these were all known facts.)

The man gazed at me with immensely increased interest. His eyes sparkled.

"Oh, oh," said he, to his companion, "have you heard this? By Jove, it is worth hearing!"

And, turning to me before the other one had had time to put in a word, he said: "Of course, in that case, it is a little different. You are not one of those foreigners who come over here either to exploit us or to pity us—a plague on them! And even if you had not the privilege of being here in the grand days, you know the truth."

"Don't I!"

"And you tell the truth, in that book of yours?"

"I hope I do."

"And what is your dominant impression of Germany as you see it today? Do you like us?"

"I admire you," I replied, with the spontaneity of conviction: "I admire you—the real, faithful Germans, I mean—even more than I did in glorious '40; even more than I did in '42, when I was waiting to welcome your armies in Delhi after what I had expected to be a triumphal march through Russia."

The man's face brightened into a most sympathetic smile.

"You are right," he said, "quite right. We are good people: hard-working, honest, kind, and peace-loving. We never wanted this war. It is those swine from abroad who forced it upon us. You know that, don't you? And we would have won, too. For although we love peace, we fight well, when we must. We would have won, had it not been for the traitors."

"I know. Three times the Führer offered England an honourable peace, and his collaboration in the building of a happy Europe. And three times she refused—obeying the orders of her masters, the Jews. I know it is no fault of yours. And . . . can I speak still more frankly? Will your friend here have no objection?" I said, alluding to the other man sitting at our table.

"He? Surely not. He is an old comrade. With us you are perfectly safe." I hoped I was. One never knows. But I spoke.

"I can never get accustomed to the sight of the ruins." said I. "Wherever I go, they cry out to me the story of the martyrdom of the great nation that could have arrested the decline of the superior races; saved the whole world. And the more I think of that, the more I hate those who, in or outside Germany, have worked to bring about the disaster."

"You mean the Jews?"

"The Jews, undoubtedly. But still more, those Aryans who believed the Jewish lies, or who allied themselves to the forces of international Jewry for petty motives of their own; all those who, in or outside Germany, betrayed National Socialism or fought it openly."

"And of all, whom do you hate the most?"

"The traitors of whom you yourself spoke a while ago: those who, in spite of being pure-blooded Germans, have secretly worked against the Führer during this war and who, now, sit in high positions, thanks to the conquerors' protection."

"Good! Well said! Yes, those are the rascals that must go first, when the day of reckoning comes."

"I am waiting for that day."

"And I! And not only I—millions!"

And the man's eyes suddenly hardened, and I saw in them a flash of ferocity—which I welcomed. "At last," thought I, "here is someone with whom I need not bother to moderate my style. Here is someone who will follow me to the end; someone whom the sight of that deep-seated Mediterranean barbarity of mine—that lingering trace of the immemorial non-Aryans who flourished before the Greeks and Latins on the shores of the Inner Sea—would not frighten; a Northerner who, once stirred, could match any Southern European in cold-blooded violence."

And I smiled.

* * *

The man swallowed his glass of beer, ordered another one, and then turned again to me.

"So you have seen what those rascals have done to our poor country, haven't you?"

"I have seen Hamburg," I replied; "I have seen Hanover, Frankfurt, Essen, Cologne, Koblenz, Saarbrücken; I have seen Stuttgart and Ulm. And I know the towns of the Russian Zone—Berlin, Dresden, and the others—are in the same state; that it is everywhere the same."

"Have you seen Düren?"

"No."

"It is my native town. Not far from here. Between Cologne and Aix-la-Chapelle. Can you imagine how many innocent people, men, women, and children, they killed there in one single night with their confounded phosphorus bombs? Twenty-two thousand! And not killed outright, mind you. No, but burnt alive—stuck, and literally frizzled to death, in the melting tar of the streets all ablaze, all but a few. I was there—on leave from the army—and had a narrow escape. I *saw* that hell with my own eyes, and will never forget it. It was on the 16th of November 1944. You should see the place now: a heap of ruins. Like the rest of Germany."

"I will never forget," he again said, after a pause: "and never forgive."

And again, I caught in his eyes that flash of elemental ferocity.

I smiled faintly, recalling in my mind the ever-vivid memory of my first journey through Germany, of my first glimpse of those ruins of whole cities, and of my appeal to the implacable Force Who rules the Universe with mathematical harmony—to the Inaccessible One,[1] deaf to the voice of pious fear or tardy remorse: "Mother of Destruction,

---

[1] Durga, one of the names of the Nature Goddess, both creative and destructive, means in Sanskrit "inaccessible."

avenge this country!"

"Yes," said I, to the man, in a most sincere outburst of feelings very similar to his although they sprang from a different source, "I too shall never forgive those rascals their cruelty and their vile hypocrisy; their sitting as judges over so-called 'war criminals,' at Nuremberg, after having themselves done *this*—as though *this* were not a war crime far more horrible than all their alleged charges against National Socialism. I shall never forgive them their smugness, their pretences of righteousness, their lies about 'justice' and 'liberty' coupled with their fanatical mania of 're-educating' all those who do not believe as they do. Who are *they* to re-educate people, anyhow? Who are they to talk of morals, and 'humanity' and what not?"

"So you hate them just as I do, don't you?"

"Yes, just as you do—if not still more."

"But you say you were in India. You have not suffered what we have suffered here. You have not seen *that* hell."

"No; but I thought of it all the time. It haunted me. I travelled from place to place not to think of it, and could not. And then came that nauseating trial—that crime, if there ever has been one. As soon as I came back to Europe, I heard them congratulating one another over it, as though it had been an act of justice—the swine! And that is not all. The savage destruction of that National Socialist Germany which I had looked up to for twenty years; the hanging of the finest men of Europe as "war criminals," even *that* fades away before the one thought which I can never cast aside: the thought of what they *would have done* to my Führer himself—the one among my contemporaries whom I have ever worshipped—if they had been able to lay hands upon him. I shudder at the idea . . ."

"Yes; the devils!" replied the man. And his eyes blazed. "But," he added in a whisper, to be heard of me alone. "Don't fear: *he* is alive—and in excellent health."

"I know," said I.

"And *he is* coming back," continued the man, in a still lower whisper. "When the Day of divine Vengeance dawns, you will see him."

"Perhaps—if the Gods judge me worthy," I replied. And my face beamed. "See him! See him at the head of the promised Last Battalion—the 'Third Power'"—said I, recalling both spoken and printed words that had given me new life and new impetus, even after my coming to Germany. "But where is that mysterious 'Third Power'? Do you know?"

The man's eyes took on an expression of superhuman ferocious joy. His face became beautiful and terrible, like that of a war god of old. "*I* am the 'Third Power,'" said he, with exultation, without even caring this time to lower his voice; "I am the Last Battalion; I am the divine Vengeance that will descend upon those rascals like the lightning, and finish them forever—both the Western lot and the Eastern lot, which is even worse; I, and millions like me. Don't expect it from abroad. No, it is here—unseen, unsuspected, but waiting, ready to strike at the first signal. It is here, and it will come from here. It will rise out of Germany's own soil, from a thousand places at a time, like the lava of a thousand volcanoes, that nobody can hold back, and it will roll all over Europe in waves of flame and fire before they have time to turn around. The hatred of the Nation who had done no harm to them, and whom they have tortured and humiliated, gagged, and robbed and cut to pieces—and reviled—in the sole hope that they would enjoy the earth alone; that hatred is the 'Third Power,' I tell you. There is no other."— "And we need no other," he added, emptying his glass, "That will finish them."

"Unless the atom bomb finishes the whole earth before," put in the other man sitting at our table. It was the first time I had heard him say something.

"The atom bomb will do a good deal of our dirty work for us," replied the first speaker. "Don't worry, my friend; the swine will use it on each other without bothering to waste it on us—it is too expensive. We will only step into their game when they imagine they are about to end it. And watch then, what happens, atom bomb or no atom bomb! Watch, for it will be worth seeing. Not like 1940, oh no! Much better!"

And his heavy shoulders shook with a loud, defiant laughter. And his eyes gleamed with that ferocious joy that *I* am said to radiate, at times, when speaking or thinking of our enemies' future abasement. I was looking at him with the admiring interest of a beautiful woman looking at herself in a mirror. Yes, that rough, uncouth, outspoken man would understand my indignation at the thought of all the sufferings imposed upon those who think and feel as I do. He would never tell me—or tell others—that I am "awful." What a relief to meet such a one after three years of contact with squeamish humanitarians of all degrees of falsity!

The man ordered three more glasses of beer, insisting that I should have one too, and then pursued:

"Much better, yes! I was then in France, with the army. I marched down the streets of Paris and under their famous 'Arc de Triomphe.'

Those were splendid days. I marched right through the country, down to the Spanish frontier. I enjoyed myself. We all did. We ate. We drank. We had a fine time. Grand days, I tell you! But we behaved as gentlemen. We did harm to nobody. More still: our iron discipline protected the vanquished against possible excesses on our part. In Lyons, I saw one of our soldiers shot for having helped himself to a wristwatch adorned with diamonds, in one of their shops. We kept order among ourselves. And we brought order to the countries we ruled. We were generous and merciful to the conquered—until, of course, they started killing us by the dozen in the streets, after sunset, for nothing at all. Then, we just had to take steps. Who would not have? We lost the war. Many of us failed to get out of France as quickly as we would have liked to, and fell prisoners to the French. I was one among them—and wounded. You should have seen how they treated us! Worse than pigs!"

"I have heard accounts from other prisoners, especially from some of those who had served in the Waffen SS, and who happened to be captured at that time," said I.

"Yes, those—our finest boys—they handled worse than any account can possibly describe. How many of them never came back from their hellish concentration camps or their slave labour settlements in the middle of Africa? How many of them, after being 'liberated,' were forced to sign contracts for years of service in their 'foreign legion,' and sent off to Indo-China and other places to die of tropical diseases? God only knows. But set *them* aside. We fared badly enough, we common soldiers of the *Wehrmacht*. I would tell you all that I went through personally, if this place were not closing at three o'clock and if it were not now nearly a quarter to three.

"Well, they kept me till the end of 1948. It is only three months since I came back home. And the oppression I have seen here—whatever be the 'zone'—I don't believe the world has ever seen before; not in Europe, at any rate. Nice ones to talk of 'liberty' and 'justice,' these damned Democrats! They have tied us down, hand and foot, so that we cannot move; and gagged us, so that we cannot protest, while they plunder our country right and left, carry away our factories piece by piece, cut down all our woods, take our coal, our iron, our steel, whatever we have, and make people believe, on the top of it all, that we are the cause of the war—the confounded liars!

"But I tell you, the day of reckoning is coming; that grand day that you and I, and our friend sitting here, and thousands of others are awaiting; the day when we shall see those Johnnies run for their lives, in every 'zone' whichever it be, and curse their destiny for ever having brought them to Germany; the day when you will see the 'Third Power' at work; when *I* shall be in Paris once more. But I shall not be the same man. And Paris will be in ruins. So will many other places that we spared this time. We will spare nothing and nobody, next time. We will show these rascals what the kind, peaceable, harmless Germans *can* become, when exasperated by years of inhuman treatment. Yes, they used to call us '*sales Boches*,' and we just laughed, as one laughs at children's naughty pranks. This time, we will not laugh. Oh, no! I, at least, will not laugh!"

And suddenly raising his voice, and rolling before me eyes that *were* those of a wounded wild beast maddened with pain, or those of a Stone Age war god athirst for blood—inspired eyes, in which the lust of murder (as old and as strong as the lust of copulation) shone in all its barbaric splendour—he said: "I shall spare none of these bastards, this time, when I go back as a conqueror. But I shall cut the throat of each and every one I catch, do you hear?—*like that*" (and, in a horrible gesture, he passed the back of his hand across his own throat three or four times) "and I shall watch their eyes beg me for mercy, and shall remain as deaf as stone and as hard as stone; I shall watch life slowly leaving them while I look straight into their faces, until the end. And that will still be kindness, compared with what I have seen them do to us, in 1944 and 1945."

I gazed at that outburst of elemental fury in a man of my own race and of my own ideals, with that mixed feeling of religious awe and elation that had once possessed me while I stood on the slippery deck of a ship, in the midst of a storm on the North Sea, or by one of the lava streams at night on the slopes of erupting Mount Hekla.

I half closed my eyes, and smiled to bitter memories which, one day—I now knew—would seem to me like the recollection of a nightmare in the glory of daylight: the tragedy of Nuremberg; the tragedy of all Germany in ruins; and all the horror of the relentless persecution of National Socialism, of which I had seen a little, and heard a lot more. And I remembered that I had called for divine Vengeance, during my very first journey through the martyred Land. "Goddess colour of the stormy Ocean and colour of the starry night, Dark Blue One, Mother of Destruction," I thought, as I looked at the frightful face in front of me, "hast Thou answered my call? Art Thou Thyself gazing at me through these ferocious eyes, promising me Thy slow, exact, passionless vengeance, for all those I love?"

I recalled in my mind Hekla's thick lava, moving at the rate of three meters a day, and burning everything on its way. Equally slow was the gradual swelling of that mighty ocean of hatred against the persecutors of all I stood for; equally slow, and equally irresistible, and equally indiscriminate in its divine, impersonal destructiveness. But that ocean was conscious, to some extent. Through each one of its molecules, it could speak to me—as it did now—and I could speak to it. It understood me. For, although I stood above it, when I liked, I still was, myself, a part of it, and knew its language, and could make its rolling waves rise and rush forth at my voice.

I held out my hand to the terrible, simple-hearted "tough," and smiled once more—not merely, this time, to the abstract idea of divine vengeance, but *to him*. "Right!" said I, "quite right! Oh, you don't know how much I am in sympathy with you! But don't forget to 'liquidate' these damned anti-Nazis out here, before you proceed to chastise the outer world. They are the first cause of the loss of the war, and the originators of all Germany's sufferings."

"Certainly! You don't imagine that we are going to leave any of these traitors behind, do you? No fear! They will get what they deserve all right."

But the man's eyes softened as he took my hand in his big, rough, strong hands. He looked at me with a face in which the murderous expression had completely vanished, giving way to a frank, kind, almost affectionate smile. And, turning to his comrade, he said—while still holding my hand in his—"I like this woman. She speaks the truth."

"And writes it!" I replied, laughing.

"Yes, I had forgotten about your book."

"I am not speaking only of my book," said I. "I am speaking of *these*. Now I know that you will not betray me, I suppose I can show you one—and give you one (or more) if you are interested . . ."

And I produced from my bag a paper about twelve inches long by eight inches wide, one of the five thousand leaflets—my latest supply—of which I had already distributed the greatest number. "But," said I, "be careful that nobody sees you reading it."

"That's all right! Don't fear."

He unfolded it, saw the large swastika filling about a quarter of the page. "Oh oh! Here is something!" he said. He cleverly turned over the portion of the paper bearing the sacred, and now most dangerous Sign and read the printed writing:

German people,
What have the Democracies brought you?

During the war, phosphorus and fire.
After the war, hunger; humiliation; oppression;
> dismantling of the factories;
> destruction of the forests;
> and now—the Ruhr Statute!

But, "Slavery is not to last much longer."
Our Führer is alive, and will soon come back with untold power.
Resist our persecutors!
Hope and wait.
>> Heil Hitler!
>>> S.D.

"By Jove, it is true—could not be more true!" said the man. "And you wrote that?"

"Yes."

"And what does 'S.D.' mean?"

"My initials, standing for Savitri Devi. My full name is Savitri Devi Mukherji."

The man laughed, "Written and signed, eh! That's splendid." "You can have a look at this," he added, turning to his friend and handing the paper over to him. And to me, he said in a whisper: "It is a dangerous game you are playing, my dear lady. Beautiful, but dangerous. Only pray you don't get 'pinched' one of these days. And now . . . another glass of beer, won't you?"

"But . . ."

"Yes, yes, you must have one; to the success of your mission; to the return of the great days; to *his* return . . ."

"Right."

"Waiter, three more beers!"

"But we are closing," said the waiter.

"Never mind! Come along! It will not take five minutes."

The waiter hurried back. The man paid. We lifted our glasses, speaking in a low voice:

"To the destruction of the enemy!"

"To the resurrection of Germany!"

"To Adolf Hitler, *Weltführer!*"

I felt tears rising to my eyes as I uttered these words, recalling in my mind the happy time when I was expecting to see the German army break through at Stalingrad, and march through High Asia into India, along the old Conquerors' Way, uniting the whole of the Aryan world.

"What are you thinking about?" the man asked me.

"About the glorious days."

"They will come back," said he, putting one hand on my shoulder; "Or rather, I should say, greater days will come; the New Order but . . . no traitors this time, and no Jews."

The waiter came up to us, "We are closing," he said; "I am sorry."

"Would you like to have more of my papers?" I asked the two men.

"I would like a couple of them," replied the one who had hardly spoken up till now. I gave him a few.

"How many have you got?" asked the other man.

"I do not know. I had, originally, five thousand. But I have distributed quite a number already. I might have a few hundreds left."

"Five thousand are very few for all Germany," said he. "Use them sparingly. This one you gave me is enough. A thousand people will read it. Dozens will copy it and distribute it in their turn."

We got up. We shook hands.

"By the way," the man said at last to me, "I did not think of asking you your nationality. In spite of your foreign accent, I completely forgot you are not a German. What are you?"

"An Aryan," I replied with a smile. "Is that not sufficient?"

"Yes, it is." The man also smiled.

"Heil Hitler!" said I, in a whisper, as we parted, without daring to lift my arm in salute, as we were in a public place.

"Heil Hitler!" replied the two men.

* * *

Since then, I have often recalled the more than human force concentrated in that man; the bitterness, the resentment, the hatred of a whole people that has suffered beyond measure, and that he embodies. Yes, *that* is the force we will let loose upon this half-ruined continent, next time.

Vox populi, vox Dei. That rough, sincere German, fundamentally good but roused to murderous violence by excess of foul treatment, *is* the German people. Through his voice, the blood of the unknown thousands of Germans martyred for the love of the Nazi Idea since 1945, cries for vengeance. It *is* a divine voice. In it, rings the spell that will bring down the whole structure both of Democracy and of Communism. Nothing can silence it, nor weaken its magic power.

Chapter 11

THE CONSTRUCTIVE SIDE

"Denn was hier verkündet werden mußte, war eine neue
Weltanschauung, und nicht eine neue Wahlparole."

—Adolf Hitler[1]

"Der Nationalsozialismus ist eine Weltanschauung, die in schärfster
Opposition zu der heutigen Welt des Kapitalismus und seiner
marxistischen und bürgerlichen Trabanten steht."
—Gottfried Feder[2]

Carved out in Pentelicus marble above the Ionic colonnade of the "Gennadios Library," in modern Athens, one can read the words: "Hellenes are all those who share our culture." I do not remember and have not, here in prison, the opportunity to find out which not exceedingly ancient Greek internationalist first wrote that foolish sentence. But I am pretty sure it is the utterance of one of those many—far *too* many—idle thinkers, improperly styled "philosophers," of the Alexandrian or perhaps even of the Roman period, *i.e.*, of the time Pagan Greece was already decadent. No Greek of the classical days would have been so silly as to believe that any human being, provided he could speak Greek and quote Greek poets, and exhibit Greek manners and acquired tastes, could be called a Hellene. Even the rough, illiterate, but intelligent and manly Greeks of the darkest days of all in the evolution of the Greek people—the days of the Turkish domination—knew better than that, for they were anything but decadent. Unfortunately, it is not classical Greece, but that internationalised, levantinised, brilliant but enervated Greece of Hellenistic and still later times that influenced Rome, and, through Rome, Europe. And, unfortunately also, in addition to this unhealthy influence, came a still more pernicious

---

[1] "For what had to be proclaimed here was a new worldview, not a new election slogan" (Adolf Hitler, *Mein Kampf*, I, ix, p. 243; cf. Mannheim, p. 223).

[2] "National Socialism is a worldview that stands in sharpest opposition to the present-day world of capitalism and its Marxist and bourgeois satellites" (Gottfried Feder, *Das Programm der NSDAP and seine weltanschaulichen Grundgedanken* (Munich: Franz Eher, 1932), p. 64) [Trans. by Ed.].

one, namely that of Christianity. Still more pernicious, I say, for in the new religion, the false doctrine of the equal possibilities of all men was not only broadened, but strengthened; sanctioned on the ground of alleged superhuman authority.

It is no wonder that, when Europe ceased to be pious without ceasing to be foolish, she started seeking for the equivalent of that equalitarian inspiration which Christianity had so long given her, once more in decaying Hellenistic thought. America followed Europe, with a vengeance. Of all possible quotations from ancient Greek thinkers, the one that the super-Democrats of the New World found the most fit to figure above the pillars of the Library of the Archaeological School run by them in Athens, is precisely the one which I recalled at the beginning of this chapter. An anticipation, I suppose, in their minds; and an encouragement, also. From the depth of a past that is not very remote, but that *looks* so, in the eyes of a hotchpotch community hardly two hundred years old, the voice of the Greek-speaking internationalist (who might have been anything but a pure Greek himself, if he lived at the time I presume) tells them: "Yes, provided he has become familiar with the works of Homer, Aeschylus, and Plato, even a 'Yank' can become 'a Hellene'—somewhat as a Pole, or an Armenian, even a Jew, settled in the USA, who speaks English, reads American papers and American novels, and enjoys American films, becomes 'an American.' Why not? It is culture that makes nationality. In other words, it is what one knows and what one is accustomed to think that makes what one is."

Christianity—as all other-worldly religions based upon revelation—had gone a step further. It had set up the idea that it is what one believes that determines, finally, what one is. And still today, strictly speaking, in the Christian conception, community of culture itself is overshadowed by the idea of common allegiance to moral and metaphysical dogmas. *Any* man, provided he believes in salvation through Jesus Christ with all its implications, is—in theory at least—according to it, to be treated as the equal of any other man who believes the same, to the extent that he can marry and give his children in marriage in that other man's family, whatever be his race and the state of his health. Culture comes second. But I say: "In theory at least"; for, to most people, it is still a real or supposed "community of culture" that is the more important factor of Democratic equality. Community of religious beliefs comes in, with pious individuals, as a part of the cultural link.

But, if Christianity never succeeded in uniting all men and mixing all races on the basis of common beliefs about the other world—if, for instance, to this day, it has not been able to break down the colour bar in the countries where it exists—its slow and steady influence has succeeded in making many of those who believe in "equality through culture" extend to all mankind, even to obviously inferior races, the possibility of sharing with the Aryan, sooner or later, "a common culture." This distorted attitude is at the back of the deplorable mania of "educating the natives," of the most non-Aryan colonial countries, along European lines. And I repeat: no man of Aryan blood could probably ever have brought himself to believe—as our Democrats and Communists do—that *any* people (of whatever race) can, "through education," imbibe the modern culture of Western Europe, if centuries of Christianity had not subconsciously prepared him to do so, by teaching his fathers that all *souls* are equal in the eyes of the Christian God, and that souls count, not bodies.

The fact that, by civil as well as, in the case of coreligionists, by religious law, everywhere in the world save in caste-ridden India, in primitive societies admitting strict sexual "taboos," and in countries in which an effective colour bar exists, anybody can marry anybody, only proves how powerfully the great international religions of equality—Christianity and Islam, both sprung from Judaism—have prepared the ground for the modern Democratic outlook, the logical outcome of which is, ultimately, Communism. The most democratic and cosmopolitan ancient Greek, for whom Hellenism meant just Hellenic culture, detached from Hellenic nationality and race, would never have gone to that length. He would never have admitted that a Chinese, for instance (highly civilised as he may be, in his own style) or an African, could "participate in Greek culture" however well he might be able to quote Homer by heart. And he would have been shocked at some of the marriages that take place in modern Europe. Humanity has greatly degenerated since the influence of Jewry—through Christianity, in the whole world, and through Islam, in the Near and Middle East and in Africa—has added itself, on an unprecedented scale, to the already existing forces of disintegration. But the root of the decay lies in the attitude expressed in the old sentence which I quoted above, *i.e.*, in the attitude that consists of underestimating or altogether neglecting the basic physical factor in culture as well as in nationality. What one knows, and even what one seems generally to think and to do, does *not* determine in any way what one is. On the contrary, it is one's physical background that determines one's intellectual and moral tendencies and the real meaning of what one thinks and does and chooses to remember or forget. And more than one's economical or geographical *milieu,* one's physical background is one's total ancestry—one's race; one's blood.

The Founder of National Socialism came, first and foremost, to remind the world of this forgotten, but all-important truth; to destroy the dangerous illusion that has misled Western consciousness ever since the decay of classical Heathendom; to denounce the foolishness of any attempt to "Germanise" even Aryans that are not of pure Germanic stock (let alone non-Aryans) and to proclaim, in defiance of twenty-four centuries of error, that "language and customs cannot replace blood."[1]

* * *

The foundation of new Germany as Adolf Hitler has laid it, can be admired in the concise wording of the fourth of the famous *Twenty-Five Points* that contain in a nutshell the whole programme of the National Socialist Party: "He alone can be a citizen of the State, who is one of the people. He alone can be one of the people, who is of German blood, whatever be his religion. No Jew, therefore, can be one of the people."[2]

Even among the early National Socialists themselves, very few realised how enormous a revolution had just been started when, on the 24th of February 1920, in an impressive mass meeting at the Hofbräuhaus, in Munich, the Führer, for the first time, uttered these words in public. Four years later, he was to write in *Mein Kampf* that the mission of the National Socialist movement was "neither to found a monarchy nor to establish a republic, but to create a German State."[3] And indeed, not only was this the first time in the history of the German people that the conception of a real German State ever was put forward, but it was, as far as I know, the first time in the evolution of the world that the conception of a national State of any description was proclaimed, in full knowledge of its practical and philosophical implications and in full awareness of its importance. It was certainly the first time that the creation of such a State was willed for the welfare of a practically homogeneous *Aryan* population.[4] The age-old Indian caste

---

[1] *Mein Kampf*, II, ii, p. 428 ff; cf. Mannheim, p. 389.

[2] "Staatsbürger kann nur sein, wer Volksgenosse ist. Volksgenosse kann nur sein, wer deutschen Blutes ist, ohne Rücksichtnahme auf Konfession. Kein Jude kann daher Volksgenosse sein" (*Das Programm der NSDAP*, Point 4).

[3] "Ihre Mission liegt nicht in der Begründung einer Monarchie oder der Festigung einer Republik, sondern in der Schaffung eines germanischen Staates" (*Mein Kampf*, I, xii, p. 380; cf. Mannheim, p. 346).

[4] Comprising, if not only people of unmixed Germanic or Nordic stock, at least Aryans only.

system, based upon the self-same racial principles as the new German régime, was devised for the harmonious development of many races living in one immense country under the intended political as well as spiritual domination of an exceedingly small Aryan minority. The only other modern civilised people, fairly homogeneous, whose native religion and tradition—combining ancestor worship, hero worship, and Sun worship—are conducive to the formation of a proper national State, the Japanese, are not Aryans at all.

In Western Antiquity, the concept of race was stressed far more than it has been ever since; for the germs of decadence had not yet so firmly set in. Race consciousness, as distinct from culture consciousness, was something that really did exist. No man, for instance, could take part in the Olympic Games unless he could prove that he was of Hellenic blood. A mere cultural "Hellene" would not have been admitted—any more than, in India, to this day, a man of a low caste (or altogether outside the pale of the caste system) would be admitted into the innermost part of a Hindu temple or into a feasting hall "for Brahmins only," whatever be his "culture." Yet, not even then was the idea of racial integrity set up as the foundation of national life; as the dominant factor, both in culture and politics. In the far North, the Aryan in all his purity was practically alone; the possibility of intermixture was too remote, too unthinkable for him to feel the danger of it. In the Mediterranean regions, he was already, to a great extent, blended with the Minoan and Etruscan elements, the civilised pre-Hellenic and pre-Latin natives of Southern Europe. Pure blood meant no longer, objectively, what it still meant in the "Hyperborean" world, whence the Hellenes and their manly gods—Ares, the Warrior, and fair-haired Apollo, and other personifications of strength and beauty, life and light—had once come. In India, alone in the midst of numerous and prolific populations entirely different from himself both physically and culturally, the Aryan soon discovered that his only hope of survival lay in his systematic upholding of race consciousness and purity of blood as a principle and as a duty. He found that out, and acted accordingly only because he was "cornered"; because he felt that it was, for him, a matter of life or death.

Generous and tolerant by nature, open-minded, sympathetic towards foreign things—anything but "arrogant," in spite of what his enemies might say—the Aryan never seems to have fully awakened to racial consciousness *unless* he realised that he was "cornered."

For the first time in the West—for the first time in the world in a pre-eminently Aryan land—Adolf Hitler has roused in him that sense of danger, and thereby brought him back to his forgotten healthy ancestral outlook on life; made him realise, in spite of twenty-four centuries of false teachings, that blood, and not artificially acquired "culture," not artificially accepted morality, is the real link among men; nay, that any culture, any morality that is out of keeping with one's racial genius, has no roots and no meaning; does not exist. Standing boldly alone against the downward rush of time—against that immemorial, slow process of decay inherent in human history; nay, defying it where it is the fiercest, *i.e.*, near the *end* of a great historical Cycle—he re-installed the natural, the eternal order of values that had God alone knows how long been reversed in men's minds and customs, and he proclaimed that the new German State was to be edified, not upon community of "culture," or of religion, or of beliefs or of interests of any sort, irrespective of race, but, on the contrary, *upon community of race irrespective of religion*—irrespective of everything. *That* was indeed a revolution; the beginning of a truly New Order. Even more; that was, as I have said before,[1] a call to resurrection; *the* only possible call to resurrection: *"Deutschland erwache!"*—"Germany, awake! Freed at last from the grip of the death-forces that are planning your destruction (for they well know that, as long as *you* are alive, they cannot rule the world unthreatened) arise! Arise, and take the lead of the reborn Aryan race!"

* * *

And, to all those who understand its implications, it was a call to resurrection not addressed to Germany alone but to all pure-blooded Nordic people beyond the technical boundaries of the Reich; nay, it was a call to all people of Indo-European stock—Indo-*Germanisch,* as they say in German—to shake off the yoke of unhealthy philosophies imposed upon them through political, religious, or cultural channels, never mind how and never mind when, by the sly, subtle, patiently destructive, the jealous genius of Judaism. Our *"Deutschand erwache!"* meant also: *"Arier, erwachet!"* More still; it was, even beyond the pale of aristocratic Aryandom, a call to all those also lovable races that are worthy to live honourably under the Sun, and to those whom Nature has appointed to rule, in their own distant spheres; an appeal to all to give up the foolish teaching of equality through "common culture" with which the Jew has infected the West, and the West, in its turn, the

---

[1] Page 14.

whole world; and to follow the new—and old; perennial—teaching of harmony in inequality and diversity; of purity of blood and originality of culture at every level of the natural hierarchy of races; of obedience to the will of the Sun that has "put every man in his place, and made people different in shape, in colour, and in speech"[1] for the fulfilment of the particular task divinely appointed to each one. It was a call for the remoulding of every State into a national one, on a racial basis, according to the genius and requirements of the people whose welfare it is to be the custodian.

As I said, few people were then—as few are now—aware of the universality and eternity of National Socialism. Some were, however. The Führer himself was, as go to prove several passages in *Mein Kampf* which allude to the laws of Nature as the ultimate foundation of our *Weltanschauung*.[2] So were—and so are still—a few of his both German and foreign followers. So were, and so are, some of the most intelligent non-Aryans whom I have met. In 1941, a Japanese residing in Calcutta told me, "We look upon your National Socialism as . . . the Shintoism of the West." Whoever has studied that immemorial religion of Japan, Shinto, or "the Way of the Gods,"[3] especially in the new political form given to it in the eighteenth century by thinkers and patriots such as Motoori and Hirata, cannot help being impressed by the meaning of that apparently strange statement. What the man wished to say was that, for the first time to his knowledge, a great nation of the Christian West had shaken off the anti-national spirit of Christianity—nay, the anti-national spirit of all philosophy prevalent in Europe since the decadence of Pagan Antiquity, with the sole exception of that of Nietzsche—and boldly gone back, for its inspiration, to a doctrine of blood and soil much similar, in its essence, to that which the proud Land of the Rising Sun has never forsaken in spite of all internationalist influences.

---

[1] King Akhnaton's Longer Hymn to the Sun (circa 1400 BC).

[2] ". . . die Menschen . . . ihr höheres Dasein nicht den Ideen einiger verrückter Ideologen, sondern der Erkenntnis und rücksichtslosen Anwendung eherner Naturgesetze verdanken"—"men . . . owe their higher existence, not to the ideas of a few crazy ideologues, but to the knowledge and ruthless application of Nature's stern and rigid laws" (*Mein Kampf*, I, xi, p. 316; cf. Mannheim, p. 288), and ". . . unsere neue Auffassung, die ganz dem Ursinn der Dinge entspricht"—". . . our new conception which corresponds wholly to the primal meaning of things" (*Mein Kampf*, II, ii, p. 440; cf. Mannheim, 399) [Trans. by Ed.].

[3] An article of mine on Shintoism—unfortunately much abridged, and thereby robbed of a great part of its consistency by the editor—has appeared in the magazine *New Asia* in 1940.

Yes, our brave Allies of the Far East, would to God we had won this war together! You would have controlled the whole of the Mongolian world, you, the *"Herrenvolk"* of Asia, the nation of Tojo and Yamagata, and above all, of Toyama. In all the West including Russia—including the vanquished USA—the Führer's word would have been the law and his spirit the source of inspiration. And some Brahmin, entirely devoted to our cause and supremely intelligent— uniting the suppleness and unscrupulousness of the East to his ancestral Aryan virtues—and in close touch both with Berlin and Tokyo, would have taken charge of India and South Asia.[1] This was the world we wanted—the grand world of which we dreamed during this struggle. It meant, no doubt, the undisputed supremacy of Germany. And that is precisely why most non-German Aryans did not want it, although it meant, also, unlimited possibilities of free and healthy development for Aryan mankind wherever it is to be found at its best; nay, free and healthy development for all worthy races, each one in its place. It meant life and resurrection: the Führer's gifts. And I say, repeating here one of my statements before my judges at Düsseldorf on April 5th, 1949—I, one of Hitler's non-German followers—the Man and the Nation that brought the world such gifts had every right to rule. The Aryans who grudged them that right have betrayed the cause of their own race.

* * *

But nowhere, or nearly nowhere, is any noble race represented in its absolute purity by more than a small minority of individuals. Even in Sweden where the Germanic type—the tall, well-built, blond, blue-eyed or grey-eyed man—is by far the commonest, one cannot say that it is the only type to be found. There *are* Swedes in whose physical appearance one detects racial characteristics, Aryan, no doubt, but other than Germanic. And what is true of Sweden—racially one of the purest countries in the world—is still more so of the rest of Europe. "Unfortunately," writes the Führer himself, "the kernel of our German nation is no longer racially homogeneous."[2] Anyone who has travelled at least in western and southern Germany is compelled to admit he is

---

[1] This is not an allusion to Subhas Chandra Bose, who was not a Brahmin, but to Savitri's husband A.K. Mukherji.—Ed.

[2] "Unser deutsches Volkstum beruht leider nicht mehr auf einem einheitlichen rassischen Kern" (*Mein Kampf*, II, ii, pp. 436-437; cf. Mannheim, pp. 395-96).

right. And the more one goes southwards, the more that beautiful Nordic type—which is, uncontestedly, *the* Aryan type in its utmost purity—becomes rare. The truth is that, wherever the Aryans have settled in Europe (save in Germany and Scandinavia, that were covered with ice until very recently)[1] they found previous inhabitants, sometimes primitive, as in England, sometimes highly civilised, as in Crete and the Aegean Isles, with whom they intermingled at a very early date. But the Celts, and later Saxons, interbred far less with the original non-Aryan population of Great Britain (which they pushed into the hilly parts of the country) than the Hellenes and Latins did, with the Minoans and Etruscans of South Europe. Whence the cleavage that one notices, to this day, between North and South Europe. As for Germany, its population has surely ceased to be as homogeneous as it was in the days when Hermann defeated Varus' legions. Still, it comprises a fairly high proportion of pure Germanic types—many of exceeding beauty—and its elements that cannot be styled as strictly Germanic, or Nordic (mixed Celtic and Nordic, mostly) are anyhow Aryan. Intermixture with the old non-Aryan Mediterranean stock (pre-Hellenic and pre-Latin) has only occurred on a very restricted scale, and very late in history, through occasional marriages between Germans and southern Europeans. So has interbreeding with the Semitic race, fortunately. Even before the rise of National Socialism, there seem to have been fewer half-Jews and quarter-Jews in Germany than in the rest of Europe, with the exception of the Scandinavian countries, of Italy and, I must say, of Greece and the Balkan States (and Eastern Europe in general) where the Jew has always been looked upon as a foreigner—and an unpleasant one at that—tolerated, but never welcome.

In spite of her lack of homogeneity, Germany was racially pure enough to appreciate the grandeur of Hitler's message. And perhaps *because* of that lack of homogeneity—and certainly because of the presence of Jews in her midst, whose despicable rôle during and after the First World War was well-known—she was more ready to respond to it than any of those Nordic countries which had not had, for a very long time, the good fortune of feeling themselves in real danger. It was therefore natural that National Socialism should have originated in Germany, and found among Germans—save for a few brilliant

---

[1] According to the *Cambridge Ancient History*, vol. 1 (Cambridge: Cambridge University Press, 1924) the whole North of Germany was covered with ice up till about 15000 BC, South Scandinavia up till 10000 BC, and North Scandinavia up till 5000 BC.

exceptions[1]—its most devoted, most consistent, and most intelligent exponents. There was more to it. The only great European nation who, two thousand years ago, not only resisted the levelling influence of imperial Rome—the metropolis of a no longer Aryan world—but defeated her armies in open conflict; the one who resisted Christianity, surely the most stubbornly if not also the longest,[2] was predestined to give birth to the greatest European of all ages and to be the first resurrected Aryan nation—the first to bear upon its flag the sacred Sign of the Sun, and in its heart, once more, the everlasting ideals of Nordic Heathendom.

But that is not all. It was—and it is—the aim of National Socialism to regenerate the race by a systematic sex policy and a type of education that would make such a policy more and more easy to apply in practice. "The German Reich," says Adolf Hitler, "must not only select out of the German nation only the very best of the original racial elements and preserve *them,* but it must slowly and surely raise them to a position of dominance."[3] This is possible in Germany because there *is,* there, a minority which represents the original Aryan in all his purity. It is possible in other lands also, to the extent that these retain racially pure elements, for "every crossing of races leads sooner or later to the decay of the hybrid product, so long as the higher portion of the cross survives, united in racial purity. It is only when the last vestige of the higher racial unit becomes bastardised that the hybrid product ceases to be in danger of extinction. But a foundation must be laid of a natural, if slow, process of regeneration, which shall gradually drive out the racial poison; that is, given that a foundation stock of racial purity still exists and the process of bastardisation is arrested."[4] If

---

[1] Such men as Vidkun Quisling, Knut Hamsun, Sven Hedin, and a few others.

[2] In the midst of the fourteenth century, Prussia was still to a very great extent Heathen.

[3] "*Das Deutsche Reich soll als Staat alle Deutschen umschließen mit der Aufgabe, aus diesen Volke die wertvollsten Bestände an rassischen Urelementen nicht nur zu sammeln und zu erhalten, sondern langsam und sicher zur beherrschenden Stellung emporzuführen*" (*Mein Kampf,* II, ii, p. 439; cf. Mannheim, p. 398).

[4] "*Jegliche Rassenkreuzung führt zwangsläufig früher oder später zum Untergang des Mischproduktes, solange der höherstehende Teil dieser Kreuzung selbst noch in einer reinen irgendwie rassenmäßigen Einheit vorhanden ist. Die Gefahr für das Mischprodukt ist erst beseitigt im Augenblick der Bastardierung des letzten höherstehenden Rassereinen.*

"Darin liegt ein, wenn auch langsamer natürlicher Regenerationsprozeß begründet, der rassische Vergiftungen allmählich wieder ausscheidet, solange noch ein Grundstock rassisch reiner Elemente vorhanden ist und eine weitere Bastardierung nicht mehr stattfindet" (*Mein Kampf,* II, ii, p. 443; cf. Mannheim, p. 401).

the representatives of such a stock are, at first, alone encouraged, and then, alone allowed, to breed, while the others—the already bastardised—are more and more discouraged and finally forbidden to do so, a time is bound to come in which the Aryan, in all his original strength, intelligence, and beauty, far from having to struggle for his very survival in an increasingly degenerate world, will automatically take his place as *the* ruling element in a natural hierarchy of restored races. And *that* is the first and foremost aim of the National Socialist Movement: to reinstall the Aryan—the natural aristocrat from every point of view—to the position of power and honour which Nature, in her impersonal wisdom, has intended him to occupy, not merely in Europe but in the world at large. The Führer has expressed this in no uncertain terms: "This world is undoubtedly going through great changes. The only question is whether the outcome will be the good of Aryan humanity, or profits for the eternal Jews,"[1] and: "For the world's future, the important thing is . . . whether Aryan man holds his own or dies out."[2]

But first, the Aryan must once more become worthy of his exalted rôle, both physically and from the point of view of character. To that end were conceived the selective sex policy of the Third Reich, and the National Socialist education.

The erroneous belief that a link of common culture is sufficient to create nationality, goes hand in hand with all the fallacies concerning "individual freedom," in particular with the idea that "one's body is one's own," to be used as one pleases, for personal edification in asceticism or for personal lust. It is the glory of National Socialism to have exposed and fought this idea, along with the other; to have proclaimed that the individual belongs to his race, whatever "culture" he may choose to acquire, and that the individual's body belongs to the race, at the expense of which no man or woman is free to sin.[3]

The negative side of our population policy—the sterilisation of the

---

[1] "*Sicher aber geht diese Welt einer großen Umwälzung entgegen. Und es kann nur die eine Frage sein, ob sie zum Heil der arischen Menschheit oder zum Nutzen des ewigen Juden ausschlägt*" (*Mein Kampf*, II, ii, p. 475; cf. Mannheim, p. 427).

[2] "Für die Zukunft der Erde liegt aber die Bedeutung nicht darin, ob die Protestanten die Katholiken oder die Katholiken die Protestanten besiegen, sondern darin, ob der arische Mensch ihr erhalten bleibt oder ausstirbt" (*Mein Kampf*, II, x, p. 630; cf. Mannheim, p. 562).

[3] "Es gibt keine Freiheit, auf Kosten der Nachwelt und damit der Rasse zu sündigen"—"There is no freedom to sin at the expense of future generations and thus of the race" (*Mein Kampf*, I, x, p. 278; cf. Mannheim, p. 254) [Trans. by Ed.].

unfit; the painless elimination of idiots, lunatics, incurables, and, in general, of all people whose life is a burden to themselves and to others—has raised enough indignation in this hypocritical world, which Christianity and like teachings have striven to make, for the last two thousand years, a safe place for the weaklings and the sick, and all manner of dregs of humanity. But our positive attitude to sex, and the subsequent constructive side of our population policy has met, perhaps, with more opposition still. Everywhere in the West, outside National Socialist circles (the East is accustomed to arranged marriages and does not feel half so shocked at our views) I have heard the same remark: "You cannot force a man and a woman to love each other just because it forwards your programme of racial regeneration, can you?" But there is no question of "forcing" them. The National Socialist régime never "forced" anybody in these matters. However, it is only natural that two young and healthy people of the same race should desire and love each other, provided they have the opportunity to meet. All that a wise national State can do, is to give such people ample opportunity of coming in touch with one another, while strongly forbidding all undesirable unions. And that is all that *was* done, in that beautiful new Germany which the advocates of "individual freedom" have reduced to ruins, and persecuted, and enslaved, to the extent they could.

The Nazi policy of racial regeneration was buttressed, from the beginning, by a parallel system of education comprising "first, the cultivation of healthy bodies"[1] and then the development of mental capability. At the same time as it pursues the policy of healthy birth which I have tried to describe, "the State must see to raising the standard of health of the nation by protecting mothers and infants, prohibiting child-labour, increasing bodily efficiency by compulsory gymnastics and sports, laid down by law, and by extensive support of clubs engaged in the bodily development of the young"[2] says Point Twenty-One of the Party Programme. And anyone who ever was even slightly acquainted with National Socialist Germany knows how faithfully that ideal was put into practice, and with what splendid

---

[1] "... so muß auch im einzelnen die Erziehung zuallererst die körperliche Gesundheit ins Auge fassen und fördern ..." (*Mein Kampf*, II, ii, pp. 451; cf. Mannheim, p. 408).

[2] "Der Staat hat für die Hebung der Volksgesundheit zu sorgen durch den Schutz der Mutter und des Kindes, durch Verbot der Jugendarbeit, durch Herbeiführung der körperlichen Ertüchtigung mittels gesetzlicher Festlegung einer Turn- und Sportpflicht, durch größte Unterstützung aller sich mit körperlicher Jugend-Ausbildung beschäftigenden Vereine" (*Das Programm der NSDAP*, Point 21).

results. I have already spoken of the physical perfection of the German youth trained under the Third Reich.

But that is not all. Next to the formation of strong and beautiful bodies comes the formation of character, the cultivation of the natural Aryan virtues: courage, self-reliance, will-power and determination, readiness to assume responsibility, readiness to self-sacrifice; fortitude, self-control, truthfulness; and absolute devotion to one's ideals and to one's leaders. Kindness, too, is to be encouraged; not weakness, not sentimentality, not that hypocritical squeamishness which disgusts us so much in our enemies the Democrats, but real kindness; the culmination of manly qualities, as Nietzsche himself says; the natural generosity of the strong. Even our opponents have to concede that this is true. Aldous Huxley, in his *The Perennial Philosophy*—that most disappointing book, of which many passages never would have been written, had the war taken a different turn—admits that the teaching of love and kindness towards living creatures was stressed in Nazi education. The love of woods, of flowers, of Nature in all her beauty—of the concrete body of the Fatherland—was also stressed; for our *Weltanschauung* is, as I have said before, the modern and Nordic form of the everlasting Religion of Life.

Contrarily to the educational ideals prevailing to this day in the capitalistic world—and already in medieval Christian education—strictly intellectual training is to come, according to our programme, only *after* the formation of character and the cultivation of bodily perfection. It is to come in its proper place, in the natural order, for man is first an animal of a particular species and race; then, a man with the moral possibilities of his race, and then only, a "cultured" man, adding to his other sound qualities the final touch of acquired knowledge, not as an end in itself but as a help and a stimulus to creative thought. We are, here, brought back to this basic idea which I have tried to express previously and which is a part and parcel of our philosophy (as of every sane outlook on life): the important thing is not what one knows, or even does, but what one *is*. This is true from the national as well as from the individual standpoint. "The national State," writes our Führer, "must act on the presumption that a man of moderate education, but sound in body, firm in character, and filled with joyous self-confidence and power of will, is of more value to the community than a highly educated weakling."[1]

---

[1] "Der völkische Staat muß dabei von der Voraussetzung ausgehen, *daß ein zwar wissenschaftlich wenig gebildeter, aber körperlich gesunder Mensch mit gutem, festem*

Another extremely important feature of our Nazi education (and of our whole system) is its absolute opposition to the pernicious "feminism" of our epoch—that product of decadence, of which the effect is nothing less than a still further lowering of the level of the race.

We hate the very idea of "equality" of man and woman, forced upon the Western world more shamelessly than ever since the time of the First World War. For one, it is nonsense. No male and female of the same living species endowed by Nature with complementary abilities for the fulfilment of complementary destinies, can be "equal." They are different, and cannot be anything else but different, however much one might try to give them the same training and make them do the same work. It is also a nefarious idea; for the only way one can, I do not say make man and woman "equal"—that is impossible—but force them, willy-nilly, into the same artificial mould; accustom them to the same type of life, is by robbing woman of her femininity and man of his virile qualities, *i.e.*, by spoiling both, and spoiling the race.[1] I do not deny that there are and always have been isolated instances of women more fitted for manly tasks than for motherhood, or equally capable of both. But such exceptions need no "feminism" in order to win for themselves the special place that Nature, in her love of diversity, has appointed to them. Around about 3200 before Christ, Azag-Bau, a wine merchant in her youth, managed to raise herself to such prominence as to become the founder of the Fourth Dynasty of Kish.[2] In those days, women did not vote—nor did men, by the way— any more in Sumeria than elsewhere. Nor did they, in general, compete with men in all or nearly all walks of life, as in modern England and the USA. Curiously enough, the most fanatical female feminists are, as a rule, those in whom virile qualities are the most lacking. Masterful women, as Nietzsche remarks, are not feminists. Most remote Azag-Bau, or Queen Tiy of Egypt, or Agrippina, or, nearer our times, the little known but most fascinating virile feminine figure of Mongolian history, Ai Yuruk, who spent her life on the saddle and, along with her father Kaidu,[3] "held the grazing lands of

---

Charakter, erfüllt von Entschlußfreudigkeit und Willenskraft, für die Volksgemeinschaft wertvoller ist als ein geistreicher Schwächling" (*Mein Kampf*, II, ii, p. 452; cf. Mannheim, p. 408).

[1] In modern English literature, no author has exposed the feminist fallacy more brilliantly than D.H. Lawrence, in nearly all his works.

[2] *Cambridge Ancient History*, vol. 1.

[3] Son of Kuyuk, son of Ogodai, son of Genghis Khan.

mid-Asia for nearly forty years,"[1] all would have burst out laughing at the idea of "women's emancipation" and all the twaddle that goes with it—in fact, at all the typically democratic institutions that our degenerate world so admires.

But exceptions need no special education; or if they do, they educate themselves. Our National Socialist education for the present and future welfare of a healthy community, was—and will still be, when the time comes to enforce it once more—based upon the acceptance of the fact that men and women have entirely different parts to play in national life, and that they need, therefore, an entirely different training; that "the one aim of female education must be with a view to the future mother."[2] We did not "force" every woman to become a mother. But we gave every healthy woman of pure blood the necessary training and every opportunity to become a useful one, if she cared to. Girls were taught to consider motherhood as a national duty as well as an honour—not as a burden. They were trained to admire manly virtues in men, and to look upon the perfect warrior as the ideal mate, as is natural. Not every girl, also, could marry every man, even within the Party. The greater the man's qualifications, the greater were the woman's to be. For instance, a girl who wished to become the wife of an SS man—a great honour—had not only to prove that she was of unmixed Aryan descent (as every marriageable German was expected to) but also to produce a diploma attesting that she was well-versed in cooking, sewing, housekeeping, the science of child welfare, etc., in one word, that she had been tested and found fit to be an accomplished housewife.

This does not mean that, in a National Socialist state, women are not to be taught anything else *but* domestic sciences and child welfare. In new Germany, they were given general knowledge also. And Point Twenty of the Party Programme, which stresses, among other things, that "the understanding of the spirit of the state (civic knowledge) must be aimed at, through school training, beginning with the first awakening of intelligence,"[3] is to be taken into account in the

---

[1] Harold Lamb, *The March of the Barbarians* (London: Robert Hale Ltd., 1941), p. 244.

[2] "Das Ziel der weiblichen Erziehung hat unverrückbar die kommende Mutter zu sein" (*Mein Kampf*, II, ii, p. 460; cf. Mannheim, p. 414).

[3] The whole text of Point Twenty is as follows: "Um jedem fähigen und fleißigen Deutschen das Erreichen höherer Bildung und damit das Einrücken in führende Stellung zu ermöglichen, hat der Staat für einen gründlichen Ausbau unseres gesamten Volksbildungswesens Sorge zu tragen. Die Lehrpläne aller Bildungsanstalten sind den

education of girls as well as of boys. Also, seldom was there, on the part of any State, a more sincere and serious attempt to provide every child with the maximum possibilities of development and advancement. "We demand the education of gifted children of poor parents, whatever their class and occupation, at the expense of the State," said the Führer, again in the same Point of his programme. And he kept his word to the letter and gave the German people, in that line as in others, even more than he had promised, as his enemies themselves are forced to admit.

* * *

If one were to define its aim and its spirit, and its essential contribution to the regeneration of mankind, in one sentence, one should say that National Socialism has set up the conception of the natural and therefore eternal aristocracy of blood and of personal value, against that of the artificial aristocracy of class and capital; that it stands for the divinely decreed human hierarchy, against all the false barriers established by man. For that is the meaning of the doctrine of race and personality, those "two pillars supporting the whole edifice"[1] of the National Socialist *Weltanschauung*.

There is, properly speaking, no nationhood apart from racial homogeneity. A country of many races is not and can never be a nation in the sense we understand that word. To call it one might be expedient, if one wishes to give the whole population the temporary

---

Erfordernissen des praktischen Lebens anzupassen. Das Erfassen des Staatsgedankens muß bereits mit dem Beginn des Verständnisses durch die Schule (Staatsbürgerkunde) erzielt werden. Wir fordern die Ausbildung besonders veranlagter Kinder armer Eltern ohne Rücksicht auf deren Stand oder Beruf auf Staatskosten"—"In order to make possible higher education and thus advancement to leadership positions for each capable and industrious German, the state must undertake a fundamental reconstruction of our entire system of public education. The curricula of all educational institutions must accord with the requirements of practical life. The understanding of the spirit of the state (civics) must be aimed at by the schools from the first awakening of intelligence. We demand the training at state expense of specially gifted children of poor parents regardless of their class or occupation" (*Das Programm der NSDAP*, p. 21) [Trans. by Ed.].

[1] "... *die völkische Weltanschauung ... nicht nur den Wert der Rasse, sondern damit auch die Bedeutung der Person erkennt und mithin zu den Grundpfeilern ihres ganzen Gebäudes bestimmt*"—"The folkish worldview ... not only recognises the value of race, but also the significance of personality, which it makes one of the pillars of its entire edifice" (*Mein Kampf*, II, iv, pp. 499-500; cf. Mannheim, p. 448) [Trans. by Ed.].

illusion of unity in view of some definite practical purpose[1] (in view, for instance, of coalescing different races against forces which one has, one's self, good reasons to fight). But that will not alter the fact that this feeling of unity will remain an illusion so long as the population consists of separate races.

In a racially homogeneous nation—a *real* nation—any idea of class, whether based upon acquired nobility, or upon wealth, or learning, is artificial and anti-national. It only hinders the spontaneous feeling of racial solidarity, on which healthy nationhood rests, for "one can only be proud of one's nation, if there is no class of which one must feel ashamed."[2] Hence National Socialism, the most aristocratic of all political philosophies, presents itself, in practice, in any homogeneously Aryan country at least, as the philosophy of a pre-eminently *popular* movement, standing for the rights of the workman and of the peasant as much, if not, in reality, much more, than Communism.

It would indeed do good to most Communists of Aryan blood, before they foolishly insult him and fight us, to acquaint themselves with all that our Führer has done in Germany for the rehabilitation of manual work, and the welfare and happiness of the labourers. It would do them good to know that the German factory worker, miner, mechanic, engine-driver, was—in general—*and is still* a better National Socialist than the doctor, lawyer, or University professor. As a foreign working woman who had the good luck to live in Germany before the war once told me, it was the people—not the "bourgeois," not the self-styled "intelligentsia"—"who lifted their right arms the most spontaneously, the most sincerely. As for the capitalists—they always looked upon Hitler with suspicion, if not with definite enmity."

The truth is that, in order to understand the depth and philosophical soundness of National Socialism, to appreciate its eternal value, one needs a broader and more living culture, as well as a more synthetic type of intelligence, and more sensitiveness to beauty than the average doctor, lawyer, or professor—let alone the average capitalist—

---

[1] While, for example, a Hindu's nationality is in reality his caste, I myself often spoke of "the Hindu *nation*" in propaganda pamphlets destined to unite all Hindus against the anti-racial, egalitarian—pre-eminently democratic—influence of Islam and Christianity (that has done a good deal in India, willingly or not, to prepare the way for Communism). It seemed to me, then, the only practical way to fight those forces. [See Savitri Devi, *A Warning to the Hindus* (Calcutta: Hindu Mission, 1939) and *The Non-Hindu Indians and Indian Unity* (Calcutta: Hindu Mission, 1940).—Ed.]

[2] "*Ein Grund zum Stolz auf sein Volk ist erst dann vorhanden, wenn man sich keines Standes mehr zu schämen braucht*" (*Mein Kampf*, II, ii, p. 474; cf. Mannheim, p. 427).

generally possesses. While, on the other hand, one does not need to understand the depth of National Socialism in order to love Adolf Hitler. One needs only to feel the power of his love. And that is exactly what the humble folk of Germany did. To them he was—and is—their benefactor, their friend, their saviour; the one man, within centuries, who had really loved them more than himself, more than anybody or anything, and who had done for them what only love (when allied to genius) can do. Most "intellectuals" were not alive enough, not instinctively, spontaneously responsive to vital forces, human and superhuman, to a sufficient degree, to feel the same. (Those few who were, and are so, in spite of being "intellectuals," are the Führer's best followers.) As for the capitalists, they knew, with the sure instinct of worldly-wise, businesslike men, that the triumph of National Socialism meant the end of their power, of their class, of their world order, forever—far more certainly and more completely than even the triumph of Communism ever would.

The strength of National Socialism lies in its appeal to the very best of Aryan men and women in *and* outside Germany, and in its hold on the German masses. It owes the former to Hitler's personality and to its own objective value—both theoretical and practical—as a doctrine. It owes the latter to Hitler's personality, and to the prosperity and happiness that the German people enjoyed under his régime, and that they have not forgotten; to the fact that, thanks to his unbending determination, the magnificent programme which he had set before the world on the 24th of February 1920, *was* carried out to the full—contrarily to those, far less radical and far less exalted, of so many politicians.

* * *

Apart from the policy of racial regeneration through marriage regulations, health regulations, and that new educational system of which I have spoken, what did the programme comprise? In one word, the liberation of the people from the thraldom of capitalism, through a series of laws concerning income, property, production. No régime—not even that of Soviet Russia—has done more than ours to exalt useful and honest work as the sacred duty of every man and woman. None has done more to make work an obligation for all. And, especially, none has done as much to render that obligation, at the same time, a pleasure.

"It must be the first duty of every citizen of the State to work with his mind or with his body. The activity of the individual should not clash with the interest of the community, but must proceed within the frame of the community and for the general good,"[1] states Point Ten of the Party Programme. And Point Eleven is but the logical corollary of it: We therefore demand "the abolition of all incomes obtained without work and without toil."[2]

Not just *any* work, but, as I have said before, useful, constructive work that has some value; that is neither a mere drudgery—reluctantly accepted because it is the only means to keep the individual's body and soul together, while it is, every minute, resented as a loss of time and energy—nor some activity, however "interesting" it be, of which the only positive result is an increase of the individual's bank balance; still less some form of exploitation of other people's weaknesses or of other people's vices, for the financial benefit of a few "clever" ones; but solid production of useful or beautiful material goods or of wholesome ideas, or some activity forwarding the necessary organisation of production, or that of national uplift or national defence; work of which the result is, ultimately, the nourishment and strengthening of men's bodies, or the formation of men's character, and of culture, such was "the first duty of every citizen of the State" in National Socialist Germany—and such will again be, I hope, the first duty of every man and woman in a future National Socialist Europe. Every law or regulation in connection with labour of any sort, was inspired by this idea. And every law was efficiently enforced.

The abolition of the "slavery of interest"[3] put forward as an article of the Party Programme, in Point Eleven and following; the "ruthless confiscation of war gains," stressed in Point Twelve, on the ground that "personal enrichment during a war must be regarded as a crime against the nation";[4] the nationalisation of big business;[5] the sharing out of the

---

[1] "Erste Pflicht jedes Staatsbürgers muß sein, geistig oder körperlich zu schaffen. Die Tätigkeit des einzelnen darf nicht gegen die Interessen der Allgemeinheit verstoßen, sondern muß im Rahmen des Gesamten und zum Nutzen aller Erfolgen" (*Das Programm der NSDAP*, Point 10).

[2] "Abschaffung des arbeits- und mühelosen Einkommens" (*Das Programm der NSDAP*, Point 11).

[3] "Brechung der Zinsknechtschaft" (*Das Programm der NSDAP*, Point 11).

[4] "Im Hinblick auf die ungeheuren Opfer an Gut und Blut, die jeder Krieg vom Volke fordert, muß die persönliche Bereicherung durch den Krieg als Verbrechen am Volke bezeichnet warden. Wir fordern daher restlose Einziehung aller Kriegsgewinne."—"In view of the tremendous sacrifice of blood and treasure demanded of a nation by every war, personal enrichment through war must be regarded as a crime against the nation. We demand, therefore, the total confiscation of all war profits" (Point 12) [Trans. by Ed.].

[5] "Wir fordern die Verstaatlichung aller (bisher) bereits vergesellschafteten (Trusts) Betriebe"—"We demand the nationalisation of all businesses that have (hitherto) been amalgamated (trusts)" (*Das Programm der NSDAP*, Point 13) [Trans. by Ed.].

profits of wholesale trade;[1] the "extensive development of provision for old age"[2] by the State, and the Land Reform, of which I shall say a few words, as well as the drastic prosecution and "punishment with death of usurers, profiteers, etc.,"[3] were not merely desiderata, intended to impress the public in political meetings, during the struggle of National Socialism for power. They became realities, as soon as Hitler became the uncontested head of the Third Reich; with the immediate result that, in a cleansed atmosphere, a new life started for the German people. Not only were the six and a half million Germans, up till then unemployed, given a livelihood, but an immense—unprecedented—enthusiasm for public welfare, a spirit of healthy competition in disinterested service for the good of others, filled everyone's heart and, in particular, the hearts of the young men and girls. And within an amazingly short time, the war-torn, downtrodden Germany of the 1920s was once more a leading power—nay *the* leading power in Europe.

Work in the fields, in the mines, in the factories recently wrested from oppressive foreign control; work along those magnificent *Autobahnen*, the building of which will remain, forever, one of the grand material achievements of the Third Reich; work in the home, where the women felt themselves useful to the whole nation as they never had before; work in the schools, in which for the first time, a programme of education in the right national spirit was at last set forth; work in every useful line, was *compulsory*. Compulsory on paper, *and* in practice also. Anyone who just did not want to do his bit was forced to do it—and a little more, in addition—in a concentration camp— unless he chose to leave the country. But there was hardly anyone who did not want to do his bit; who did not joyfully come forward to do it. Never was "compulsory" work so little of a burden, so much of a pleasure. For now the Germans felt, as they never had before, that *they*—and not a gang of idle rich men; and especially not a parasitic gang of rich aliens (not even Aryans, let alone Germans)—were the

---

[1] "Wir fordern Gewinnbeteilung an Großbetrieben"—"We demand profit sharing in all big businesses" (*Das Programm der NSDAP*, Point 14) [Trans. by Ed.].

[2] "Wir fordern einen großzügigen Ausbau der Alters-Versorgung" (*Das Programm der NSDAP*, Point 15).

[3] "Wir fordern den rücksichtlosen Kampf gegen diejenigen, die durch ihre Tätigkeit das Gemeininteresse schädigen. Gemeine Volksverbrecher, Wucherer, Schieber u.s.w., sind mit dem Tode zu bestrafen, ohne Rücksichtnahme auf Konfession und Rasse"— "We demand ruthless war upon all those whose activities are contrary to the common interest. Common criminals, usurers, profiteers, etc., must be punished by death without regard to creed or race" (*Das Programm der NSDAP*, Point 18) [Trans. by Ed.].

lords of their own land and of their own destiny.

Just as, in most countries, every male citizen has to spend a year or two (or more) in the army, so, in the Third Reich, every able-bodied young man or woman between sixteen and eighteen was expected to join some section of the *"Arbeitsdienst"* (labour service) for six months, and thereby to offer some positive contribution to the nation's welfare, in addition to that which his or her usual activities might have constituted. Students, for instance, would go, under a leader, to work in the fields, along with the farm lads—to plant potatoes, to help bring in the harvest—or, in the case of girls, to help housewives with large families in their cooking, washing, and other domestic work. This was compulsory, no doubt. But it was anything but a drudgery—so much so that, apart from the general *"Arbeitsdienst"* that was for *all* young people, the students had a voluntary one of their own, whose members would, for a time, work as factory labourers, tramway drivers, etc., for the sheer sake of experience and service. I have spoken to many men and women who were enrolled in that regular army of peace. Not one of those I met has anything but pleasant memories of those months of non-professional service. And many have told me that they were "unforgettable months," "the best time they ever had." The work was done joyfully, nay, enthusiastically—as play would have been. Indeed, the general atmosphere of the country was one of joyous earnestness, of wholehearted, *youthful* activity. The self-confidence, the uncompromising spirit and the hopes of youth, had taken the place of the hesitations, the doubts, the pessimism and "defeatism" of bygone years. And work—no longer a curse even when compulsory—had become play; pleasure.

* * *

It would be superfluous to expatiate in detail upon the numerous laws promulgated under the Third Reich for the protection and welfare of the labourers and small traders. In a book like this, which is by no means a technical study but just a profession of faith, there is no point in doing so. Moreover, it would be impossible for me, here in jail—systematically deprived of books and kept out of contact with the other political prisoners—to obtain the precise references which I would need for such a task.[1]

---

[1] For references, I have to rely upon my sole memory. It is good, no doubt, but has its limitations.

But the Land Reform is something too important not to be mentioned with some comments. And our Communist opponents have stressed too much in their propaganda, all that has been done in Russia and in Russian sponsored areas for "the welfare of the peasant," for me not to say something of our efforts in the same line.

Point Seventeen of the Party Programme had laid down, already as early as 1920, the spirit and the main features of the Land Reform: "We demand a Land Reform suited to our national requirements; the passing of a law for confiscation, without compensation, of land for communal purposes; abolition of interest on land loans, and prevention of all speculation on land,"[1] an explanation of which was given by the Führer on the 13th of April 1928.[2] A more detailed account of the policy of National Socialism as regards land and agriculture is to be found in the Party Manifesto of the 6th of March 1930, in which the reasons why farming "did not pay" in Germany before the creation of the Third Reich, are analysed, and the new land regulations set out. These regulations, like the rest of the laws that were promulgated by or under the inspiration of Adolf Hitler, were intended to free the people—here, the peasants—from the grip of the capitalist exploiter under any form, be it the selfish middleman between the farmer and the consumer—the middleman whose extravagant profits did not allow the peasant any decent living—or the moneylender, or the commercial concerns that sold to the peasant what he required in order to carry on his work efficiently, and that were, in Germany before 1933 as in many other countries, mostly owned by Jews. They gave every facility, every possible encouragement and help, every freedom to the peasant provided that he was a German and that he worked "in the national interest." For the land being "a home, as well as a means of livelihood," only members of the German nation, *i.e.*, people of German blood, were allowed to possess land in Germany, which is only natural.

"The National Socialist Party stands for private ownership," the Führer has said on several occasions, in particular, in his declaration of the 13th of April 1928, explaining the attitude of the Party with regard to the agriculturists. And no Nazi has ever contested—as the Communists have—the right of the individual to possess property (land or anything else) and to transmit it to his children. But, "to the right to hold property, however, is attached the obligation to use it in the

---

[1] *Das Programm der NSDAP*, Point 17.
[2] *Das Programm der NSDAP*, Point 17, note.

national interest."[1] And, in the case of land, special courts were set up to enforce this obligation. And a farmer who, through bad farming, according to the judgement of those courts, was not acting "in the common interest," could be expropriated *with a suitable compensation.*

Land, under the Third Reich, could in no way become the object of speculation.[2] The law concerning expropriation *without* compensation, "for communal purposes," as stated in Point Seventeen of the Party Programme, was, in fact, directed, in the Führer's own words, "against the Jewish companies given to speculation on land."[3] Whoever owned land had to cultivate it himself, or to give it up (in exchange of a compensation, whenever the land was acquired legally) for the settlement of other farmers willing to cultivate it. The State had a right of pre-emption on every sale of land, in order to see to it that no land should thus become, for somebody, the source of an unearned income. It was also strictly forbidden to pledge land to private moneylenders.[4] And necessary loans for cultivation were granted on easy terms by associations recognised by the State, or by the State itself. And the dues to the State were to be paid according to the extent and quality of the land. There were no hard and fast rules regarding the amount of cultivation expected from each farmer.[5] It depended largely upon local factors concerning the land itself. Laws of inheritance prevented the subdivision of land, or the accumulation of debt upon it.[6] Finally, the middleman's business was transferred to agricultural associations,[7] under State control. And everything was done to raise the farming class, not only economically but also educationally.

These few details are enough to show that the National Socialist land policy was not only in no way less conducive to the peasants' prosperity than that of the Communists (as our opponents of the Red Front like to pretend) but, indeed, far more so. It thoroughly protected the peasant's interests without curtailing anything of his right to own private property and to inherit it, as well as to buy and sell. It left him an immense amount of initiative in the management of his own affairs, while safeguarding the interest of the community through strict State

---

[1] Party Manifesto of 6 March 1930.

[2] Point 17 of the Party Programme. Cf. Party Manifesto of 6 March 1930.

[3] The Führer's Declaration, Munich, 13 April 1928 (quoted in *Das Programm der NSDAP*, Point 17, note).

[4] Party Manifesto of 6 March 1930.

[5] Party Manifesto of 6 March 1930.

[6] Party Manifesto of 6 March 1930.

[7] Party Manifesto of 6 March 1930.

control wherever that was necessary. Nay, that very State control was, at the same time, the surest protection of the peasant against possible exploitation by clever money-makers. For what I said about the other laws and regulations foreseen in the Party Programme already before Hitler's rise to power, is also true of those concerning land and agriculture: they were *not* just laws "on paper," but were enforced. Indeed, no régime—not even the Communist—was as drastically opposed as ours to the grip of the money-makers on the land, and as ruthless in its endeavour to break it. Many of the "poor Jews" interned during the time it lasted, especially in Eastern Germany, were prosecuted not "just for being Jews," as simple people are inclined to believe, but for dabbling in shadowy speculations on land, or lending money to farmers at exorbitant rates of interest, and so forth; for being, in one word, the exploiters of the people. Once freed from them and from their imitators, the German peasant no less than the labourer of the towns was able to work with the feeling that it was "worthwhile"; that he and his family, and the people at large, of whom he was a part, would draw the maximum benefit from his toiling year after year. Young people of all social conditions—sons and daughters of manual labourers, of professors, of generals, of humble shopkeepers, of men in high office—would come regularly and help him in the fields as members of the *Arbeitsdienst*, and make him realise more and more that he and they, he and the townsfolk, were one blood and one people—one nation. The joyful, hopeful, self-confident atmosphere of the towns spread to the countryside as well, in spite of the concealed, though thoroughly organised opposition that a great number of ecclesiastics set up, in many places, against National Socialism, taking advantage of the peasant's ignorance or of his acquired prejudices.[1]

* * *

Another most positive contribution of the National Socialist régime to the renaissance of Germany—and of Europe—lies in its effort to cleanse the press, as well as all forms of art and literature, and to build a new healthy and beautiful culture upon the ruins of the decadent,

---

[1] I have heard, in villages of the Mosel region (around Treves) people criticising National Socialism as "anti-Catholic" and Alfred Rosenberg as "anti-Christ" under the influence of the clergy, as one can imagine.

pseudo-culture of the capitalistic world; its effort to raise the moral as well as intellectual and aesthetic standard of the adults, no less than of the young men and women. No aspect of National Socialist rule (save, perhaps, our struggle against Jewry) has been more bitterly and more foolishly criticised, not only by our deadly opponents but by "public opinion" in the world at large. And yet that stubborn fight for truth, and for the triumph of whatever is the healthiest and the best in the Aryan race, is something of which every Nazi can be proud—even if, for the time being, we failed.

Without a thorough purging of the press, no renaissance would have been possible after 1933—no renaissance ever will be possible. For, so long as the journalist writes just to get paid—regardless by whom, and on behalf of whom, and for what ulterior purpose—and not because he feels the urge to enlighten or uplift his readers, then, I say, the "clever" ones, of whatever race or creed, who are in control of the money will remain, also, in control of people's minds and, to the extent the "masses" have a say in national and international affairs, in control of the destiny of nations. For the reading masses are foolish—pre-eminently gullible—and the knowledge of the conventional symbolism of script has never made them less so. On the contrary, it has given them the dangerous illusion of free thought while enslaving them to the written word more than they ever had been to any tangible power. No one has pointed out more brilliantly—and sarcastically—than our Führer the evil influence of that self-styled "intellectual" or "enlightened" press, controlled by Jewish money. "The *Frankfurter Zeitung*," states he (and this is only one instance among many), "always writes in favour of fighting with 'intellectual' weapons, and this appeals, curiously enough, to the least intellectual people."[1] "It is just for our semi-intellectual classes that the Jew writes in his so-called 'intelligentsia' press."[2]

There were only two ways of dealing with the plague: either eliminate the press altogether, or else, use the incurable propensity of the newspaper readers to believe all that is printed for the triumph of

---

[1] "Für diese Leute war und ist freilich die 'Frankfurter Zeitung' der Inbegriff aller Anständigkeit. Verwendet sie doch niemals rohe Ausdrücke, lehnt jede körperliche Brutalität ab und appelliert immer an den Kampf mit den 'geistigen' Waffen, der eigentümlicherweise gerade den geistlosesten Menschen am meisten am Herzen liegt" (*Mein Kampf*, I, x, p. 267; cf. Mannheim, p. 244).

[2] "Gerade für unsere geistige Halbwelt aber schreibt der Jude seine sogenannte Intelligenzpresse" (*Mein Kampf*, I, x, p. 267-68; cf. Mannheim, p. 245).

the National Socialist Idea, by allowing the papers to print *nothing* but what was conducive to the strengthening of the new spirit, or at least, what was in no manner opposed to it. Of the two courses, the second was undoubtedly the easiest at the same time as the most profitable. One cannot teach people to think for themselves in a day. But if, while they are learning to do so, they must have something to believe, let that be the truth rather than lies. So the second course was taken. The press was not eliminated, but controlled, as foreseen by Point Twenty-Three of the Party Programme demanding, "legal warfare against conscious political lying and its dissemination in the press."[1] All editors of newspapers in German and their assistants had to be "members of the nation," *i.e.*, to be of German blood. Papers in other languages, or even foreign papers in German, could be published with the permission of the Government. But no non-German was allowed to influence the German press, either financially or otherwise, the penalty being (if any such transaction was found out) "the suppression of the newspaper and the immediate deportation of the non-German concerned with it."[2]

It is easy to criticise such a policy, advocating the "right of the individual to express himself freely," and what not. But one should first realise that, had a similar national press policy been applied in England (from the English point of view, that goes without saying) England never would have declared war on Germany in 1939; there would have been no bombardments, no ruins, no millions of dead—nothing of that immense misery that everyone deplores—but a happy Europe in which the two great Aryan nations, Germany and England, would have collaborated in a friendly spirit for the welfare of both of them and of the whole Aryan world. Such a result—at least I believe—would have been well worth obtaining at the cost of a little less liberty to lie. And then, also, I cannot help knowing that those Democrats who blame *us* for not having allowed the German papers to publish propaganda against our views, when we had power, are the self-same people who have been persecuting us for the last four years, on the sole ground that our outlook on life is diametrically opposed to theirs; the self-same people who sentenced me to three years' imprisonment for

---

[1] "Wir fordern den gesetzlichen Kampf gegen die bewußte politische Lüge und ihre Verbreitung durch die Presse" (*Das Programm der NSDAP*, Point 23).

[2] "... jede finanzielle Beteiligung an deutschen Zeitungen oder deren Beeinflussung durch Nicht-Deutsche gesetzlich verboten wird und fordern als Strafe für Übertretungen die Schließung eines solchen Zeitungsbetriebes sowie sofortige Ausweisung der daran beteiligten Nicht-Deutschen aus dem Reich" (*Das Programm der NSDAP*, Point 23).

writing and spreading "Nazi propaganda." Their "liberty of conscience" and their "right of the individual to express himself" are the most ludicrous humbug—so coarse and clumsy that anyone gifted with a shadow of common sense can see through it. The least said about those lies the better.

* * *

Along with the cleansing of the press took place the thorough purging of art and literature, in order to forward the growth of a healthy national culture, such as was really impossible in the enervating atmosphere that modern capitalism has created. This was also laid out, in principle, in Point Twenty-Three of the Party Programme: "We demand legal prosecution of all tendencies in art and literature of a kind likely to disintegrate our life as a nation, and the suppression of institutions which militate against the requirements above mentioned."[1]

The world, accustomed by its whole education to call any cleverly written rubbish a manifestation of the "intellect"—encouraged to do so by the Jewish press, as one can well imagine—and trained to admire "intellect" above everything, burst out in loud indignation when, on the evening of the 10th of May 1933, in the presence of the Reich Propaganda Minister Dr. Goebbels—one of the finest, sincerest, *and* most intelligent National Socialists who ever lived—the students of Berlin made a public bonfire of a lot of books, mostly but not all written by Jews, which came under the ban as decadent or pernicious literature. "What!" cried out the foreign press, "Going back to the intolerant fanaticism of the Middle Ages? Returning to barbarity! Burning books! How outrageous!" The newspaper-reading apes of the whole so-called civilised earth echoed the indignation. The more smeared they happened to be with cheap "learning" and the more puffed up with unjustified "intellectual" pretences, the more horrified they were at the news of the paper and printing ink holocaust, the more they ranted against Dr. Goebbels, against the Führer, against the German students and the Nazi Party, and (whenever they had the opportunity) against the isolated non-German Aryans, like myself, who

---

[1] "Zeitungen, die gegen das Gemeinwohl verstoßen, sind zu verbieten. Wir fordern den gesetzlichen Kampf gegen eine Kunst- und Literatur-Richtung, die einen zersetzenden Einfluß auf unser Volksleben ausübt und die Schließung von Veranstaltungen, die gegen vorstehende Forderungen verstoßen" (*Das Programm der NSDAP*, Point 23).

understood the meaning of the holocaust and greeted it with cheers.

The same frantic outcry was heard when the Third Reich banned as decadent, and dangerous to the moral health of the German nation, all the queer, sickly, distorted productions on canvas or out of stone which, before Hitler's rise to power, used to pass as "art." And still greater horror was expressed when doctors and professors of Jewish origin, and German "intellectuals" whose outlook was too obviously opposed to the National Socialist way of life, were dismissed from service. It reached its highest pitch, as one would expect, when a sufficient number of rich Jews, whom the Nazi Government had magnanimously allowed to leave Germany with all their money and valuables, settled in England, in America, in India, all over the world, and nourished the anti-Nazi propaganda more lavishly than ever.

Yet, it was an artificial indignation—as artificial indeed as any parrot's lesson. For half the people who took part in the world-wide chorus against the "Nazi persecution" of "art and culture" had not the faintest idea of the meaning of these two words. They just called "art" whatever was advertised to them as such in the Sunday editions of the daily papers dealing with Miss So-and-so's latest "psychological" novel and Mr. So-and-so's exhibition of oil paintings. The other half would simply have detested the sight—or the sound—of most of the stuff banned in Germany, had they seen it, or read it, and would have cried out wholeheartedly: "A jolly good thing it *was* banned!" had they been sure nobody would have overheard them. They joined in the parrots' chorus only because they were afraid of being taken for "rustics"—"barbarians"—if they did not.

The truth is that whatever was banned was really not worth keeping. The truth is also that, in the domain of art and culture as in all others, we National Socialists did not only ban, and forbid; and destroy. We also created. In fact, we only destroyed in order to be able to create, with the collaboration of a reborn people, untrammelled by unhealthy examples and depressing memories. And nothing would have served our propaganda so much, perhaps, as a series of double art exhibitions all over the world: in one hall, all the bizarre specimens of ultra-modern art which we banned—unnatural curves, contorted shapes, nightmarish expressions; queer human faces, supposed to be all the more rich in deep hidden "meaning" that they appear the more insane or idiotic to the unprejudiced eye—and in the other . . . the finest works of Arno Breker. And an explanatory notice addressed to the sincere observer: "We have come to destroy that, in order to create *this*." That would have been Nazi propaganda indeed! And of the best kind. I wish such a double exhibition had been organised in every town of the world where there was a German Consulate.

What can be said, in this connection, of painting and sculpture, is no less true of music and literature. But many will say, "What about science? No civilised government can ban 'scientific' publications—and persecute a scientist like Sigmund Freud, on racial grounds. And banish Einstein, one of the greatest brains of all times."

Yes, I know; Freud and Einstein, the two instances that are automatically brought forth to damn us, every time the question of our attitude to "culture" arises. It is curious how few people are in a position to speak of these two scientists, even when they use their names as weapons against us. Millions have *read* some of the works of Freud (or some extracts from them) it is true, but only for the sake of vicarious sexual excitement—not out of thirst for scientific information; not as one should read them, if at all. As for Einstein, however fashionable it might have been to talk about his "theory of relativity" in the 1920s (when "simplified" explanations of it were to be found even in ladies' magazines), nobody but a handful of highly specialised mathematicians and physicists can boast of understanding his scientific innovations. All that lay people know is that he is "a great brain"—which is undoubtedly true. And we are barbarians for not appreciating such greatness, when it happens to manifest itself in a Jew.

There is a fundamental error, a thorough misconception, at the root of this attitude to us. It is not true that we do not recognise or appreciate such intellectual greatness as that of Einstein, in a Jew. We recognise it wherever it might be. But that is no reason why we should allow a Jew to hold a professorship in a German University—(or in a University in any Aryan National State, at that) any more than we would a Chinese or an Arab with similar qualifications. If nationality be, first and foremost, a matter of race (as it undoubtedly is) and if, as is natural, only nationals of a country, *i.e.*, people of that country's blood, should be allowed to occupy responsible posts there, then surely no Jew should be permitted to retain such a post, whether it be in the educational line or in the government, or elsewhere, in an Aryan country. The world should understand that there was, in our attitude, no personal hostility towards Einstein as a scientist. There was just the fact that we could not betray both the letter and the spirit of the Party Programme for the sake of anybody. And the "intellectuals" should blame us all the less as, science being above frontiers, it matters little, from *their* point of view, whether the "theory of relativity" be expounded from Berlin, New York, or Jerusalem.

The case of Sigmund Freud is a little different on account of the popularity of his works, and of the deplorable influence they have upon the lay people, especially the young. It is true that the lay people have no business reading them, and it is no fault of Freud's if they do. Still, the fact remains that, unless strictly confined to the perusal of specialists, those works are dangerous—"likely to disintegrate" a nation's life. They had—and have—not only in Germany but all over the world, wherever they are available in translations, a pernicious influence upon the young men and women who seek in them an opportunity of pondering over sex-pathology and of discovering, in their own lives, sex problems, real or imaginary, of which they would otherwise never have thought. The man, therefore, to the fact of being a Jew, added that of having—maybe unwillingly; but that makes no difference—a disintegrating influence. One really cannot blame the students of resurrected Germany for making a bonfire of his books along with many others, less technical in their suggestiveness. One cannot blame the Nazi government, either, for expelling Freud from Germany, a little roughly.

The attitude of National Socialism to far-fetched monstrosities or pretentious platitudes in art; to far-fetched "problems," analysed in loose and lazy style, to mysteries about nothing, *bizarrerie*, childish exhibitionism in literature; to artificial sex-quack[1]—"sex on the brain," as Norman Douglas would have said—to the cheap eroticism of people who have nothing better to think of, is a joyous, boisterous, defiant "Goodbye to all that!" and a triumphant feeling of riddance. We Nazis have no interest in and no sympathy for the ugly, sickly, foul-smelling capitalistic world, which we are out to kill, and which will die anyhow, even if we have not the pleasure of striking the last blow at it. Facing the future—work and song; faith, struggle, and creation—we breathe in the beauty of our tangible ideals like a gush of fresh, invigorating air from the woods after some oppressive nightmare. Yes, goodbye to all that! Or rather, "Away with all that!" What have we in common with this world of parrots shrieking meaningless words at the top of their voices, and of monkeys scratching their genitals? The culture, of which we laid the foundations during the first brief years of our power, will be something entirely different from what the modern intellectuals call "culture."

---

[1] Savitri probably means "*Quackelei*," i.e., silly talk, nonsense, prattle.—Ed.

* * *

But an entirely new culture can hardly be conceived among people who retain the same religion as before. The Programme proclaimed at the Hofbräuhaus states, it is true, that "the Party as such stands for a *positive* Christianity."[1] But, as I have said before—and as all the most intelligent National Socialists I met have admitted to me—it was well-nigh impossible, in 1920, to say anything else, if one hoped at all to gather a following. And it also remains true that the very fact of replacing, as we did, the link of common faith by the link of common blood—the creedal conception of community by the racial one—is contrary to the spirit of Christianity, no less than to its practice, always and everywhere, up to this day. It remains true, in other words, that if whatever religion that is "a danger to the national State"[2] is to be banned, then, Christianity must go—for nothing is more incompatible with the fundamental principles upon which rests the whole structure of any National State.

However, apart from the fact that this could not be *said* in a political programme in 1920—or even in 1933—it could still less be *done* in a day. Christianity could not be too openly and too bitterly opposed, before the Nazi philosophy of life had become widely accepted as a matter of course; before it had firmly taken root in the subconscious reactions of the German people, if not also of many foreign Aryans, so as to buttress the growth of the new—or rather of the eternal—religious conception which naturally goes hand in hand with it. Until then, it would have been premature to suppress the Christian faith radically, however obsolete it might appear to many of us. "A politician," our Führer has said, "must estimate the value of a religion not so much in connection with the faults inherent in it, as in relation to the advantages of a substitute which may be manifestly better. *But until some such substitute appears, only fools and criminals*

---

[1] "Die Partei als solche vertritt den Standpunkt eines positiven Christentums . . ." (*Das Programm der NSDAP*, Point 24).

[2] "Wir fordern die Freiheit aller religiösen Bekenntnisse im Staat, soweit sie nicht dessen Bestand gefährden oder gegen das Sittlichkeits- und Moralgefühl der germanischen Rasse verstoßen"—"We demand the freedom of all religious denominations in the state, so long as they do not endanger its existence or militate against the ethical and moral feelings of the Germanic race" (*Das Programm der NSDAP*, Point 24).

will destroy what is there, on the spot."[1]

One had to prepare the ground slowly, by creating anew a thoroughly Aryan soul in the young people, through their whole education; and, at the same time—for the elder folk—by giving a precise meaning (as National Socialistic as possible) to the expression "*positive* Christianity." That is what Alfred Rosenberg has endeavoured to do in his famous book, *The Myth of the Twentieth Century*.[2] His "positive Christianity" is something indeed very different from the Christianity of any Church, nay, from the Christianity of the Bible, based as it is solely upon Rosenberg's interpretation of what is obviously the least Jewish in the New Testament and upon Rosenberg's own National Socialist philosophy. The Christians themselves soon discovered that it was no Christianity at all. And of all the prominent men of the Party, Alfred Rosenberg is surely the one whom they dislike the most to this day—although they are probably wrong in doing so, for there were and still are National Socialist thinkers far more radical than he. And he was, moreover, far too much a theoretician to be a real danger to the power of the Churches.

But it is certain that, under all this talk about "positive Christianity," there was, from the beginning, in every thoughtful National Socialist, the feeling that Germany in particular and the Aryan world at large need a new religious consciousness, entirely different from and, in many ways, in vigorous contrast to the Christian one; nay, that such a consciousness *is* already lurking in the general discontent, disquiet, and scepticism of the modern Aryan,[3] and that the Nazi Movement must sooner or later help it to awake and to express itself. Although he too speaks of "positive Christianity" and insists on the fact that "nothing is further removed from the intentions of the NSDAP than to attack the Christian religion and its worthy servants";[4] and although he

---

[1] "Für den Politiker aber darf die Abschätzung des Wertes einer Religion weniger durch die ihr etwa anhaftenden Mängel bestimmt werden als vielmehr durch die Güte eines ersichtlich besseren Ersatzes. Solange aber ein solcher anscheinend fehlt, kann das Vorhandene nur von Narren oder Verbrechern demoliert werden" (*Mein Kampf*, I, x, pp. 293-94; cf. Mannheim, p. 267).

[2] Alfred Rosenberg, *Der Mythus des 20. Jahrhunderts* (Munich: Hoheneichen, 1930).

[3] This fact has been most forcefully pointed out by Gustav Frenssen in his magnificent book *Der Glaube der Nordmark* [*The Faith of the Northland*] (Stuttgart-Berlin: Georg Truckenmüller, 1930).

[4] "Es kann nicht genug betont werden, dass der NSDAP nichts ferner liegt als die christliche Religion und ihre würdigen Diener anzugreifen" (*Das Programm der NSDAP*, p. 17).

is very careful to separate the Movement from every endeavour to revive the old Germanic cult of Wotan,[1] Gottfried Feder cannot help mentioning that slowly rising new consciousness, and "the questions, the hopes, and the wishes whether the German people will, one day, find a new form by which to express their knowledge of God and religious life," if only to say that such questions, hopes, etc. are "far beyond the frame even of such a revolutionary programme as the one National Socialism proclaims."[2]

And it is no less certain that, although no attempt was ever made officially to overthrow the power of the Churches and to forbid the teaching of the Christian doctrine, books inspired through and through, not by the desire to revive any particular Cult of old—that of Wotan or any other God—but by the love and spirit of eternal Nordic Heathendom, some of which are exceedingly beautiful, were published under the Third Reich, and read, and sympathetically commented upon in Nazi circles; and that this was the first time that the real Heathen soul of the North—the undying Aryan soul—fully realised, after nearly fifteen hundred years, that it is alive; more so, that it is immortal, invincible. I have already quoted Heinrich Himmler's short but splendid book, *The Voice of the Ancestors*, that masterful condensation of our philosophy in thirty-seven pages, which only an out-and-out Pagan could write. It contains, among other things, a bitter criticism of the Christian attitude to life—meekness, self-abnegation, delectation in the feeling of guilt and misery; "aspiration towards the dust"—and, in opposition to it, a profession of faith of the proud and of the strong and free: "We do not exhibit our faults to anyone, we Heathens—least of all to God. We keep quiet about them; and try to

---

[1] "Die Partei als solche verbittet es sich jedenfalls, mit Wotanskultbestrebungen identifiziert zu werden . . . "—"The party as such refuses to be identified in any way with the endeavours of the Wotan cult . . ." (*Das Programm der NSDAP*, p. 62) [Trans. by Ed.].

[2] "Alle Fragen, Hoffnungen und Wünsche, ob das deutsche Volk dereinst einmal eine neue Form finden wird für seine Gotterkenntnis und sein Gotterleben gehören nicht hierher, das sind Dinge von säkularer Bedeutung, die auch über den Rahmen eines so grundstürzenden Programmes, wie es der Nationalsozialismus verkündet, weit hinausgehen"—"All questions, hopes, and desires as to whether the German people will find once again a new form for their knowledge and experience of God do not belong here, among things of secular meaning, and are far beyond the frame even of such a revolutionary programme as the one National Socialism proclaims" (*Das Programm der NSDAP*, p. 62) [Trans. by Ed.]. Savitri translates "Gotterleben" as "religious life" where "experience of God" would be more appropriate—Ed.

make good for our mistakes."[1]

Of the many other books of similar inspiration, I shall recall only two far less well-known than Alfred Rosenberg's famous *Mythus* but, I must say, far more radical, and deserving undoubtedly more, both the pious hatred that so many Christians of all persuasions waste upon that work and the wholehearted admiration and gratitude of all real modern Heathens: one is Ernst Bergmann's *Twenty-Five Theses of the German Religion*,[2] and the other, Johann von Leers' *History on a Racial Basis*.[3] There, the incompatibility of the National Socialist view of life and the Christian is shown as clearly, once for all, as any uncompromising devotee of either of the two philosophies could desire:

> A people that has returned to its blood and soil, and that has realised the danger of international Jewry, can no longer tolerate a religion which makes the Scriptures of the Jews the basis of its Gospel. Germany cannot be rebuilt on this lie. We must base ourselves on the Holy Scriptures which are clearly written in German hearts. Our cry is: "Away with Rome and Jerusalem! *Back to our native German faith in present-day form!* What is sacred in our home, what is eternal in our people, what is divine, is what we want to build."[4]

And Thesis Two of the *Twenty-Five Theses*—the number seems to have been chosen to match the *Twenty-Five Points* of the National Socialist Party Programme, so as to show that the "new" (or rather eternal) "German religion" is ultimately inseparable from the creation in Germany of a true National State—the second "thesis," I say, states that the German religion is "the form of faith appropriate to *our* age which we Germans *would have today, if it had been granted to us to have our native German faith developed, undisturbed, to the present time.*"[5] As for Christianity, it is frankly called "an unhealthy and unnatural religion, which arose two thousand years ago among sick,

---

[1] "Wir kommen nicht zu Gott, zu klagen, wir Heiden—weil wir unsere Fehler nicht den Leuten zeigen—am wenigsten aber Gott. Wir suchen unsere Fehler abzulegen und zu wachsen" (*Die Stimme der Ahnen*, p. 31 [cf. *The Voice of the Ancestors*, pp. 34-35—Ed.]).

[2] Ernst Bergmann, *Die 25 Thesen der Deutschen Religion. Ein Katechismus* (Breslau: Hirt, 1932).

[3] Johann von Leers, *Geschichte auf rassischer Grundlage* (Leipzig: Reclam, 1934).

[4] *Die 25 Thesen der Deutschen Religion.*

[5] *Die 25 Thesen der Deutschen Religion*, p. 9.

exhausted, and despairing men, who had lost their belief in life,"[1] in a word, exactly the contrary of what the German people (or, by the way, *any* Aryan people) need today.

I do not remember any writer having more strongly and decisively pointed out the contrast between the everlasting Aryan spirit and that of Christianity and, especially, having more clearly stressed the nature of the Aryan religion of the future. There is no question of reviving the Wotan cult, or any other national form of worship from Antiquity, as it was *then*. The wheel of evolution never turns backwards. The religion of resurrected Germany can only be that which *would have been* flourishing today, as the natural product of evolution of the old Nordic worship, had not "that Frankish murderer Karl," as Professor Bergmann calls Charlemagne, destroyed the free expression of German faith and forced Christianity upon the Germanic race by fire and sword, in the eighth and ninth centuries; or rather, had not Rome herself fallen prey to what her early emperors called "the new superstition," introduced by the Jews. And what can be said of the new German religion is no less true of the desirable new religion of every regenerate Aryan people, organised under a real national State.

The only international religion—if such a thing is to exist at all—should be the extremely broad and simple Religion of Life, which contains and dominates all national cults and clashes with none (provided they be true cults of the people, and not priestly distortions of such); the spontaneous worship of warmth and light—of the Life energy—which is not the natural religion of man alone, but that of all living creatures, to the extent of their consciousness. In fact, all the national religions should help to bring men to *that* supreme worship of the Godhead *in* Life; for nowhere can Divinity be collectively experienced better than in the consciousness of race and soil. And no religion definitely stamped with local characteristics, geographical or racial, should ever become international. When such a one does—as Christianity did; as Islam did—the result is the cultural enslavement of many races to the spirit of that one whence the religion sprang, or through which it first grew to prominence. An Indian Muslim, to the extent he is thoroughly Muslim, is outside the pale of Indian civilisation.[2] And, to the extent he accepts Christianity, a European

---

[1] *Die 25 Thesen der Deutschen Religion*, p. 9.

[2] This is an idea which I have expressed many times, during my long struggle in India against those religions of equality that do not take racial factors into account. The immemorial non-Aryan cults and customs of India, however, were never put in any sort of *bondage* to the finer Aryan culture of the Sanskrit-speaking invaders, for the latter *did*

accepts the bondage of Jewish thought. And a Northern European, to the extent he accepts Christianity, and especially Catholicism, accepts, in addition to that, the bondage of Rome. Germany, the first Aryan nation that has rebelled on a grand scale against the Jewish yoke—cultural, no less than economical—is also the first Nordic nation to have shaken off, partly at least, in the sixteenth century, the less foreign (while Aryan[1]) but still foreign bondage of Rome. Nothing shows better the spirit of the religious revolution—of the religious liberation—slowly preparing itself under the influence of National Socialism, than the outcry of Ernst Bergmann which I have quoted above: "Away with Rome and Jerusalem! Back to our native German faith in its present-day form!"

* * *

The same inspiration—the same quest of the eternal Aryan faith under its present-day Germanic form—fills Johann von Leers' *History on a Racial Basis* which I mentioned. There too one finds, applied to the domain of religion and culture, that passionate assertion of the rights of the Aryan North which constitutes, perhaps, the most characteristic feature of National Socialism on the political plane. For a political awakening of the type that Adolf Hitler provoked, stirring a whole nation to its depth, cannot go without a parallel awakening in *all* fields of life, especially in that of culture and religion—of thought, generally speaking. There too, one finds—based this time upon the extensive researches of Herman Wirth in ancient lore—a protest against the idea, current in all the Judeo-Christian world, that the old Aryan North was something "primitive" and "barbarous"; and a vision of the future in which Germany in particular and the Aryan race at large will rise again to unprecedented greatness, having rediscovered their glorious, eternal collective Self. The passage of Johann von Leers' book which comes a few pages after his tribute to Hitler as "the greatest regenerator of the people for thousands of years"[2] is worth quoting *in extenso*:

---

admit the principle of the *inequality* of races and the importance of the racial factor in religion. The non-Aryan cults and customs were allowed to survive. They exist in India to this day.

[1] To the extent the metropolis of the Roman Empire, with the multifarious race-mixtures that took place there and the resulting conflicting influences, can still be termed "Aryan."

[2] *Geschichte auf rassischer Grundlage*, p. 67.

After a period of decadence and race-obliteration we are now coming to a period of purification and development which will decide a new epoch in the history of the world. If we look back on the thousands of years behind us, we find that we have arrived again near the great and eternal order experienced by our forefathers. World history does not go forward in a straight line, but moves in curves. From the summit of the original Nordic culture in the Stone Age, we have passed through the deep valleys of centuries of decadence, only to rise once more to a new height. This height will not be lesser than the one once abandoned, but greater, and that, not only in the external goods of life. . . . We did not pass through the great spiritual death of the capitalistic period in order to be extinguished. We suffered it in order to rise again under the Sign that never yet failed us, the Cross of the great Stone Age, the ancient and most sacred Swastika.[1]

The form and particulars of a modern Aryan religion destined to rule consciences in the place of obsolete Christianity are not yet laid out—and how could they be? But the necessity of such a religion could not be more strongly felt and expressed; and its spirit and main features are already defined. It is the healthy religion of joy and power—and beauty—which I have tried to suggest in the beginning of this book. In other words, it is the eternal aspect of National Socialism itself or (which means the same) National Socialism extended to the highest sphere of life.

I have previously recalled the Führer's words of wisdom concerning the growth of a new religion, better adapted than Christianity to the requirements of the people, namely, that "until such a new faith does appear, only fools and criminals will hurry to destroy what is there, on the spot."[2]

In 1924—when he wrote *Mein Kampf*—he obviously felt that the time was not yet ripe for such a revolution.

From what one reads in the famous *Goebbels Diaries*, published by our enemies in 1948 (and therefore, no one knows to what extent genuine) he would appear to have been in perfect agreement with the Reich Propaganda Minister's radical opposition to the Churches at the same time as with his cautious handling of the religious question

---

[1] *Geschichte auf rassischer Grundlage*, pp. 76-77.
[2] *Mein Kampf*, I, x, pp. 293-94; cf. Mannheim, p. 267.

during the war. As long as the war was on, it was, no doubt, not the time to promote such changes as would, perhaps, make many people realise too abruptly that they were fighting for the establishment of something which, maybe, they did not want. But, when victory would be won, then, many things that looked impossible would be made possible. According to the *Diaries*, the Führer was even planning, "after the war," to encourage his people, gradually, to alter their diet, with a view to doing away with the standing horror of the slaughterhouses[1]—one of the most laudable projects ever seriously considered in the history of the West,[2] which, if realised, would have at once put Germany far ahead of all other nations, raising her conception of morality much above the standard reached by Christian civilisation. He was certainly also planning the gradual formation of a religious outlook worthy of the New Order that he was bringing into being. Already, the most devotedly radical among the active Party members, the *corps d'élite*; the SS men—were expected to find in the National Socialist *Weltanschauung* alone all the elements of their inner life, without having anything to do with the Christian Churches and their philosophy. And if one recalls, not the Führer's public statements, but some of the most striking private statements attributed to him, one feels convinced that he was aware of the inadequacy of Christianity as the religion of a healthy, self-confident, proud, and masterful people no less than any of the boldest of the National Socialist thinkers, nay, no less than Heinrich Himmler himself and those whom he had in mind when he repeatedly wrote, in his brilliant booklet, *"Wir Heiden"*—"We Heathens."

I know that the sayings attributed to a man, either by an admiring devotee in a spirit of praise or by an enemy, in a spirit of hatred, are, more often than not, of doubtful authenticity. Yet, when, while quoted in order to praise the one alleged to have uttered them, they in reality condemn him, or when, while quoted as "awful" utterances, with the intention of harming him, they in reality constitute praise; and when, moreover, they happen to be too beautiful, or too true, or too intelligent

---

[1] "An extended chapter of our talk is devoted by the Führer to the vegetarian question. He believes more than ever that meat eating is wrong. Of course he knows that during the war, we cannot completely upset our food system. After the war, however, he intends to tackle this problem also" (*The Goebbels Diaries*, 26 April 1942). [Cf. *The Goebbels Diaries, 1942-1943*, ed. and trans. Louis P. Lochner (New York: Doubleday, 1948), p. 188.—Ed.]

[2] Only once was the slaughter of animals forbidden on a wide scale, by order of the Indian Emperor Ashoka (3rd century BC).

for the reporter to have invented them wholesale, then one can, I believe, accept them as authentic or most probably so.

Of the many books written purposely to throw discredit upon our Führer, I have only read one through and through; but that one—the work of the traitor Rauschning, translated into English under the title *Hitler Speaks*—I read not merely with interest, but with elation, for it is (much against the intention of its author) one of the finest tributes paid to the Saviour of the Aryan race. Had I come from some out-of-the-way jungle and had I never even heard of the Führer before, that book alone would have made me his follower—his disciple—without the slightest reservation. Should I characterise the author of such excellent propaganda as a scoundrel? Or is he not just a perfect fool: a fellow who joined the National Socialist Movement when he had no business to do so, and who recoiled in fright as soon as he began to realise how fundamentally opposed his aspirations were to ours? His aspirations were, apparently, those of a mediocre "bourgeois." After he turned against us, he did not actually lie; he did not need to. He picked out, in the Führer's statements, those that shocked *him* the most—and that were likely to shock also people who resemble him. And he wrote *Hitler Speaks*, for the consumption of all the mediocre "bourgeois" of the world. As there are millions of them, and as the world they represent was soon to wage war on the Führer, the book was a commercial success at the same time as an "ideological" one[1]—the sort of success the author had wanted: it stirred the indignation of all manner of "decent" *Untermenschen* against National Socialism. But one day (if it survives) a regenerate Aryandom will look upon it as the unwilling tribute of an enemy to the greatest European of all ages.

And Hitler's words about Christianity, reported by Rauschning in the fourth chapter of his book, would be admired—not criticised—in an Aryan world endowed with a consistently National Socialist consciousness, for they are in keeping with our spirit—and ring too true not to be authentic. "Leave the hair-splitting to others," said the Führer to Hermann Rauschning before the latter turned renegade:

> Whether it is the Old Testament or the New, or simply the sayings of Jesus according to Houston Stewart Chamberlain, it is all the same Jewish swindle. It will not make us free. A German Church, a German Christianity, is a distortion. One is either a German or a

---

[1] There were five printings of the book in English up till 1940. And probably others *after* that date.

Christian. You cannot be both. You can throw the epileptic Paul out of Christianity—others have done so before us. You can make Christ into a noble human being, and deny his divinity and his rôle as a saviour. People have been doing it for centuries. I believe there are such Christians today in England and America—Unitarians, they call themselves, or something like that. It is no use. You cannot get rid of the mentality behind it. *We* do not want people to keep one eye on life in the hereafter. We need free men, who feel and know that God is in themselves.[1]

Indeed, however clever he might have been, Rauschning was not the man to concoct *this* discourse out of pure imagination. As many other statements attributed to the Führer in his book, this one bears too strongly the stamp of sincerity, of faith—of truth—to be just an invention. Moreover, it fits in perfectly with many of the Führer's known utterances, with his writings, with the spirit of his whole doctrine which is, as I said before, far more than a mere socio-political ideology. For, whatever might be said, or written, for the sake of temporary expediency, the truth remains that National Socialism and Christianity, if both carried to their logical conclusions—that is to say, experienced in full earnest; *lived*—cannot possibly go together. The Führer certainly thought it premature to take up, publicly, towards the Christian doctrine as well as the Churches, the attitude that the natural intolerance of our *Weltanschauung* would have demanded; but he knew that we can only win, in the long run, if, wherever essentials are concerned, we maintain that intolerance of any movement sincerely "convinced that it alone is right."[2] And he knew that, sooner or later, our conflict with the existing order is bound to break out on the religious and philosophical plane as well as on the others. This *is* unavoidable. And it has only been postponed by the material defeat of Germany—perhaps (who knows?) in accordance with the mysterious will of the Gods, so as to enable the time to ripen and the Aryan people at large, and especially the Germans, to realise, at last, how little

---

[1] Hermann Rauschning, *Hitler Speaks: A Series of Political Conversations with Adolf Hitler on his Real Aims* (London: Thornton Butterworth, 1939), p. 57.
[2] "Die Zukunft einer Bewegung wird bedingt durch den Fanatismus, ja die Unduldsamkeit, mit der ihre Anhänger sie als die allein richtige vertreten und anderen Gebilden ähnlicher Art gegenüber durchsetzen"—"The future of a movement depends upon the fanaticism, indeed the intolerance, with which its adherents uphold it as alone correct and forward it past other similar formations" (*Mein Kampf*, I, xii, p. 384; cf. Mannheim, pp. 349-50) [Trans. by Ed.].

Christianity can fulfil their deeper aspirations, and how foolish they would be to allow it to stand between them and the undying Aryan faith implied in National Socialism.

That Aryan faith—that worship of health, of strength, of sunshine, and of manly virtues; that cult of race and soil—is the Nordic expression of the universal Religion of Life. It is—I hope—the future religion of Europe and of a part at least of Asia (and, naturally, of all other lands where the Aryan dominates). One day, those millions will remember the Man who, first—in the 1920s—gave Germany the divine impetus destined to bring about that unparalleled resurrection; the Man whom *now* the ungrateful world hates and slanders: our Hitler.

Imprisoned here for the love of him, my greatest joy lies in the glorious hope that those reborn Aryans—those perfect men and women of the future Golden Age—will, one day, render him divine honours.

Chapter 12

THE HOLY FOREST

"Es mag sein, daß heute das Geld der ausschließliche Regent des Lebens geworden ist, doch wird dereinst der Mensch sich wieder vor höheren Göttern beugen."

—Adolf Hitler[1]

"The walls, in this house, are as thin as paper; every word can be heard, especially at this time of the night, when everything is quiet. And the fellow who lives on the first floor is a treacherous swine. Used to pretend to be a National Socialist, once—when it paid. But went and joined the SPD[2] as soon as the Occupation started. And now, goes about denouncing us. So be careful what you say." This is what Herr A had told me, the night before, as I sat by him in a comfortable easy chair after a tiring journey from one end of Germany to the other. "But," he added, "tomorrow I shall take you to the forest. There, we can talk freely."

And we were now walking uphill towards the forest. In fact, we were already practically in it. We were only walking farther and farther away from the road—away from possible onlookers, away from possible listeners, possible traitors, possible spies. And I thought to myself, recalling what someone had said in the first German town I had visited: "Indeed this is 'the land of fear.' Unfortunate Germany! For how long?"

We walked on and on without talking. I had never met Herr A before. I had come to him recommended by other Nazis from abroad, with whom he was in touch without having, either, actually met them. And all he knew of me was that I had spent long years in India; that I was "*in Ordnung*,"[3] *i.e.*, myself also a Nazi; and that I was prepared to take part, directly or indirectly, in any underground activities aimed at strengthening the National Socialist spirit and undermining the

---

[1] "It may be that today gold has become the exclusive ruler of life, yet the time will come when man will again bow down before higher gods" (Adolf Hitler, *Mein Kampf*, II, ii, p. 486; cf. Mannheim, p. 436) [Trans. by Ed.].

[2] The Social Democratic Party, revived and sponsored by the Allied occupation.

[3] In order—Ed.

influence of the Occupying Powers in present day Germany. So he had many things to tell me, and I many things to tell him. But we waited.

It was a bright September morning. Through the branches of the trees, still thickly covered with green leaves, the Sun projected patterns of light upon the ground and upon us—patterns that moved, as the breeze stirred the leaves—and birds were singing. The more we walked towards the interior of the forest, the more I felt elated. After the hundreds of miles of ruins that I had been seeing, day after day, ever since I had entered Germany, to find myself in that inviolate sanctuary of peace was refreshing. And the knowledge that Herr A and I were there alone, and that we had come to seek aloofness from the venal treachery of man; silence; secrecy; and heart-to-heart communion with each other in our grand, impersonal ideals, made it all the more so. I was aware that the hidden Godhead of the Forest—the unseen, still, invincible Soul of the Land—was our ally. And indeed it was.

A couple of deer ran past gracefully at some hundred yards' distance from us, and disappeared in the thickness of the trees. I admired the beauty of their flight. I wanted to ask Herr A if, like the English friends who had sent me to him, and like myself, he disapproved of the chase as of all cruel sports, both on moral and on aesthetic grounds. I remembered a Jew who had declared, in a tea-party in Iceland, where I happened to be present, that such sports "should be encouraged" as they provided "a convenient outlet for man's natural destructive instinct" which was, according to him, "more suitably exercised against animals than against people." To which I had replied in indignation that, if one's natural destructiveness must have an outlet, it was far more suitable to direct it against dangerous human beings rather than innocent animals. And when the man had asked me whom I called "dangerous human beings" I had answered defiantly "People like yourself," setting against me the whole company—Icelanders (anything but Jews) but people with a Christian outlook. I wanted to relate that episode to Herr A. But I did not. I could not bring myself to break the silence. And I felt that Herr A was thinking of things in comparison with which all personal episodes were unimportant. We continued to walk, without speaking, for about half an hour. Dead leaves and dead twigs creaked under our feet.

At last, Herr A spoke. "Nobody can hear us here," said he. "Now we can talk. Would you like to sit down, or would you mind us going still a little farther into the forest?"

"Let us go a little farther," said I; "I like walking."

He asked me a few questions about my background, my childhood, my life as a student, both in Greece and in France; he asked me when and how I had come to National Socialism, and how long I had lived in India, and what I had done there during the war, and how I had come to know the people who had recommended me to him. I replied faithfully. He told me something of his own life and struggle; of his beautiful birthplace, in Sudetenland; of his pious upbringing; of his conversion from Christianity to National Socialism.

"You are right," he told me, "when you say that the two philosophies can never go together. You had the privilege never to have been a Christian. I ceased to be one in 1933."

"I was one, outwardly, till 1929."

"What do you mean by 'outwardly'?"

"I mean that I used to go to church on Sundays. But I had never believed in the teaching of any Church. I used to go to the Greek Church, not because it was Christian, but because it was Greek; because I had there an opportunity of meeting the other Greeks of the French town where I was brought up, and of hearing Byzantine singing, which I love; and because I knew that the Church, as an organisation, had done a lot to keep Greek nationality alive during the four centuries Greece remained under the Turks. Also because, however sorry I was, at heart, that the Greeks had ever taken to Christianity at all, in the past, I considered that the foreign creed had irretrievably become a part of the national culture of a modern Greek. I don't think so now. I have not thought so for many years—not since 1929, as I said."

"What did you do in 1929?"

"I spent forty days in Palestine. I wanted to know, not from books but from experience, the birthplace of the religion that had overrun Greece and nearly the whole of the Aryan world. I saw it thoroughly, from one end to the other. I saw the Jews there—the people whom my pious aunt[1] (my English mother's sister) used to call 'God's chosen ones.' Not that I had never seen any before. I had seen many. But it is one thing to meet an occasional Jew in France or in England, or even in Athens, and another thing to see hundreds, thousands of them in a land in which they were already settling twelve centuries before Christ or so; in a land that one can no longer separate from their history. I had never felt myself in such a foreign atmosphere as in those picturesque and dirty streets of the old Jewish quarter of Jerusalem; also as in the

---

[1] Nora Nash—Ed.

very churches of the place, and its sites of Christian pilgrimage. How could people of pure Aryan blood, nay, descendants of the Vikings, like my pious aunt and my own mother, thought I, bring themselves to accept a God said to have chosen such a nation as that one as 'his own'? How could the Greeks have gotten accustomed to calling him 'their' God, even outwardly—for I knew that, inwardly, they had always been far less Christian-like than the English—and that, through a teacher such as Paul of Tarsus, of all men, a hater of life and of beauty? It may well be that his Church had helped to preserve Greek nationality under Turkish domination. But before that, it had ruined the Greek race and what was left of the Greek spirit—as it had ruined the Aryan spirit in all other Aryan countries, more or less. I could no longer lie. I could no longer force myself to believe that this religion was an indispensable part of any national inheritance. There was too much Jewry irredeemably mixed up with it for me to tolerate it any longer. I had always been a Nature worshipper, a Sun worshipper, at heart. I would now be one openly. And I retained this attitude ever since."

"Why did you go to India?"

"To see a land in which the old Aryan religion had resisted victoriously, to this day, the efforts both of Islam and of Christianity to wipe it out; in other words, a land of Aryan culture, free from the influence of the Jew—so I thought, at least. I had read a few books about the caste system. I could not help feeling a connection between that heroic effort to keep Aryan blood pure (and the blood of every race) in that land of many races, and the amazing survival of the Aryan Gods of old. I wished to see that system at work with my own eyes; to study it. I could not help noticing that the principles that had guided the immemorial Aryan lawgivers in their insistence on purity of blood, in that distant tropical country, were exactly the same as those which the Führer proclaimed in our times—for the first time in the West since decay had set in. I had just read *Mein Kampf* and was already, in the full awareness of my Aryan pride, a devoted admirer of Adolf Hitler."

"Did you not wish to see, also, Hitler's own land?"

"Oh, do not again tear open the lasting wound in my heart! Too many people have done so already, first of all the generous, detached, all-understanding Indian who gave me his name and protection that the British might allow me to leave India in the beginning of the war. I was to go to France. From France, I would have come here. I had introductions; everything I needed. I would have broadcast on behalf of the Propaganda Department, and put all my heart and soul in my messages. But Italy joined the war a fortnight too soon. And so the last Italian ship, which I was to take, never sailed. Of course I should have come *before* the war. I intended to. I never meant to remain in India more than two or three years—not fifteen.[1] But it is not always possible to do as one has planned. And not easy to come from ten thousand kilometres away. When the war once broke out, it was impossible, in spite of all my efforts.

"I have told you what I did during the war. Whatever it might have amounted to, it was nothing compared with what I could have done here."

"It was the best you could do, in the circumstances. And it was useful. And now you have come to us, and you are welcome. You can also be useful, if you know how to be careful and patient."

"Still, in former days, I would have seen the Führer."

"You will see him, one day."

"So you too believe he is alive?"

"I do not 'believe' it; I know it."

"Do you know where he is?"

"Yes."

"Where?"

"I cannot tell you now. But a time will come when you will know."

"And see him?"

"Surely."

"And feel his divine eyes rest upon me, be it only for a minute or two! And hear his voice—his own voice—address me!"

"And tell you that he is pleased that you were among us in 1948, in the darkest days. Yes, why not?"

My eyes brightened at the thought of this happiness. And I blushed. Herr A smiled to me as he would have to a little girl, although I am as old as he, in fact a year or two older. "Don't I know," said he, "what you want? I can read your thoughts."

"Then, you know at least that I am sincere."

"That, I do! I knew it as soon as you opened your mouth. But sincerity is not sufficient, in times like these. You also have to learn how to wait, how to keep calm, and how to hide your feelings, also, if you do not want to get into trouble one fine day and—which would be worse—to get others into trouble along with yourself. Be careful, very careful. You seem entirely to lack the sense of danger."

---

[1] Savitri's first sojourn in India lasted only a little more than ten years, from May 1935 to November 1945.—Ed.

"I was aware of danger when I crossed the border with my trunk full of those leaflets which I showed you; acutely aware of it indeed."

"Yes. But you forgot all about it as soon as you felt that you had safely come through. You should not forget. Danger is lurking everywhere, in this unfortunate country. People can denounce you for nothing, in the sheer hope of securing safety for themselves. You do not know who is a friend and who is a traitor."

"But surely no Nazi would harm me."

"Certainly not. But you do not know who is really a Nazi and who is only speaking as one, in order to trap you. Be careful. Bribery and fear are the weapons of our enemies; powerful weapons. Our proud Germany has become, under the Occupation, the land of fear."

For the hundredth time I recalled in my mind my arrival at Saarbrücken, my first evening in the midst of a German family, and those self-same words, which I heard there for the first time: "*Das Land der Angst*"—"the land of fear."

"But," said I, "the faithful minority, the genuine German National Socialists, they stand erect in the midst of that general terror . . ."

Herr A gave me a beautiful, proud smile.

"Yes," said he, "*we*, the wide-awake, the steadfast; the true followers of him you love and revere. . . . You have defined us in your leaflets. We are 'the gold in the furnace.' The weapons of the agents of the death forces have no power against us."

* * *

I looked up to him admiringly. The words he quoted might have been mine, no doubt. But the pride was his. And so were the hardships endured these three and a half years: the loss of his home and of all he possessed; and his sufferings as a soldier on the front and as a prisoner of war abroad. And it was his indomitable will that had overcome those sufferings, and kept him erect and expectant, strengthened instead of disheartened in the depth of disaster and destitution; ready to seize the mastery of the future at the first opportunity. In his tall and handsome figure walking by my side against the sunlit background of the forest; in his virile countenance brightened by large, deep blue eyes, I beheld a living representative of that golden minority that I love; that I had come to Germany in order to seek and serve; of that minority which is, in my eyes, *the* real German nation, for whom Hitler dreamed such glory, such power, and such happiness. Herr A was Hitler's people welcoming me. I had not felt so happy for a long time.

"Would you like us now to sit down," said he.

"Yes."

We reclined upon a mat of dead leaves, at the foot of a tree. A ray of sunshine struck Herr A's ash blond, glossy, wavy hair, and made it shine like gold. His face was stern. His eyes, looking in the distance, were as hard and cold as steel. I too, looked straight in front of me at the play of light and shade in those hundreds and hundreds of trees; at their varied shades of green; at a patch of blue sky, visible through the intricate branches. We were silent for a moment, as though under a spell. I felt the soul of that forest *in* me. I was a part and parcel of that endless life. And I knew Herr A felt the same. (I have never met a National Socialist who does not feel the same as I do about Nature.) He turned to me and his hard eyes softened. And his mouth, which had expressed up till then nothing but concentrated willpower and pride, smiled faintly. "Are you comfortable?" he asked me.

"I am happy."

"Do you know where we are? In *which* forest?"

And without giving me the leisure to answer or even to think, he pursued: "We are in the outskirts of the Hartz, the great sacred forest of all times. It stretches on, from here, for kilometres and kilometres, right into the Russian Zone. Is it not beautiful?"

"It is."

"'They' have cut down whole portions of it, the devils. One day, I shall show you: whole hilltops robbed of their verdant, age-old mantle; acres and acres of land, in which you will see nothing but stumps of felled trees. At one time, in their first fury of plunder and desecration, in 1946, 'they' were cutting down ten thousand trees a day. And goodness only knows what the Russians have been doing on the other side of the forbidden border—although they have enough wood in their own country without spoiling ours. That is what 'Occupation' means."

"I know," I replied: "I have seen some of the damage 'they' have wrought in the Black Forest. And believe me, I hate 'them' as fiercely as you, although I am not a German. I shall never forget the massacred woods, nor the cities in ruins, nor that splendid faith of ours, for which I lived twenty years, shattered in the hearts of millions. Shattered, and replaced by what? Blank despair—like that which I myself experienced until this year in the spring; for one cannot have loved our ideals and then love different ones. I shall never forget that moral ruin added to the material."

Herr A's cold blue eyes looked straight into me inquiringly. "Have *you* ever really lost faith?" he asked me.

"No," said I. "And yet, in one way, yes. Of course, I never lost my devotion to the Führer, nor my faith in his mission. I always believed, or rather always knew, that one day his principles would triumph, for they are rooted in truth. What is rooted in truth never perishes. But I had given up all hope to see them triumph in my lifetime."

"Did you ever give up your willingness to act?"

"Never."

"Why, since you had no hope?"

"First, because I hated those millions of fools who had obediently swallowed the Jew's horror tales (which never impressed *me,* anyhow, and would not have, even if they had all been true) and fought against the Führer. I hated those who have been persecuting his faithful ones ever since the capitulation. I would have given anything, done anything to witness their destruction and to rejoice over it. Then, I realised that the faithful ones were more numerous than I had imagined. Hope came back to me, as I have already related to you. Then, I saw the ruins of Germany and could no longer remain away from here in freedom and security. No. Even if I had still believed that the New Order could not be restored in my lifetime; even if there were no hope, still, I would have come—come, at least to suffer with Hitler's people, if I could do nothing more useful; come to share their hardships and their dangers; to be persecuted with them. I would have crossed the frontier on foot, clandestinely, from the nearest village in France, if I had not, this time, been granted an entrance permit."

Herr A took one of my hands in his, and pressed it, and smiled. "There is no moral ruin for the strong," he said, triumphantly; "and material ruin does not count, in the long run. I have not only never lost faith in our ideals but, even in 1945 when, a prisoner of war in the USA I was told of the capitulation, I knew that one day we would rise again; and that I would live to witness our second rising, more irresistible, more glorious than the first, and more lasting. I knew *then* that the Führer was alive. Something told me."

The forest continued to breathe and to sing all round us, in grace, in majesty, in the superb indifference of things everlasting. "The felled trees will grow again," I said. "It might take a long time—a hundred years, two hundred—for the holy Hartz to look like itself once more. But what are two hundred years in the life of the Land?"

"We too will rise again," replied Herr A. "Like the divine Forest, we too are eternal. We too have our roots in the soil. The world does not yet know what real National Socialism is. It will, soon."

"How soon?"

"In less than two years' time—surely in less than three—you will see the beginning of our second struggle for power."

"How I wish I could believe you! So soon! Yet, would it not have been better if there had been no capitulation, no disaster? Why, after all, why could we not win this war? Whose fault is it, according to you, that we lost it; that Germany is occupied, plundered, terrorised; that our Hitler's name is slandered all over the stupid world; that the best men of the Party were killed as 'war criminals'; that you and I have to come here, miles away from the town, to speak freely?"

"Ours," replied Herr A.

"You mean to say that the Nazis in power were not ruthless enough? I have always said that myself. There would have been no trials for so-called 'war-crimes,' had there been no Jews left to bear false witness against our people."

"Not ruthless enough, not merely towards the Jews," observed Herr A, "but towards a number of good-for-nothing fellows who had crept into the Party, and towards the traitors in high position. Not critical, not discriminate enough; not suspicious enough. The facts you told me last night about Rommel's briefcase are significant. And the other information you obtained abroad about that pack of traitors in the German railway services, sending regular dispatches to the London War Office concerning our troop movements and so forth, while pretending all the time to be sincere National Socialists, is no less eloquent. We must not blame the Occupation authorities if those rascals now have good posts as a reward for their doings and if they go about denouncing us to increase their income still a bit more. We must blame ourselves for not finding them out in time and 'liquidating' them before they did irreparable mischief."

"We had," said I, "a too high opinion of human nature. We were too generous."

"Too slack, too stupid, and too self-centred," replied Herr A.

"But the Party members . . ."

"I have told you: there were all sorts of fellows in the Party besides genuine National Socialists," said Herr A. "Three-quarters of them had not the right spirit. Had it been otherwise, we never would have lost the war."

And he started discussing some of the prominent members of the Nazi Government. He was bitter in his criticisms.

"Look at that creature, Schacht," said he. "Can you call *that* a Nazi? The slimiest type of traitor. And to think we tolerated such a man twenty years without being able to see through him!"

"Capable, but characterless," said I. "He should have been a Democrat from the start. But he is an exception, you must admit."

"I should think so! Still; look at Ley, a man who never should have been in high position. Look at Baldur von Schirach; the reputation he had . . ."

"I have heard all that," said I. "Oh, don't tell me any more! I don't wish to know. They were both among the Führer's early followers. And one died a martyr at Nuremberg. And the other is, to this day, in captivity, in our enemies' hands. Leave them in peace. Whatever might have been their weaknesses, they suffered enough to expiate them a thousand times."

"A Nazi should have no weaknesses," said Herr A. And his bright eyes were as hard as stone. And I felt that he despised me a little for the sympathy I had shown the two men.

We remained some time without speaking. The many noises of the forest were the same as before: songs of birds and rustling of leaves; the fall of a pebble at the swift passage of a lizard. I saw another couple of deer run past in the distance. But I was neither looking nor hearing with the same restfulness as before—that restfulness without which one cannot remain in touch with the soul of living Nature. I looked up to Herr A once more, and I did not know what to think. "Have you not a good word to say of any of them?" I asked at last; "Not even of Hermann Göring? Not even of Dr. Goebbels, the embodiment of devotion to our Führer?"

And I thought of Göring's fine, frank face. And sentences from his speeches at Nuremberg—at the Party rally in September 1935, and, ten years later, before our victorious enemies—came back to my memory; unforgettable sentences, everlastingly true. And I thought of Goebbels' eloquence also, and of his death with all his family, worthy of the heroic Age; and of Göring's death in honour and dignity—and in defiance of the iniquitous judgement of our persecutors.

"Göring was both able and sincere, and I respect him," said Herr A. "Still"—he added—". . . too much luxury, too much money . . ." as though this were nearly a disqualification in his eyes. "As for Goebbels, he was undoubtedly one of the best ones," he said, "although none were perfect—none but the Führer himself."

He paused for a while and then addressed me again. "You mentioned the martyrs of Nuremberg," said he. "Shall I tell you of two among them, the most misjudged, the most hated by the world at large, but worthy men, whom you should admire?"

"Tell me."

"Himmler, and Streicher."

Herr A's choice did not astonish me. In fact, I expected to hear these two names from him.

"I have never shared the prejudices of the God-forsaken world—or even of many Germans—about these men," said I. "I remember the passage of *Mein Kampf* relating how Julius Streicher, in a gesture of unselfish, true patriotism, dissolved his own previous party and asked his followers to join the Führer, in the beginning of the struggle.[1] I always liked that generous attitude of his. And I like his uncompromising spirit, also; his one-pointed effort to free this country from the unseen yoke of the Jew; and his last gesture, and two last words—'Heil Hitler!'—at the tragic hour of death, after going through still more suffering, perhaps, and greater humiliations than the others, at Nuremberg. Poor Streicher! And I know Himmler's task was a heavy and a thankless one. Yet he did it well."

"Right," replied Herr A. "And have you ever read his little book, *Die Stimme der Ahnen*? It is not well known; not even published under his own name. But if you can ever get a copy, read it. You will then understand what a man he was."

And he added in a lower voice: "A real Heathen; a man *you* would have been happy to meet. A man who would have understood you, too, for he had the right view of things and hated half measures. So did Streicher, in fact. And so did Goebbels. He too was a man from the people."

* * *

Herr A uttered those last words with particular emphasis. One could feel that, in his estimation, it was easier for a camel to pass through the eye of a needle than for a person born and bred in a "bourgeois" atmosphere to make a good National Socialist. For Herr A could not forget the enormous influence of upbringing upon *most* human beings. He did not speak of the exceptions. "Yes," he repeated after a pause, "only among the people—the workmen, the peasants; those who know and accept real life—are the qualities of the race to be found, unmarred. The workman is healthier than the 'bourgeois.' His blood is purer—in general—and therefore stronger; more valuable. All or nearly all 'intellectuals' are perverts in some way or another. All are

---

[1] *Mein Kampf*, II, viii, p. 575; Mannheim, p. 514.

more or less hopelessly sick. Cut them down, as a class. Suppress classes. They are incompatible with a society dominated by the national (*völkisch*) ideal which is, before anything else, racial. And the leaders of the people should be men of character and of experience; men who have lived and suffered, and learnt; whose personality has been forged by the Gods upon the anvil of hardship, like that of the Führer—not men of books; theoreticians; men who do not know mankind, and who can neither love it nor hate it."

"I have always said that myself," I replied—strange as it might seem to many, who believe that one's education determines one's being, in all cases. "No one is more contemptuous of unthinking 'intellectuals' than I. I want people who think for themselves, or at least who trust and follow those who *do* think—and who really love them. And of all such ones I met, nine out of ten come, as you say, from the working classes."

I was perfectly sincere. And Herr A felt it. He gazed at me with warm, understanding approbation, and was silent.

The birds continued to chirp, and the leaves to rustle, and the Sun to throw moving patterns of light upon the mossy ground and upon our faces. I felt safe, and at rest. All was so beautiful and so peaceful around us. Herr A pressed my hand and smiled at me gently. "Are you happy, here?" he asked me.

"Yes," said I. "I love forests. And to know that this one is a part of the famous Hartz makes it all the more lovable to me. I feel on a holy spot."

"So you really love our Germany, don't you? Not merely with your brain, but with all your heart." And his large, limpid eyes, that could, at times, be so hard, looked at me with tenderness. "You are right," he added; "see how lovely she is!"

"She is, indeed," I repeated. "Yet, it is not her beauty alone that moves me. The whole world is beautiful. But she is my Führer's land. Her people are *his* people, whom he loves more than himself, more than anything on earth. And that is why I love them. That is why I came, when all was lost."

Herr A again pressed my hand in his and looked at me so gently that my heart ached.

"You are a woman," said he, smiling; "a young, loving woman. I know it. How old are you?"

"Nearly forty-three."

"Nearly twenty-three," replied Herr A.

"About the age I was," said I, "when I first realised all that National Socialism meant to me."

"That is to say, all that Adolf Hitler meant and still means to you," said Herr A mercilessly.

"Is it not the same thing?" asked I, suddenly flushing crimson.

"Yes, it *is*."

"It is," he repeated after a pause, "and always shall be. For not only is our *Weltanschauung*, as you say so well, the modern form of the everlasting Religion of Life and Light—of health, and strength, and beauty—but *he* is the one modern Man of action in Whom God—"the Heat-and-Light within the Sun," to use the expression you quoted last night—manifested Himself. I believe that. And so do a few others who understand, who feel the truth."

"I believe it too. *I know it*, because I love Him. And I have never loved anyone in that way, but Gods. Oh," said I, in a new outburst of enthusiasm, stretching out my arms as though I would reach the ends of the earth, "I wish I could say it freely, write it, proclaim it, stick it on all the walls: 'Hitler is divine; our glorious, our beloved Führer *is* the cosmic Soul, the Spirit of the Sun, born for the first time in the West since immemorial Antiquity to stay the decay of creation.' I wish the world could rise and praise him—and love him—at my voice!"

"The broad world—nay, his own Fatherland that he so loves—will listen to no one. It will learn the truth as it has always learnt: through bitter experience, through remorse, through despair; through the way of blood and tears. Germany is learning already. As for you, continue to love him and serve his ideals, in small as well as in great things. Continue to love his people. Are you not happy to feel that some of them, however few, think and feel as you do, and are waiting and working with you for his triumph?"

"Surely I am. And it is a joy for me to feel myself, just now, in this holy forest—away, far away from the impure world created by his enemies; alone with one of his sincere followers."

Herr A gazed at me more tenderly than ever, and spoke in a low, caressing voice: "I too am happy with you in this solitude, united to you in the love of all I adore and stand for and live for. There is no link like that one. Had you been a little different, I would have perhaps tried to bring you nearer to myself. But I shall never do so; for you have been put aside to live for gods alone."

"My husband always said the same."

"A wise, very wise, and noble man," said Herr A.

We were silent for a few minutes and then, overwhelmed by the feelings that had been roused in me, I suddenly said in a low voice, with such appealing gentleness that I was myself surprised at the sound of it: "You must have seen 'him.' Have you ever had the privilege of speaking to 'him'? Oh, do talk to me about 'him'!" Herr A understood—knew—that I meant: about Adolf Hitler.

"I have seen him and greeted him several times, but only spoke to him once," he said. And his face was beaming with a strange light, as though inspired.

"Do tell me!" said I.

"Well, it was in Berlin, long ago—before his coming to power. He had just been addressing a meeting and spoke individually to many people. I was then a student, and I had been attending the meeting with other students. We went up to him, some eight or ten of us. And he shook hands with each one of us, and spoke to us in turn. He told us that he relied upon us; that we were to be the builders of new Germany. But it is not so much his words that impressed me, as it is himself, especially his eyes. 'His divine eyes,' you said. You are right: large, deep blue, magnetic eyes, he has; eyes that look straight into one's soul or straight into infinity; full of heavenly light. No one could see those eyes and remain unmoved. No one could hear his warm, convincing, compelling voice; no one could behold his countenance—stamped with unbounded willpower; brightened with the holy radiance of inspiration; softened with kindness—without loving him. No one—at least no German—could come in close contact with him even once, even for five minutes, and not become his follower."

He paused a minute, as though lost in a dream, or watching some inner vision. The words he had uttered would have thrilled me anywhere. But there, in the midst of the sacred forest, the Hartz, they took on a beauty, a solemnity that lifted me above myself and above the world, to the realm of the eternal.

But Herr A was again speaking—speaking freely in this sanctuary of peace where no profane ears could hear us, no enemy watch us; where we lay, for a while, outside the pale of persecution: "Yes," he was saying, "you are right, entirely right: Adolf Hitler *is* National Socialism; He *is* Germany; He *is* the Aryan race; the 'god among men' as you write in your paper; the living Soul of the race—our Hitler!"

He was no longer the same man. He was transfigured, as though the very spirit of the forest and of the blue sky had entered him, overshadowing his individual spirit. And I too, probably, looked more than myself. He took my hand in his, and I looked up to him with tears in my eyes.

* * *

We remained a long time without speaking, absorbed in our feelings, in tune with each other through the great One who filled our consciousness; in tune with the majestic trees, with the soul of the Hartz, the soul of all woods, abode of silent, inexhaustible strength and life—with the invincible soul of the Land he so loved. Ascending the pure blue sky, the Sun shed his rays more and more directly upon the treetops above our heads.

At last, Herr A spoke: "You told me last night," said he, "that you are a worshipper of 'the Heat-and-light within the Sun,' of the Energy that is Life; in other words, that you are a Heathen like myself and like the few others of us who really know the meaning of what we profess to stand for. Have you never longed to see the spirit of our philosophy exalted in a public cult?"

I thought I had heard the self of my youth, of my childhood, of always—my eternal self—speaking to me in the Führer's sweet language.

"I have longed for that all my life," said I, "and travelled all my life in search of its nearest equivalent, without really finding it." (I nearly said: "I have longed for that all my lives, and sought it in all the countries of this and other planets, without yet finding it.")

Herr A looked at me intently and spoke: "The public cult of Life and sunshine, as you have dreamed it," said he, "will flourish here in Germany, the cradle and the stronghold of National Socialism—during your lifetime and mine. One day, somewhere on the edge of this very forest, men will behold the temple of the new Soul. I have planned it; and I shall build it after we are free once more; after 'he' comes back; in other words, after the new soul awakens in earnest and takes consciousness of itself."

He was silent for a while, and spoke again. ("Was it he, Herr A, or was it more than he? Was it the consciousness of the future, was it reborn Germany speaking to me through him?" thought I.)

"The new Aryan soul that will pray and sing and dream in the temple of Life, is now slowly taking shape," he said; "the collective soul that will uphold the Religion of Life and Light, the one religion that can minister to the aspirations of man in a permanent National Socialist State. I shall describe to you the temple as I have conceived it. I have hardly ever spoken of this to anybody. But you will understand me, I am sure."

"I hope so."

And he unfolded before me his beautiful dream. He described to me a splendid structure of granite, against a hill, in the midst of the woods.

He evoked, before my eyes, the altar of the Sun—a huge cubic monolith bearing the holy Swastika, the Sign of the Sun, in the centre of a broad open platform, reached by a monumental staircase from within the temple, and upon which fire, lit directly from the sun rays through a convergent glass or crystal, would burn day and night—and the stately services to which the warrior-like sound of trumpets would call the population, not at ten or eleven o'clock, but at sunrise and sunset, on ordinary Sundays, and on the great festive days of the Sun—the equinoxes and the solstices—natural, regular landmarks in cosmic life, and on the great national anniversaries, landmarks in the history of the race, days on which the people have taken consciousness of their greatness in some great action.

And I listened to the wonderful conception, more and more moved as Herr A spoke. I was a Sun worshipper all my life, and I was all my life a National Socialist—knowingly, for the last twenty years. And I had been aware all the time, at the bottom of my heart, that the everlasting Religion of the Sun and the modern *Weltanschauung* of power and beauty, of purity of blood, bodily perfection and mental virility—the eternal and the modern philosophy of the Swastika—were the same. And all my life I had dreamed of a modern cult expressing this fact. And lo, at last, a man was telling me that my dream would become a living reality, at least that it would inasmuch as that depended upon him; and that man was none other but one of the faithful National Socialists in downtrodden, persecuted Germany. I felt as though, through Herr A, her worthy son, it were Germany herself speaking to me in her martyrdom: "Trust Me, the Führer's Nation; The Power of the Sun, Whom you worship, will again raise Me from the abyss. And I shall make your dream a reality from Ocean to Ocean. I shall establish the cult of strength and joy—of youth—all over the subdued world!" And the words of one of our beautiful Nazi songs came back to my mind: ". . . for Germany belongs to us today, and tomorrow the whole world."[1]

I gazed at Herr A. "I have never heard of any conception as beautiful as this," said I sincerely. "When did you first think of this 'German temple' of yours?"

"In 1936."

"And what did you do about it then?"

"Nothing."

"But why? Why did you not try to bring the scheme into being,

---

[1] "denn heute gehört uns Deutschland, und morgen die ganze Welt."

under the great One who would have understood it and appreciated it better than anybody else?"

"But he would have been the only one to understand it and appreciate it," said Herr A.

And I recalled what my wise husband had told me sometime in early 1941—and then, not for the first time: "There is one man, and one alone, in the wide world, who would fully understand and appreciate your conception of religion and life, and that is . . . the Head of the Third Reich. You should have gone straight to him instead of coming and wasting your time in the East."

And the old sadness, and the old feeling of inexpiable guilt again made my heart ache. The knife was again thrust into the unhealed wound.

But Herr A spoke once more. "The time was not ripe, then," said he. "It is not ripe now. But it will soon be. It will be, when the German people have walked to the end along the way of blood and tears, and learnt to value that which so many of them considered lightly."

"And what did they consider lightly?" I asked.

"Hitler's words, Hitler's love, Hitler's spirit," replied Herr A. "They are only now beginning to realise what a man lived in their midst; lived for them alone."

"But would not the public cult of Life, as you understand it so well, would not your 'German temple' as you planned it in your mind, have helped them to realise all that?"

"No. The new soul must slowly emerge out of unconsciousness before it can express itself in a public cult. It must emerge out of new dwellings, new schools, new factories, new centres of physical training, new life. The ever-burning high altar of the Sun, bearing the sacred Sign both of Life and of National Socialism, can only be the culmination of the future city in which the new life will be an everyday reality, accepted as a matter of course. We were gradually building that splendid new life, when the vile Jew stirred up the whole world against us, and forced war upon us."

And he described some of the features of the world that would have been if National Socialist Germany had not been defeated in 1945—of the world that will come into being tomorrow, one day, never mind when, if, with the help of the invisible forces that govern all things, we succeed in imposing our will upon men.

I was beaming with elation. "You have described," said I to Herr A, "that which, all my life, I have dreamed and longed for, thought impossible, and regretted never to see: modern civilisation at its best, modern industry in all its efficiency, in all its power, in all its grandeur; modern life with all its comforts *and*, along with that, the eternal Heathendom of the Aryans; the religion of living—physical and supraphysical—perfection, of 'God residing in pure blood' to repeat the words of Himmler; the religion of the Swastika which is the religion of the Sun; efficiency and inspiration; iron discipline coupled with enthusiasm; work, a parade; life, a manly hymn; military schools and up-to-date dwellings in the midst of trees; blast furnaces and Sun temples. That is the super-civilisation according to my heart. That is, that always was my conception of true National Socialism applied in practice. And to think that I had to come to defeated, downtrodden, martyred Germany, to find at last someone to express the same dream even better than I ever have!"

"Only through the experience of disaster and oppression, through years of martyrdom, could Germany grow to realise to the full the greatness of her Saviour and of all He stands for, and prepare herself to follow Him in absolute faith. She cheered Him, formerly, in the sunshine of victory, and her devotion was skin deep. Where are they now, those millions, whose lifted arms and joyous faces can be seen in the pictures of 1933 and 1935? Where are they? But now, the increasing thousands who long to shout 'Heil Hitler' from the bottom of the abyss, although they are not allowed to do so, mean it, with all their hearts. They will adore the holy Swastika, symbol of Life, in the Sun temples of the future. They will build the new world—the Golden Age world—which Hitler wanted."

"But could not that have happened without all this misery?"

"No. Only bitter experience teaches nations, as it teaches individuals."

"What would have happened, according to you, if by chance we had won this war?"

"Herr Schacht would still be Finance Minister of the Reich. And more millions of good-for-nothing people all over the world—some of them not even pure Aryans, strictly speaking—would be calling themselves National Socialists, without having anything in common with our beautiful way of life; without understanding the basis of it. The system would perhaps be in the process of decay through corruption *from within*. And once it collapsed (for it surely would have, in time) it could never have flourished again. A system that becomes rotten from within never does. Christianity, for instance, never will."

"And now?"

"Now the world at large thinks us dead. Let people believe it! It is better to be alive, and believed dead, than dead or dying, and believed alive. It is even sometimes expedient to be thought dead. The more our enemies believe us so—the more the Occupying Powers are convinced that they have succeeded in 'de-Nazifying' Germany—the better for us. The more they believe us incapable of rising again, the freer we are to take consciousness of our strength, and to organise ourselves, and to get ready. The more silence, the more oblivion there is around us, the easier it is for us to move about in peace, and to do what is needed of us in these times of trial, of suffering, and of preparation.

"We are few. But we have never been so alive as we are now—never so convinced of the absolute justice of our cause, of the absolute soundness of our principles; never so aware of the greatness of all we stand for.

"Wait. And learn how to work in silence, in effacement, forgotten by others, forgetting yourself. Learn how to live, faithful to our ideals, without speaking of them. Learn how to live for our Führer alone, without stirring when you hear men either praise or condemn him. Remain proud and worthy of being a National Socialist, without letting the hostile or indifferent world know that you are one. Then, and then alone, you can be useful in our ranks."

"But when shall I see, at last, the triumph that our comrades deserve, if I don't? And that new world which you say is nigh? When shall I witness the public cult of life among the regenerate Aryans?"

"In less than ten years' time. And you will see the beginning of the new rising in less than two, or at most three, if I am right. Great changes are to take place sooner than people think."

* * *

Thus we conversed, lying in the moss at the foot of the trees, in the sunny solitude of the holy forest, in communion with those living trees, with the birds, the deer, the Sun and sky above; with the maternal earth on whose bosom our bodies lay—Germany's earth.

I often wish I had hearkened more strictly to Herr A's words of prudence and wisdom. I would not now be here, in jail, but would still be useful—and in many more ways than one. Still, as Herr A said, "people learn through experience alone."

But I remember that warm September day spent in the Hartz, as a moment of beauty that nothing can alter—one of those unforgettable contacts of mine with the invincible soul of Germany.

We had been sitting there for who knows how many hours, when at last Herr A said: "It is perhaps time for us to go. My wife will be waiting for us."

"Let us use and enjoy the freedom of the woods yet five minutes longer," said I; "let us stand and sing any one you like of our old songs, as we would have, in former days, after a meeting of the NSDAP. No political gathering could have made me feel in tune with Germany's living élite more vividly than I have here, today, through your contact."

"You are right," said Herr A. "I too, feel the solemnity of this moment; your devotion represents, in my eyes, the homage of the whole Aryan race to our Germany."

So we stood, with our right arms outstretched towards the Sun, in that green solitude, the symbolical two of us—he, the Führer's compatriot, and I, the Aryan woman from far away, the first fruits of the Race's reverence and love. And we sang the Horst Wessel Song. The manly tune and words that once accompanied the march of the German army across Europe, filled the grand sunlit stillness of the holy Forest, abode of peace.

And we were calm, although intensely happy, in the awareness of the eternity of all we stand for.

Chapter 13

ECHOES FROM THE RUSSIAN ZONE

> "So ist die marxistische Lehre der kurzgefaßte geistige Extrakt der heute allgemein gültigen Weltanschauung. Schon aus diesem Grunde ist auch jeder Kampf unserer sogenannten bürgerlichen Welt gegen sie unmöglich, ja lächerlich, da auch diese bürgerliche Welt im wesentlichen von all diesen Giftstoffen durchsetzt ist und einer Weltanschauung huldigt, die sich von der marxistischen im allgemeinen nur mehr durch Grade und Personen unterscheidet."
>
> —Adolf Hitler[1]

> "... die Frage der Zukunft der deutschen Nation [ist] die Frage der Vernichtung des Marxismus ..."
>
> —Adolf Hitler[2]

I have never visited the Russian Zone of Germany—unfortunately. I wish I had. I would have, in fact—or would have at least tried to, on the sly—had I not been arrested in the British Zone before I could put my project to execution. And it is perhaps just as well—from the standpoint of my possible usefulness in the future—that I was arrested on this side of the "iron curtain" rather than on the other.

But I have met quite a number of people who have been in the Russian Zone, and some who actually live there. And I can never forget the impression they left upon me. The first one I encountered was a young woman, tall and beautiful, dressed in a very simple dark blue coat, and bearing an expression of infinite anxiety upon her face. She sat by my side in a train leaving from Hanover, and we started talking to each other. Her father, she told me, was a German, her

---

[1] "Thus the Marxist doctrine is the condensed spiritual extract of today's generally prevalent worldview. For this reason alone, any struggle of our so-called bourgeois world against it is impossible, indeed laughable, since this bourgeois world is in essence permeated by the same poisonous stuff and adheres to a worldview that in general differs from Marxism only in degree and personalities" (*Mein Kampf*, II, i, p. 420; cf. Mannheim, p. 382) [Trans. by Ed].

[2] "The question of the future of the German nation is the question of the annihilation of Marxism" (*Mein Kampf*, I, iv, p. 171; cf. Mannheim, p. 155) [Trans. by Ed].

mother a woman from the Baltic States, a Lithuanian, I believe. Her father had known Sven Hedin. We talked about Sweden—where she had lived for a time—and about that great friend of Germany and of the Führer. Then, all of a sudden, after a long pause, she asked me: "Do you believe in the power of thought?"

"I do," I replied.

"Then, think of me intensely this evening at about eight o'clock," she said. "I shall then be on the border."

"You are going to the Russian Zone?"

"Yes. And I am afraid."

"Why don't you stay here, if you believe it is not safe for you to go?"

"I once lived there," she replied. "I could not stand the atmosphere, and came away. But I could not take my two children with me. They are there still. And I have had no news of them for a long time. I feel restless. I want to see them again at any cost."

There was controlled, but intense emotion in her voice, and tears in her large blue eyes appeared as she spoke.

"I shall think of you, and pray for you with all my might this evening at eight o'clock," said I. We were on the morning of the 26th of October 1948. Then I asked her about the Russian Zone. "Tell me," I said, "how are things there; worse than here?"

"Much worse."

In the course of our conversation, I had already made sure that she was a Nazi at heart. I asked her, nearly in a whisper: "How about the 'old' spirit, there?" She smiled faintly.

"Outwardly, it looks as though it is dead," she said. "But it lives in the secrecy of our hearts, even though we do not speak, even to one another, for fear of hidden listeners. Men who are—or pretend to be—drunk, sometimes sing the old songs. In such cases, the Russians say nothing."

"And how about Communism? Got many German adherents?"

"None whom I know," she replied. "Those it once had have changed their minds, after seeing what it meant in practice."

"So, if, one day, things took an unexpected turn, you would all be ready to welcome the rebirth of the New Order?"

"Most certainly," she said. And her face took on an expression of ineffable longing. "But when? When?"

"Perhaps sooner than we think."

"Oh, if only you could be right!" she whispered.

Very quietly, I gave her one of my leaflets. She slipped it into a magazine and read it, pretending to be reading the magazine.

"Where did you manage to get that printed?" she asked me, in a voice hardly perceptible, when she had finished.

"Abroad," said I.

She squeezed my hand. "I wish I could take your whole stock with me," she said. "But I dare not. I shall keep that one paper, however. We shall copy it over and over again, be sure. Thousands will read it."

"So," said I, "you *are* alive, in the Russian Zone!"

"How can it be otherwise? Did you imagine for a moment that we could forget? Never!"

One of the sentences in my leaflet had caught her attention. She pointed it out to me. "You say so yourself, don't you?" she whispered: "We are the gold in the furnace . . ."

"You are indeed," replied I.

She looked at me intently and said: "*We* are—including yourself. Your turn too will come, to bear witness to the truth we stand for, in suffering, as all other genuine National Socialists."

I felt honoured far beyond my merits by that mark of confidence from one who had already lived three and a half years in the midst of persecution. I did not know that the woman's words were prophetic. The following station was my destination. I got down, saluting my friend of an hour, for the last time, perhaps. And I thought of her on that evening, and many times since.

Later on, on my way to Mainz, I met a student who had also lived in the Russian Zone, and after talking to him some time, I asked him the same question: "Is it really worse than in West Germany, as so many people say?"

"Dear me," exclaimed the youth; "I should think so!"

"In the Western Zones it is bad enough," I said.

"Yes. But at least we can grumble."

"Only to a very small extent," I replied. "Go and say, for instance, in any public place, that the National Socialist régime was wonderful and that you would like nothing better than to see it come back; and watch what happens—that is to say, if there is any policeman or police informer lurking about. Or just try to salute a friend at the corner of the street in the former manner . . ."

"Yes," said he, interrupting me, "of course, if you go that far. But one can express much of one's feelings without going that far. And one does. We have, for example, been talking now, for over half an hour, and we understand each other, don't we? You know me enough to trust me at least to some extent; your last words prove it. And I think I know what you are."

"But, I said nothing at all."

"You don't need to 'say' it. Nobody ever 'says' it. But again, you are allowed to let everybody know it, if you choose to do so. While 'there,' it is different."

"But," I replied, "what precisely irritates me the most, not merely here, in the French Zone, but in the whole of Western Germany (I never was in the Eastern area), is that ban on my free speech; that reticence, that constant repression forced upon me."

"You say that because you come from the free world outside unfortunate Germany, and because you have never yet crossed the border between the Western Zones and the Eastern Zone. There, behind the 'iron curtain,' you could not say a quarter of what you have said now during our short conversation, without being asked to get down at the next station and to follow the policeman waiting there to take you up."

"But if nobody overheard me?"

"In the Russian Zone, somebody always does overhear. There are informers everywhere, and you can never tell who is who. Parents cannot trust their own children, nor a brother his brother, nor a man his wife. Here, National Socialism is persecuted. There, it is crushed."

"Inwardly also?"

"Outwardly. Inwardly, no power on earth is in a position to crush it."

"And how do the people react to this?"

"They are quiet—outwardly; much quieter than here, in the Western Zones. They suffer more."

I asked him the same question as I had, some months before, to the woman in the train from Hanover: "How about the Communists, there?" The answer was the same: "There *are* no Communists, in the Russian Zone—save a handful of fellows who suck up to the Russians for what they expect to get out of them, materially. There would be none anywhere, in Germany, if only they all could have a taste of what Communism means, for six months or so, as we have had, for four years. Communism," he added after a pause, repeating that which I have said myself so many times, "sounds like salvation, and is, indeed, perhaps, the nearest approach to salvation, for people who are both primitive and exploited, like the peasants of Russia—or China—were for centuries. If such people are, in addition to that, of an inferior stock, it will appeal to them all the more. But no highly-civilised, organised, and *conscious* people of a superior race, especially no people who, like we, have once experienced National Socialism, can possibly take to such a system. Even the Russians who have had a glimpse of our régime during the short time their country was occupied by us, cannot help feeling all the difference between the Communist point of view and ours."

"And do you believe they would have been easily kept within the pale of a National Socialist world, if Germany had won this war?"

"With time, and adequate propaganda, and education, why not?" said he.

"And what about those social reforms which, they say, the Russians have introduced into the Russian Zone: the division of the land among the peasants and so forth, of which such a fuss is made abroad by Communist sympathisers?"

"Oh, that!" said the student, with a wry smile, "another piece of deceit! The peasants of Eastern Germany fare worse, now, than they ever did before. Whether the land is supposed to be theirs or not, it makes no difference. They are slaves upon it. They are compelled to give up to the Government a certain amount of goods fixed beforehand, and the same whether the crops have been plentiful or scanty, with the result that, after a bad season, they have to buy food from peasants of more fortunate areas so that they can give the Government dues and still eat. Sometimes, they even have to buy from others the very goods—potatoes, for instance—that they are expected to give as a tax. You should visit the Zone yourself, and make a thorough inquiry."

"I would like to. But how can I go? I have no permit."

"If you are willing, I shall try to arrange for you to go on the sly, with relatives of mine returning there. Only when you have seen the place will you be able to understand how justified you are in your wholehearted praise of the German National Socialists of *all* the Zones. Only then will you know how right you are when you say: 'Four Zones, but . . . still one people, and in that people's heart one Führer—*the* Führer.'"

I saw the young man again. I was received in his home. I had made up my mind to try my chance and do as he had suggested. But my arrest upset my plans.

* * *

There is a place not far from Hanover, called Celle. In the station, as in most German stations of any importance, there is a "Catholic

Mission" that provides food and shelter for the night to people who cannot afford to go to a hotel. That is one of the spots where one can watch the daily arrival of refugees from the Russian Zone. I spent a couple of nights there myself, as well as at the Catholic Mission of the Hanover station, and thus got in touch with many of them.

I shall always remember a lad of fourteen, whom I met at Celle—an intelligent, but still childish face, with large pale blue eyes that looked up to me, full of tears, with heart-rending entreaty, as I put my hand upon his shoulder, in a gesture of sympathy.

But I could do nothing for him. "He crossed the border two days ago," the lady in charge of the Mission told me, "and now we are sending him back. What else can we do? He has no relatives, no friends who could take charge of him in the British or any other of the Western Zones; no work; no money." (How gladly I would have taken charge of him, had I not been, myself, but a homeless wanderer, living and carrying on my activities, on the few scraps of jewellery I had left, with no prospects of finding any work however much I tried!)

"What prompted him to come over?" I asked, when the unfortunate boy had eaten his last morsel and was taken to the train.

"Fear," said the lady in charge. "They were looking for him to send him to work in the mines, somewhere far away—'in the Urals,' he says. And he does not want to go. He wants to remain in Germany and continue to go to school."

"Who are his parents?"

"People who both played an active part in spreading National Socialism in their town, in former days, apparently. His father was taken away to Siberia and never heard of again. His mother works and maintains him the best way she can. He has two young brothers."

"The same attempt to uproot National Socialism everywhere," thought I; "the same savage persecution of the élite of the world, from one end of Germany to the other! And it does, definitely, look worse in the Russian Zone than in the Western area, I must admit." Turning to the lady in charge I said: "And there was nothing, really, that you could have done for the kid? Absolutely nothing?"

"Alas no."

"You could not have sent him to a refugee camp?"

The lady in charge looked at me as one looks at a person who does not know what he or she is talking about.

"Have you visited any of those refugee camps?" she asked me.

"No," said I. "I wished to. But I was told I needed a special permission. I was thinking of applying for one on the ground that I am writing a book about Germany."

". . . as a consequence of which you would never be granted a permit," she replied, ". . . that is to say, not unless the Occupation authorities felt sure that you would shut your eyes to all that they wish to keep concealed concerning the conditions of life in their relief camps. But you are not a woman to shut your eyes to things, or to hide the truth when you know it. I can understand that, from your conversation during these two or three days. I can even understand more about you, I believe. A very, *very* definite reason for 'them' to give you no admittance to their 'charitable' institutions in this unfortunate land."

"What reason?"

She hesitated. I knew her first impulse would have been to say: "You are a National Socialist." But she did not say that, although she was practically sure it was true. She said: "You are a *real* friend of Germany"—which meant the same. "Our friend, and a writer; then surely no permit for you, my dear lady!" she added jokingly. "But if you could see some of those camps you would not think of sending a young boy there."

"Still, perhaps better than slave labour in the mines," I ventured to say.

"I am not so sure about that," she replied enigmatically. "Moreover, there *is* no place in the refugee camps. Do you know how many people cross the border every week on an average?"

"Five thousand, I was told in Hanover, by an Englishman in a responsible position in the Labour Department, at 'Sterling House.'"

"That is the official figure," she said. "In fact, there are many more than that. And their position—and ours—is becoming more and more acute."

Two women stepped in at that moment—two more from the Russian Zone—and asked for something to eat. While they sat and ate, I talked to them.

They were not refugees. They were people who lived with their families in the Russian Zone, and who came regularly to see relatives and to buy food across the frontier. I asked them, as I did every other person from the forbidden area, how they fared there.

"Life is hard," they told me, "not so much for such people whose sympathies were, from the beginning, actively and obviously with the Red Front, as for us, who were connected with the NSDAP."

"Connected only," the other woman put in at once. "For had we distinguished ourselves by any special activity, or held any special position in the Party, we would not even enjoy that small amount of tranquillity. My husband was an SS man. He fell a prisoner to the Americans during the last year of the war and only came home in '47. Well, he is not allowed to take up his former job in civil life as an electrician. He must work on the roads—break stones and dig—for the sole reason that he was a militant Nazi."

"The Democrats do such things here, too," I said. "Not that I want to defend the Reds. I never was a Communist, goodness me! But I can tell you many instances of similar oppression on this side of the Elbe."

"I believe you. Yet I doubt whether they could match those of the Russian Zone," she replied unconvinced. "You have no idea what we suffer over there—all Germans, but especially we National Socialists."

During the time I remained in Celle we got to know one another better. One day, as we were alone, I took out of my pocket a padded jewel box, opened it, and placed it before my new friends. A pair of golden swastikas—the earrings I used to wear in Calcutta and in London—gleamed before their eyes on a background of dark blue velvet. The two women repressed a cry of joyous surprise. "How beautiful!" they exclaimed, almost together. "But where on earth did you get those?"

"In India. One can buy any number of them in the jewellery shops, there. The swastika is a widespread religious symbol held in veneration by all Hindus—who dimly remember the Nordic origin of the civilisation they glory in to this day. It is the sacred Sign of the Sun."

"We too call it *'Sonnenrad'*—the 'Wheel of the Sun.' But you don't wear those here, in Germany?"

"I do . . . under a shawl thrown over my head, which I take off indoors, when I know that I can trust the people I am visiting."

"Do you know what would happen if you were caught with those in the Russian Zone?"

"What?"

"You would be sent off to Siberia at once."

I paused; and then, producing two of my leaflets, I said: "And what would they do to me if they caught me distributing *these*?"

There was another cry of surprise and then, deep silence, while each of the two women read the words of defiance.

"Never cross the border," said finally one of my new friends; "'they' would kill you. How many of these did you distribute in the Western Zones?"

"Ten thousand, up till now."

"Without getting into trouble! Marvellous! And how long have you been doing that?"

"Over eight months."

"You could not have done it eight days in the Russian Zone. 'They' have spies everywhere. 'They' are devils. Worse than the Western Democrats, I tell you. But you can give us some of your papers. We know whom to give them to."

"But how will you cross the border with them?"

"No fear as far as we are concerned," said the other woman. "We come and go every fortnight. The guards on the frontier know us."

"And I can trust you to distribute those leaflets at your own risk?"

"Every German in the Russian Zone misses National Socialist rule, not just we, who supported it from the beginning. You can rely upon us."

I gave them each a couple of hundreds of my leaflets, as I had given several other sympathetic people returning to the forbidden area.

When they had left, I showed my Indian earrings to the lady in charge of the Mission, a little cautiously. "I hope you don't object to my having them," I said: "You see . . . they are Indian . . ."

Her face brightened as she saw the immemorial Sign. She smiled. But, along with joy, there was an ineffable nostalgia in her smile. She gazed at the symbol of National Socialism. "I, object?" she said at last. "You don't know me. I too love that Sign . . ."

"Do you, really?" I replied, overjoyed. "I had thought . . ."

I had thought—and still think—that no consistent person can be a Catholic and "love that Sign." And the woman would not have been in charge of this station mission had she not been, at least outwardly, a Catholic. So I wondered . . . She was probably no sincere Catholic after all. Or she lacked consistency—as so many people do. But she did not leave me time to wonder.

"Shhush!" said she, in a whisper, putting her fingers to her mouth. "I am not supposed to talk frankly to you. And this is not the place. But when you come back to Celle, come to my house. If I cannot myself put you up, I know friends who will gladly do so. And then we shall talk. I am beginning to know you—and to like you."

But I was arrested before I could go back. I never saw the lady again. She must have read about my case in the daily papers—or heard of it on the wireless: "Sentenced to three years' imprisonment for Nazi propaganda . . ." And she probably thought: "Not surprising."

* * *

But all these people, whether hundred percent National Socialists or not, had always been sympathetically inclined towards our régime; they were, at least, never hostile to it. Yet, there seem to be, in the Russian Zone no less than in Western Germany, quite a number of men and women who previously hated National Socialism but who, now, bitterly regret they did not support it with all their might. I repeat: I have not lived in the Zone. But I can assert that there are many such Germans among those who come across the border, whether with the intention of remaining in the Western areas, or on short periodical visits.

I shall recall one instance only: that of a young woman whom I met at the "Catholic Mission" in the Hanover station. This woman could hardly have been more than thirty—thirty-five at the most. She had a frank, pleasant face. She told me she was living in the Russian Zone. I introduced myself as a writer, and told her of my intended journey over the border in order to complete my book on Germany.

She gazed at me with genuine interest and said: "Don't go! It is only courting trouble. You don't know what a life we live, over there."

"That is just what I would like to see for myself," I replied.

"The knowledge is not worth the risk," she answered. "You might never come back. You are English, aren't you?"

"Half-English."

"Whatever you be . . . You are not a Communist?" she asked.

"Anything but one!"

"Well, in that case, don't go! They will seize on the slightest pretext to charge you with espionage on behalf of the Democracies and to send you off to some place whence you will never return."

"But I am no Democrat either!" said I. And then, realizing that I had perhaps spoken too much, I added: "I take no interest whatsoever in politics. As a writer, I am only concerned with men and women and their lives." The lie was a clumsy one. But she did not seem to notice it.

"If you care for people's welfare, you should take interest in politics," she replied. "But think twice before you support or fight any movement—weigh the pros and cons carefully." And she added in a low voice: "Never do what I did. I betrayed my country without knowing what I was doing."

I suddenly had a glimpse of the whole tragedy of that woman's life. She was one of those thousands whom I had hated so intensely; one of those of whom I had so often said: "They should all have been 'liquidated' in time." But I controlled my feelings, looked at her with curiosity, and answered enigmatically:

"Many have betrayed their country without knowing what they were doing during this war, and not only among the Germans. And they have betrayed the Aryan race, which in my eyes is worse."

The woman looked strangely into my face and asked me, hesitatingly: "Are you also one of them?"

"Oh, not I!" I burst out in protest—I could nearly say "in indignation." "I knew where my duty lay. And there lay my heart also. I was on the right side from the beginning—years before the war."

"I see you *are* interested in politics after all," said the woman, with a pinch of irony. But her face soon became serious, nay, sad, once more.

"You were on the right side without being a German," she resumed, "while I . . . Oh, had I only known!"

"Is it indiscreet to ask what you did?" said I.

"I fought against Hitler," she replied; "I was in an underground organisation whose aim was to undermine his power and to bring about his downfall. We were deceived into believing that he was the cause of the war and the original source of all our misfortunes—he, our saviour! Oh, had I but known!"

Every word of hers was like a knife-thrust into my heart. With implacable clearness, I pictured that woman busying herself with shadowy propaganda against the inspired Leader whom I so loved; I imagined her secretly informing the Russians of whatever she knew of his efforts to defend Germany (as so many other traitors had informed the Western Democracies)—doing her best to bring about the ruin of the National Socialist Order, the downfall of all I admired, revered, praised, defended, all those years. Did she perchance fancy that her tardy remorse would efface that criminal past of hers in my eyes? I hated her with bitter hatred. And my first impulse was to say: "Well, remain, now, under the darling Communists whom you yourself called and longed for, and enjoy them to your heart's content! You don't know how glad I am to behold that distress upon your face. You are not the first one I see—nor the last, I hope. I am only sorry I cannot meet the whole lot of you, one by one, and enjoy the sight of each one's present-day misery. The Third Reich, which you betrayed, spared you. May those for the sake of whom you betrayed it not spare you, but slowly grind you out of existence, you and all the other wretched anti-Nazis! You don't deserve to see the daylight!"

But I did not utter these words. I only felt them spring from my heart in indignation and hatred, as I gazed at that woman.

She was pretty, and well-built. She looked healthy. Under a broad, intelligent forehead, her two large grey eyes were fixed upon me, while the curls of her glossy reddish-brown hair moved in the wind. There was such a depth of despair in those eyes that I shuddered. But still, I hated her.

Then, in a flash of imagination, I recalled the stern and beautiful face of the Man she had betrayed—and probably reviled in speech, countless times—the Führer's face, as sad as hers, but of a different sadness; a face conscious of the tragedy of the whole world led to its ruin by its own folly, and its enemies' lies; conscious of the eternal tragedy of better mankind exploited by the clever rogues of an inferior nature, but aware, also, of the endless potentialities of the misled Aryan; the face of the Saviour who hoped because he loved, and who stands above defeat because he knows the everlastingness of the truth for which he fought. And I felt as though He stood between us—He, our loving Hitler—and was saying to me: "Don't crush her still more under the weight of your indignation. Don't hate her! For my sake, don't! Whatever she might have done against me, she is one of my people. Help her to come back to me."

Tears filled my eyes; and I was a while without speech. Then, I said slowly: "What is done is done. But the endless future is there, before you. Germany is not dead; will never die. Tell me: what would you do *now*—tomorrow, next year—if the Führer came back?"

"I would stand by him fanatically, in the new struggle, glad if an honourable death cleansed me of my shameful past activities," she replied, her eyes also moist with tears. And she added with entreaty: "I know you can hardly believe me. You don't trust me. You look upon me as a traitor, which I am, or rather which I *was*. But if you could realise what agony I have lived, all these four years, you would believe me. And you would not hate me."

A tear slowly rolled down one of my cheeks.

"Who am I," said I, "to hate you? I have no right to do so. As an Aryan and as a lover of truth, I came from the other end of the world to bear witness to my Führer's greatness in this martyred Land. And you are one of his people. And you love him—now. Don't you?"

A flash of unearthly joy brightened her pale face—the joy of unexpected redemption.

"I do!" she replied passionately.

I took her to a place where nobody could watch us and asked her: "Would you like to *do* something for him?"

"What can I do, now? It is too late."

"It is never too late, as long as the spirit is alive. Listen: can you distribute a few of these among the men and women across the border who, like yourself, once fought against National Socialism, but now repent for what they have done?"

And I took out of my bag a bundle of leaflets wrapped up in a fashion magazine.

She read one and asked me: "Who wrote this?"

"I."

"And you are sure he is alive?"

"Practically sure. I know it from several sources."

"Oh," said she, with infinite yearning, "if only you were right! I shall take as many of those leaflets as you can give me, and distribute them among my friends."

"Are you not afraid to cross the border with them?"

"No. I am never searched now. The guards know me. Moreover, they know I have worked against all this in bygone years. But they do not know how I regret it."

I gave her the whole bundle. "Good luck to you," said I.

"I shall never forget our meeting in this station," she replied. "I hope to see you again, one day, if I am not caught and sent to Siberia to work till I am dead. I don't think I shall be. But one never knows. Well, if I am, I shall expiate my past."

"Don't look to the past," said I; "look to the future—for we have a future. I assure you we have. *Auf wiedersehen!*"

She looked at me as though she wanted to say something more. She turned her head right and left to see whether anybody was paying attention to us from a distance. Then, she lifted her right hand in the ritual gesture, as I would have, myself, in a lonely place, in the presence of someone of our views.

"Heil Hitler!" she said.

It was perhaps the first time in her life that she greeted anyone sincerely with those words and that gesture. I replied with the same gesture, repeating the forbidden, sacred words: "Heil Hitler!" And I recalled in my heart the Führer's sentence: "One day, the world will know that I was right."

And I was filled with an immense joy, as though I had played a part—a tiny part—in the making of a new Germany, more strongly, more genuinely united than ever under the sign of the Swastika.

* * *

I have said so before: they can dismember Germany, terrorise her people, starve them, humiliate them, vilify them in the eyes of a world of charlatans and imbeciles; they can forbid the *Horst-Wessel-Lied*, and all the other songs of the glorious days; forbid the Nazi salute, and all external manifestations of love for Adolf Hitler. They can never kill the Nazi spirit, or the German soul—the first national soul awake in an Aryan nation, foreshadowing the birth of the future soul of Aryandom. Let them maintain four 'Zones' in the place of the one Reich—as long as the invisible Powers allow them to do so. Four Zones there might be but, still one people, one heart, one German consciousness and—whether alive or dead, in the flesh—one Führer, of whom nobody speaks (in public at least) but of whom everybody thinks and whom, more and more, everybody reveres.

To the unsympathetic foreigner come to occupy their country and to try to "convert" them, the Germans might show but an extreme outward politeness, and an absolute indifference to the fate of National Socialism and of its Founder. But the intelligent occupants themselves are not deceived. A French official in Baden-Baden, Monsieur P, once told one that a paper in Cologne had published an article discussing the question whether the Führer is alive or not. "There was a 'queue' waiting to buy the paper on that day," said he. "There would be! There is nobody but Hitler in their minds."

And, as soon as the Germans are really in distress, their thoughts automatically rush back to him, "not only the Leader of his people, but their Saviour," as Hermann Göring once said.[1] In the dark days of hunger and destitution, in Treves and several other towns, I was told, one found the two forbidden words written upon the walls: "Heil Hitler!" as though to say: "Yes, in 'his' time we were happy, while now . . ." And during the tragic blockade of Berlin, the crowd from the starving Western sectors, roused by prolonged hardships, did not oppose Communist power with newly learnt Democratic slogans. No. Those dead words, corresponding to nothing whatsoever in the German heart, if ever learnt at all for the sake of immediate expediency, were forgotten in the twinkling of an eye. And on the 13th of September 1948 the crowd marched to the Brandenburg Gate singing the Horst Wessel Song, and tore down the flag of the Hammer and Sickle shouting "Heil Hitler!"—despite the terrible penalties that awaited all those on whom the Russians managed to lay hands.

"Heil Hitler!" is the cry of Germany's heart to this day, in whatever "Zone" it be.

---

[1] Speech at the "*Parteitag*" of Nuremberg, 15 September 1935.

* * *

The feeling of bitterness and resentment that one encounters in those who live in the Russian Zone is partly due, no doubt, to the hard conditions of life that prevail there. But it is also, and more still, due to the knowledge of the thoroughness and stability of Communism, compared with Democracy; to the consciousness of its hold on a large section of mankind, and its irresistible expansion. The Germans of the Western Zones—I mean, not the docile slaves of the Jews, but the genuinely intelligent and wholeheartedly German people, *i.e.*, the National Socialists—might be persecuted: not allowed to air their views freely; not allowed to greet one another publicly in the former manner, or to have pictures of the Führer on the walls, in their own houses; not allowed to hold certain posts, or even to work at all, if they are known to have been prominent or at least enthusiastic members of the NSDAP in recent years. Yet, they are too intelligent not to realise the weaknesses of Democracy; not to see how shallow, how inconsistent, nay, how childish is the "philosophy" upon which it lies, compared with ours; not to think: "Such a system cannot last. It carries in itself the germs of its own destruction. Its very inconsistency—or rather its hypocrisy—is its death-warrant." The Democrats, even when they persecute us, are too stupid for us not to despise them, as I have already said many times. The *naïveté* with which they proceed to "reform" us would be sufficient to make anybody laugh. We know what they want us to say. We say it. And we are amused to see how readily they believe that we really mean it. We deny (outwardly) whatever we can of the acts of ruthlessness—the so-called "war-crimes"—attributed to us, letting the simpletons remain convinced that, *if only* we believed that such "crimes" really took place, we would be the first ones to renounce National Socialism. And when we see how firmly convinced they are of our fundamental "humanity"—when we see how readily they take all but the most obviously, the most blatantly thorough amongst us for lovers of half-measures like themselves—we think: "What fools!" As though we ever cared—as though we care, now—what acts of violence took place for the sake of our triumph; as though we mind a little ruthlessness, when it is expedient! In you, our persecutors of today, what revolts us is the hypocrisy, not the violence; the way you find excuses for your crimes, not your crimes themselves; the spirit in which you do things, not the things you do—not even your atrocities upon us; we would understand those, if only you called them acts of vengeance and not acts of justice. You don't know us! You never will. Continue to lull yourselves into believing that you have "converted" us—"awakened" in us the natural "humanity" that our "monstrous" Nazi education had silenced for a while—you bumptious imbeciles, you self-styled "crusaders to Europe," and keep on being fooled, as long as we judge it expedient to nod our heads at your sermons! Tomorrow—next year, the year after—when our opportunity comes again, we will show you fast enough how silly of you it was to judge us by your own standards. We will teach you what Nazis are, if you do not know by now! In the meantime, keep your illusions.

In the Russian Zone, things are different. There—from what I imagine from my few contacts with Germans who live there; for I repeat: I have not lived there myself—persecution seems to be not only more ruthless (it is ruthless enough in Western Germany) but more intelligent, and more difficult to avoid. The Communists know that we are as one-pointed, as purposeful, as uncompromising as themselves, and that therefore they cannot trust us, whatever we might tell them. They might try to "convert" a few of the younger ones among us. But they do not try for long. They do not believe in wasting their time. They either subdue us materially, and terrorise us into silence, or "liquidate" us. They understand us better than the Democrats ever will, and consequently, dislike us without reservations. As I said before, they, and not the Democrats—not the men spontaneously drawn to half-measures—are our real enemies.

The National Socialists of the Russian Zone realise that only too well. And at times, under the heel of those real enemies, so well organised and so strong, they experience a feeling of dejection verging on despair. We have lost this war. We all know that. But in the West of Germany, many of us still believe that the Democracies *and* the Bolsheviks won it together. In the Russian Zone, we are all convinced, for the last four years, that the Bolsheviks alone are the victors.

Moreover we feel—and that, not only in the Russian Zone, but also in the areas under Franco-Anglo-American control, and outside Germany—that we are, with Communism, in the presence of something altogether out of proportion with Western Democracy; of something grim and formidable, not the last sign of life in a dying world, but the swelling tide of a new, great wave in the history of man. And we feel—we know, from our intuition of history (and those of us who possess a sound historical background know it all the more definitely from logic as well as intuition)—that this new great movement in the evolution of man is unavoidable. We could not stop it. The Democracies will still less be able to do so. *Nothing can stop it.*

It has to come, whether one likes it or not, just as, sooner or later, night has to take the place of daylight. We know this is the last leap of mankind along its age-old, fated path towards disintegration—unavoidable doom. We know that doom must come, before resurrection. We—the children of resurrection—can do nothing, before the world has trodden the path of death to its very end. We can only be ready and wait—"hope and wait,"[1] as the Gods, through my humble agency, told the German people. There is nothing else to be done. Our time of grand outward activity lies in the past and in the future. At present, we can only watch—keep our spirit alive—and pray; keep ourselves in contact with one another and with the eternal Source of our inspiration: the truth we stand for, and the godlike Exponent of that truth, our Führer, living forever, whether he be materially alive, or dead and immortal; somewhere on earth, or in Valhalla.

And, while we know we can just now *do* nothing, we can see everywhere around us, near and far, increasing instances of that power of Communism which seems, at present, boundless. In the Western Zones we feel that, sooner or later, the Occupation will have to go. We can imagine the last lorry full of soldiers rolling across the frontier, and the general sigh of relief at the news. It might not be tomorrow morning, but every German, let alone every National Socialist, feels that it must be, that it *will be* one day. In the Russian Zone, at times at least, one feels that such a day might, perhaps, never come. Moreover, in the Western Zones, the end of military control would mean the end of control altogether, over Germany. Nothing can keep the country down, once the troops of occupation are gone. In the Russian Zone, even if the troops of occupation did go, a burdensome control would still remain, an effective control, like that over so many other countries in which "popular republics"—*i.e.*, Russian-sponsored republics—have been established. For how long? As the Communists have taken over Russia and are ruling it still, after so much distrust and scepticism on the part of the world, in the early years of their régime, so they will take over Germany, the whole of Europe, the world—who knows?—and rule it, no one can tell for how long; one wonders, sometimes, in despair, if not forever. They seem to be thoroughly well organised, already, in the Russian Zone. That is to be expected. Communism—the latest great lie of the everlasting Jew; the last mass-onrush of mankind towards final decay and death, under the impulse of the age-old enemy of the natural order—is nothing but Democracy carried to its bitterest

---

[1] "*Hofft und wartet!*"—the last words on the posters I stuck up in Germany.

conclusion; Democracy endowed with our merciless logic and our unbending thoroughness. It is, on the broadest possible scale, the display of our qualities and of our efficiency put to the service of the philosophy of death *par excellence*.

Those same qualities were once used to forward the cause of Christianity in the days the Catholic Church was all-powerful. Democracy—the sickly régime of half-measures—is, to a great extent, devoid of them. For it is but the bridge between Christianity and Communism, or, if one prefers, the expression of Christian civilisation grown old and pining for rest—for "security"; that is the Democrats' pet word—in reality, pining for disintegration and death. But Communism, the latest and, maybe, the last expression of the irresistible tendency of mankind towards disintegration, has taken on those qualities once more. And, thanks to them, it is everywhere undermining the artificial democratic structure, causing great alarm among the comfortably settled Jews of capitalistic countries. For although it is itself, undoubtedly, a Jewish product—Marx's "historical materialism" applied to government—more and more numerous are the Jews who are experiencing genuine fear at the sight of its expansion. These Jews wanted Communism to destroy Christian civilisation, in order to bind the Aryan race more tightly than ever to their yoke. They did not imagine that the upheaval might drag *them*, also, to their doom, in the process. Now, they fear it might be so. "Communism is evolving," they say; "it is no longer 'genuine' Communism."

And maybe it is not, in many instances. In 1930, a certain Keralian Communist was, to my knowledge, cut off from the Communist Party—excommunicated—for three years, for having called a man a "dirty Jew" in a Russian tramway car. Today—I hear—many Jews who had helped the Russians to fight Germany during this war were "liquidated" under one pretext or another as soon as the war was finished. Does this, perchance, mean that, in the eyes of many Russians at least, this war was not the struggle of Communism against National Socialism (as the Jews had wished) but just that of Russia against Germany—an ordinary war between two Aryan nations for vital space, as so many conflicts in the past, and no "crusade" whatsoever?

And—I hear also—there are, in Germany today, Communist groups from which Jews are excluded.[1] How is one to characterise such Communism that admits—and insists upon—racial distinctions?

---

[1] An apparently well-informed Communist woman interned in Werl has told me so. I have not had the opportunity to check the truth of her statement.

Perchance, as a disguised form of National Socialism? And that is what the Jews fear. And that is what we hope.

But in the meantime, there reigns an implacable tyranny in the Russian Zone—a tyranny aiming at the uprooting of National Socialism in the name of purely Marxist principles, no less ruthlessly than we would ourselves try to crush any *Weltanschauung* standing in our way, if we were in power; a tyranny, of which we can well envy the thoroughness while hating the purpose.

* * *

And beyond the boundaries of the Russian Zone and of Germany, and of Europe, the power of Communism is becoming every day more formidable, more irresistible. Who will oppose it? The Western Democracies, or their worthless tools, the less objectionable Oriental rogues who exploit the gullibility of the Democracies for the sake of sheer personal profits?—less objectionable, I call them, for they are at least frank enough to put forward no "ideology" at all; no justification of their unholy alliance with the world's greatest deceivers.

The Communists have conquered China. When, before that, they had tightened their hold on Poland and Czechoslovakia, the Western Democracies had become alarmed. Those "poor Czechs" and those "poor Poles" had already suffered so much from us "Nazi beasts!" It was really not fair that our deadliest enemies the Reds should continue our work—and (they say) improve upon it—after we were crushed! It made the Western Democracies feel as though they had fought their stupid war and defeated us for nothing. Or rather, it made things look as though they had fought it as complacent henchmen of the clever Communists, and as though the Communists had won it, and not they—which is, of course, the truth. As a consequence, they had been thoroughly alarmed. But Poland and Czechoslovakia are insignificant countries compared with China and its five hundred million people. True, the Chinese are not Europeans. But that should never come into account with broadminded gentlemen devoid of "racial prejudices"— believers in quantity, not in quality—as our persecutors the Democrats pretend to be. And China is far away. But that too is a blunt excuse for indifference. No country is far away, in our epoch. And the fact is that General Mao Tse-Tung's victory is a very great event; the beginning of a worldwide change, the rising of a mostly if not entirely Communist Asia—and that, whether the short-sighted Democracies care to be alarmed or not.

For Communism in China means, very soon, Communism in Indo-China and in India, and perhaps in Japan. The Japanese, the victims of America's first atom bomb and, since then, the object of endless humiliations under American occupation, have a great grudge against the Western Democracies. And who would not have, in their place? In Malaya, in Indonesia, the irresistible ideology of the Hammer and Sickle is spreading like wildfire. It is the end of the "white man's burden," forever. It would be lovely to revisit the East and hear what the white man thinks while packing his things to go away—that self-same white man who, during this war, used to talk with such naïve, undeviating hatred, about "Fascist beasts," and "Nazi monsters." Perhaps he is now beginning to wonder whether it would not have been better, after all, to support Hitler unwaveringly. How glad I would be to remind him of his recent propaganda of slander against us who did support him; to point out to him, mercilessly, all that he is now "in for," and tell him with a sneer: "It serves you right!" I have no love for him. Let him and his friends in Europe and America—those who poured fire and phosphorus over Nazi Germany—bleed and groan for centuries under the whip of their ex-"gallant Allies!" "But what about us, Hitler's faithful ones?" I hear, within my heart, the voices of my comrades say: "Do you want *us* also to perish, for the pleasure of gloating over our persecutors' plight? The Communists too are our persecutors." And I think of those genuine National Socialists whom I met in the stations near the border of the Russian Zone.

If I were the Führer's last follower, then, yes, I would desire nothing else but vengeance. I would live only to see, one day, and to enjoy, the annihilation of that Europe who hated and betrayed her Saviour; who tortured and killed those who loved him; who would have tortured and killed him, had she been able to lay hands on him in 1945. If I were the last Nazi, I would myself help the Communists to inflict upon the ungrateful continent all the suffering the Democrats inflicted upon us, and still more, if possible. I have more imagination than most people—even than most Orientals—and this could prove handy. But I am *not* the last—far from it. "There are millions like yourself, in martyred Germany," Sven Hedin told me, on the 6th of June 1948. He was too courteous to say: "There are millions much better than you." But I know there are. I have met them, in that Land of suffering and of glory—of death and resurrection—during my year's stay. Rather than see one of those endure permanent servitude, I would, if I could, spare the whole continent—spare the people I hate or despise, in order to save those whom I love and admire; renounce vengeance if, at the cost of that sacrifice, Hitler's New Order can be given a chance to rise again out of the ruins of the world.

There is no doubt that Communism will soon be the uniting force of the whole of Asia and of all the non-Aryan races in general. More so: millions among the Aryans have already adhered to it; millions more will. And the Democracies, in their coming struggle with their former allies, will have to reckon with a formidable Fifth Column force within their own people. Add to this the fact that, not being "totalitarian," they possess none of those characteristics that make for strength in the Communists as well as in us.

As a result, unless *we* step in against them and beat them, or at least come to some agreement with them, the Communists will win the battle and remain the masters of the world for good. There is no doubt about that.

But *why should we* step in against them, if the outcome is to be a Democratic victory? Do we wish to help those hypocrites who only allow us to live on the condition they believe they will one day "convert" us, and who, up to this moment, persecute us—who, I am told, *now*, after four years, are sitting as judges in Hamburg in a new "war crimes trial" over thirty-five *more* German women, formerly in service at Ravensbrück; who look as if they intend to pursue their "de-Nazification" campaign forever? Most certainly not.

How distressing life would be for us in a Communist world, we all know from the instance of the Russian Zone of Germany. And yet, a *permanently* Democratic world—in which, like now, all (including the Communists) would enjoy freedom of expression, save we—would be no better, if not still worse. The real reason why the Germans feel, perhaps, less inclined, at times, to despair in the Western Zones than in the Eastern, is *not* that Democracy is better than Communism, or even that it allows them more freedom; it is just that we feel that Democracy is weaker and less stable than Communism. Hell is less horrible— seems less horrible—when one knows, or thinks, it is soon to come to an end. It is the hope of Democracy's unavoidable downfall and of our resurrection that sustains our spirit under the triple oppression of the French, British, and Americans. In the Russian Zone, we feel the formidable power not only of Communist Russia, but of Communist Asia, hanging over us; the threat of the masses of inferior humanity brought together and increasingly organised, mechanised, made supremely efficient for the work of disintegration appointed to them by the Gods in the last days of the last historical Cycle; the threat of the powers of Darkness coalesced, not against Democracy which will be easily crushed anyhow, but against *our* survival, and *our* possible rule in the future. But that is surely no reason why we should help our Western enemies, the Euro-American Plutocracies, to crush the power of Russia so that *they* might continue exploiting the world for themselves and for their real masters the Jews. Why on earth should we? We despise them. We loathe them. Their rule—the rule of the Control Commission in West Germany—if less harsh, is even more humiliating than that of the Russians. We shall not help them against the Russians, nor the Russians against them, unless . . . it is expedient from *our* point of view. Which attitude will be expedient, when the time comes? That, none—or very few—of us can tell, just now. All we can do, at present, is to remain firm in our National Socialist faith, and to wait. To wait for the hour of the Gods.

Our faith is unshakable. We know we are right. We know our dreams are in accordance with the unchangeable dictates of Nature and that we are, in all our activities, "co-workers with the Creator," to quote a scriptural expression. We know nothing can stand in our way, in the long run. Still, we feel, sometimes, that the way is long, and our lives short. Will those of us who are now in their forties live long enough to see "the Day of freedom and of plenty"—the rise of a National Socialist world out of the ruin and desolation brought by the coming struggle between our enemies? Nobody knows.

In the meantime, the shadow of the Communist danger no longer looms on the horizon. It is approaching. The absorption of China by the Communist forces, six months ago, is the beginning of the end of Democratic capitalism. A blessed good riddance! But for whose benefit, ultimately: that of Communism, the race-levelling order, the rule of quantity to a no lesser degree than Democratic capitalism itself, the system of the "common man" of all races? Or ours? That of the eternal Jew—whom the bastardised "common man" will gladly serve, under an illusion of freedom—or that of higher humanity? "For the future of the world, the important question is . . . whether Aryan humanity will hold its own or die out."[1] Never have those words of our Führer rang so true as today.

---

[1] "Für die Zukunft der Erde liegt aber die Bedeutung . . . darin, ob der arische Mensch ihr erhalten bleibt oder ausstirbt" (Adolf Hitler, *Mein Kampf*, II, x, p. 630; cf. Mannheim, p. 562).

Chapter 14

AGAINST TIME

"The four castes were established by Me, by the different distribution of natural characteristics and capacities."

—Bhagavad-Gita[1]

"When society reaches a stage where property confers rank, where wealth becomes the only source of virtue, passion the sole bond between man and wife, falsehood the source of success in life, sex the only means of enjoyment, and when outer trappings are confused with inner religion . . . then we are in the Kali Yuga—the Dark Age."

—*Vishnu Purana*[2]

"Es mag hier natürlich der eine oder andere lachen, allein dieser Planet zog schon Jahrmillionen durch den Äther ohne Menschen, und er kann einst wieder so dahinziehen, wenn die Menschen vergessen, daß sie ihr höheres Dasein nicht den Ideen einiger verrückter Ideologen, sondern der Erkenntnis und rücksichtslosen Anwendung eherner Naturgesetze verdanken."

—Adolf Hitler[3]

Given the poor quality—not to say the hopeless quality—of mankind taken *en masse* anywhere in the world in our epoch, there can be no doubt that if the main aim of propaganda is to win over the greatest possible *number* of people, irrespective of race, health, character, and intellectual capacity—irrespective of physical and mental worth—Communism has immense advantages over National Socialism, and far greater chances of immediate success.

First, it appeals to the most elementary, not to say elemental,

---

[1] Bhagavad-Gita, 4:13

[2] Condensation of a long descriptive passage in Book IV, ch. 24, translation by H.H. Wilson (London, 1840).

[3] "At this point, someone or other may well laugh, but this planet once moved for millions of years through the ether without human beings, and it may one day do so again, if men forget that they owe their higher existence, not to the ideas of a few crazy ideologues, but to the knowledge and ruthless application of Nature's stern and rigid laws" (*Mein Kampf*, I, xi, p. 316; cf. Mannheim, 288 [Trans. by Ed.]).

aspiration of man: to the desire to "live well," i.e., to live in comfort and plenty. "Workers of the world, unite!" say the Communists. Unite to what end? To wrest power from the hands of those who now exploit you, and to better your lot; to eat every day to satisfaction; to live in healthier conditions; to have an increasing share in that wealth which you have been producing, up till now, only for others to enjoy. And when you once have all that, what then? Then, you will "live"—eat, drink, and breed for your individual satisfaction and enjoyment. Individual enjoyment, provided it is not an obstacle to the next door neighbour's equally legitimate pleasure, is the supreme aim, the great end of life, in this philosophy centred around man as an economic unit. The one thing that counts, in the eyes of the Communists, is neither country nor race but "mankind"—the sum total of all human individuals who, just because they are "human," *i.e.*, because they have two legs only and no tails, have "equal rights" and equal duties; the right to "enjoy"; the duty to work in order to earn that enjoyment. And the economic problem, on the solution to which depends, finally, the possibility of enjoyment for all individuals in the world, is the main, nay, the only problem, as well-being (material, or anyhow, always conditioned by material circumstances alone) is an end in itself.

It is so because man, in the light of the Communist *Weltanschauung,* is just a privileged animal—believers in a certain theory of biological progress say: the remote descendant of a monkey. (I would say—if I could, as the Communists do, consider the whole of mankind as one mass of interchangeable units—the degenerate descendant of the Gods, in the more or less rapid process of becoming a monkey.)

It seems strange, at first sight, that the upholders of such a philosophy put at least as much stress as the Christians upon the unbridgeable abyss between man—the one creature towards which we are supposed to have "duties"—and animal. The Communists, of course, do not attribute the difference to man's immortal "soul" but rather to his capability for speech and to his "reason." The fuss they can make over that precious "reason," which so many Communist recruits from the inferior races (and often also, alas, from the superior ones) seem to lack so hopelessly, is indeed incredible.

But the more one thinks of it, the less this appears strange. Christianity, humanitarian Free Thought—that half-way reaction against Christianity, in other words, that decadent form of Christianity—which supply the philosophical basis of both modern Democracy *and* Communism, are essentially man-centred creeds. Islam is also. Obviously *all* creeds directly or indirectly derived from Judaism or from Judaic inspiration—and perhaps, also, most creeds of non-Aryan origin, even when they have no connection whatsoever with Judaism—are man-centred. It would be more difficult to tell for certain whether *all* life-centred creeds, ancient and modern, are of Aryan origin or, at least, ultimately traceable to Aryan inspiration. If one could prove that they are, one would thereby put forward the most eloquent of all arguments in favour of the inherent superiority of the Aryan race, that fundamental National Socialist dogma, debated and criticised with such bitterness everywhere outside our circles. Anyhow, many of the historic life-centred religions and philosophies, if not all, are most definitely of Aryan origin.[1]

The Jewish origin of Communism—Marxism—is no secret to anyone. One must therefore expect such a philosophy to be man-centred. The fact that it is, perhaps, more cynically so than any other—especially than the otherworldly creeds that stress so strongly the dignity of man's "soul"—makes it all the more repellent in the eyes of the real artist, but all the more attractive to the human beasts, *i.e.*, the majority of men.

The human beast—the human being of our times, in the process of becoming a beast—is only too glad to be told that his tendency to beastliness is natural and commendable, and that his superiority over other animals lies only in the fact that, through "reason," he can enjoy the goods of the world better than they, and, in particular, exploit them (the beasts) better than any of them can the species on which it preys. The average man of the superior races feels it is generous of him to be a Communist. *He* might spontaneously believe in a duty of kindness towards all life, but his centuries of Christian upbringing are there to influence his subconscious mind and suggest to him that he surely "must" devote himself "first" to "all men." The fellow from the inferior races is delighted to be offered an equalitarian, man-centred philosophy that gives him the illusion that nothing is above him, while the whole of subhuman living Nature lies under him, in his power, existing only for his needs and for his pleasure. By the way, man-centred philosophies always had more success in this world than life-centred ones. Inferior races who are taught to believe in life-centred religions never live up to them, as a rule. The treatment of animals—even of the cow—among

---

[1] Sir Wallis Budge suggests very strongly that the Religion of the Disk is. It is difficult to *prove* how far it owes its existence to Mitannian (*i.e.*, Aryan) influences, but it is certain that King Akhnaton its Founder was to a greater extent than any other Pharaoh of Aryan blood. See Budge's *Tutankhamon: Amonism, Atonism and Egyptian Monotheism* (London: Martin Hopkinson, 1923), pp. 114-15.

the low castes of India, is a typical illustration of this fact. And the superior races themselves, I am sorry to say, have often given up life-centred religions for man-centred ones, as the wholesale conversion of Northern Europe to Christianity proves only too well.

The appeal of Communism, today, is, in many ways, similar to that of Christianity fifteen hundred years ago. Its reign will not last so long—fortunately—for we are now nearer to the end of the present historical Cycle, and both events and thought currents succeed one another more rapidly. Moreover, the form under which the eternal Religion of hierarchised life will finally reassert itself and win, namely National Socialism, is already in existence. Nevertheless, in the short period of trial and preparation in which we are living just now, Communism is bound to obtain a considerable amount of cheap success.

* * *

Another great point in favour of such immediate success is that Communist propaganda addresses itself not to an *élite*, but to *all* men of every race, of every civilisation, of every tradition, and especially to those who have reasons to feel themselves exploited and downtrodden, *i.e.*, to the immense majority of mankind. Following the example of Christianity and Islam—the two great international religions of equality sprung from Judaism—and of the Democratic creed popularised by the French Revolution for "the liberation of all peoples," Communism states that there are, between human beings, no natural, irreducible differences, due to blood, but only artificial differences due to environment and education—due, ultimately, to economic factors. In other words, our bitterest opponents believe that a young Negro, a young Chinese, a young Eskimo, and a young Jew, brought up together from early childhood in England or Germany, and educated in the same English or German schools and Universities, will have, in the same circumstances, practically the same reactions as any Englishman or German who received the same education. The apparently unlimited adaptability of quite a number of non-Aryan races to what is commonly termed "modern" life—*i.e.*, to organised life, as evolved by the scientific genius of the European Aryan—is greatly responsible for the credit given to that absurd belief among thousands of people who should know better. How superficial, how purely *external* that adaptability is, nobody seems to care, either because people have lost the capacity of distinguishing between the essential and the secondary, or, rather because the external—the secondary—alone matters in their eyes; because they consider *that* to be the essential, reversing spontaneously, in their consciousness, the natural scale of values—another sign of universal decay in our times.

The most "adaptable" man—outwardly—whether in the West or in the East, is, naturally, the Jew. Whether in India or in Iceland, everywhere he goes, he wins the same praise for that extraordinary suppleness, from the population in the midst of whom he settles and thrives: "He is *like one of us*"—which means that, in Iceland, he eats Icelandic food and shows a taste for winter sports—and for Icelandic girls—while in India he manages to become the "pal" of the worst type of Indian—of the casteless product of uncritical "western" education—and pretends to relish everything Indian, from Sanskrit philosophy (the spirit of which he is the last person to be able to share, however much of a scholar he be) down to curry sauce and Indian sweets and gregarious life. In addition to that, he is a remarkable linguist. The result is, everywhere, the illusion that the Jew *can* become a native of the place where he chooses to live, and an outcry of horror at the assertion of the contrary by a handful of racially conscious, intelligent, and proud Aryans. The internationalist myth, and the legend of the "poor Jew," go hand in hand with the belief in "man" as a mentally homogeneous species in which any unit contains the same possibilities as the other, whether Jew or Gentile, Negro, Chinese, Maltese, or Scotch, or pure German or Swede. Communism is based and thrives upon that lie. Nothing analogous could have thriven a few millenniums ago. Each race had, then, its pride; was conscious of its unique position in the broad scheme of creation, of its irreplaceable character. But now that two thousand years of Christianity—another Jewish product—have subtly but surely deprived most people of their sense of racial dignity in the name of an otherworldly ideal; and now that years of Democratic education have filled the simpletons with an unhealthy admiration for "intellect" and a no less unhealthy aspiration towards "individualism," the world is ready for the next step: the universal levelling of mankind through mixture of blood on the largest possible scale, in the name of a philosophy that no longer crushes the body (as early Christianity did) but despises it; that looks upon it purely as an economic unit—a producer and consumer of food—and an instrument of personal enjoyment; that reduces it to something of lesser account than the animal body, in a way, for the Communists who proclaim that *all* men have equal possibilities and equal rights, and deny the natural hierarchy of races among human beings, will admit, on the other hand, without difficulty, that a thoroughbred Persian kitten, for instance, or a pedigree puppy, has a greater potentiality for beauty—greater inherent value—than an ordinary one and represents a natural feline or canine aristocracy.

But the natural human aristocracy is a small minority. And those of its members who are conscious of their value as representatives of a superior race are fewer still. The great majority of men and women—especially those of the inferior races—like a philosophy that denies racial aristocracy and reduces the exceptional individual (who can never be denied) to a product of purely economic factors coupled with the play of circumstances. They like it, because it flatters them. Because each human worm who accepts it is entitled to think himself the potential equal of anybody, and to say to himself: "If only circumstances had been a little different, who can tell what a great person I would have become?" The insignificant "I" of millions of nonentities at once looks less insignificant in the eyes of each one of them. A lovely theory! Not merely the economic salvation of all men, but the moral salvation of the worthless in their own estimation; an illusion of greatness appealing both to the stomachs and to the vanity of the subhuman masses—the proper *Weltanschauung* for inferior races. No wonder the inferior races rush to it like flies to honey—and, along with them, quite a number of kind-hearted "humanitarians," and of uncritical victims of clever propaganda belonging to the superior races, unfortunately.

These would not be in such a hurry to respond to it, if they could fathom the grim reality that lies at the back of that resounding appeal "to all men"; at the back of that talk about freedom, about unhampered personal development, material welfare, "education," and enjoyment. That grim reality, the workers of the Russian Zone of Germany—many of whom, in their Communist zeal, at first welcomed the Russians as "liberators"—will all tell you what it is: the worst type of servitude; compulsory work, without the redeeming satisfaction of feeling oneself useful to anything or anybody one loves; work for some distant, abstract, ever-grabbing foreign power; compulsory leisure, filled with standardised amusements; compulsory standardised "culture"; the lowering of the level of life, not only for the capitalist and the "bourgeois" or so-called such, but for those labourers themselves who happened to have tasted some kind of material civilisation; the creation of an artificial and detested equality between them and people who have always lacked the very elements of modern comfort. On the other hand, the death of all originality, of all creative thought.

The labourers and working women of the Russian Zone will tell you that the Russian invaders were dumbfounded at the sight of the "luxury" which the humblest mechanic enjoyed in National Socialist Germany. They had always been told that, outside the USSR, all was misery, hunger, oppression of the proletariat and so forth. When, even in her material collapse, Nazi Germany gave them a glaring proof that it was *not* so, they could not believe their own eyes. With childish naivety, they took all Germans for "capitalists." The German labourers took them for savages, and their system for something hateful, the likes of which they could not have imagined in the most awful nightmare.

But, of course, the German labourers—and the English, and the Scandinavian, and the Dutch, and the French—are, numerically, a negligible minority in the wide world. The Communists, following the example of the Democratic parliamentarians, rely upon numbers to bring about their triumph. Minorities, however inherently valuable, do not count in their eyes when they are minorities of opposition. Numbers—our enemies hope—will soon crush them out of importance if not out of existence. The German labourers might grumble, or rather (for grumbling is forbidden in the Russian zone) feel indignant in their hearts, and curse Communism. But the Chinese coolie, the wretched Indian sweeper, the man who digs coal out of the mines of Giriya, the woman who collects cow dung in the streets of Calcutta and sells it a few *annas* a basket, for fuel; the labourer who toils in the tea plantations of Assam, in the rubber plantations of Malaya and Indochina, in the sugar plantations of Java; the docker and the rickshaw driver of Singapore, Saigon, and the ports of the Yellow Sea, all welcome—or will soon welcome—the message of Communism *and* its application as something wonderful. And who can blame them? Who, but a supremely intelligent and astonishingly well-informed person would *not* do so in their place?

And one must not forget that, wretched as they might seem, and worthless as they might be, taken individually, *they* are the majority; *they* are the "workers of the world" to whom the famous call for union is addressed; *they* are the "humanity" for whom Communism is preparing a better life. Our *Weltanschauung* of the natural élite, our message of pride and power, our dream of a godlike humanity, is not, and can never be, addressed to them. The *Communist Manifesto* is. The first, the *sine qua non* condition to be a National Socialist, is to be an Aryan, and a healthy, intelligent, fully conscious one, in addition; a worthy specimen of higher humanity. The only condition one needs, in order to be a Communist, is to be a "human being"—a mammal walking on two legs, without a tail, capable of speech, and assumed to be "reasonable," whether or not so in reality, it matters very little.

Now, two-legged mammals without anything to recommend them, outnumber pure-blooded Aryans, bodily and mentally worthy of the name of "human élite," by a hundred to one. And even among the pure Aryans, those who are susceptible of being misled by "humanitarian" propaganda—because of centuries of Christianity, followed by a long Democratic education have killed in them all sense of racial pride—outnumber by far those who have retained the capacity to think for themselves, and to think as Aryans. Is it any wonder, if we were unable to get a permanent hold upon so-called "world-opinion," quite apart from the disastrous effect of the calumnies which Jewish propaganda poured out against us under every possible form? And is it any wonder that the Russians won the war through Communism, and are now rising in power at the expense of their idiotic dupes, the degenerate Aryans of the West, already docile servants of the Jews for many decades?

Not only is this no wonder, but it is, as I have tried to point out in another book,[1] within the natural order of things.

One cannot understand the significance of the momentous events of our times, in particular of the temporary defeat and persecution of National Socialism, if one does not constantly bear in mind the fact that we have been, for the last six thousand years or so, living in the last of the four great periods into which the wise men of olden days agreed to divide every complete historical "Cycle," *i.e.*, every complete creation, or rather manifestation in time, from its beginning in perfection to its final dissolution. One cannot realise the meaning of contemporary happenings unless one realises also that we have now come to the last part of that last, shortest, and fiercest period in the natural development of our Cycle—to the end of what the Sanskrit Scriptures call the "Kali Yuga," *i.e.*, the Dark Age, and that there *is* no hope until this humanity, as we know it only too well, meets its doom in some final crash. Until then, man as a whole is bound to become more and more monkeyish, and to follow the latest suggestion of the death forces with increasing zeal. Communism is the most thorough, the most complete, the typical expression of man's lure of disintegration; the most logical, the most extreme philosophy of death. Democracy, and older Christianity—of which, as I said, Democracy is only the decadent form—are also products of the death forces, but less cynical, and less masterful ones. The "Kali Yuga" was not yet so "advanced" when they were invented.

---

[1] *The Lightning and the Sun*, ch. 1, "The Cyclic View of History."

There was place, in them, for some redeeming inconsistency. In the Medieval Christian Church, there was still place for racial pride (although this *was,* really, against the grain of the faith); and in modern Democratic civilisation one enjoyed, until 1939, the possibility of expressing, at least, one's adhesion to the philosophy of natural values—the Philosophy of the Swastika—without running the risk of being imprisoned for it. That possibility still exists, to a very small extent, outside unfortunate occupied Germany. Though it is practically impossible to publish books, or to make public speeches in praise of the Nazi ideology, one can stand for it privately, to the knowledge of all one's neighbours, even of those who are against it—the last shadow of freedom.

Under a Communist Government, even that shadow would vanish. It has vanished wherever the logical *Weltanschauung* of disintegration inspires the all-powerful ruling machinery. And this is natural; this is within the merciless logic of historical evolution. It cannot be otherwise. And it is also natural—and unavoidable—that a degenerate humanity such as the one we know should prefer the yoke of Communism to our call to real freedom. Being what it is, it is incapable of appreciating that which we understand by "freedom"—just as apes would be unable to appreciate the membership of a learned society, if such an honour were offered to them.

The Communists will win; must win—for the time being—whether by force of arms or through the effect of their propaganda, it makes little difference. This is also natural—unavoidable.

But this should not distress us. They—the exponents of the philosophy in accordance with the tendency of Time—will win, and pass: be annihilated by Time. We, the followers of Him Whom I called, in other writings of mine, "the Man against Time"[1]—the exponents of a Golden Age philosophy—will rise upon their ruins and rule, once more, a world, not of apes, but of regenerate, godlike men, Aryans in the full sense of the word.

* * *

For, if Communism has many advantages over National Socialism from the point of view of immediate success—if it centres its propaganda around man's elemental needs and lusts; if it admits all

---

[1] *The Lightning and the Sun*, ch. 3, "Men in Time, Above Time, and Against Time."

men to its fellowship; if it uses deceit as its strongest weapon, giving people the illusion of freedom, while enslaving them more completely than any ancient absolutism has ever done—still it is doomed, in the long run. What is not founded in eternity is always doomed. And of all modern "isms," alone our Hitler's beautiful teaching—the Philosophy of the Swastika—is founded in eternity. It alone can stand the test of persecution and, which is more, the test of time.

It is, I repeat, a Golden Age philosophy in the midst of our age of gloom; the philosophy of those who stand heroically against the downward current of history—against Time—knowing that history, that moves in circles, will one day forward their lofty dreams; the philosophy of those few who, instead of allowing themselves to be drawn along by the general downward rush, forgetful of the hope of eternal Return, prefer to fight an impossible battle and to fall, if necessary, but to feel, when the new dawn comes, that they have called it, in a way, through the magic virtue of action for the beauty of action; who, if the dawn is not to shine in their lifetime, will still act against the growing tide of mediocrity and vulgarity, for the sole joy of fulfilling the inner law of an heroic nature.

The characteristics that appear, today, the most disadvantageous to our creed, from the standpoint of worldly success, are the very ones that justify its claim to be the latest expression of everlasting truth, and that will assure its triumph and domination, in the long run. First among these, is its Aryan exclusivity; its appeal to the best, to the élite of mankind alone—to which all its adherents belong by birthright—and, to the most generous, the most heroic, the most disinterested feelings in each one of its adherents, according to that principle of natural hierarchy, and therefore of discrimination, of natural privilege, upon which it is founded: the principle of Race and Personality.

It would be, no doubt, absurd to say that National Socialism does not appeal *also* to man's legitimate aspiration to healthier as well as more pleasant material conditions of life. It does. It always did, from the beginning. The immediate solution which Hitler gave to the appalling unemployment problem that was threatening the whole economy of Germany in the 1920s and early '30s, did, perhaps, more for the success of the Movement than anything else. And the material prosperity of Germany under Nazi rule, and the excellent social laws that were then promulgated and enforced (the laws for the welfare and education of children, for instance) are remembered to this day, in the martyred Land, like features of a lost paradise. "In Hitler's days, we lived well." "In Hitler's days, we could have as many children as we liked: the State helped us to bring them up, or rather brought them up for us, and so beautifully!" "In Hitler's days, food was cheap, and laws were wise, and well applied; there was plenty, then, and there was order. Those were splendid days." "We never were so happy as under Adolf Hitler," such talk one hears today everywhere, in every "Zone," as soon as one enjoys the people's confidence. And I am sorry to say that, from what I gather from their talk, there are quite a number of Germans for whom nostalgia for the National Socialist régime seems to be nothing else but the nostalgia for a period of material happiness—of cheap and good food, fine clothes, lovely lodgings, wealth and merriment. But such people are not—and never were—National Socialists. They are—and were already in the days they used to hail the Führer in the streets—but members of that immense animal-like majority of human beings who can, and do, "live on bread alone," and who have no real allegiance to anybody or anything but their stomachs. They are not to be neglected, or despised. Many of them have been useful, and many more will again be so, when better times come back. The fact alone that they can breed healthy children of pure blood, capable of fighting for higher ideals, one day; the fact that they can themselves fight for that better mankind of which they represent the physical side, is a great point in their favour. But don't call them National Socialists. They are not. The National Socialist ideology appeals, in man, to far more than such people contain in their mental and emotional makeup. It appeals to the finest elements of character: *to absolute selflessness*; to the thirst of sacrifice for something infinitely greater than one's little individuality; to courage, fortitude; to uncompromising love of truth for truth's own sake; to the love of better mankind—of the higher brotherhood of Aryan blood—for the sake of its inherent value, of its all-round beauty and endless possibilities. It appeals to intelligence—real intelligence; not the mere smearing of bookish information—to one's capacity to think for one's self and to draw one's conclusions from the facts of life; to one's capacity to read the meaning of the world in the unfolding of universal history, and to detect, in the tragedy of all past ages, the basic everlasting truths which Adolf Hitler proclaimed in our times. It appeals to one's sense of beauty; to one's aspiration towards that perfect comeliness and that integral truth which are one and the same, on all planes, and in all walks of life.

In other words, while any German could be a member of the NSDAP, and while any Aryan could, and can still, take pride in the National Socialist *Weltanschauung* as the natural creed of his race, only superior individuals of Aryan blood—men and women without blemish—can be real, full-fledged Nazis. Stupidity, shallowness, meanness, pusillanimity—weaknesses of any kind—are incompatible with our glorious faith.

I was once told that there are not more than two or three million absolutely reliable National Socialists in the whole of Germany. It may be that there are not more than ten thousand in the rest of Europe, and not more than two hundred among the non-German Aryans of the rest of the globe. But that fact—if it be a fact—will never induce us to lower the moral and physical standard up to which a person is to live, if he or she is to have the right to be called a National Socialist. For in this age of the exaltation of quantity, we are the only ones who consistently put forward the Golden Age ideal of quality before all. And to forsake that ideal, or even to compromise with the contrary current outlook on life, would be to deny ourselves, to deny our Movement, and the very mission of our godlike Führer.

Individual value—personality—is rare enough. But many people who do not possess it are pleased to believe that they do. And therefore a philosophy that would put stress on personality alone would not be thoroughly unpopular—on the contrary. But our creed puts emphasis upon blood *also*. It is, as I have said in the beginning of this book, the eternal creed of Life and Light, viewed in our modern world of technical achievements, from the standpoint of the Aryan race of which the Nordic or Germanic people are, today, the purest representatives. It is an essentially Nordic philosophy; there is no getting away from that fact. And it is *that*, more than anything else, which has made it so unpopular, not merely among a great number of non-Aryan Orientals, but also among many Europeans who, though untainted by any admixture of Jewish blood whatsoever, are obviously anything but pure "Nordics." People, as a rule, resent being told—or given to understand—that they are by nature inferior to any privileged aliens. To a philosophy such as ours, they are bound to prefer Communism and its indiscriminate appeal to all men of all races. Every vain individual from any one of the numerous varieties of inferior mankind, feels that he (or she) can "get somewhere" with such a convenient *Weltanschauung,* while in a world dominated by us, he would always remain outside the privileged minority. "In his place," we say. But one of the characteristics of the Dark Age—of our age of decay—is precisely that both worthless individuals and inferior races are less and less willing to remain "in their places"—and more and more indignant at the idea of being put back there by force. Consequently, the children of all the *Untermenschen* of the world, from the aborigines of Central Africa to those of the hills of Assam, to whom the Christian missionaries have taught the doctrine of the "equal dignity" of all human souls, the Latin alphabet, and discontent, are the first to jump at the new opportunity offered to them by the Communists. Communism appears to them—or will soon appear to them—as applied Christianity. And who can blame them? They are right. Christianity carried to its logical limits, under modern material conditions, can lead nowhere except to Communism. The Jewish doctrine of Marx is, at our stage of historical evolution, the prolongation of the doctrine of Jesus "son of David," King of the Jews. True, the Kingdom of Jesus was "not on earth," while the Communist paradise is (in theory at least). But that too is natural. For, as I said, history follows a downward evolution.

The truth is that vanity is the pet defect of nearly all men and women, while the capacity to face facts with detachment and to stand for truth even against one's interest, is the privilege of an infinitesimal minority. In reality, National Socialism does address its message to all men—it would to all thinking creatures outside mankind, if there were any on our planet—for it is *true*. And truth is independent of the qualifications of whoever might grasp it. It is men's personal or collective vanity that stands in the way of their proper appreciation of it. Their vanity, and their jealousy, too; that hatred of their betters that has also its origin in wounded vanity.

* * *

I have said: only an all-round superior individual of Aryan blood can be a real Nazi; and alone people of Aryan blood can look up to National Socialism as something theirs by birthright. But all thinking men and women can acknowledge the soundness of our principles; the eternity of that natural order in harmony with which our Führer has planned the socio-political structure of new Germany. Even a non-Aryan *can* admit it; and some do, if very few. But he would have to be not merely a fine individual of his race but an exceptional one, or, at least, a person brought up within the pale of a *true* tradition, entirely different from that which has imposed itself upon Europe, through Christian civilisation; a tradition based, precisely, upon our age-old principles of divinely ordained racial hierarchy.

A sincere National Socialist who is neither a German nor even a Northern European—a pure Aryan, say, from the Mediterranean shores, who readily admits that an unmixed Nordic type of man or woman is a finer specimen of the race than he himself and three quarters of his compatriots—is rare enough. For such an objective attitude implies more detachment than most people can afford. But a non-Aryan capable of admitting the biological truths laid down in *Mein Kampf*, knowing fully well that *he* (or she) can never expect even a second rate place amidst the natural élite of mankind, should be, in all probability, still more unusual. And yet such people can be found. I have recalled, in the beginning of this book, the story of that young Indian servant of the Maheshya caste of West Bengal who told me, in the second year of this war "*Memsaheb*, I too admire your Führer, not merely because he is triumphant but because he is struggling to replace, in the West, the Bible by the Bhagavad-Gita"—which was, of course, amazingly true if taken to mean: the *spirit* of the Judeo-Christian tradition by that of ancient wisdom, rooted in the idea of racial hierarchy.

"But," said I to the boy, "*you* are not an Aryan; only Brahmins and Kshatriyas count as such among Hindus. What is that to you?"

And the illiterate village lad of Bengal answered: "Maybe I am not an Aryan, but *I know my place*. All souls are reborn into bodies at the level they deserve. That does not alter the fact that the Scriptures are true and that men are divided into different castes—different races—the first duty of each one of which is to keep its blood pure. If I do my duty faithfully now, in this life, maybe I shall one day be reborn among the high castes, provided I become worthy to be an Aryan."

More than seven years later, in a luxurious restaurant in Stockholm, I met a pure Nordic woman—the finest type of Aryan, physically—who asked me, when she noticed the Wheel of the Sun—the sacred Sign of National Socialism—gleaming on each side of my face, "Why do you wear that 'symbol of evil'? Those earrings of yours are 'horrid.'" Immediately, I recalled the swarthy face of the lad of the Tropics, and his words—profession of faith of many primitive millions living for thousands of years under a social system based upon the self-same principles as National Socialism: "I am not an Aryan, but I know my place—and I know the truth; and I admire your Führer." Never, perhaps, did I so bitterly hate that religion of equality, sprung from Judaism and first preached by Jews, that has, for so many generations, silenced the old pride of Nordic humanity. Never perhaps did I feel so keenly what a shame it is for Aryans—and especially, for those of pure Germanic stock—to deny their own God-ordained superiority, and renounce their privileges, while in caste-ridden India, millions of non-Aryans lucky enough to have escaped the influence both of Christianity and of democratic education, still believe in the natural hierarchy of races and look upon the Aryan as the lord of creation.

* * *

A racially hierarchised world in which every man would "know his place"—and, like the Indian lad, look up to the Man who, standing alone against the current of dissolution, proclaimed anew, in our times, the everlasting principles of the natural order—is not impossible. In fact, it is bound to come after the final period of chaos that will, one day, close this cycle; the period of chaos that it is the very business of Communism to bring about.

In such a world, every nation, whether Aryan or not, would be organised under a national State. Every race would have its pride and its sense of duty, and would avoid intermixture as the greatest source of physical and moral evil. The noblest non-Aryan races would be the allies of the Aryan, in view of the creation and maintenance of a world order inspired by a deep sense of obedience to the eternal decrees of Nature. The alliance of Germany and Japan, during this war, was a symbol foreshadowing such a collaboration in friendship and dignity, but necessary aloofness in the domain of breeding; a mutual understanding, a knowledge of each other's culture, to the extent that is possible, without the slightest desire of ridiculous imitation on either side. The "internationalist" tendencies of our decadent age would be—will be one day—in a world evolved anew according to our principles, replaced by something which seems now entirely utopian—impossible—the mentality of the "nationalist of every land."

I remember how I surprised the psychiatrist sent to examine me before my trial when, in answer to the question as to "why" I had thought it worthwhile to risk my freedom, if not my life, for a country that was "not mine," I replied describing myself first as "an Aryan, grateful to Germany for having staked her all for the awakening of Aryan consciousness and pride in every worthy person of my race," and then as "a nationalist of every land." And yet, in this strange expression lies all the difference between the non-Russian Communist and the non-German National Socialist; the secret of the immediate success of Communism as opposed to the temporary failure—but to the triumph, in the long run—of National Socialism.

The German Nazi is a German patriot before all. The Russian Communist might be an "internationalist" but might also be—and, from reports from Soviet Russia, often is—a Russian patriot using the Communist ideology, so popular outside Russia, for the benefit of

Russian imperialism; thinking, in a mistaken manner, that such an ideology *can* be used in such a spirit.

But the *foreign* Communist is pre-eminently an "internationalist"; a believer in "mankind" before nationhood, in mankind as a privileged species, united (at the cost of never mind what disgraceful blendings) in view of the ever-increasing exploitation of living Nature for the greatest enjoyment of the greatest number of human beings—which means, ultimately, the cheapest and coarsest enjoyment. While the foreign Nazi is either just an Aryan in whom the consciousness of race dominates and absorbs the narrower consciousness of fatherland or else—in the case of a minority within a minority—that, of course, *and* at the same time, a "nationalist of every land"; a person who, in a clear vision of world history, admires the working of those everlasting principles which Hitler has proclaimed over and over again; who, through his understanding of many cultures of different times, feels, with direct intuitive certitude, that man can reach his higher goal— which is to reflect the eternal, individually *and* collectively—*only through oneness with his nation, i.e.*, with his race; that *only* by developing in himself the soul of his race can he expect to know and understand and love the soul of other races and, ultimately, the soul of multifarious, hierarchised mankind and of the whole scheme of life, ordinate in its various manifestations, one in its infinite diversity. He (or she) is also a person who looks up to Germany as to the Führer's Land; the one Aryan Nation who bore witness to these truths in the midst of the hostile, decadent world of our age, at the cost of her very existence on the material plane. A person who, for that reason, would welcome German leadership as the expression of the divine right of these Aryans who proved themselves the worthiest.

Needless to say, there are many more non-Russian Communists than non-German Nazis, and there always will be until, out of the ruins of the present world order, the new Day dawns—"the Day for freedom and for bread," to quote the words of the Horst Wessel Song, giving them a symbolic meaning; the Day both of material prosperity *and* healthy beauty, manly thought, and manly joy—true freedom within order—the Day of the rule of best, for the coming of which National Socialist Germany fought and died (in appearance), and will rise in glory from the dead.

Then, many will feel for Hitler's beloved people the same admiration as I and a few other foreigners do now, in the darkest days of persecution.

* * *

But it is not only its aristocratic conception of life and racial exclusivity that make our Ideology unpopular. It is also our blunt frankness about our aims and objects—and methods; the fact that we never tried to conceal what we really wanted, nor what we are prepared to do (or have already done) in order to attain our ends in the shortest time possible.

National Socialism being, as I said before, a Golden Age philosophy, and this present-day humanity being at the last stage of its downward process towards degradation—in the gloomiest period of the Age of Gloom—it is clear that what *we* want is not what nearly all other people want.

What nearly all people want is a "secure" world—a world in which every one can pursue his petty pleasures in peace. What we want is, pre-eminently, a beautiful world. The two conceptions often clash. Let them clash. We do nothing to hide the fact that they are bound to clash as long as our contemporaries remain, physically and mentally, what we know them to be. We do nothing to win their sympathy and collaboration by telling them lies. In order to maintain such a co-operation, we would have to continue lying until, in the end, some of us might begin to lose sight of the glaring, uncompromising ideal of truth set before us. The collaboration of the submen is not worth our taking that risk. Moreover, we hate lies as a weapon—save when they are absolutely indispensable. We much prefer bare, brutal, force, the weapon of true warriors. When true warriors are temporarily exhausted, or wounded, or in chains, the only thing for them to do is not to try deceit, but to prepare themselves in silence to become strong once more—and to wait.

We never tried to hide or to excuse our ruthlessness, which is a consequence of our earnestness. On the contrary, we have always said we would stop at nothing in pursuit of the mission appointed to us by Nature, which is, to bear witness to our Golden Age truth against the spirit of these degenerate times. And we have proved it. We have done what we said. And we are ready to do it again.

People do not like that trait in us. They say we are "awful," if not "odious." The Communists are not "awful" because they never say what they wish to do, and never do what they say. Also because they never tell their opponents how much they hate them or despise them, before they have crushed them. They do not defy them *before* fighting them, as warriors have always done.

What they—or rather what the Jews who inspired their movement—want, and what most people want, is also not exactly the same thing. "Security," yes; the Jews, and those Communists who serve Jewish interests without knowing it, and the average man in the street, all want that. But the man in the street wants it that he might enjoy his insignificant little life without worries; the Communist wants it as the supreme goal of a humanity for which the economic side of life is everything, because he loves such a humanity as it is, or—if he be a Russian Communist—perhaps because he fears the German National Socialists' "*Ostpolitik*," Germany's natural expansion at *his* expense in the struggle for vital space. The Jew wants "security" so that, amidst docile, unthinking, and ever-content masses, he and his race might forever remain "at the top." It is not at all the same thing. But it can be, and is, called by the same name, and presented in such a manner as to look the same thing.

In fact, the whole power technique both of the Communists *and* of the Democrats consists in making people feel "free" while prompting them, quietly, to behave like obedient puppets; in making them believe that they think for themselves and act according to the dictates of their own feelings, while, all the time, they only think and feel what the guiding force of the system suggests to them through the press, the radio, the films, and other channels, and act as *it* wants them to. The guiding force of the system is the unseen Jew.

I would say more: this is, under one form or another, the natural power technique of all *Weltanschauungen* of disintegration. It was, and still is, the secret of the hold of the Christian Churches upon people. For Christianity is also such a *Weltanschauung*. Like Communism, like Democracy, it is based upon lies and, what is more, upon Jewish lies. A notoriously anti-Nazi English authoress[1] once told me—before she knew who I was—about what she calls "the main lies of the Jews": first, that *they* are the Chosen People; second, that the Bible is entirely theirs; third, that a man of their race is "the only Son of God." The woman was clever enough to detect these impostures. But other Jewish lies had so thoroughly influenced her mind without her even suspecting them, that she was incapable of freeing herself from all the Christian and Democratic twaddle about the "dignity of all men" and so forth, and about the "horror" of brutal force (but of course, only when *we* use it). And she was violently against us.

Communism is only, perhaps, still a little more deceitful than the

---

[1] Miss B. Franklin.

earlier philosophies of Jewish inspiration and that, even when it is no longer used by Jews but by Russian imperialists. Still then, its Jewish character sticks to it. It is the source of its strength, as opposed to our philosophy. Not only the man in the street, but the better type of foreign Communist will run forth to fight for hidden Russian imperialism as readily as others do for hidden Jewish capitalism—without knowing it. While the foreign Nazi who is prepared to fight and die for the Germans because they are Hitler's compatriots and first collaborators, *knows* fully well what he (or she) is doing.

But, if it be an advantage *now*, from the standpoint of numbers, this deceit upon which Communist power is established will prove fatal to it in the long run and, perhaps, help to prepare the coming of our day. True, millions are ready to die for something which does not interest them at all, provided they do not know it, and remain convinced that they are dying for something else, which they do value. But, "one cannot deceive all people for all times"—not even great numbers of people for all times. A day is bound to come when they will find out that they are being tricked. Some seem to have found it out already, to a greater or lesser extent. There have been repeated "purges" in the Communist party, since Stalin has come to power and, curiously enough, an impressive proportion of the eliminated members were Jews—"Trotskyists," putting stress upon "world revolution" rather than upon the immediate interests of the Soviet State. The Marxist principles are, doubtless, there still, rammed into everyone's head. Principles are not so easily disposed of as people. Yet, there is a definite tendency, if not towards "Russian nationalism" in the sense that word might have had once, at least towards the systematic strengthening of that particular Euro-Asiatic Bloc (more Asiatic than European) that constitutes the Soviet Union—a tendency that might well, one day, end in a pan-Mongolian policy, to the disappointment of many simple Marxist "idealists" both of Aryan *and* of Jewish blood.

On the other hand, the nationalist attitude of certain German Communists is still more significant. It does not tally at all with their professed faith. As for the racial discriminations which, I am told, a few German "Communist" circles are beginning to admit today, well . . . what is Communism with racial discriminations amongst an overwhelmingly Aryan population, if not, as I remarked before, National Socialism in disguise? That hated National Socialism! Surely history—in all times but especially in ours—is "the greatest of ironists."[1]

---

[1] Ralph Fox, *Genghis Khan* (London: John Lane, 1936), p. 13.

In the long run—and perhaps much sooner than we ourselves dare to believe—our consistent frankness will pay. Our Führer has once said: "One day the world will know that I was right." And his words will receive in time a glaring confirmation, however widely unpopular we and our *Weltanschauung* might still be today.

* * *

One has always to come back to the cyclic theory of history for a satisfactory understanding of the momentous happenings of our epoch. I repeat—believing one can never put too much emphasis upon the fact—our outlook on life, our socio-political views, our conception of government are not "out of time," but pre-eminently "against time," which is quite different. However strange this might sound to those who judge it from a narrow, purely political angle, National Socialism is the everlasting Religion of Life—the unshakable truth about life which in a Golden Age would appear to everybody as evident as daylight—applied, on the material plane, at the very epoch which is *the* remotest from the Age of perfection: at the end of a great historical Cycle. It was bound to be misunderstood, hated, betrayed, reviled, rejected; in all appearance, to fail. And the age-old death tendency, the lust for disintegration inherent in all evolution in time, was bound to triumph today in Democracy; is bound to triumph, still more completely, tomorrow, in Communism, the logical and ruthless outcome of the Democratic principles in a technically advanced age; the system based upon the precedence of quantity over quality; upon economics at the expense of biology; upon the ideal of "man" as a producing machine for the greatest material benefit of the greatest number of worthless human units, as opposed to that of man as a warrior fighting to impose his faith in superhumanity upon the racial élite of mankind and the rule of that élite upon the world. The forces of disintegration were and are bound to win, I say. *But only for the time being*—only until this wretched humanity meets its unavoidable doom, and the new Day dawns.

For nothing can break the endless cycle of life and death, death and life: the law of everlasting Return, true on the socio-political plane as on all others. As surely as the Sun will rise tomorrow morning, National Socialism will come to power once more. As surely as spring will bring forth its green grass, its violets and its fruit blossoms and its tender blades of growing corn after the apparent death of Nature in winter, so will our ideal—of health, strength and beauty, of order and manly virtues—Adolf Hitler's ideal—again inspire the natural aristocracy of the world. As surely as birth follows death in the everlasting cosmic Dance of destruction and creation, martyred Germany will rise once more from her ashes, and again take the lead of the Aryan race. United, in spite of all efforts to dismember her; fully aware of her value and of her divine mission; in possession of the strength of eternal youth—of that "will to power" that has characterised her people from the far-gone ice age to the present day—again she shall stand, and again she shall march, exultant, defiant, irresistible. And again the Horst Wessel Song, now forbidden in its very birthplace, shall resound along the great international highways, and in the streets of conquered capitals.

We who believe in Adolf Hitler and in his mission need fear nothing from a Communist victory in the coming titanic conflict between our persecutors of East and West. The technically undeveloped races of Asia and Africa might well find Communism wonderful for a change. But in a world dominated by Communism, the growing discontent of the people of Northern Europe and, in general, of all the technically more advanced and also more thinking nations of Aryan blood, would be enough to provoke, in our favour, such a reaction as no amount of coercion could halt. A complete Democratic victory, won without our help (supposing that it were possible) would be far worse: it would amount to a much more subtle and more demoralising enslavement. But the strength of Communism is so great in the world that even a dubious victory of the Democracies would be impossible without our collaboration. And our collaboration would mean the overthrow of the Democratic order immediately after the war—or perhaps before—and the reinstallation of *our* socio-political order, stronger than ever. In other words, in the near future, the Democracies will just have to choose between our iron rule and that of the Communists. And we will be the ultimate victors in any case; the victors in a ruined world, no doubt; the only men erect, and composed—nay, beaming with joy, after all our sufferings—amidst the remnants of a scattered and frightened pack of monkeys. But who cares? Triumph will be just as sweet, just as elating to us. For we count; not the monkeys. And Germany, once so prosperous, which they tore and smashed, could hardly be more ruined than she is already, whatever happens.

We will not try to "convert," "reform," "re-educate" the submen. Oh, no! Of that, their prototypes, our present-day persecutors, can remain quite sure. Remembering all we suffered since 1945 under the rule of our inferiors—the rule of deceit and slander, of threat and bribery—remembering the torture of our comrades in their concentration camps; the agony and death of the martyrs of Nuremberg, and the victims of a hundred other iniquitous "war crimes" trials; the martyrdom of all Germany; the mental agony of our beloved Führer who witnessed those horrid days, facing alone the frenzied hatred of the ungrateful world he had wanted to save, we shall just broadcast to the survivors of that world our supreme ultimatum: "Hitler, or hell!" and make it hell for all those who will still think themselves clever enough to resist us, openly or secretly. But not as long a hell as that which we endured, and are still enduring. For they will not have, to sustain them, a faith in their cause comparable with our faith in National Socialism. Nor such a horrible one either. For we shall afford the luxury of mercy, when we rule the earth: we will despatch the troublesome fools as quickly as possible.

And then, when the last opposition is broken—if there *be* any opposition; for all I know, after the Third World War there might not be any—then, I say, *our era*; the actual Golden Age of a new Cycle; a hierarchised world (in which every regenerate race and every animal species shall be healthy and happy and beautiful) governed by a minority of living Aryan gods, according to the everlasting Nazi principles. And our beloved Führer—whether in the flesh, as I dare hope, or in spirit only—*Weltführer,* even more completely and more lastingly than if, pushing through Russia and High Asia and further still at the head of the German Army in 1942, he had entered Delhi and received the sworn allegiance of East and West in the glittering marble hall in which once stood the famous Peacock Throne.

* * *

Is this a superb but insane dream? Many would think so, as they look around and behold the present-day wretchedness of the dismembered Land—the "Land of fear," in which Adolf Hitler's beloved name is uttered only in whispers. I would think so myself, if I did not firmly believe in the cyclic Law of Time, and if I were not convinced that the end of this degenerate humanity and the following new beginning are drawing nigh. The study of world history has more and more confirmed me in that belief. And that belief has helped me to bear the sight of the ruins of Germany without losing heart. "Mortar and stone," as I said once, "it can all be rebuilt. As long as the Nazi spirit remains alive, nothing is lost."

I have tried to keep that spirit alive against the dictates of our persecutors, in the name of the dictate of my heart, of the inner law of an unbending nature, and of the birthright of the superior races to thrive and to rule. In appearance, I failed—as *we* failed. All I have done is to win for me a sentence of three years' imprisonment. But an all-powerful inner certitude tells me I have not failed (any more than *we* have); tells me that in three hundred years to come—perhaps much sooner—the whole of the Aryan world will look up to Adolf Hitler as I have done all my life, and render homage to this nation of his to whom I have come, in these atrocious times, to show a sign of love. I am, today, the first fruits of the love and reverence of future Aryandom for its Saviour; the first fruits of the world's grateful tribute to National Socialist Germany.

Once, on one of the vine-clad hills that border the river Saar, I stood alone, my right arm outstretched, upon the ruins of a "bunker" blown up three years before by the invading Americans—the "crusaders to Europe," champions of the Christian and Democratic values against National Socialist Heathendom, Aryan Heathendom. I stood, facing the east—facing Germany—and sang the immortal Song: "Standards high! Close the ranks! Storm Troopers, march with a calm and firm step! Comrades whom the Red Front and the Reaction have shot, march in spirit within our ranks!"

The Sun shed His rays upon me. And the joy of defiance shone in my face. Also, the joy of future triumph. The "crusaders" of the dark forces had blown up that "bunker" and hundreds of others; poured fire and brimstone over all Germany. But could they keep the martial words of the forbidden Song from resounding under the blue sky, over the sunlit landscape? Could they keep *me*—a non-German Aryan—from remaining faithful to Hitler's Germany in her defeat and ruin and martyrdom? Could they suppress, one day, in the future, the allegiance of a better world to the Führer and to his ideals and to the people he loved so much—that allegiance which I foreshadowed and symbolised in my humble way?

The music of the Song poured out of me as a magic spell—as the death warrant of Germany's persecutors in the name of the higher justice of future Aryan humanity.

The Aryan world's future justice is that justice to which I appeal today, against the decrees of those who hate us. The Aryan world's future allegiance to the Führer, is my life-long love, on a scale of millions of people, and for centuries—the greatest "German miracle."

I might have failed, materially, and for the time being. But I am the first sign of that miracle, sent to Germany by the Gods, as a token of love; the promise of the endless admiration of the best, in near and distant times to come. In the midst of her temporary defeat and humiliation, I am Nazi Germany's living, lasting victory.

In spite of all contrary appearances, we did not fail; we cannot fail. Truth never fails.

Heil Hitler!
(Finished in cell no. 49 of the Werl prison, on the 16th of July, 1949)

INDEX

A, Herr, 223-42
Aeschylus, 183
Agrippina, 195
Ai Yuruk, 195-96
Akhnaton, Pharaoh, ix, 1, 11, 11 n1, 51, 53, 53 n1 & n2, 60-61, 169, 169 n1, 188 n1, 267 n1
Amon, 51, 51 n1, 53, 60, 61, 267 n1
Apollo, 93, 186
Ares, 186
Arminius (Hermann the Cheruscan), 171, 190
Asmus, Lotte, xi
Ashoka, Emperor of India, 219 n2
Aton, 267 n1
Ay, Pharaoh, 53 n2
Azag-Bau, 195

B, Frau (Herta Bothe), 76, 76 n1, 78, 79
B, Fräulein, 163, 164, 165, 166, 168
Baldur the Fair, 87
Belgion, Montgomery, 72, 72 n1
Bergmann, Ernst, 10, 10 n1, 215, 215 n1, 216, 217; *Die 25 Thesen der Deutschen Religion*, 215 n1, 215 nn3-5
Bishop, General, 109 n1
Bose, Subhas Chandra, 189 n1
Bothe, Herta (Frau B), 76, 76 n1, 78, 79
Brasillach, Robert, 8 n1

Brauchitsch, Walther von, 20 n1
Breker, Arno, 60, 155, 209,
BT (Ben Topf), 39, 39 n1, 40-41, 48, 49
Budge, Wallis, 267 n1
Burnouf, Eugène, 1 n2

Canaris, Wilhelm, 16
Chamberlain, Houston Stewart, 220
Charlemagne, 54, 216
Cheetham, Beryl, xii
Christ: see Jesus
Churchill, Winston, ix, 20-21 n1
Cromwell, Oliver, 137 n1

David, King of Israel, 277
de Gaulle, Charles, 124
Dietrich, Otto, 13
Dior, Françoise, xii
Douglas, Norman, 3, 3 n1, 211
Durga, 174, 174 n1

E, Frau (Hertha Ehlert), 74, 75, 76-77, 78-79, 88, 114, 114 n1
E, Fräulein, 158-162, 168
Eckart, Dietrich, 13, 14
Ehlert, Hertha (Frau E), 74, 75, 76-77, 78-79, 88, 114, 114 n1
Einstein, Albert, 210
Erhard, Ludwig, 103 n3

F, Herr, 156-58

Feder, Gottfried, ix, 182, 213-14; *Das Programm der NSDAP*, 182 n2, 185 n2, 193 n2, 196-97 n3, 200 nn1-5, 201 nn1-3, 203 nn1-2, 204 n3, 207 n1-2, 208 n1, 212 nn1-3, 213-14, 213 nn3-4, 214 n1
Fox, Ralph, ix, 283 n1
Franklin, Miss B, 282, 282 n1
Frenssen, Gustav, 213 n2
Freud, Sigmund, 210, 211

G, Monsieur (Rudolf Grassot), 109, 109-10 n1, 130-136, 130 n1, 132 n1
Gantry, Muriel, iv n1
Genghis Khan, vi, ix, 195 n3, 283 n1
Gieseking, Walter, 59 n1
Goblot, Edmond, 131
Goebbels, Joseph, 10, 10 n2, 16, 208, 218, 219 n1, 232, 233
Gopal, Ram, iii, iii n3, 33, 33 n1 & n2, 37
Göring, Hermann, xv, xv n2, 72-73, 73 n1, 79, 232, 256
Gowan, Herbert H., ix
Grassot, Rudolf (Monsieur G), 109, 109-10 n1, 130-136, 130 n1, 132 n1
Grese, Irma, 79

H, Frau (Anna Hempel or Irene Haschke), 78, 78 n2, 79, 88
H, Herr (Friedrich Horn), 81-85, 81 n1, 85 n2, 88, 163-68
Halder, Franz, 20 n1
Hall, H.R., ix
Hamsun, Knut, 191 n1

Hancock, Tony, xii
Haschke, Irene: see Frau H
Hedin, Sven, xi, 17, 33-34, 58, 73 n1, 191 n1, 244, 262
Hempel, Anna: see Frau H
Hepp, Eugène, 95
Hermann the Cheruscan (Arminius), 171, 190
Himmler, Heinrich, ix, 4 n1, 143, 143 n1, 214, 214 n2, 219, 233, 240
Hirata Atsutane, 188
Hitler, Adolf, vi, vii, ix, xiii, xv, xv n2, xvi, xvii, xviii, 1, 2, 3, 4, 5, 6, 7, 8, 9, 11, 12, 13, 14, 15, 16, 17, 18, 19, 20, 20 n1, 21, 22, 25, 26, 27, 29, 30, 31, 33, 34, 35, 36, 40, 41, 42, 43, 44, 45, 46, 47, 48, 49, 50, 51, 53 n1, 58, 59, 60, 61, 62, 63, 64, 66, 67, 68, 75, 89, 90, 91, 92, 93, 94, 99, 106, 119, 123, 134, 135, 139, 140, 142, 143, 144, 145, 147, 150, 151, 153, 154, 156, 159, 160, 162, 165, 167, 168, 170, 172, 173, 180, 181, 182, 185, 186, 187, 188, 189, 190, 191, 192, 194, 197, 198, 199, 201, 203, 204, 205, 206, 208, 209, 212, 217, 218, 219, 219 n1, 220, 221, 221 n1, 222, 223, 226, 227, 228, 229, 230, 232, 233, 234, 235, 236, 237, 238, 239, 240, 241, 242, 243, 244, 253, 254, 255, 256, 257, 259, 262, 264, 265, 273, 274, 275, 276, 277, 278,

279, 280, 283, 284, 285, 286, 287, 288; as divine being, xv-xvi, 5, 222; *Mein Kampf*, ix, 1 n3, 2 n1, 3 n2, 7, 14 n1, 51 n2, 68 n1, 89 n1, 123 n1, 130, 130 n2, 139 n2, 142 n1, 143 n2, 147, 149, 150, 165, 165 n4, 166, 170 n2, 182 n1, 185, 185 n1, 185 n3, 188, 188 n2, 189 n2, 191 n3, 191 n4, 192 n1, 192 n2, 192 n3, 193 n1, 194-95 n1, 196 n2, 197 n1, 206 n1-2, 218, 218 n2, 221 n2, 223 n1, 226, 233, 233 n1, 242 n1-2, 264 n1, 265 n3, 278; religious views, 219-21; survival rumours, xvii, 175, 180, 227, 230; as *"Welt-führer"* (World-Leader), xvi, 15, 157, 180, 286
Hohenzollern, August-Wilhelm von, Prince of Prussia, 81
Homer, 183, 184
Horemheb, Pharaoh, 53, 60
Horn, Friedrich (Herr H), 81-85, 81 n1, 85 n2, 88, 163-68
Hugo, Victor, ix, 100 n2
Huxley, Aldous, 194

Jesus, 68, 82, 183, 220, 277
Jordan, Colin, xii

Kaidu Khan, 195
Kali, 33, 42, 47-48, 77, 173, 178
Kaliar, Mahavir, 79-80
Koch, Ilse, 116
Krebs, Hans, 151
Krishna, xv

Kuyuk Khan, 195 n3

Lamb, Harold, ix, 196 n1
Lawrence, D.H., 195 n1
Leconte de Lisle, Charles Marie, ix, 126, 143-44, 144 n1
Leers, Johann von, 215, 215 n2, 217, 217 n2, 218, 218 n1
Ley, Robert, 232

M, Frau, 162
M, Herr, 162-63
Mao Tse-Tung, 261
Marx, Karl, 260, 277
Mohammed, 35
Motoori Norinaga, 188
Mukherji, Asit Krishna (Savitri Devi's husband), x, 43, 92-93, 128, 172, 189 n1, 226, 235, 239
Mussolini, Benito, 92

Nash, Nora (Savitri Devi's aunt), 225, 225 n1
Nietzsche, Friedrich, 9, 58, 88, 153-54, 162; *Beyond Good and Evil*, 162 n1; *The Will to Power*, 88, 188, 194, 195

Ogodai Khan, 195 n3

P, Monsieur, 256
Paul of Tarsus, 220, 226
Petrie, Flinders, 60
Plato, 183
Potocki de Montalk, Count Geoffrey, iii, iii n5

Quisling, Vidkun, 191 n1

R, Mr., 84, 84 n1
Racine, Jean, ix, 91, 91 n1, 170, 170 n1
Rama, 7, 150
Rauschning, Hermann, 219-21, 220 n1, 221 n1
Rommel, Erwin, 231
Roosevelt, Franklin Delano, 72
Rosenberg, Alfred, 9-10, 9-10 n1, 167, 205 n1, 213, 213 n1, 214
Rousseau, Jean-Jacques, 11-12
Royall, Kenneth, 85
Rundstedt, Gerd von, 20-21 n1

S, Fräulein, 62-66
Sacco, Nicola, 23
Savitri Devi, her name, iii n1; first sojourn in India, 227 n1; *And Time Rolls On: The Savitri Devi Interviews*, 73 n1; *Defiance*, iii-x, xiii, 166 n1; *Gold in the Furnace*, iii-xii, xiii; "Hitlerism and the Hindu World," 5 n2; *Impeachment of Man*, vi, 99 n3; *The Lightning and the Sun*, v-vi, viii, x, 71 n1, 272, 272 n1, 273, 273 n1; Nazi propaganda leaflets, 18, 18 n1, 32, 32 n1, 34, 179-180, 259, 259 n1; *The Non-Hindu Indians and Indian Unity*, 198 n1; Shintoism essay in *New Asia* (1940), 188 n3; *A Warning to the Hindus*, 198 n1
Schacht, Hjalmar, 16-17, 17 n1, 71 n4, 232, 240
Schirach, Baldur von, 232
Schlageter, Leo, 136

Shiva, 50
Sörensen, Wulf, ix, 4 n1, 143, 143 n1, 214, 214 n2, 233
Soustelle, Georgette, 124, 124 n1, 125
Soustelle, Jacques, 124, 124 n1, 125
Squire, Charles L., ix
Stalin, Josef, 283
Streicher, Julius, 72, 233

Tilak, Lokamanya Bal Gangadhar, 4 n2, 149 n1
Tiy, Queen of Egypt, 195
Togukawa Iyemitsu, 54
Togukawa Iyeyasu, 54
Tojo Hideki, 189
Topf, Ben (BT), 39, 39 n1, 40-41, 48, 49
Toyama Mitsuru, 189
Truman, Harry S., 99
Tutankhamon, Pharaoh, 53, 267 n1

Van Roden, E. Lewy, 85
Vanzetti, Bartolomeo, 23
Varus, Publius Quintilius, 190
Vassar, Veronica, iv n1, viii
Vickers, Edward, vi, viii, 20-21 n1
Vishnu, xv, 265
Vivekananda, Swami (Narendranath Dutta), 33, 42

W, Fräulein, 56
W, Herr (Gerhard Wassner), 86-87, 88, 120, 120 n1
W, Pastor, 160-62
Wagner, Richard, 58-59
Waldeck, Friedrich, Prince of,

81
Waßner, Gerhard (Herr W), 86-87, 88, 120, 120 n1
Watkin, E.I., 137
Weitz, Dr. 95, 109 n1
Wessel, Horst, 136

Wirth, Herman, 217
Wotan, 213, 213 n4, 214, 216,
Wright, Elwyn, 33, 33 n3, 153, 153 n1

Yamagata Seigo, 189

About the Authoress

SAVITRI DEVI (1905-1982) is one of the most original and influential National Socialist thinkers of the post-World War II era. Born Maximine Julia Portaz in Lyons, France on 30 September 1905, she was of English, Greek, and Italian ancestry and described her nationality as "Indo-European." She earned Master's Degrees in philosophy and chemistry and a Ph.D. in philosophy from the University of Lyons.

A self-described "nationalist of every nation" and an Indo-European pagan revivalist, Savitri Devi embraced National Socialism in 1929 while in Palestine. In 1935, she travelled to India to experience in Hinduism the last living Indo-European pagan religion. Settling eventually in Calcutta, she worked for the Hindu nationalist movement, married a Bengali Brahmin, the pro-Axis publisher Asit Krishna Mukherji, and spied for the Japanese during World War II.

After World War II, Savitri Devi embarked upon an itinerant, ascetic life. Her two chief activities were tireless witness on behalf of National Socialism and caring for homeless and abused animals.

Savitri Devi influenced such leading figures of post-war National Socialism as George Lincoln Rockwell, Colin Jordan, William Pierce, and Miguel Serrano. In 1962, she took part in the Cotswolds camp, where the World Union of National Socialists (WUNS) was formed.

Her sixteen books include *A Warning to the Hindus* (1939), *L'Etang aux lotus* (*The Lotus Pond*) (1940), *A Son of God: The Life and Philosophy of Akhnaton, King of Egypt* (1946), later republished as *Son of the Sun* (1956), *Akhnaton: A Play* (1948), *Defiance* (1951), *The Lightning and the Sun* (1958), *Pilgrimage* (1958), *Impeachment of Man* (1959), *Long-Whiskers and the Two-Legged Goddess* (1965), *Souvenirs et réflexions d'une Aryenne* (*Memories and Reflections of an Aryan Woman*) (1976), and *And Time Rolls On: The Savitri Devi Interviews* (2005).

Savitri Devi died in England on 22 October 1982.

About the Editor

R.G. FOWLER is Archivist of the online Savitri Devi Archive (www.savitridevi.org) and General Editor of the Centennial Edition of Savitri Devi's Works, which also includes *And Time Rolls On: The Savitri Devi Interviews*, *Defiance: The Prison Memoirs of Savitri Devi*, *Forever and Ever: Devotional Poems*, and *The Lightning and the Sun*.